IN DEFENCE OF WAR

IN DEFENCE

OF

WAR

BY

NIGEL BIGGAR

OXFORD

UNIVERSITY PRESS

Contents

Acknowledgements

First and foremost I thank my wife, Ginny Dunn, for enduring long stretches of silence over several years as I laboured to craft this book. Her patience and support, and her cheerful refusal to take my little academic woes with the grand seriousness they sometimes demanded, were a godsend.

My colleagues at Christ Church Cathedral shouldered my share of canonical responsibilities during two periods of research leave, one in 2009 and the other in 2011; and Dr John Perry, the McDonald Post-Doctoral Fellow in Christian Ethics and Public Life, carried out my normal examining and teaching duties in Trinity and Michaelmas Terms 2011. I owe a debt of gratitude to them all.

Next I thank Alonzo McDonald and the McDonald Agape Foundation, who, since 2008, have supported my work through the McDonald Centre for Theology, Ethics, and Public Life.

Early drafts of this book were the subject of round-table conferences at the University of Notre Dame in September 2009 and at the University of Virginia in April 2012. It was both a privilege and an enormous help for the manuscript to receive such expert and critical attention before it reached maturity. I am most grateful to Michael Perry and Paul Weithman for arranging the former, to Charles Mathewes and Philip Lorish for the latter, and to the others who also took time out of busy academic lives to read and comment: James Childress, Scott Davis, Kelly Denton-Boraug, Eric Gregory, Roger Herbert, James Davison Hunter, Timothy Jackson, Ross Kane, Cathy Kaveny, Robin Lovin, Mary Ellen O'Connell, Atalia Omer, Daniel Philpott, Jean Porter, Jerry Powers, Matthew Puffer, and Nick Wolterstorff. Charles Mathewes was especially generous in offering written comment on the whole manuscript.

Many friends and colleagues have served to strengthen particular chapters. Mark Coffey guided me into the most recent writings of Stanley Hauerwas for the purposes of Chapter One. Patrick Bury assured me that Chapter Two's account of motivation in combat is not risibly idealistic. To

Chapter Four Hew Strachan contributed detailed comment on a variety of points and Gary Sheffield his intimate knowledge of General Haig's plans for the Battle of the Somme. Christopher Tyerman told me everything I needed to know about St Bernard of Clairvaux for Chapter Five. To Chapter Six, David Bentley and Jeremy Hill, formerly legal advisors in the Foreign and Commonwealth Office (FCO), contributed their expertise in international law. Commodore Neil Brown, RN educated me in the laws of war and Georg Ringe drew my attention to the Radbruch formula. Chapter Seven was improved in response to comments by Simon Walters out of his experience in the Middle Eastern reaches of the FCO. Distinguished former members of that same Office—Michael Crawford, Iain Mathewson, and Peter Jenkins—educated me on the issue of terrorism and weapons of mass destruction. Almost everything that I know about oil and Iraq I learned from Derek Brower. Werner Jeanrond joined forces with me to wrest decent English sense from von Clausewitz's subtle German text.

Others who have given aid include: Hugh Beach, John De Bono, David Fisher, Andrew Hurrell, Edwina Moreton, William Shawcross, and Jonathan Wright. James Offen far exceeded the call of duty to furnish me with a suitable photograph of a Blomfield 'Cross of Sacrifice' for the front cover; and Tom Perridge, Lizzie Robottom, and Carla Hodge at Oxford University Press have applied their professional magic to conjur a handsome volume out of the bare manuscript.

For all this help I am enormously grateful. Without it, *In Defence of War* would have been much the poorer. Whether it should have been better still is my responsibility.

Some of what follows has been drawn from previous publications. Section III of Chapter One comprises a version of 'Specify and Distinguish! Interpreting the New Testament on "Non-Violence"', *Studies in Christian Ethics*, 22/2 (May 2009), which has been expanded and revised in the light of 'The New Testament and Violence: Round Two', *Studies in Christian Ethics*, 23/1 (February 2010). Elements of Chapter Two derive from 'Forgiving Enemies in Ireland', *Journal of Religious Ethics*, 36/4 (December 2008) and 'Reinhold Niebuhr and the Political Possibility of Forgiveness', in Richard Harries and Stephen Platten, eds, *Reinhold Niebuhr and Contemporary Politics: God and Power* (Oxford: Oxford University Press, 2010). Both Chapter Two and Chapter Six contain passages that echo 'The Ethics of Forgiveness and the Doctrine of Just War: A Religious View of Righting Atrocious Wrongs', in Thomas Brudholm and Thomas Cushman, eds, *The*

Religious in Responses to Mass Atrocity: Interdisciplinary Perspectives (Cambridge: Cambridge University Press, 2009). Chapter Six also contains traces of 'On Giving the Devil Benefit of Law in Kosovo', in *Kosovo: Contending Voices on Balkan Interventions*, ed. William Joseph Buckley (Grand Rapids: Eerdmans, 2000). Minor parts of Chapter Seven first drew breath in 'Invading Iraq: What are the Morals of the Story?', *International Affairs*, 87/1 (January 2011), and (with David Fisher) 'A Debate on the Iraq War and Reflections on Libya', *International Affairs*, 87/3 (May 2011). I thank Sage Publications, Wiley-Blackwell, Oxford University Press, Cambridge University Press, and Wm B. Eerdmans & Co. for their kind permission to use these materials in the present work.

Abbreviations

9/11	al-Qaeda terrorist attacks on New York and Washington, 11 September 2001
BND	Bundesnachrichtendienst, German intelligence agency
CBW	chemical and biological weapons
CPA	Coalition Provisional Authority
EU	European Union
FCO	Foreign and Commonwealth Office
IAEA	International Atomic Energy Agency
ICISS	Canadian government's International Commission on Intervention and State Sovereignty
IFHS	Iraq Family Health Survey
IRA	Irish Republican Army
JIC	Joint Intelligence Committee
MI6	British Secret Intelligence Service
NATO	North Atlantic Treaty Organization
OPEC	Organization of the Petroleum Exporting Countries
OSCE	Organization for Security and Co-operation in Europe
R2P	Responsibility to Protect
RAF	Royal Air Force
RN	Royal Navy
UK	United Kingdom
UN	United Nations
UNMOVIC	UN Monitoring, Verification and Inspection Commission
UNSC	UN Security Council
UNSCOM	UN Special Commission on Iraq
UNSCR	UNSC Resolution
US	United States
USSR	Union of Soviet Socialist Republics
WHO	World Health Organization
WMD	weapons of mass destruction

Introduction

Against the virus of wishful thinking

Why write yet another book on the justification of war? Why not a book on the arts of peacemaking instead? Surely peace, not war, should have first claim on our attention and reflection and creative intelligence.

I cannot deny the truth of this statement, nor the force of the questions preceding it. I cannot deny them, since I know that war is horrendous and that working to prevent its outbreak—even if in the end that should prove justified—is our first and most urgent duty. *A fortiori* as a Christian I cannot deny these things.

Nevertheless, I confess that I do not have it in me to write a book about peace. Maybe in due course I shall have; but I do not have it now. Now, as for most of my life, it is war that captures my imagination. I read nothing so voraciously as military history. Wherever I go, if there is a battlefield or a war cemetery, I will make a point of visiting it: Waterloo, Bull Run, Antietam, Gettysburg, Gallipoli, Ypres, the Somme, Jerusalem, Gibraltar, Maleme and Souda Bay in Crete, Leningrad, Malta, El Alamein, Assisi, Rome, Normandy.

Whence the fascination? I grew up in a country haunted by the two world wars. As a child I played in my grandmother's air-raid shelter, and I heard about the German bomber that had crash-landed in the adjacent field only twenty years before. I attended a school and a university college where the names of the war dead cascade down whole walls. A brother of my father's father left Scotland for France one September day in 1915 and was killed three weeks later at the battle of Loos. He was twenty-one years old. My mother's youngest brother flew out over the Burmese jungle on another September day in 1944 and was never heard of again. He was twenty-two years old. My father himself volunteered in 1943, aged thirty, and spent the next two-and-a-half years in Italy first manning an anti-aircraft gun and then, when there were no more enemy planes left to shoot at, carrying a stretcher.

To date I have been granted fifty-eight years, and I have enjoyed nothing but peace. No one has rudely interrupted my easy life and commanded me to pick up a weapon and use it against another human being. Yet all that separates me from the previous two generations that were fated to go to war is an accident of history or an act of inscrutable Providence. I am very, very fortunate, and I remember that by remembering them.

But I do not remember them just to stoke my gratitude. I also wonder what I would have done in their shoes, how I would have reacted to the kinds of thing that they experienced. And in particular I wonder how my Christian faith would have coped—what difference it would have made—when confronted by the terrible and urgent demands that war makes.

War therefore exercises my imagination to an extent that peace does not. I do not claim this as a virtue. I merely state it as a fact from which I cannot escape, but which therefore defines (for now) my vocation. The arts of peacemaking certainly deserve attention, and others who are differently located and called should reflect on them. In the meantime, however, it is my task to think and write out of the place—historical, cultural, emotional, imaginative—that has, with all its many limitations, been given me. I have inherited a certain fate, and I must honour it.[1]

So here is another book on the moral justification of war. It is not a text-book, for there are several good instances already available. There is of course Michael Walzer's famous modern classic, *Just and Unjust Wars*.[2] But there is also A.J. Coates's *The Ethics of War*,[3] which is far less well known but actually clearer, more systematic, and more deeply rooted in the classical tradition of just war thinking. More recently, Brian Orend has given us a comprehensive exposition and updating of just war thinking in *The Morality of War*;[4] the British Methodist pacifist, David Clough, has engaged in methodical debate with the American Roman Catholic advocate of just war, Brian Stiltner, in *Faith and Force*;[5] Charles Guthrie and Michael Quinlan have offered a suc-cinct introduction to just war thinking in *Just War. The Just War Tradition:*

---

1. The notion is W.H. Auden's: 'Remember the noble dead/And honour the fate you are,/Travelling and tormented,/Dialectic and bizarre' ('Atlantis', in W.H. Auden, *Collected Poems*, ed. Edward Mendelson [London: Faber & Faber, 2007], p. 314).
2. Michael Walzer, *Just and Unjust Wars. A Moral Argument with Historical Illustrations* (New York: Basic Books, 1977, 1992, 2000, 2006).
3. A.J. Coates, *The Ethics of War* (Manchester: Manchester University Press, 1997).
4. Brian Orend, *The Morality of War* (Peterborough, Ontario: Broadview Press, 2006).
5. David L. Clough and Brian Stiltner, *Faith and Force. A Christian Debate about War* (Washington, DC: Georgetown University Press, 2007).

Ethics in Modern Warfare;[6] C.A.J. Coady has published the wider-ranging *Morality and Political Violence*;[7] and David Fisher has brought his experience as a senior civil servant to bear on the matter in *Morality and War: Can War be Just in the Twenty-first Century?*[8]

What follows is not a textbook, but a series of essays on particular topics. For the sake of readers who are not already well acquainted with just war thinking, especially in its traditional form, let me pause here briefly to set out its basic criteria. These fall into two classes, one regarding the justice of going to war in the first place (*ius ad bellum*) and the other regarding justice in the course of fighting (*ius in bello*). The six criteria of *ius ad bellum* are: just cause, legitimate authority, right intention, last resort, proportionality, and prospect of success. The criteria of *ius in bello* are proportionality and discrimination. In the shadow of the invasion of Iraq in 2003, some would now add a third class of criteria regarding justice in the aftermath of war (*ius post bellum*). Since I think that these are already implicit in the *ad bellum* requirement of right intention, I do not accept the proposal.

This book comprises a series of essays, which means that each chapter is intelligible by itself and can be read independently of the others. Therefore, those readers who have no particular interest in, say, Christian pacifism or liberal individualism should feel free to pass over the chapters devoted to those topics. Nevertheless, what follows is a series rather than a collection, at least because there is a logic to the order of their presentation. More importantly, however, there is a consistent point of view that finds expression in all of them, and there are concerns that are common to several parts. One concern that is shared by every chapter is to defend the doctrine of just war. By 'just war' I do not refer to war that is simply or perfectly just; and I certainly do not refer to a war that is holy. 'Just' here means 'justified'—on balance and all things considered. No human action or enterprise is pure and unblemished; but that is not to say that no human action can ever be right. No war waged by human beings will ever be simply just; but that is not to say that no war can ever be justified. What is more, even when it is justified—and even when it is therefore considered to be commanded by God—war is always waged by one set of sinners against another, and never by the simply righteous against the simply

6. Charles Guthrie and Michael Quinlan, *Just War. The Just War Tradition: Ethics in Modern Warfare* (London: Bloomsbury, 2007).
7. C.A.J. Coady, *Morality and Political Violence* (Cambridge: Cambridge University Press, 2008).
8. David Fisher, *Morality and War: Can War be Just in the Twenty-first Century?* (Oxford: Oxford University Press, 2011).

unrighteous. For that reason justified war can never be holy in the sense that it carries with it a divine *carte blanche*. Such a view is not universal, but it is certainly (Augustinian) Christian.

To say that war can be right is not to deny that it causes very terrible evils. An evil comprises something painful or harmful; and, while no one should *want* to cause pain or harm, the experience of finding oneself in the position of being morally obliged to mete evil out is not at all uncommon. Due care of a wilfully errant child requires a parent to punish him—that is, deliberately to impose something painful upon him, in order to prompt second thoughts about his conduct. And sometimes justice or prudence requires employers to sack employees or make them redundant, knowing full well that this will cause them the considerable harm of the loss of livelihood. It can be justified to cause evil, and justified war causes evils that are very terrible.

This admission is honest, but it is not honest enough. Much of the discussion that follows is abstract, as thinking must be. Thinking seeks to make sense of things, to order them; and this requires standing back—abstracting—from the immediate experience of concrete particulars. Human beings are so made that this intellectual grasp or ordering is very important to them. It matters enormously to us that things make sense; and in many realms—not least the physical—we have found that, curiously, reality is so made as to correspond to our desire for intellectual ordering. Of all the kinds of intellectual ordering in which we engage, the one that is most important to us is, arguably, moral. It matters most of all to us that how we live and what we do are good and right. Accordingly, moral thinking seeks to make sense of human conduct by ordering it in terms of normative principles and rules. This is as it should be. The danger, however, is that intellectual tidiness with its careful logic, clear concepts, and nice distinctions ceases to do justice to the intractable messiness of flesh-and-blood human experience—that it buys clarity at the expense of reality. Since one of the main concerns of this book is to test the practical realism of its preferred analysis of the morals of war, and since it will argue that war can be morally justified, let me posit here two flesh-and-blood instances of the evils of war, in the hope of keeping subsequent thinking honest. The first belongs to a war whose justice is highly controversial:

> There was so much of Duncan Crookston missing that he didn't seem real. He was half a body propped up in a full-size bed, seemingly bolted into place. He couldn't move because he had nothing left with which to push himself into

motion except for a bit of arm that was immobilized in bandages, and he couldn't speak because of the tracheotomy tube that had been inserted into his throat. Every part of him was taped and bandaged because of burns and infections, except for his cheeks, which remained reddened from burns, his mouth, which hung open and misshapen, and his eyes, which were covered by goggles that produced their own moisture, resulting in water droplets on the inside through which he viewed whatever came into his line of sight.[9]

Duncan Crookston was a corporal in the US Rangers, who was blown up by an improvised explosive device during the 'Surge' in Iraq in 2007. He died on the eve of his twentieth birthday.

The second instance of the evils of war belongs to one whose justice is almost universally celebrated:

> The never-ending detonations—soldiers waving to us, begging for help, the dead, their faces screwed up but still in agony—huddled everywhere in trenches and shelters, the officers and men who had lost their nerve—burning vehicles from which piercing screams could be heard—a soldier stumbling, holding back the intestines which were oozing from his abdomen—soldiers lying in their own blood—arms and legs torn off—others, driven crazy, shouting, swearing, laughing hysterically. But also there were civilians lying by the roadside, loaded with personal belongings...and still clinging to them in death. Close by a crossroads, caught by gunfire, lay a group of men, women, and children. Unforgettable, the staring gaze of their broken eyes and the grimaces of their pain-distorted faces. Destroyed prams and discarded dolls littered the terrible scene.[10]

The witness here was *Oberfeldwebel* Hans Erich Braun; the place and date, the Falaise Pocket, 1944; the victims, a mixture of occupying German troops and innocent French civilians; and the deliberate agents of this gross carnage, American artillery and bombers fighting against Hitler's tyranny. War, even when justified, causes very terrible evils.

That is true. However, if war usually causes terrible evils, peace sometimes permits them. If advocates of justified war need to be honest about the horrendous character of the practical implications of their reasoning, then so do their opponents. For the sake of balance, therefore, let me present two flesh-and-blood instances of the evils of peace. Here is the first:

---

9. David Finkel, *The Good Soldiers* (London: Atlantic Books, 2009), pp. 206–7.
10. Paul Fussell, *The Boys' Crusade. American G.I.s in Europe: Chaos and Fear in World War Two* (London: Weidenfeld & Nicolson, 2003), pp. 63–4.

In late March, eyewitnesses... reported that several groups of up to 50 suspected government opponents were arrested, lined up, blindfolded with their hands bound, and shot in front of their families. Other detainees were doused with petrol and set alight... The bodies of some of those executed were reportedly tied to tanks by government forces and dragged through the streets or were left hanging from electricity pylons... Several of the refugees interviewed described incidents involving... soldiers throwing patients and others out of hospital windows... A former member of the armed forces... saw some 30 to 35 men being pushed into the water. They were blindfolded with red cloths, their hands tied, and weights attached to their feet... One 21-year-old former soldier... stated that... several thousand detainees were being held... of whom small groups were executed daily. Guards read out the names of a group of detainees, who were then led outside, lined up against palm trees and executed by firing squad using machine guns.[11]

Now follows the second instance:

When it got dark, the shooting stopped. There was a lot of screaming, shouting, people were crying out for help in the warehouse. Many were wounded. As I lay down, the right-hand side of my body got soaked in blood. I couldn't stand it any longer, so I got up from the blood and pulled a dead body underneath me to lie on top of it. When dawn started breaking, [my neighbour] Zulfo Salilović got up to urinate and have a drink of water. I tugged at his coat and told him, 'Stay down,' and he said, 'I can't hold it in any longer.' A machine-gun burst cut him in half and he fell down. I covered myself with two dead bodies and stayed underneath for twenty-four hours. During the day I heard someone calling 'Salko, Salko'. He repeated it about twenty times. [Then someone said,] 'Fuck your Turkish mother. You're still alive.' There was a rifle shot. You couldn't hear the voice again. Afterwards a truck and mechanical shovel appeared. They started tearing down the side of the warehouse facing the road, then they started loading. They loaded until nightfall. The shovel came very close. I was thinking, 'This is the end for me. All that fear has been in vain,' but you have to keep hoping whilst you're still alive. And then I heard someone say, 'Park the shovel, wash the tarmac and cover the dead bodies with hay. It's enough for today.'[12]

The first instance of the evils of peace was recorded in Amnesty International's report on the suppression of the Shi'a revolt in southern Iraq by Saddam Hussein's regime in 1991. The second instance comprises the testimony of

11. Amnesty International, *Iraq: Human Rights Violations since the Uprising* (London: Amnesty International, 1991), pp. 6, 7, 8–9.
12. Jan Willem Honig and Norbert Both, *Srebrenica: Record of a War Crime* (London: Penguin, 1996), p. 56.

Hakija Huseinović, one of the few survivors of the massacre of seven thousand Bosnian Muslims by Serbian forces at Srebrenica in 1995. These are instances of evil, of course; but why do I describe them as evils of *peace*? I do so, because the first was the indirect consequence of the decision by the United States and its allies *not* to continue fighting the Iraqi regime after it was expelled from Kuwait; and because the second was the indirect consequence of the *refusal* by European and American governments to use armed force against the Bosnian Serbs. This is the dilemma: on the one hand going to war causes terrible evils, but on the other hand not going to war permits them. Whichever horn one chooses to sit on, the sitting should not be comfortable. Allowing evils to happen is not necessarily innocent, any more than actually causing them is necessarily culpable. Omission and commission are equally obliged to give an account of themselves. Both stand in need of moral justification.

This book's choice is to defend the doctrine of justified war. But against what? The answer to that question reveals the author's British, and somewhat European, location. Early 21st-century Britain is an arena for conflicting narratives about war. One of these is the liberal-left story that has dominated since the late 1960s. This tells of a British empire that was 'imperialist' and therefore basically rapacious, and whose vain and foolish essence was laid bare in the futile, criminal slaughter of the First World War. Such a reading of the past generates a strong suspicion of patriotism and of the military, and a strong presumption against war, especially military intervention elsewhere in the world, and most especially unilateral intervention without the authority of the United Nations and in cahoots with the United States.

This presumption against war—especially by Western nations—is even stronger on the European continent, whose dominant power, Germany, is now virtually pacifist. Identifying the reason for this needs no research. After launching two world wars in the space of a single generation, and after being shaken to its foundations by defeat in the first and reduced to rubble in the second, it is hardly surprising that contemporary Germany is strongly inclined to turn its back on war completely. One expression of this renunciation can be found in the permanent exhibition at the *Deutscher Soldatenfriedhof* at Maleme in Crete. After telling the poignant and tragic tale of three young brothers, who as German paratroopers descended upon Crete on 20 May 1941 and were all killed before the day's end, the exhibition draws the moral that war is evil and must be renounced always and everywhere.[13] It does not pause to distinguish between what is evil and what is wrong. Nor does it ask what young Germans, fighting in the service of the Nazi regime, were doing by dropping out of the skies onto part of Greece in 1941, and by what right they did it. Nor does it consider how the Cretans and their Anglo-Saxon allies should have responded to them.

There is every reason to avoid war, of course, if war *may* be avoided. The evils it causes are indeed terrible. However, the Maleme exhibition and those who think along its pacifist lines assume that war is so terribly evil that it may never be morally right to engage in it. Consequently, when faced with grave and persistent injustice, they are convinced a priori that there must be a non-belligerent solution. Thus, after hearing me argue that the 2003 invasion of Iraq might have been justified as the means of ending an intolerably atrocious regime, one member of my audience exclaimed, 'But there *had* to be a better way!' That in fact there *was* a better way is certainly possible. But why did there *have* to be one?

There *has* to be a better way to respond to grave injustice than by waging war, *if* one adopts something like Rousseau's faith in human nature. In this view, human beings are basically well intentioned and only do wicked things to other people because they themselves have been victim to a distorting social or political or historical environment. The way to get them to stop doing wicked things, therefore, is by reasoning with them sympathetically and patiently, even to the extent of addressing their legitimate grievances. There is not a little truth in this, of course. Sometimes an aggressor is indeed impelled by the rage of his Inner Victim; and sometimes those oppressed by an aggressor bear some responsibility for what they suffer. We are often implicated in each other's sins. Nevertheless, victims, too, retain moral responsibility, which obliges them to proportion their justified resentment and retaliation, and to restrain the latter from waxing into fresh forms of injustice. Even if it is true that Germany was the victim of unbridled vengeance at the Treaty of Versailles in 1919, that does not justify Hitler's invasion of Poland in 1939; and even if Britain colluded in Versailles's vindictiveness, that does not undermine her decision to oppose the Nazi invasion of France in 1940.

Besides, not all abuse perpetrated by one human being against another *is* motivated by a sense of outraged innocence. Sometimes it is motivated by the sheer pleasure of domination or by the self-exonerating need for a racial

---

13. At least, this was what the exhibition said when I visited it in April 2003.

scapegoat. It seems empirically self-evident to me that not all human beings are well motivated or well intentioned—and it seems so as much from internal reflection as from external observation. The light of Augustine's psychology penetrates more deeply than Rousseau's. We may be rational creatures, but we are also—and primarily—creatures of love or desire; and when desire throws off reason's control, we become creatures of passion; and when we are creatures of passion, we lose the ability to contain ourselves out of respect for justice toward others. Whether and how far someone is redeemable from the grip of malevolent or negligent passion is often hard to say; and in the meantime other people continue to suffer at its hands. So in the light of this less optimistic but, I think, more empirically accurate view of human beings, I do not suppose that the perpetrators of grave and persistent injustice can always be deflected from their course by ever more patient reasoning. I do not believe that there always *has* to be an available pacific solution. One major target of this book, therefore, is 'the virus of wishful thinking'.[14]

This optimistic and virtually pacifist point of view, however, is only one that informs my cultural context, and it does not go unchallenged. In contemporary Britain there still runs a rival, more realist narrative. The fact that she entered the war against Hitler only after bending over backwards to avoid it, and the fact that she ended it as one of the victors, gives contemporary Britons an almost unassailable (and largely unassailed) example of a justified war and an object lesson in the need (sometimes) to use armed force. Moreover, since her empire was more far-flung than Sweden's and more long-lasting than Germany's, since reconstruction after the Second World War involved mass immigration from colonies far beyond Europe, and since her post-war withdrawal from formal empire ran in parallel with the assumption of a global role in the Cold War, Britain has never entirely lost a sense of direct responsibility for global order. Just after the turn of the millennium I asked the director of military operations in the Ministry of Defence why it was still politically acceptable for a British government to send its troops overseas to the likes of Sierra Leone, in contrast to most of its European counterparts. His answer was that the continuing legacy of the empire means that, even in the early 21st century, the British are still accus-

---

14. The phrase is Michael Burn's and it appears in his autobiography—as fascinating, eloquent, courageous, and wise as it is little known—where he reflects with unflinching candour upon his early admiration for Hitler (*Turned Toward the Sun: An Autobiography* [Wilby, Norwich: Michael Russell, 2003], pp. 70, and 69–78, 148).

tomed to having their soldiers fighting and dying in foreign parts. Indeed, at one point during the writing of this book British newspapers were headlining the conclusion of Operation Panther's Claw in Afghanistan, where 3,000 British troops had been involved in fighting the Taliban. What were the British doing in Afghanistan in 2009? No longer defending the North-West Frontier, as they were on the three previous occasions that they intervened there—in 1839–42, 1878–80, and 1919—but combating an Islamic terrorism that, thanks to Britain's imperial past and post-war immigration, now ties Britain to the fate of Pakistan.

This realist tradition is where I stand, and it is partly against its pacifist rivals, whether Enlightenment or Christian, that I seek here to defend the doctrine of just war. I do not deny that war involves horrendous evils, which ought to be strenuously avoided if they can be—and if they may be. I do not believe, however, that all war *may* be avoided. I do not believe that international conflict is always the product of a failure of understanding or that it is always the equal responsibility of all parties. Nor do I believe that every international player always negotiates in good faith. Sometimes conflict is decisively the fruit of one party's greed for power or ethnic contempt or delusory paranoia or fetid resentment; and sometimes it bursts into open warfare because that party really is not open to persuasion or to honest (as distinct from tactical) negotiation. Some people really do not want peace. Or at least, they do not want it enough. Or they want it only on their own, seriously unjust terms. The position that I oppose here is the one attributed by Andrew Roberts to Lord Halifax, namely, '[t]he Whiggish view that there was a rational solution to all problems and all that was needed was to find a modus vivendi comfortable to all parties' and that these parties 'were rational... [and] sincerely wanted to reach solutions'.[15] My opposition to this is not a priori but based on historical experience. As I shall argue in Chapter Four, the decisive causes of the First World War were not cultural forces common to all parties, or the nature of international structures, but the moral attitudes and choices of individuals: the slaughter in the trenches is primarily attributable to the thinking and decisions of the military and civil leaders of Wilhelmine Germany and Austro-Hungary. And as I shall argue in Chapter Six, one reason why it was right for NATO to go to war against Serbia over Kosovo in 1999 was that Slobodan Milosevič saw negotiations only as a way of pursuing his aggressive policies, not as an occasion to agree

---

15. Andrew Roberts, *The Holy Fox. A Life of Lord Halifax* (London: Papermac, 1992), p. 115.

to change them. I am a realist, therefore, about the fact of intractable human vice on the international stage. Of course, as a Christian I do not believe that anyone has a monopoly of vice; but the fact that its spread is wide does not make it even. If all are somewhat culpable, some might still be more culpable than others. And while it is beyond human competence to pronounce any human being to be ultimately irredeemable, it is presently the case that some people cannot be talked out of grave wrongdoing and that they must therefore be forced out of it.

As I believe in the fact of gross and intractable wickedness, so I believe that punishment is necessary and that it has a basic, broadly retributive dimension. As I shall explain in Chapters Two and Five, I do not think of retribution as necessarily or properly vengeful. I think of it merely as a hostile response to wrongdoing, which might and should be proportionate. Retribution is important because wrongdoing needs to be contradicted, fended off, and reversed. Not to contradict it and fend it off and try to reverse it is to imply that it does not matter and, therefore, that its victims do not matter. Just war is an extreme form of retributive punishment.

If I am a realist, however, I am a Christian realist, not a Hobbesian one. That my anthropology is not optimistic does not make it cynical. I do not believe that human beings are driven only by the fear of pain and death and the desire for security. That is not merely cynical, but empirically false. It seems to me empirically true that human beings can also be powerfully driven at least by a hatred of injustice, and sometimes even by a love for justice. And while I believe in the fact of sin and the need for retributive punishment, for coercion, and sometimes for violent coercion, I also believe that retribution, even when coercive and violent, should be qualified by forgiveness. I say 'qualified', not 'displaced'. How this is possible, logically and practically, I shall explain in Chapter Two.

I am not a Hobbesian realist, but a Christian one. Does that make me a Niebuhrian? Not simply. Ever since I first read Reinhold Niebuhr I have been impressed—as have many others—by the power of his Christian anthropology to illuminate the ambiguous human—even spiritual—depths of political relations and international affairs. I have also been impressed by his robust honesty about the ineradicable fact of power in human, and especially social, relations. Nevertheless, as I have explained elsewhere,[16] I consider

---

16. Nigel Biggar, *Behaving in Public: How to Do Christian Ethics* (Grand Rapids: Eerdmans, 2011), pp. 3–5, 9.

Niebuhr to be theologically deficient. The problem is not exactly, as some have put it, that he replaces theology with anthropology; for his anthropology is evidently theological in a certain sense. No, the problem with Niebuhr is that his theology is insufficiently personal. What I mean by this is that his concept of God is too abstract and remote, too incapable of acting in flesh-and-blood history to give moribund humans any ground for hope in the face of death and of the greater part of injustice that lies beyond historical remedy. My complaint against Niebuhr, then, is that he was too Bultmannian. In contrast, I am more Barthian. The God in whom I believe is a living, loving, intending, acting reality, who is capable of incarnation, real death, and bodily resurrection. I confess that I cannot really see the point in believing in any other kind. As a consequence, my Christian realism is stronger on eschatological hope than Niebuhr's—stronger because I feel no need to equivocate about its grounds or its content.

In part, then, when I describe the viewpoint of this book as 'realist', I mean that it is realistic about human nature. It is neither optimistic nor cynical. Human beings are capable of loving what is good and doing what is right, sometimes with heroic courage. Equally, however, they are capable of becoming so wedded to evil that sweet reason, for all its patience, cannot detach them. That is one, *anthropological* sense of 'realist', which applies generally in what follows. However, there is another, ontologico-moral sense that applies intermittently. *Moral* realism takes the view that human understanding of what is good and right is preceded by, and responsible to, a moral order that is rooted (somehow) in the nature of things—in objective reality. This moral realism is undergoing something of a renaissance among contemporary moral philosophers, by no means all of whom are theists. Nevertheless, since monotheists (such as Christians) believe in a basic unity of things that is originally given (by God) and not made (by Man), they are logically bound to be moral realists. From this it follows that a Christian doctrine of just war cannot regard positive international law as the final word. International law has considerable authority, but its authority is not final. This is because all positive law must ultimately answer to the moral law that is given in the nature of things. This is a major theme in Chapter Six, but it also surfaces in Chapters Five and Seven.

This book defends the doctrine of just war from a position of anthropological and moral realism, and it does so against a virtual pacifism that depends on an optimistic anthropology. However, not all pacifism is generated primarily by faith in the natural goodness of human beings. Christian pacifism, for example, is primarily moved by the normative example of Jesus, and so by faith in the *super*natural power of *God* to purge the world of the human vices that foster war. This theological pacifism is often supposed to have been the original stance of the Christian church, from which it was seduced by the growing opportunities for wielding political power in the course of the 4th century AD; and Augustine's early articulation of just war thinking at the turn of the fourth and fifth centuries is often regarded as the prime symptom of the church's lapse from its pristine state of grace. Whether any theory of just war may claim the title 'Christian' at all is controversial, therefore, and those that believe that it may, must fight for the right. This has always been the case, but it is all the more so now, when pacifism has come to dominate the academic discipline of Christian ethics. That is one reason why the opening chapter of this book in defence of just war is devoted to an argument against the claim that Christianity is properly pacifist. But the other, more significant reason is that the Christian version has been, and remains, a very influential species of pacifism in general.

To some extent the following three chapters take their cue from the first, addressing some important issues that it raises. Since the norm of love for the neighbour is central to the moral teaching of Jesus—and, indeed, to that of St Paul—any theory of just war that wishes to call itself 'Christian' will have to follow Augustine in arguing that the use of violent force can be a form of 'kind harshness'. That it can be kind is straightforwardly plausible with regard to the neighbour who is the innocent victim of attack; but its plausibility is not so obvious with regard to the neighbour who is himself the unjust aggressor. Chapter Two tries to make this plausibility clearer, and it does so by arguing that the use of violent force can be qualified by love in its most characteristically Christian form—namely as forgiveness.

Whether Christian or not, pacifists tend to object to killing *as such*. But killing comes in different moral kinds, as common sense and law both recognize. One significant differentiating factor—at least according to non-utilitarian moral theologians and philosophers—is the killer's intention. Enter the theory of double effect. This holds that one may deliberately perform an act that one knows will possibly, probably, or even certainly cause evil, provided that one does not *intend* that evil. As I interpret it, to intend something is to desire it actively. To actively desire someone's death is incompatible with loving them. Therefore we should not intend to kill another person, though we may choose to perform an act that will possibly, probably, or certainly cause that person's death, provided that that is not what we wanted and that we accept the risk of killing with manifest reluctance and proportionate reason. The implication of this way of thinking, however, is that soldiers should never intend to kill their enemies. Is this *really* plausible? Chapter Three argues that it is.

One of the most cogent criticisms of just war thinking that has been made by Christian pacifists—and by others, too—is that it cannot demonstrate with any precision or certainty that the good, which it intends or achieves, outweighs the evils, which it seeks to stop and which its belligerent means themselves partly cause. This brings us to the issue of proportionality, which Chapter Four considers in terms of a battle and a war now widely regarded as grossly disproportionate—the Somme and (Britain's prosecution of) the First World War. I examine the concept of proportionality, analyse it into different kinds, reckon the most popular kind to be impracticable, and judge that both the battle and the war were proportionate, all things considered.

So far I have described the stance taken in this book in terms of two kinds of 'realism', one anthropological and the other ontological-moral. Chapters Two, Three, and Four all manifest a third kind: *practical*. I am concerned that just war theory's moral prescriptions be realistic—that they be realizable in practice. That concern makes a strong appearance both in Chapter Two's consideration of the plausibility of considering the grim business of war as an expression of love, and in Chapter Three's consideration of the plausibility of requiring soldiers not to intend to kill their enemies. It also makes an appearance in Chapter Four, where I argue that, notwithstanding its very terrible and very massive evils, Britain's war against Germany in 1914–18 was justified. What this implies is that the requirement of proportionality, while constraining justifiable killing, can nevertheless be highly permissive of it. For those of us who advocate just war, this is a sobering fact.

Not every critic of the tradition of just war thinking is impelled by pacifist convictions. David Rodin is a liberal philosopher, whose searching philosophical critique finds just war thinking incoherent, even while he withholds himself from a pacifist conclusion. At the heart of his argument is an assumed right of the individual to freedom from harm, and an individualist view of the conditions of its forfeiture. Any contemporary theory of just war that wishes to be credible must meet Rodin's objections. This I attempt to do in Chapter Five.

This chapter represents a break with the first half of the book, since, instead of responding to the pacifist critique in Chapter One, it sets out a fresh array of criticisms. It also represents the beginning of the book's second half, since the remaining two chapters build on its response to Rodin. Basic to that response is the argument that, while his critique tells against legally positivist and Walzerian-liberal versions of just war thinking, it inadvertently confirms the early Christian tradition. Basic to that tradition is the view that positive law, however important, is subject to a higher, natural law. Illegality, therefore, need not amount to immorality. Chapter Six considers the implications of this for military intervention motivated by humanitarian concern, and for the authority of international law, with special reference to NATO's war against Serbia over Kosovo in 1999.

Intervention is also the subject of the seventh and final chapter, although here the focal instance is even more controversial, namely the Anglo-American invasion of Saddam Hussein's Iraq in 2003. It seems that most people—at least in the circles where I move—view the Iraq invasion as obviously, simply, gravely, and wickedly wrong. To me, however, its overall moral quality has never seemed either obvious or simple. Indeed, it has seemed very complicated, and at different times I have found myself arguing for and against it. In this chapter, therefore, I strive to lay this troubled ghost to rest. At the same time and of more general importance, through this particular analysis I seek to show how the various criteria should be ordered, so as to construct a coherent and comprehensive judgement about the justice of war.

I

Against Christian pacifism

Pacifism is popular. In much of the West, and especially in Western Europe, war's undoubted evils are barely distinguished from its sheer wickedness. Even among those who concede that going to war might sometimes be right, many impose such stringent conditions as to make theoretical justification amount to practical pacifism.[1] And then there are those who are principled pacifists, regarding all war everywhere as wrong.[2]

In the Western world, and probably beyond, one of the oldest traditions of pacifism is Christian. While it has never been dominant in the Christian religion, it has persisted; and while non-religious pacifisms now abound, the Christian version remains important and has seen its influence grow in recent decades. My intention in this opening chapter is to argue against it.

I. Stanley Hauerwas

The leading living exponent of Christian pacifism is Stanley Hauerwas. A Methodist, Hauerwas has been heavily influenced by the Mennonite tradition; a Protestant, he has taught at one of the leading Roman Catholic universities in the United States,[3] and his influence reaches some considerable

---

1. See Nigel Biggar, 'Between Development and Doubt: The Recent Career of Just War Doctrine in British Churches' and James Turner Johnson, 'Just War Thinking in Recent American Religious Debate over Military Force', in Charles Reed and David Ryall, eds, *The Price of Peace. Just War in the Twenty-First Century* (Cambridge: Cambridge University Press, 2007).
2. Some use 'pacifism' to refer to a variety of positions, ranging from the absolute prohibition of war to the justification of certain kinds under demanding conditions. This seems to me confusing, since such a broad definition embraces just war doctrine. Therefore, I reserve 'pacifism' to refer to the refusal of all kinds of violent force in all circumstances.
3. That is, the University of Notre Dame.

way into Catholic circles;[4] and an academic, his reach extends into grass-roots churches.[5]

One would expect Hauerwas, as a Christian, especially of a Protestant and theologically orthodox kind, to have given his pacifism a strong biblical foundation; but here expectation meets with disappointment. In the whole body of his work, there is no rigorous attempt to justify his position biblically. He observes that, in the stories of Jesus' temptation in the wilderness, Jesus is shown to refuse the role of 'military messiah . . . to try and free Israel, if necessary by violent means, from her masters',[6] and from this he infers a general rejection of 'dominion . . . peace through coercion . . . violence'.[7] He does not pause to consider, however, whether the latter should be understood strictly in terms of the former—that is, whether the dominion, coercion, and violence that Jesus rejected should be *specified* in terms of religious nationalism. Instead, he just assumes that Jesus' espousal of 'non-violent revolt' amounts to a challenge to 'the violence of the world' in general.[8] Further, Hauerwas assumes that the Sermon on the Mount's enjoining the forgiveness of enemies amounts to 'non-violent love',[9] that 'self-giving' love is always 'non-resistant',[10] and that Jesus' crucifixion issues in the absolute ethical norm that any injustice should be suffered.[11] For sure, these are all widely held assumptions, but, as I shall argue in Chapter Two, they are mistaken.

Hauerwas's disinclination to grapple closely with the biblical text might be viewed as evidence of a certain hermeneutical sophistication. On one occasion he admits disarmingly that Christian non-violence cannot be justified by any particular biblical text or group of texts: 'The text of the Bible

---

4. When I was teaching in the Republic of Ireland in 2006 I received an email from a young Irish Roman Catholic theologian who, recently removed to California, reported his surprise at the extent of Hauerwas's influence among his peers.

5. As Richard Hays writes, '[Hauerwas's] popular works . . . have received far wider attention in the church than is customary for works by academic theologians' (*The Moral Vision of the New Testament: A Contemporary Introduction to New Testament Ethics* [Edinburgh: T. & T. Clark, 1996], pp. 253–4).

6. Stanley Hauerwas, *The Peaceable Kingdom. A Primer in Christian Ethics* (Notre Dame: University of Notre Dame, 1981), pp. 81, 83–4.

7. Ibid., pp. 78–9.

8. Stanley Hauerwas, *Matthew* (London: SCM Press, 2006), pp. 182, 225.

9. Hauerwas, *Peaceable Kingdom*, pp. 75–6.

10. Stanley Hauerwas, 'Epilogue: A Pacifist Response to the Bishops', in Paul Ramsey, *Speak Up for Just War or Pacifism: A Critique of the United Methodist Bishops' Pastoral Letter, 'In Defense of Creation'* (London: Pennsylvania State University Press, 1988), pp. 159.

11. Ibid., p. 160.

in and of itself does not require pacifism. Rather, only a church that is non-violent is capable of rightly reading, for example, Romans 13.'[12] As he puts it elsewhere, only those who already participate in the non-violent politics of the Kingdom of God are in a position to interpret the text of the Bible correctly:[13] 'you cannot rightly read the Sermon on the Mount unless you are a pacifist'.[14] In addition, he asserts that Christian non-violence is unintelligible apart from presuppositions about Jesus Christ and about the Christian church.[15] Hauerwas is correct, of course, to claim that the biblical text can sustain a variety of interpretations, and that each interpretation is bound to be shaped by the interpreter's spiritual posture, moral commitments and experience, and prior theological views. However, while it might be obvious to Christian pacifists that only pacifist practice can unlock the true meaning of the biblical text, it is not so obvious to Christian just warriors. So how is this difference in view to be negotiated, if not (in part) by reference to the biblical text, to the interpretations it will wear, and to those that it will wear best? When Hauerwas tells us that the meaning of a text is not *limited* by the original intent of its author, he is both right and wrong.[16] He is right that it is not fixed; he is wrong that it is not channelled. If the meaning of a text is not in some sense objective, standing over and against the reader and his tradition and limiting what they can read out of it, how can it challenge their assumptions?[17] And if it cannot challenge them, what remains of its authority? As for theological presuppositions, of course certain Christological and ecclesiological views make principled non-violence rational. But those views are not the only ones available. Therefore we need an *argument* for why we should choose the former over the latter. And we need an *argument* that shows why pacifist practice and experience get the best sense out of the text. It is not enough for Hauerwas to assert, 'I believe the narrative into which Christians are inscribed means we cannot be

---

12. Stanley Hauerwas, 'Can a Pacifist Think about War?', in *Dispatches from the Front: Theological Engagements with the Secular* (Durham, NC: Duke University Press, 1994), p. 118.
13. Stanley Hauerwas, 'Why "The Way the Words Run' Matters: Reflections on Becoming a 'Major Biblical Scholar"', in Stanley Hauerwas, *Learning to Speak Christian* (London: SCM Press, 2009), pp. 96, 104.
14. Stanley Hauerwas, *Unleashing the Scripture. Freeing the Bible from Captivity to America* (Nashville: Abingdon, 1993), p. 64.
15. Hauerwas, 'Can a Pacifist Think about War?', p. 120.
16. Hauerwas, 'Why "The Way the Words Run" Matters', p. 102 n. 20.
17. Hays makes the same point when he writes that it follows from Hauerwas's position that 'the classic Protestant idea that Scripture can challenge and judge tradition is simply an illusion' (*Moral Vision*, p. 263).

anything other than non-violent . . . non-violence is simply one of the essential practices that is intrinsic to the story of being a Christian.'[18] We need an
argument that takes the form of a careful negotiation between experience,
coherent theology, and a rational construal of the text.[19]

Hauerwas's cavalier dismissal of the constraining authority of the biblical
text does not sit easily with his complaint about the deployment in its interpretation of the distinction between private and public forms of retaliatory
violence—a distinction that is crucial to just war theory's claim to be
Christian. 'That such a distinction has seemed to many a "natural" reading
of the Sermon [on the Mount],' he writes, 'reflects a politics quite different
from the church I think must exist if we are to avoid importing foreign
categories to shape the reading of the Gospel.'[20] Quite what the distinction
is foreign *to* remains unclear. Is it foreign to the politics normative in the
Christian community or to the biblical text? Elsewhere, however, the text
itself appears to be accorded normative authority, as when Hauerwas tells us
that the distinction between the private person and the bearer of a public
office does not appear in Matthew's gospel and 'is unknown to Jesus'.[21]

I do not mean to say that Hauerwas's Christian pacifism is lacking any
good theological reason. In part, it is driven by an admirable determination
to give practical expression to faith in the providential activity of God and
hope for his eschatological resolution of history into peace at the end of
time. 'Violence,' he diagnoses, 'derives from the self-deceptive story that we
are in control—that we are our own creators—and that only we can bestow
meaning on our lives, since there is no one else to do so.'[22] Instead, Christians
repudiate this story, because, trusting in God, 'we are no longer driven by
the assumption that we must be in control of history, that it is up to us to
make things come out right'.[23] We 'seek not so much to be effective as to be

---

18. Stanley Hauerwas, 'Whose Just War? Which Peace?' in *Dispatches from the Front*, p. 137.
19. I agree with Richard Hays's criticisms of Hauerwas's 'freewheeling' treatment of the Bible, as
    manifested in his lack of 'a coherent hermeneutical position' and of 'detailed exegesis or sus-
    tained close reading' (*Moral Vision*, pp. 254, 258. See also p. 259). Hauerwas's response to Hays
    in 'Why "The Way the Words Run" Matters' is glib and barely begins to grapple with any of
    the difficult questions raised.
20. Hauerwas, 'Why "The Way the Words Run" Matters', p. 111 n. 40.
21. Hauerwas, *Matthew*, pp. 59, 73. Confusingly, Hauerwas goes on to argue in two opposing direc-
    tions at once: on the one hand, that Jesus enjoins his disciples to leave behind their 'public
    responsibilities' (e.g. as sons to parents); but on other hand (following Bonhoeffer) that no one
    is ever a private person but is always constituted by responsibilities, and that the Christian
    exercise of responsibility eschews evil means in resisting evil (Hauerwas, *Matthew*, p. 73).
22. Hauerwas, *Peaceable Kingdom*, p. 94.
23. Ibid., p. 87.

faithful'.[24] Non-resistance is right, 'not because it works, but because it anticipates the triumph of the Lamb that was slain'.[25] Hauerwas is determined that God's peace should not be simply other-worldly and future, but that it should take mundane and present form.[26] It is 'not some ideal, but an actual way of life among a concrete group of people . . . a possibility amid a world at war'.[27] As he rightly says, '[t]he decisive issue is how we understand the eschatological nature of God's peace'.[28] Or, to put it more exactly, the decisive issue is whether or not we regard God's peace as—at least in part— a *present* reality.

Hauerwas's *bête noire* here is Reinhold Niebuhr, for whom the Gospel's ideal of pure, disinterested love cannot constitute a practicable social ethic, since this must concern itself with the doing of justice, sometimes by way of coercion. For sure, the aspiration to love can help raise justice above sheer political expediency,[29] and hope for love's realization beyond history is necessary to sustain the struggle for justice here and now. Nevertheless, history remains tragic—the realm where only limited good can be achieved by way of morally ambiguous coercion, which invariably involves selfish interest.[30] Against this, Hauerwas insists that coercive, retributive justice must not displace Jesus' justice of forgiveness and reconciliation in politics;[31] and that the peace that Christians seek is not an impossible ideal, but 'a present reality', since God is 'the present Lord of the universe'.[32]

There is much to commend in the position that Hauerwas takes here. To believe in the God who wears the face of Jesus is to believe in a superhuman power that is at work in the world to recover it from sin and deliver it to fulfilment. It is to believe that the world's salvation does not lie entirely, or primarily, in human hands; and that it does not lie wholly in the future, but is already coming to be. What is more, to believe that Jesus' teaching and life show how human beings should behave, so as to concur with and mediate

24. Ibid., p. 104.
25. Hauerwas, 'Epilogue', pp. 160–1.
26. Stanley Hauerwas, 'Should War Be Eliminated? A Thought Experiment' (1984) in Stanley Hauerwas, *The Hauerwas Reader*, ed. John Berkman and Michael Cartwright (Durham, NC: Duke University Press, 2005), p. 410.
27. Ibid., p. 418.
28. Ibid., pp. 418–19.
29. Hauerwas, *Peaceable Kingdom*, pp. 139–40.
30. Ibid., pp. 139–41, 145.
31. Stanley Hauerwas, 'Jesus, the Justice of God' in *War and the American Difference. Theological Reflections on Violence and National Identity* (Grand Rapids: Baker, 2011), pp. 100–6.
32. Hauerwas, *Peaceable Kingdom*, p. 142. See also Hauerwas, 'Epilogue', pp. 163–4.

the divine saving power, is to make normative a certain kind of forgiving love for others. None of this, however, entails the pacifist repudiation of violence always and everywhere. It does entail that forgiveness be displayed as appropriate; but I shall argue in the following chapter that different kinds of forgiveness are appropriate in different circumstances, and that one kind is compatible with the use of violent force. It also entails that the human defence of justice may not be conducted by any means and at all costs, and that there will be occasions when its champions must lay down their weapons and pray God to defend what they themselves may defend no longer. But this, as we shall see, is exactly what the Christian doctrine of just war requires.

In his critique of Niebuhr, Hauerwas obscures the main point of contention between them. It does not lie in the possibility of the present realization of Christian love, nor in the tragic quality of human social life. Niebuhr, like Hauerwas, believes that Christian love can manifest itself here and now—by qualifying justice with mercy. Hauerwas, like Niebuhr, recognizes a tragic dimension to human history, as when he writes: 'we cannot deny that in certain circumstances it may be necessary to watch others die unjustly... That our death and the death of others might be required if we are faithful to that cross cannot be denied, but it would only be *more* tragic if we died in a manner that underwrites the pagan assumption that nothing is more tragic than death itself.'[33] No, the crucial point of contention lies in their conceptions of justice. Niebuhr sees justice, especially outside interpersonal relations, as inevitably self-interested and coercive; whereas Hauerwas thinks that this sinful justice should be replaced here and now by the kind of justice that God has displayed in Jesus Christ—that which forgives, in order to reconcile. As I shall explain later, I think them both mistaken to assume that Christian love is properly disinterested and that forgiveness must be an alternative to coercion.

Hauerwas's repudiation of war is not only fuelled by theological convictions and assumptions about the proper nature of love and forgiveness. It is also fuelled by assumptions about the nature of political motivation. Thus he tells us that even liberal nation-states fight wars 'for state interest',[34] and that in general the nation-state:

33. Hauerwas, 'Epilogue', p. 180. The italics are mine.
34. Hauerwas, 'Whose Just War? Which Peace?', p. 138.

is the history of godlessness... For what is war but the desire to be rid of God, to claim for ourselves the power to determine our meaning and destiny? Our desire to protect ourselves from our enemies, to eliminate our enemies in the name of protecting the common history we share with our friends, is but the manifestation of our hatred for God.[35]

The sweeping rhetoric of this theological critique overreaches the historical data. Insofar as Romantic nationalism is a religion substitute, and insofar as it has enchanted some nation-states, the critique is cogent. But nation-states existed before Romantic nationalism was born,[36] and not all nation-states since have been nationalist. And the fact that states fight wars in their own interests is only ethically conclusive if all self-interest is immoral—which it is not.

II. John Howard Yoder

Anyone reading Stanley Hauerwas, especially on matters to do with war and peace, will quickly become aware of his debt to John Howard Yoder, to whom he often defers. As might be expected of the most influential Mennonite theologian of modern times, Yoder's articulation of Christian pacifism is more fully developed than Hauerwas's, and his biblical grounding of it is far more thorough.[37]

The main burden of Yoder's classic text, *The Politics of Jesus*, is to argue that Jesus is immediately relevant to social ethics.[38] Focusing on the Gospel of Luke, Yoder discovers in Jesus' teaching and practice a consistent political dimension. In responding to the second temptation in the wilderness, Jesus repudiated the idolatries of 'political power hunger and nationalism'.[39] He rejected 'the Zealot option... of anti-Roman violence'[40]—as well as violence against Jews judged guilty of apostasy or collaboration with the

---

35. Hauerwas, 'Should War be Eliminated?', p. 421.
36. The historian Adrian Hastings argues this in *The Construction of Nationhood: Ethnicity, Religion, and Nationalism* (Cambridge: Cambridge University Press, 1997).
37. Hays agrees: 'Yoder's interpretation of these [New Testament] texts is informed by detailed and sophisticated interaction with historical-critical scholarship... *The Politics of Jesus* is an impressive foray by a theological ethicist into exegetical territory' (*Moral Vision*, pp. 245–6).
38. John Howard Yoder, *The Politics of Jesus: Vicit Agnus Noster* (Grand Rapids: Eerdmans, 1972), pp. 15, 23, 25. A second edition, containing a series of updating 'epilogues', was published in 1994.
39. Yoder, *Politics of Jesus* (1972), p. 32.
40. Yoder, *The Politics of Jesus: Vicit Agnus Noster*, 2nd edn (Grand Rapids: Eerdmans, 1994), p. 55.

infidel.[41] His expulsion of the merchants from the Temple in Jerusalem was an expression of 'nonviolence and non-nationalism'.[42] His 'way of the cross' involved the renunciation of 'the real option of Zealot-like kingship... the option of crusade',[43] of 'the Zealot temptation' of rebellious or revolutionary violence,[44] in favour of love—unconditional, indiscriminate, suffering injustice without complaint, absorbing hostility, forgiving.[45]

Notice how closely Yoder's political reading of the Gospel associates Jesus' non-violence with his repudiation of Zealot nationalism, insurrection, and 'political power hunger'. He could (and should) have specified the former strictly in terms of the latter, but he does not. Instead, like Hauerwas, he generalizes beyond the data: Jesus' refusal of violence in the service of politically power-hungry, religious-nationalist revolt is taken to imply a broader refusal, first, of *the principle* of violent insurrection *as such* and then, even more broadly, of the principle of using violence in *any* supposedly 'righteous political cause'.[46] Jesus rejects even 'the responsible sword',[47] even 'legitimate defense'.[48] His vision of the kingdom of God 'is crucially defined by its [unconditional] non-coerciveness'.[49] This universalizing expansion of the significance of Jesus' specific refusal of violence in a certain set of circumstances requires justification, which is not provided. And while it is undeniable that much of the ethical import of Jesus can be captured by the word 'love', provided that this is specified as love for enemies and forgiveness of sinners, what remains open to doubt is that this love is simply unconditional and indiscriminate. I myself do doubt it and I shall explain why in the next chapter.

41. Ibid., p. 57 n. 73.
42. Yoder, *Politics of Jesus* (1972), p. 50 n.36.
43. Ibid., pp. 57, 61, 90–3.
44. Yoder, 'Jesus, a Model of Radical Political Action', in Yoder, *The War of the Lamb: The Ethics of Nonviolence and Peacemaking*, ed. Glen Stassen, Mark Thiessen Nation, and Matt Hamsher (Grand Rapids: Brazos, 2009), p. 79. Against Richard Horsley, Yoder argues that the word 'Zealot', as used by Luke in his Gospel, need not refer anachronistically to a particular party in the great revolt of 66–70 AD or with historical inaccuracy to a continuous political movement. It could also have a broader reference, namely to 'the general phenomenon of subversive violence', especially as manifested in periodic messianic uprisings of the rural poor (Yoder, *Politics of Jesus* [1994], pp. 56–7).
45. Yoder, *Politics of Jesus* (1972), pp. 118–28, 134.
46. Yoder, *Politics of Jesus* (1994), p. 58. The emphasis is mine.
47. Yoder, *Politics of Jesus* (1972), p. 93.
48. Ibid., p. 100.
49. Yoder, 'Biblical Realism and the Politics of Jesus', in *Christian Attitudes to War, Peace, and Revolution*, ed. Theodore J. Koontz and Andy Alexis-Baker (Grand Rapids: Brazos, 2009), p. 313.

To Jesus' teaching and practice of unconditional love and non-violence, Yoder adds faith in God's saving activity, as manifested pre-eminently in Jesus' resurrection from the dead. He claims that the theme of trusting God for national survival *as an alternative to military action* had become 'part of the standard devotional ritual of Israel'[50] in the post-Exilic period; and that Jesus' announcing the restoration of God's kingdom without recourse to violent methods 'could very easily have been understood as updating the faith of Jehoshaphat and Hezekiah'.[51] Seen in this light, the use of violence involves an 'element of despair' in God: 'We short-circuit that providential potential when we decide to be providence ourselves, at the expense of the fellow humans on whom we inflict the violence that we claim is lesser.'[52] In contrast,

> [t]he present meaning of the resurrection for ethics is that we are never boxed in...Many 'saving' events in history were unforeseeable, unplanned, but they happened. The Resurrection was an impossible, unforeseeable new option, and it happened...[W]e are committed to confessing as relevant for our ethics that there is a power in history that reaches beyond the boxes in which we find ourselves.[53]

Yoder is quite right to suppose that faith in God should manifest itself in a readiness to wait upon Him to defend and promote goods that we ourselves cannot or may not; and that resort to immoral means in their service is an expression of faithless impatience. If this were not so, faith would be practically otiose. Nevertheless, faith does not require the abandonment of all human responsibility, initiative, and effort. Those who love God are bound to love the world that He loves; and those who love the world are bound to do whatever they can and may to see it prosper. In that sense, then, we human beings are actually called 'to be providence ourselves'. Indeed, that is perhaps the best interpretation of what is meant by describing us as 'made in God's image'.[54] The issue is not whether we should be provident, but

---

50. Yoder, *Politics of Jesus* (1972), pp. 81–2, 86. Yoder acknowledges, however, that Israel's post-Exilic ritual did not view belligerency as *necessarily* opposed to God's providence, since '[s]ometimes this [miraculous divine] preservation had included the Israelites' military activity' (ibid., p. 86).

51. Ibid., p. 88.

52. Yoder, 'A Theological Critique of Violence', in *War of the Lamb*, p. 39.

53. Yoder, 'Biblical Realism', p. 319.

54. The status of being made in God's image has been understood in a variety of ways in the course of the history of Christian reflection on Genesis 1:26. Arguably the most exegetically responsible reading interprets it in terms of the second, parallel half of the biblical verse

what the moral constraints are that should discipline our providence. Yoder assumes that all violence is intrinsically wrong and that resorting to it necessarily represents an impatient, faithless throwing off of moral constraint. This assumption, however, stands in need of argumentative support, since not everyone shares it. Just war theorists insist that the use of violence be proportioned by morally right motive and intention, and they believe that it can be. Where violence cannot be so disciplined, it must be foresworn. Even just war theorists, therefore, admit that there are times when just warriors must clamber off their warhorses and clatter onto their knees. Even in just war, faith in God can find practical expression in the heeding of moral constraints and obedience to their logic.

Anyone, like Yoder, who wants to argue for a pacifist reading of the New Testament has to reckon with the 13th chapter of St Paul's Epistle to the Romans, where the Apostle appears to say that God has authorized the use of violent force by public authorities to curb wrongdoing:

> [T]here is no authority except from God, and those that exist have been instituted by God. Therefore he who resists the authorities resists what God has appointed . . . For rulers are not a terror to good conduct, but to bad. Would you have no fear of him who is in authority? Then do what is good, and you will receive his approval, for he is God's servant for your good. But if you do wrong, be afraid, for he does not bear the sword in vain; he is the servant of God to execute his wrath on the wrongdoer. (13:1–4)[55]

Yoder's first response to this passage is to marginalize it, by asserting that there is 'a very strong strand of Gospel teaching which sees secular government as the province of the sovereignty of Satan', that there is a comparable strand in the rest of the New Testament, and that Romans 13 'is not the center of this teaching'.[56] Next, Romans 13:1–7 is to be understood in the context of chapters 12 and 13:8–10, where Christians are urged to give themselves over to 'suffering and serving love' and to leave vengeance to the public authorities ordained by God for that purpose. 'This makes it clear,' Yoder writes, 'that the function exercised by government is not the function

---

where the assertion is first made: 'And God said, "Let us make man in our image, after our likeness; *and let them have dominion* over the fish of the sea, and over the birds of the air, and over the cattle, and over every creeping thing that creeps upon the earth"' (Genesis 1:26. The emphasis is mine). That is to say, to be made in God's image is to exercise dominion on God's behalf.

55. All biblical quotations in this chapter are taken from the Revised Standard Version.
56. Yoder, *Politics of Jesus*, pp. 195–6.

to be exercised by Christians.'[57] Moreover, since Christians had no part in the government to which Paul instructed them to be subject, the text cannot imply a call to exercise the judicial or police functions. Besides, even if it did imply that, such functions need not involve the death penalty and do not amount to war.[58]

It is quite true that there are parts of the New Testament where Roman imperial government is absolutely condemned for its oppressiveness—most obviously in the Revelation to John. However, such a stance was a response to a particular set of circumstances—religious persecution by the imperial authorities—that did not obtain always and everywhere during the seventy years or so when the components of the New Testament were being written. Other parts of the New Testament take different views. The Gospels, for example, are critical of the imperial governor, Pilate, because of his political weakness rather than his indiscriminate strength, while Paul in Romans 13 expresses greater confidence that government will use its strength to defend the innocent against the guilty. It is not at all obvious, therefore, that the New Testament exhibits a predominant bias against 'secular government' in general.

As I shall argue more fully in the next section of this chapter, Paul's injunction to Christians in Rome to suffer in love rather than avenge themselves was a plea not to respond to their persecutors by taking the law into their own hands, thus posing a threat to public order.[59] Of course Paul was not arguing that Christians should exercise the judicial or police functions, because the prospect of them actually doing so was nowhere on his horizon. Whether Christian love might ever be compatible with the public bearing of the sword is a question that he raised implicitly but did not address. Still, in describing the sword's use in defence of the innocent as authorized by God—the one God, who has made himself manifest in Jesus—Paul did lay the basis for an affirmative answer. Moreover, the affirmation of Christian magistrates and policemen does amount to an affirmation of Christian executioners and soldiers. Paul's choice of metaphor for the judicial and police functions—the sword—was hardly a metaphor at all. In the circumstances of his time and place the force used to keep law and order was commonly lethal, and, since police as a distinct category of public official did not exist, it was exercised by soldiers.

---

57. Ibid., pp. 197, 199.
58. Ibid., pp. 205–6.
59. See below, pp. 42–5.

On the matter of the Christian refusal of violence in the post-Apostolic era, Yoder admits that this was associated with the rejection of the culture of the Roman empire. The early Christians were 'globally polarized' against all that Caesar and his empire meant, he tells us, because 'Caesar stood for polytheism and idolatry... Caesar was sometimes honoured in a cultic way... The life of the soldier involved regularly swearing oaths... Caesar's agents occasionally persecuted Christians... Caesar's total lifestyle was immoral and blasphemous'.[60] Still, Yoder also regards as discredited the argument that early Christians were not pacifist, strictly speaking, but only rejected military service on account of its association with idolatry.[61] This is undoubtedly true. Judging by those views that have come down to us, early post-Apostolic opposition to Christian participation in military service was not always grounded *simply* on its entailment of idolatry or on its association with a wantonly bloodthirsty culture. Tertullian, for one, can be found appealing directly to the teaching of Jesus as delivered by the Gospels. So, for example, he writes: 'Shall it be held lawful to make an occupation of the sword, when the Lord proclaims that he who uses the sword shall perish by the sword?'[62] Nevertheless, one relatively recent survey of the relevant literature—deemed 'even-handed' by the pacifist Richard Hays[63]—judges that the old consensus that the earliest Christians were overwhelmingly pacifist is *passé*, and that a new consensus has arisen. This holds that the most vociferous opponents of military service (such as Tertullian) 'based their objections on a variety of factors'; that at least from the end of the 2nd century Christian opinion and practice on the matter were divided; that throughout the 3rd century Christian support for military service grew (which is why Tertullian was provoked to write against it); and that Christian just war thinking 'stand[s] in fundamental continuity with at least one strand of pre-Constantinian tradition'.[64]

How does Yoder explain the emergence of just war thinking among Christians in the later 4th century? In part, he attributes it to the gradual

60. Yoder, 'Gospel Renewal and the Roots of Nonviolence', in *War of the Lamb*, pp. 48–9.
61. Yoder, 'The Pacifism of Pre-Constantinian Christianity', in *Christian Attitudes to War*, pp. 45, 47 n. 2.
62. Tertullian, 'On the Soldier's Chaplet' [De Corona], in *Ante-Nicene Christian Library*, ed. Alexander Roberts and James Donaldson, vol. XI: 'The Writings of Tertullian', vol. I (Edinburgh: T. & T. Clark, 1869), chapter 11, p. 347.
63. Richard B. Hays, 'Narrate and Embody! A Response to Nigel Biggar, "Specify and Distinguish"', *Studies in Christian Ethics*, 22/2 (May 2009), p. 190 n. 10.
64. David G. Hunter, 'A Decade of Research on Early Christians and Military Service', *Religious Studies Review*, 18/2 (April 1992), p. 93.

relaxation of 'primitive moral discipline'.[65] Mostly, however, he blames the
identification of divine providence with the Christian empire, which came
into being with Constantine:[66] Constantinian Christians 'now knew that
the Roman emperor and their God were allies and that the forward movement of history was enforced by the legions'.[67] Among such Christians
Yoder explicitly ranks not only Eusebius but Augustine.[68] Thus the Christian
empire produced the concept of a crusade against the infidel.[69] This account
of the genesis of the Christian tradition of just war thinking is distorted to
the point of caricature, and it implies that Yoder had not taken the trouble
to make himself familiar with the classic texts of Christian just war thinking.[70] No one who has read Augustine's *City of God* would ever align him
with Eusebius in identifying the Christianized empire with the kingdom of
God. As for the concept of a crusade against infidels, that emerged at the
very end of the 11th century AD. A hundred and fifty years later, in his seminal statement of the criteria of just war, Thomas Aquinas made no mention
of it. However, in analysing the Spanish conquest of the Americas, his 16th-
century disciple, Francisco de Vitoria, judged that war waged to propagate
the Christian religion is unjust.[71]

Moving from the genesis of just war thinking to its nature, Yoder's fundamental complaint is that it assumes that biblical truth and ordinary human
wisdom tend to coincide, does not bother to justify itself on the basis of (the
whole of) Scripture, and so both formally and materially diverges from Jesus
in the New Testament.[72] Instead, it takes its cue either from pagan sources
such as Aristotle and Cicero or from the tradition of Joshua and holy war in

65. Yoder, 'Pacifism of Pre-Constantinian Christianity', pp. 53–4.
66. Yoder, 'The Constantinian Sources of Western Social Ethics' *The Priestly Kingdom. Social Ethics
    as Gospel* (Notre Dame: University of Notre Dame Press, 1984), pp. 136–7.
67. Yoder, 'Gospel Renewal', p. 45.
68. Yoder, 'The Meaning of the Constantinian Shift', in *Christian Attitudes to War*, pp. 62–3.
69. Yoder, 'Constantinian Sources', pp. 137–8.
70. It is possible, of course, that the account that I have given here of Yoder's thought does not
    represent it at its most mature. However, 'The Constantinian Sources of Western Social Ethics'
    was published in 1984; 'Gospel Renewal and the Roots of Nonviolence', while first written in
    1984, was published in revised form in 1995; and 'The Pacifism of Pre-Constantinian
    Christianity' and 'The Meaning of the Constantinian Shift', while first published in 1983, were
    last presented as lectures by Yoder in the autumn of 1997, shortly before his death in December
    of that year.
71. Francisco de Vitoria, 'On the American Indians', in Vitoria, *Political Writings*, ed. Anthony
    Pagden and Jeremy Lawrance, Cambridge Texts in the History of Political Thought (Cambridge:
    Cambridge University Press, 1991), esp. question 2, article 4, pp. 265–72.
72. Yoder, 'Meaning of the Constantinian Shift', p. 66; Yoder, 'The Logic of the Just War
    Tradition', in *Christian Attitudes to War*, pp. 76–7.

the Old Testament.[73] One material ethical consequence of this formal orientation is that just war thinking measures itself by 'the world's standard',[74]
thus making pragmatic success the criterion of right and virtue:[75] 'once the
evident course of history is held to be empirically discernible, and the prosperity of our regime is the measure of good, all morality boils down to
efficacy'.[76] Another consequence is that, thanks to the influence of
Neoplatonism on Augustine, it assigns primary moral importance to 'the
inner attitude', thus cutting the nerve of Jesus' social ethic.[77]

To claim that Christian just war theory does not care to justify itself in
terms of the New Testament and merely defers to pagan or sub-Christian
wisdom is neither true nor fair. Augustine's early articulations of a Christian
rationale for the use of violent force are thick with biblical references;[78] and
if in his treatment of war in the *Summa Theologiae* Aquinas quotes Augustine
more often, he does not fail to attend to the New Testament as well.[79] As for
the criteria of just war reducing down to that of success, Augustine explicitly denied that success is the mark of a Christian ruler;[80] Aquinas's criteria
were all concerned with duties, not consequences; and even when consequential criteria were added in the 16th century, the deontic ones remained
basic.

The focusing of moral concern on the motivation and intention of an
act, rather than on its effects, is crucial for the justification of the use of
lethal force, and Yoder is quite right to identify it as a decisive issue.
Nevertheless, it is odd that he should complain that it hamstrings Jesus'
ethic, since so much of Jesus' teaching emphasizes the importance of internal attitude: for obvious example, 'You have heard that it was said to the men
of old, "You shall not kill…". But I say to you that every one who is angry
with his brother shall be liable to judgement' (Matthew 5:21–22a). Besides—
unless one is a consequentialist, which Jesus seems not to have been—the
determination of the moral rightness or wrongness of an act requires

73. Yoder, 'The Career of Just War Theory', in *Christian Attitudes to War*, p. 106.
74. Yoder, 'Meaning of the Constantinian Shift', p. 58.
75. Ibid., p. 70.
76. Yoder, 'Constantinian Sources', p. 140.
77. Yoder, 'Meaning of the Constantinian Shift', pp, 62, 64.
78. E.g. Augustine, 'Letter 138' (to Marcellinus), in Augustine, *Political Writings*, ed. E.M. Atkins and
    R.J. Dodaro, Cambridge Texts in the History of Political Thought (Cambridge: Cambridge
    University Press, 2001), ss.9–14, pp. 34–9; 'Letter 189' (to Boniface), *Political Writings*, ss.2–7,
    pp. 215–17.
79. Aquinas, *Summa Theologiae*, 2a 2ae, q. 40.
80. Augustine, *City of God*, Book V. 24–5.

reference to motivation and intention. The mere fact that you use a knife to cut into my flesh, with the result that healthy tissue is damaged, is not sufficient to determine the moral quality of what you are doing. You could be engaged in a disproportionate act of revenge, motivated by hatred and intending nothing but pain and harm. Or you could be undertaking an act of self-defence, motivated by reasonable self-interest and intending only to disable me from continuing an act of unwarranted aggression. Or you could be a surgeon, motivated only by care for your patient, and intending to save my life by amputating a limb whose lower reaches are gangrenous. Not even pacifists object simply to acts that result in the deaths of other people; for they themselves are prepared to perform deliberate acts of omission, which permit innocents to die at the hands of the unjust. What pacifists object to, rather, are lethal acts of commission—that is, acts that intend another's death, and which (judging by Hauerwas and Yoder) they assume must be motivated by anger or hatred. Unless inner attitude is morally decisive, therefore, it is impossible to make sense of the pacifist's position.

Another basic objection that Yoder makes to just war thinking is that it assumes that 'we have a mandate to take charge of the historical process, to help God's will triumph'—that is, to take 'responsibility'.[81] The exercise of responsibility presupposes 'the possession of power', which Yoder associates with 'pride and self-justification'. He also associates it with ideological ruthlessness:

> One seeks to lift up one focal point in the midst of the course of human relations, one thread of meaning and causality which is more important than individual persons, their lives and well-being, because it in itself determines wherein their well-being consists. Therefore it is justified to sacrifice to this one 'cause' other subordinate values, including the life and welfare of one's self, one's neighbor, and (of course!) the enemy. We pull on this one strategic thread in order to save the whole fabric.[82]

This assumes 'that the relationship of cause and effect is visible, understandable, and manageable'. Here, however, it seems that Reinhold Niebuhr was right: history has a penchant for irony:

> [W]hen men try to manage history, it almost always turns out to have taken another direction than that in which they thought they were guiding it... [Man] is not capable of discerning and managing [history's] course when

81. Yoder, 'Logic of the Just War Tradition', p. 81.
82. Yoder, *Politics of Jesus* (1972), p. 234.

there are in the same theatre of operation a host of other free agents, each of them in his own way also acting under the same assumptions as to his capacity to move history in his direction.[83]

By contrast, 'Jesus was so faithful to the enemy-love of God that it cost him all his effectiveness; he gave up every handle on history', especially 'the compulsiveness of purpose that leads men to violate the dignity of others'.[84] According to the Revelation to John, the key to the obedience of God's people is 'not their effectiveness but their patience'.[85] And '[d]oing without dominion was not for [the early Christians] a second-best alternative to glory; *it was the way to participate in the victory of redemption*'.[86]

There is a lot of wisdom in what Yoder says here. Our capacity to determine the effects of our action, and so to control the direction of history, is very limited; and when, rising up against frustration and despair, we resolve to impose our will *at all costs*, the results are ruthless and unjust. Sometimes it really is better to do nothing; sometimes prayer is (at least) less harmful than action. Nevertheless, human beings are made in the image of God to tend the world. We are made to care for what deserves to be cared for, and to flourish in its service. We are made to take responsibility *under God*—to take responsibility *while being responsible*. Therefore, in full knowledge of the irony of history and of the fragility of whatever we achieve, we must do what we *can* to defend and promote what is good—but within the limits of what we *may*. The question, then, is whether war can ever tell the difference between what can be done and what may be done, and whether it can allow the latter to govern the former. Yoder assumes not. I see no reason to share this assumption, since it seems historically and empirically clear to me that soldiers' conduct can suffer moral constraint.

Some of Yoder's criticisms of the nature of just war thinking are directed against its basic assumptions; others are more particular. Some of the latter have to do with intention. Yoder claims that the intention of soldiers is not what Christian discipleship requires: instead of laying down their lives for their friends, they intend 'to kill...to lay down somebody else's life'.[87]

---

83. Ibid., p. 235.
84. Ibid., pp. 239, 243–4.
85. Ibid., p. 238. Later Yoder became more nuanced: '[T]o follow Jesus does not mean renouncing effectiveness...It means that in Jesus we have a clue to which kinds of causation...which kinds of conflict management...go with the grain of the cosmos, of which...Jesus is...the Lord' (Yoder, *Politics of Jesus* [1994], p. 246).
86. Yoder, 'A Theological Critique of Violence', p. 39. The emphasis is Yoder's.
87. Yoder, 'The Career of Just War Theory', p. 112.

Related to this is the complaint that double effect reasoning 'constitutes a powerful intellectual apparatus contributing to a downward drift', and that '[i]t is not easy for the critic who wants to be fair to know where the line runs between careful casuistic good faith and plain cynical abuse'.[88] Yoder's reading of military motivation and intention is a priori rather than a posteriori. In combat, soldiers are primarily motivated by love for their comrades rather than hatred of the enemy—and sometimes not at all by the latter; and what they intend, strictly speaking, is to disable the enemy rather than kill him.[89] Regarding double effect reasoning, since it permits deliberate (if not intentional) killing, pacifists are bound to view it as excessively permissive and amounting to cynical rationalization. Those who do not regard deliberate killing as always and everywhere wrong, however, will beg to differ.

Other particular criticisms focus on the just war criterion of proportion: namely that before deciding to go to war or to embark on a particular military operation, one must judge that the evils caused will not subvert or outweigh the goods defended or promoted. However, writes Yoder, this wrongly assumes 'that some way exists to quantify the different values violated over against each other'.[90] Just warriors 'owe it to their own integrity . . . to possess reliable and verifiable measures of the evil they claim to be warding off and the lesser evil they are willing to commit . . . [T]he burden of proof lies with the party who says that it is probable enough to justify intervening by causing some certain lethal evil in order to reduce other projected evils.'[91] Here Yoder presses down on one of the weakest elements in just war reasoning. There is no common currency in terms of which to weigh together the evils caused (the loss of human lives, the grief of families, damage to the social and economic infrastructure, resentment of and mistrust toward the enemy) and the goods achieved (an end to atrocious oppression, the punishment of the oppressor, the possibility of a healthier political future, the removal of a threat to international peace). These evils and goods are incommensurable. If there is a rational way of deliberating about them, it is not scientific and—notwithstanding the popular metaphor of 'weighing up'—it is not quantitative. And no matter how well reasoned the conclusion of our deliberation, it is

88. Yoder, *When War is Unjust. Being Honest in Just-War Thinking*, rev. edn (Maryknoll, NY: Orbis, 1996), p. 59.
89. I develop the first claim (about motivation) in Chapter Two, and the second one (about intention) in Chapter Six.
90. Yoder, 'A Theological Critique of Violence', p. 37.
91. Yoder, *When War is Unjust*, p. 77.

certain that it is not certain. However, such imprecision and uncertainty about effects are the condition of all human deliberation about action. Yet much of the time it seems reasonable to launch the ship of action into the prevailing fog. Might it not, therefore, be reasonable to venture an act of war? Yoder might reply that the evils of war are so terrible that one needs strong reasons to incur them. That is true. But perhaps strong reasons need not be consequential ones; and perhaps the consequential reasons can be sufficiently strong without being certain. And besides, since acts of pacifist omission can also have grave effects, pacifists, too, must deliberate as best they can about the evils of peace. The burden of proof—or rather, since proof of accurate prediction in advance of events is impossible, the burden of practical reason—presses down on their shoulders too. As Michael Quinlan has written, 'where action is possible inaction is itself a choice, with its own con-sequences, its own responsibility and its own problems of unsure prediction. Abstention from or opposition to engagement in Kosovo in 1999—or in Rwanda in 1994—was not a cost-free moral option.'[92]

Finally, Yoder claims that just war theory has proven almost completely ineffectual in practice: '[t]otal war has in fact characterized our culture... there was no effective restraint in most of the Western world's experience of war. Just war theory has not been operational in any significant way in the mili-tary reality of the last centuries.'[93] This is a sweeping historical claim, which is asserted without any supporting argumentation. It is obvious, of course, that the just war tradition has failed to stop many wars that clearly fail to meet its basic criteria—for example, the medieval crusades, the Spanish invasion of the Americas, and Mussolini's invasion of Abyssinia. However, the failure to prevent unjust wars is one that the just war tradition shares with Christian pacifism. The fact that political rulers sometimes refuse to heed a morally normative view tells us nothing at all about its truth. Moreover, if just war reasoning has failed to turn some ruling heads, it has probably succeeded in turning others. There is no a priori reason to doubt that Augustine's epistolary counsel moderated the way in which military tribunes such as Marcellinus and Boniface carried out their policing func-tions. And it is quite clear that just war reasoning now informs public delib-eration in the United Kingdom and United States today, as well as the international law of armed conflict.

---

92. Michael Quinlan, 'A British Political Perspective', in *The Price of Peace*, p. 289.
93. Yoder, 'Just War and Non-violence' (1992), in *War of the Lamb*, p. 88.

III. Richard Hays[94]

Pacifism that would call itself Christian is bound to justify itself in terms of the New Testament. After all, the New Testament is a basic authority in Christian churches, and there is a rival, non-pacifist interpretation of it, which finds conditional grounds for the use of violent force. Christian pacifists therefore face a challenge from other Christians, which, if they are to behave responsibly, they should take care to answer.

Stanley Hauerwas seems cheerfully oblivious to the fraternal obligation. John Howard Yoder is not, and offers a serious response. However, far more thorough, systematic, and sophisticated yet is Richard Hays's *The Moral Vision of the New Testament*.[95] Widely showered with superlatives by biblical scholars on its first publication in 1996,[96] and rated a 'classic' and a 'masterpiece' in 2006[97] and 2007,[98] *The Moral Vision* devotes its 14th chapter

---

94. Section III of this chapter comprises an expanded and revised version of 'Specify and Distinguish! Interpreting the New Testament on "Non-Violence"', *Studies in Christian Ethics*, 22/2 (May 2009). The revision has been made in the light of Richard Hays, 'Narrate and Embody! A Response to Nigel Biggar', which appeared in the same place; and of a subsequent round of correspondence, which was published in *Studies in Christian Ethics*, 22/2 (May 2009).

95. Richard B. Hays, *Moral Vision of the New Testament: A Contemporary Introduction to New Testament Ethics* (Edinburgh: T. & T. Clark, 1996).

96. Among the pre-publication plaudits to be found on the back cover and opening page are these: 'Hays's...book...has neither peer nor rival' (Leander Keck, Yale Divinity School); 'Hays has pulled off, with a success for which I can think of no contemporary parallel, one of the most difficult tasks in theological and biblical writing today' (James Dunn, University of Durham); '[Hays's] description of the variegated ethical vision of the early church is state-of-the-art, and the application of that vision to contemporary issues is hermeneutically skillful...' (George Lindbeck, Yale Divinity School); 'A gem that sparkles on every page' (Graham Stanton, University of London); '...an extraordinary accomplishment' (Allen Verhey, Hope College); 'Hays's method and proposals will...prove a benchmark for future scholarship' (L. Gregory Jones); 'a rare and fine book' (John Riches, University of Glasgow).

97. For example, by Willard M. Swartley in *Covenant of Peace: The Missing Peace in New Testament Theology and Ethics* (Grand Rapids, MI: Eerdmans, 2006): 'Hays's *Moral Vision* is a classic for its penetrating, succinct exegesis of selected NT writings; his hermeneutical model...and his perceptive treatment of five major voices in theological ethics...Hays's treatments of Mark, Matthew, Luke-Acts, and John are incisive' (pp. 439, 441); and by Robert Morgan in *The Oxford Handbook of Biblical Studies* (Oxford: Oxford University Press, 2006), who refers to 'Hays's...subsequent masterpiece *The Moral Vision of the New Testament*' (p. 48).

98. In the first chapter of his own alternative reading of New Testament ethics, Richard Burridge writes of *The Moral Vision* that 'it has quickly established itself as the classic treatment and has been widely appreciated' (*Imitating Jesus: An Inclusive Approach to New Testament Ethics* [Grand Rapids, MI: Eerdmans, 2007], pp. 14–15).

to arguing that the New Testament forbids the use of violence under all circumstances, even when the defence of justice seems to require it. I begin with a summary of what Hays says.

Hays's hermeneutic

Richard Hays recognizes that the New Testament contains a plurality of voices, which are sometimes in tension with each other. He also recognizes, therefore, that, in order to give an account of *the* moral vision of the New Testament, one must construct synthesis out of diversity. This he does by selecting certain focal 'images' on the grounds of their wide representation across the spectrum of New Testament writings, their congruence with the ethical teachings and major emphases of the New Testament witnesses, and their highlighting central and substantial ethical concerns of the texts in which they appear.[99] The selected images are those of community, cross, and new creation, which comprise principal elements in the story of God's salvation of the world.[100] These Hays then deploys as a canon within the canon,[101] so as to order the New Testament's diverse voices, pulling some elements to centre stage and pushing others to the wings, thus producing a coherent account of *the* moral vision of the New Testament. This ordering is an act of interpretation, which inevitably involves other, extra-biblical, authorities such as tradition, reason, and experience. These, however, stand in a subordinate relationship to the New Testament, whose perspective is privileged.[102] After the hermeneutical task comes the 'pragmatic' one of working out what the New Testament's general moral vision means for specific areas of Christian practice. To be adequate, any such specific ethic must give serious and sustained attention to all three focal images.[103] Moreover, since the New Testament presents itself to us in the shape of a story, narrative texts are more fundamental than any secondary process of abstraction that seeks to distil their ethical import. It follows that an adequate ethic must give hermeneutical primacy to the paradigmatic or analogical use of the New Testament over that which operates in terms of rules or principles.[104]

---

99. Hays, *Moral Vision*, p. 195.
100. Ibid., p. 292.   101. Ibid., pp. 199–200.
102. Ibid., p. 296.   103. Ibid., p. 293.   104. Ibid., p. 295.

Hays's pacifist reading of the New Testament

Hays's pacifist argument about the New Testament's view of violence opens, predictably, with the Sermon on the Mount in the Gospel of Matthew (chapters 5–7). This he sees as Jesus' 'basic training on the life of discipleship', his 'programmatic disclosure of the kingdom of God and of the life to which the community of disciples is called', and 'a definitive charter for the life of the new covenant community'. While not taking the form of 'a comprehensive new legal code', this 'charter' 'suggests by way of a few examples the character of this new community'. And what is this character? *Inter alia*, one in which 'anger is overcome through reconciliation (5:21–6) . . . retaliation is renounced (5:38–42), and enemy-love replaces hate (5:43–8)'.[105] In sum, 'the transcendence of violence through loving the enemy is the most salient feature of this new model *polis*'.[106]

Lest it be supposed that this vision of a non-violent Christian community is confined to the Sermon on the Mount, Hays proceeds to argue that it finds confirmation in Matthew's 'overall portrayal of Jesus'. In the temptation narrative (4:1–11), for example, Jesus renounces the option of 'wielding power' over the kingdoms of the world; and (following Yoder) his deflection of the temptation to refuse the cup of suffering amounts to a renunciation of the resort to armed resistance.[107]

Hays's next move is to tackle 'various ingenious interpretations that mitigate the normative claim of this text [Matthew 5:38–48]'.[108] Among these are interpretations holding that the only violence prohibited is that in self-defence (and that violence in defence of third parties is implicitly permitted). Against these, Hays invokes the 'larger paradigm of Jesus' own conduct in Matthew's Gospel', which 'indicates a deliberate renunciation of violence as an instrument of God's will'.[109] He substantiates this by appeal to the temptation narrative, where Jesus 'does not seek to defend the interests of the poor and oppressed in Palestine by organizing armed resistance against the Romans or against the privileged Jewish collaborators with Roman authority'. He also appeals to the narrative of Jesus' arrest, where the disciple who draws his sword in defence of his master receives a severe dominical rebuke (Matthew 26:47–52). This he takes to

---

105. Ibid., p. 321.   106. Ibid., p. 322.
107. Ibid., p. 322.   108. Ibid., p. 320.   109. Ibid., p. 323.

be 'an explicit refutation' of the justifiability of the use of violence in defence of a third party.[110]

A second set of interpretations that Hays seeks to discredit are those that would limit the meaning of the prohibitions of violence in terms of their social and political context. One of these readings is offered by Robert Guelich, who argues that the scope of Matthew 5:39a ('But I say to you, Do not resist one who is evil') should be limited to a courtroom context, specifying its meaning as an injunction against seeking judicial redress against a false accuser.[111] Hays concedes that one of the illustrative injunctions in Matthew 5:38–48 does have a specifically judicial meaning (v. 40: 'and if anyone would sue you and take your coat, let him have your cloak as well'), but he denies that the others (e.g. v. 39b: 'But if one strikes you on the right cheek, turn to him the other also') can be confined to a forensic context. He points out that Guelich himself admits that verses 41 and 42 ('and if any one forces you to go one mile, go with him two miles. Give to him who begs from you, and do not refuse him who would borrow from you') cannot be so constrained.[112] Hays's case here seems cogent.

Another restrictive interpretation that Hays seeks to discredit is Richard Horsley's. Horsley argues that in the original historical setting, the 'enemies' whom Jesus exhorted his disciples to love (Matthew 5:44) referred only to 'personal enemies'—other members of small Palestinian villages who found themselves competing against one another for scarce economic resources—rather than foreign or military ones; and that Jesus' primary concern was to get the peasants to stop squabbling with each other so as to cooperate for mutual economic benefit.[113] Hays's first counter-argument is that such a reading commands no lexicographical support: the Greek word *echthroi* in Matthew 5:44, translated as 'enemies', is a generic term and is often used in biblical Greek of national or military enemies, not just of personal or local ones. His second point is that nothing in the Gospel of Matthew suggests such a precisely local social situation, and that Horsley himself acknowledges that the Matthaean context actually requires the more

---

110. Ibid., p. 324.
111. Robert A. Guelich, *The Sermon on the Mount: A Foundation for Understanding* (Waco, TX: Word, 1982).
112. Hays, *Moral Vision*, pp. 325–6.
113. Richard Horsley, *Jesus and the Spiral of Violence: Popular Jewish Resistance in Roman Palestine* (San Francisco: Harper and Row, 1987), pp. 255–73.

general interpretation of enemies as 'outsiders and persecutors'.[114]
However, Hays's main complaint is methodological, namely that Horsley
makes normative his reconstruction of the history *behind* the text, and
uses it to trump the intended meaning of the Matthaean text itself. On
the contrary, according to Hays, 'the canonical narrative context governs
the normative theological use of the text; the historical reconstruction
remains speculative'.[115]

After his defence of a pacifist reading of the Gospel of Matthew, Hays
proceeds to the synthetic task of showing that the non-violent stance of this
Gospel is echoed throughout the canonical New Testament as a whole. The
Gospels, he finds, are unanimous in portraying Jesus as a Messiah who sub-
verts all prior expectations by assuming the vocation of suffering 'rather
than conquering Israel's enemies'.[116] The Acts of the Apostles present the
martyr Stephen, praying for the forgiveness of his enemies (Acts 7:60), as the
model of a Christian response to violence. In his epistles, Paul presents God
himself as responding to his enemies, not by killing them, but by seeking
reconciliation through the 'self-giving' of his Son.[117] And while Paul writes
that 'the governing authority bears the sword to execute God's wrath
(Romans 13:4), that, according to Hays, is not the role of believers. Those
who are members of the one body in Christ (12:5) are never to take vengeance (12:19); they are to bless their persecutors and minister to their enemies, returning good for evil'. Likewise, the Epistle to the Hebrews and the
Catholic Epistles offer 'a consistent portrayal of the community as called to
suffer without anger or retaliation'.[118] Finally, the Revelation to John 'seeks
to inculcate in its readers precisely the same character qualities that we have
seen extolled through the rest of the New Testament canon: faithful endurance in suffering, trust in God's eschatological vindication of his people, and
a response to adversity modeled on the paradigm of "the Lamb who was
slaughtered"'.[119]

The concluding move that Hays makes in his synthetic argument is to
deal with certain particular texts that 'seem to stand in tension with the
central witness of the New Testament concerning violence'.[120] Prominent
among these are the passages where soldiers make an appearance. In Luke

---

114. Hays, *Moral Vision*, p. 328.   115. Ibid., p. 324 (cp. p. 328).
116. Ibid., p. 329.   117. Ibid., p. 330.   118. Ibid., p. 331.
119. Ibid., p. 332.   120. Ibid., p. 332.

3:14–15 John the Baptist does not exhort them to abandon their profession, but merely to pursue it honestly without exploiting the civilian population. In Matthew 8:5–13 and Luke 7:1–10 Jesus marvels at the faith of the centurion whose servant he has healed, but raises no questions about his military profession. In Mark 15:39 it is a centurion at the foot of the cross who is the first human character in the Gospel to recognize Jesus as the Son of God. And in Acts 10:1–11:18 the centurion Cornelius, described as 'an upright and God-fearing man', converts to the Christian faith, but there is no indication that this is supposed to involve his renunciation of military service. Hays's response to these awkward texts is to argue that they have a particular literary role, that is, 'to dramatize the power of the Word of God to reach even the unlikeliest people'. In Luke 3:12–13, for example, soldiers appear alongside tax collectors as examples of how John's preaching reached even the most 'unsavory characters'.[121] Moreover, when measured against 'a synthetic statement of the New Testament's witness', the examples of individual 'good soldiers' in the New Testament 'weigh negligibly': in the light of the vocation of the Christian community to the work of reconciliation and to suffer in the face of great injustice, 'the place of the soldier within the church can only be seen as anomalous'.[122]

After the synthetic operation comes the hermeneutical or interpretative one. Now that we have before us *an* account of *the* view of violence that the New Testament takes, how should we respond to it? First of all, we should note that testimony against violence is to be found in all four normative modes—rules, principles, paradigms, and symbolic world. What this means is that the evidence that the New Testament sets its face against any justification for the use of violence 'accumulates overwhelmingly'.[123] Therefore, given the primacy of the New Testament among ethical authorities, Christian ethics has no option but to jettison the tradition of just war thinking.[124]

One classic objection to this is that since 'the Sermon on the Mount was addressed to a marginal community outside the circle of power, its teachings cannot be directly applied in a context where Christians hold positions of power and influence, or where they constitute the majority in a democratic political order'. However, while this position reckons very seriously with

---

121. Ibid., p. 335.   122. Ibid., p. 337.
123. Ibid., p. 340.   124. Ibid., pp. 297, 341.

'the historical fact' that the political context for Christian ethics has changed dramatically from the time of the New Testament writers, 'an equally serious case can be made that, on balance, history teaches that violence simply begets violence'.[125]

There we have Hays's argument. Now let us examine it.

The soldier narratives: the thin end of the wedge

We begin our critique at the point where may be found, according to Hays, 'the one possible legitimate basis for arguing that Christian discipleship does not necessarily preclude the exercise of violence in defence of social order or justice': the narratives about soldiers.[126] As he sees it, however, the basis is 'fragile',[127] since these passages are intended to play a particular literary role, namely to illustrate the dramatically generous capaciousness of Jesus' version of the kingdom of God—its capacity to embrace even 'sinners' such as tax collectors and soldiers.

As I see it, four problems attend this interpretation. First, to say that soldiers are presented as notorious sinners is not yet to identify what their sin consists in. If one is going to assume—as Hays does—that the sin of soldiers is that of *being a soldier*, then presumably one should also assume that the sin of tax collectors is that of *collecting taxes*. Zacchaeus's story, however, makes it clear that his sin was fraud (Luke 19:8). Similarly, according to the only place in the New Testament where military sin is actually spelt out, it comprises robbery by violence and false accusation, and discontent over wages (Luke 3:12–14). Yes, indeed, this is only John the Baptist's view; but it is one that neither Jesus nor any of the evangelists seems to have felt the need to improve upon.

Similarly, second, the centurion's acknowledgement of the crucified Jesus as Son of God in Mark (15:39) and Matthew (27:54) is certainly dramatic, but not because it comes from the lips of a sinner-as-sword-wielder; rather because it comes from a sinner-as-gentile. In Luke (23:47) the centurion's testimony serves to confirm Pilate's earlier judgement of Jesus' innocence (Luke 23:14, 22). The drama here issues from that fact that these gentiles perceived what the chief priests and scribes of 'God's people' could not.

---

125. Ibid., p. 342.   126. Ibid., pp. 335–6.   127. Ibid., p. 340.

Third, the centurion at Capernaum (Matthew 8:5–13, Luke 7:1–10) and the centurion Cornelius (Acts 10:1–11:18) are not presented to the reader as 'sinners' (except insofar as they were gentiles). In the case of the former, the elders of the Jews commend him to Jesus as 'one who is worthy to have you do this [i.e. heal his slave] for him, for he loves our nation' (Luke 7:3–4). After meeting him, Jesus himself comments, 'Truly, I tell you, not even in Israel have I found such faith. I tell you, many will come from east and west and sit at table with Abraham, Isaac, and Jacob in the kingdom of heaven, while the sons of the kingdom will be thrown into the outer darkness' (Matthew 8:10b). Similarly, Cornelius is introduced as 'a devout man who feared God... gave alms liberally to the people, and prayed constantly to God'; his servants introduce him to Peter as 'an upright and God-fearing man, who is well spoken of by the whole Jewish nation' (Acts 10:2, 22); and the upshot of their encounter is that Peter exclaims, 'Truly I perceive that God shows no partiality, but in every nation any one who fears him and does what is right is acceptable to him' (Acts 10:34). Note: in both cases the drama depends on the status of these soldiers *as gentiles* and consists in the fact that Jesus and Peter transcend Jewish law by not treating them as 'unclean' (Acts 10:28).

Fourth, sinners who become Christian disciples are invariably portrayed by the New Testament as renouncing their sinful practices;[128] and Hays himself notes that, whereas the Acts of the Apostles takes care to mention that the Ephesian magicians who became 'believers' publicly burned their magic books (Acts 19:18–20), it makes no suggestion whatsoever that the God-fearing Cornelius was moved to surrender his military profession (Acts 10:1–11:18).[129] Likewise, Hays could also have mentioned that whereas the Gospel of Luke makes a point of showing that a tax collector's salvation involves the public mending of his extortionate ways (Luke 19:1–10), on no occasion does it suggest that a soldier's salvation involves the renunciation of military service as such. If the New Testament understood Jesus to mean non-violence simply, and regarded participation in the military profession as

---

128. In 'Narrate and Embody', Hays offers the counter-example of the sinful woman who washes Jesus' feet in Luke 7:36–50. My response in the subsequent correspondence in *Studies in Christian Ethics*, 23/1 (February 2010) was this: 'It's true that we're not told here explicitly that she formally renounced her former ways, like Zacchaeus. But on the assumption that the pronouncement of absolution, salvation, and reconciliation ("Your sins are forgiven... Your faith has saved you; go in peace") only makes sense as a response to repentance, albeit implicit (in her tears), the story implies that woman was not about to return to her sin'.

129. Hays, *Moral Vision*, p. 335.

intrinsically sinful, then *surely* its authors would have taken care to tell us that soldiers who became Christian disciples renounced military service? That they do not amounts to a silence that speaks volumes.

The awkward presence in the text of soldiers who are neither rebuked for their profession nor repent of it makes the stance of the New Testament canon toward the use of violent force far less 'unambiguous'[130]—and the ground for arguing that Christian discipleship could include it far more robust—than Hays supposes. His response to this awkwardness is to claim that it 'weigh[s] negligibly' in a synthetic statement of the New Testament's witness.[131] What he means by this is that the New Testament is so predominantly in favour of non-violence that these soldier stories may be discounted. The fact that they *need* to be discounted at all, of course, implies that, notwithstanding his attempt to tame them, Hays recognizes that they continue to carry non-pacifist significance. More important, his synthesis (which is already interpretation) takes it for granted that absolute 'non-violence' best captures what the New Testament is centrally and predominantly against. I shall argue below that this assumption is wrong; and that Hays is incorrect to assume that love for one's enemies and a commitment to reconciliation necessarily rule out the use of (sometimes lethal) force. Rather than brush the awkward finger aside, therefore, I will let it guide us toward a non-pacifist reading of the New Testament, which does better justice to *all* of the relevant material.

Romans 13: on not importing the 'Anabaptist distinction'

If we take our cue from the soldier narratives and suppose that the New Testament does not regard military service as incompatible with Christian discipleship, then we may infer that it has no objection *in principle* to the publicly authorized use of lethal force. This implication finds explicit corroboration in St Paul's Epistle to the Romans, when he writes that '[he who is in governing authority] does not bear the sword in vain; he is the servant of God to execute his wrath on the wrongdoer' (13:4).

It is true that Paul also enjoins members of the body of Christ not to avenge themselves but to leave vengeance to the wrath of God (12:19). Instead, they should minister to their enemies (12:20), repaying no one evil

---

130. Ibid., p. 341.   131. Ibid., p. 337.

for evil (12:17). Hays reads this along classic Anabaptist lines: the governing authority's use of force to punish the wicked is ordained by God, but 'that is not the role of believers'.[132] That role is to bear witness to an alternative society so completely governed by God as to lack need for the sword. This distinction of roles, however, is not coherent. If such a 'peaceable kingdom' were currently practicable *as an alternative* to the 'coercive kingdom', then presumably God would have ordained the former *instead of* the latter. I say 'presumably', because a benevolent God would not ordain unnecessary coercion. Since, however, God has ordained it, he evidently thinks it necessary. The implication is that, under the current spiritually and morally ambiguous conditions of this secular age, the 'peaceable kingdom' cannot be alternative; it can only be parasitic. This puts pacifist believers in the intellectually incoherent position of contradicting in principle what they depend upon in practice, and in the morally inconsistent position of keeping their own hands clean only because others are required to get theirs dirty.

Instead of this incoherent view, one might regard the non-coercive, entirely God-governed society not as a current alternative to one where the public use of force is ordained, but rather as its ideal goal. Thus the pacific ideal would so function as to qualify and discipline the current use of force, which ultimately intends it. Rather than produce two distinct classes of people—those who use the sword, and those who point to peace—it would produce one class only—those who struggle to use the sword pacifically. This, however, would bring us not to pacifism, but to the doctrine of just war.

Whether the Anabaptist distinction is coherent is one issue; whether it makes best sense of St Paul is another. Hays's interpretation gathers its exegetical force from the fact that what the governing authority is instituted by God to do—namely to execute God's wrath on the wrongdoer (13:4b: 'he [who is in authority] is the servant of God to execute his wrath on the wrongdoer' [Θεου γαρ διακονος εστιν, εκδικος εις οργην τω το κακον πρᾱσσοντι])—is precisely what the Christians at Rome are forbidden to do

---

132. Ibid., p. 331. The 1527 Schleitheim Confession, the classic statement of Anabaptist faith, puts the point thus in its sixth article: 'The sword is ordained of God outside the perfection of Christ... [I]t is not appropriate for a Christian to serve as a magistrate' (in John Leith, ed., *Creeds of the Churches: A Reader in Christian Doctrine from the Bible to the Present*, rev. edn [Atlanta: John Knox, 1973], pp. 287, 289). Stanley Hauerwas alludes to the Confession in taking up the same ecclesiological position: 'The Christian does not deny that often the state does some good through its violence; the point is rather that the sword of the state is outside the "perfection of Christ"' (Hauerwas, 'Epilogue', p. 178).

(12:19: 'Beloved, never avenge yourselves, but leave it to the wrath of God; for it is written, "Vengeance is mine, I will repay, says the Lord" ' [μη ἑαυτους εκδικουντες, αγαπητοι, αλλα δοτε τοπον τη οργη. γεγραπται γαρ, Εμοι εκδικησις, εγω ανταποδωσω, λεγει Κυριος]). This need not be read, however, as asserting a general distinction between the calling of Christians and the calling of publicly authorized sword users—and given the incoherence of such a distinction, it *should* not be so read. Rather, it should be understood as an answer to the ad hoc question of whether or not Christians should respond to their persecutors—be they pagan Romans, Jews, or other (gentile or Jewish) Christians—by avenging themselves, taking the law into their own hands, and so making themselves into a threat to public order.[133] As J.D.G. Dunn writes: 'the growing and increasingly desperate activity of the Zealots in Palestine was warning enough of how an oppressed people or persecuted minority might turn to acts of revenge... (the fire of Rome and Nero's persecution of the Christians were to follow in less than ten years)'.[134] Paul's response to the temptation facing the Roman Christians was that rather than yield to it, they should bear injustice patiently and charitably—'Be patient in tribulation' (12:12), 'Bless those who persecute you' (12:14)—trusting the public authorities to fulfil their divine commission. We may not take this to imply that Paul held all private use of violent force in defence or promotion of justice to be forbidden to Christians. We may only infer that Paul considered public order to be a sufficiently precious good that Christians should bear some injustice—and try and turn it to good—rather than conjure up an anarchy of private vendettas and provoke the brutality of public repression.

As we read it so far, then, the New Testament does not object in principle to the publicly authorized use of violence. As for its private use, we may say at least that St Paul had very strong reservations. The remedying of injustice is the proper, divinely instituted task of public authorities; and even where

---

133. Our understanding of the historical situation of the Christian community in Rome, to which Paul's letter was addressed, is uncertain. Nevertheless, there is reason to suppose that it had been involved in conflict with local Jews, and had also suffered strife between its own Jewish and gentile members, to the point of disturbing the civil peace. The Roman historian, Suetonius, reports that in 49 AD, about eight years before Paul sat down to write, the Jews living in Rome had been expelled by the emperor Claudius, because of rioting 'instigated by Chrestus' (*The Lives of the Caesars*, 'Claudius', s.25). Most scholars believe that this refers to civil disturbance caused by controversy among Roman Jews *about* Jesus and Christian claims for him.

134. James D.G. Dunn, *Romans 9–16*, Word Biblical Commentary, vol. 38B (Dallas: Word, 1988), p. 749 (commenting on Romans 12:19).

the authorities fail to complete their task—as they are bound to from time to time—private (Christian) persons should bear some injustice and respond to it constructively rather than take the law into their own hands and risk all the grave attendant evils of resultant anarchy.

Jesus' repudiation of religious nationalist revolt

St Paul's concern about the evils of private violence finds a strong echo in Jesus' teaching and practice. According to Hays, Jesus and the Gospels repudiate the use of violence, not just in self-defence, but also in defence of justice. As witness he calls the temptation narrative in the Gospel of Matthew (4:1–11), where Jesus refuses 'to defend the interests of the poor and oppressed in Palestine by organizing armed resistance against the Romans or against the privileged Jewish collaborators with Roman authority'.[135] He also appeals to the narrative of Jesus' arrest in the Garden of Gethsemane, where a disciple draws his sword in defence of his master, but Jesus, perceiving the same temptation, rebukes him (Matthew 26:47–52).[136] This Hays takes to be 'an explicit refutation' of the justifiability of the use of violence in defence of a third party.[137] Here as elsewhere, however, he generalizes beyond the evidence. The option historically available to Jesus was not an abstract 'violence in defence of third parties against injustice', but specifically private violence motivated by a conviction that Israel is *the* divinely chosen nation and by a corresponding hatred of her gentile imperial masters.

This is controversial. Not every New Testament scholar sees in Jesus' hinterland the option of violent religious nationalism (although Hays himself evidently does).[138] Richard Horsley has argued that, excepting 'the terrorism of the Sicarii directed against their own high priests', Jewish resistance

---

135. Hays, *Moral Vision*, p. 324.
136. Hays reads the disciple's offer of defence as another instance of the temptation that Jesus had earlier refused (ibid., p. 324: 'the temptation that Jesus rejects in the wilderness and again at Gethsemane').
137. Ibid., p. 324.
138. He says as much in his interpretation of Matthew's temptation narrative (see the immediately preceding paragraph). Among the good company in which this places him is Seán Freyne, the eminent historian of 1st-century Palestine. In Freyne's *Jesus: A Jewish Galilean: A New Reading of the Jesus Story* [London and New York: T. & T. Clark, 2004], he writes that 'Jesus refused to endorse the triumphant Zion ideology which viewed the nations as Israel's servants, and which was to provide a rallying call for some of Jesus' near-contemporaries in their struggle against Roman imperialism' (p. 135); 'Jesus was not prepared to share the violent response to such conditions [of oppressive imperial rule], espoused by many Jews throughout the 1st century, which eventually plunged the nation into a disastrous revolt' (p. 149).

to Roman rule during Jesus' lifetime was 'fundamentally non-violent'.[139]
Pace those interpreters who see the 'Zealots' as a continuous movement or
party straddling the first seven decades of the 1st century AD and make of
them 'a convenient foil over against which to portray Jesus of Nazareth as a
sober prophet of a pacific love of one's enemies', Horsley holds that they did
not come into existence until the winter of 66–7 AD.[140] Against this it is
reasonable to argue that the absence from Jesus' context of the 'Zealots' as a
definite party need not be taken to mean the absence of militant nationalism *tout court*. That had erupted in 4 BC and it was to erupt again in 66 AD.
While it is possible that the failure of the earlier revolt had completely discredited violent nationalism during the intervening period—and so during
Jesus' lifetime—it is *prima facie* unlikely. While crushed revolts may confirm
some—typically the middle-aged, married, and propertied—in their conviction that armed resistance is futile and counterproductive, they tend to
provide others—typically gangs of young bachelors—with heroes, an activ-
ist ideal, and a lust for revenge.[141] What is more, even if Horsley is correct in
claiming that the violence of the Sicarii was directed only at 'their own high
priests', the rule of this religious elite can hardly be considered something
entirely separate from Roman hegemony.

What the temptation and Gethsemane narratives permit us to say, then,
is only that Jesus declined to participate in violence that was not publicly
authorized and that was inspired by religious nationalism. Why he should
have done so, the text does not make explicit. We know, however, that in
Jesus' view the boundaries of the kingdom of God were defined less by
ethno-national identity than by faith—that is the implied significance of his
response to the centurion at Capernaum (Matthew 8:5–13 and Luke 7:1–
10).[142] Moreover, according to both the apostle Peter (in Acts 10 and 11) and
the apostle Paul, this was a main defining feature of the religious tradition

---

139. Horsley, *Jesus and the Spiral of Violence*, p. 117.
140. Ibid., pp. x–xi.
141. It is true that I am generalizing here on very particular ground—namely the pattern of sup-
     port for the IRA evident in County Cork in the aftermath of the failed Easter Rising of 1916.
     (See Peter Hart, *The I.R.A. and its Enemies: Violence and Community in Cork, 1916–23* [Oxford:
     Oxford University Press, 1998].) Still, I take it to be common sense that human beings who
     are old enough to have developed commitments to spouses and families and adequate liveli-
     hoods are likely to be less keen than herds of young unattached males to run the risks and
     unleash the unbiddable forces of violent revolution.
142. What is implied here is made quite explicit in Luke's story of the Apostle Peter's encounter
     with Cornelius (Acts 10:34, 45).

emanating from their Lord. It seems, therefore, that Jesus had strong theological reason to distance himself from religious nationalism.

On being discriminate about 'violence'

Beyond these reservations about its private, unauthorized use, especially as that is inspired by religious nationalism, does the New Testament manifest any more general concerns about violence? Of course it does. As Hays points out, it forbids anger, hatred, and retaliation—and the violence that issues from them.[143] However, we should not assume—as Hays does—that anger is all of one piece or that all violence is immorally angry, hateful, and retaliatory. It is not.

To begin with, an important distinction may be made with regard to anger. On the one hand, there is the anger that is both appropriate and proportionate. It is appropriate because it is the human emotion by which we take injustice seriously, recognizing it for the evil it is and setting ourselves against it; and it is proportionate because it is tempered by a loving intention to seek reconciliation. On the other hand, there is the anger that, driven by rage and indignation, intemperately answers injustice with injustice. This distinction between two kinds of anger may be made, and the Anglican moral philosopher, Joseph Butler, made it.[144] But, as Butler pointed out, so does the New Testament. St Paul, for example, implicitly distinguishes a moral kind of anger from a sinful one, when he exhorts Christians at Ephesus, 'Be angry, but do not sin; do not let the sun go down on your anger' (Ephesians 4:26). This moral anger is characterized both by a certain candour and by a certain fraternal restraint in telling the critical truth (Ephesians 4:25: 'let everyone speak the truth with his neighbour, for we are members one of another'). If we proceed to review Jesus' own conduct and teaching in the light of this distinction, then we notice that Jesus himself evidently thought that fierce anger was an appropriate response to the oppressiveness of Pharisaic religion: 'But woe to you, scribes and Pharisees, hypocrites!... Woe to you, scribes and Pharisees, hypocrites!... Woe to you, blind guides... You blind fools!... You blind men!... Woe to you, scribes and Pharisees, hypocrites!... You blind guides...! Woe to you, scribes and

---

143. Hays, *Moral Vision*, pp. 321–2.
144. Butler argues that anger or what he calls 'resentment' is a natural passion that may take either virtuous or vicious form according to circumstances (Joseph Butler, 'Upon Resentment', *Fifteen Sermons*, ed. W.R. Matthews [London: G. Bell & Sons, 1953], p. 123 [Section 3]).

Pharisees, hypocrites!... You blind Pharisee!... Woe to you, scribes and Pharisees, hypocrites!... Woe to you, scribes and Pharisees, hypocrites!... You serpents, you brood of vipers, how are you to escape being sentenced to hell?' (Matthew 23 *passim*). Further, we notice that the anger that Jesus prohibits in the Sermon on the Mount is of a specifically insulting kind: 'But I say to you that every one who is angry with his brother shall be liable to judgement; whoever *insults* his brother shall be liable to the council' (Matthew 5:22—my emphasis). The New Testament itself, therefore, implies that anger is not all of one piece: sometimes it can be appropriate or proportionate, sometimes it can withhold itself from insult, and sometimes it can be restrained by an awareness of fraternity in the midst of hostility. We may infer, then, that the New Testament forbids violence that is motivated by anger that is disproportionate, contemptuous, and issues from hatred.

What about violence that is retaliatory? The answer hangs on what is meant by 'retaliation'. In one sense any hostile response to injustice is retaliatory, a form of payback—not excluding Jesus' tirades against the Pharisees or his overturning of the moneychangers' tables in the Temple. Presumably that is not what the New Testament forbids. In a more colloquial sense 'retaliation' also connotes a touchy, vengeful reaction that lacks control by any sense of proportion or of moral duty. In such retaliation one hits back instinctively, no matter how trivial the injury; and even if one's retaliation is designed to deter and not merely to inflict suffering, it defends the self without any (fraternal) regard for what one owes the aggressor. In this light, it is noteworthy that none of the injuries with which Jesus illustrates his prohibition of retaliation is very serious. If we should understand being struck on the right cheek (Matthew 5:39) by the back of someone's left hand as a calculated insult,[145] then that is merely an offence against dignity, and relatively trivial; and as a purely physical injury being struck on one's cheek hardly rates highly. Losing one's coat to an extortionate creditor (Matthew 5:40) and being coerced into carrying military equipment for a mile (Matthew 5:41) are more serious forms of oppression, but still less than grave ones. What the text allows us to say, then, is that the Sermon on the Mount urges Christians not to respond instinctively and vengefully to tolerable injuries to oneself. In this sense, Jesus' disciples are indeed to relinquish

---

145. This is David Daube's interpretation in *The New Testament and Rabbinic Judaism* (London: Athlone, 1956), pp. 260–3, which Robert Guelich follows (*Sermon on the Mount*, p. 222) but Hays does not (*Moral Vision*, p. 326).

the 'tit-for-tat ethic of the *lex talionis*'.[146] Clearly, there is here a definite bias away from the knee-jerk returning of evil for evil, and toward more forbearing, generous, and conciliatory responses. Nevertheless, the text does not allow us to infer—as Hays does—an absolute prohibition of any violent response to injury. It does not forbid a violent response that is not motivated by touchy self-regard or vengeful anger, allows fraternity to govern hostility, observes the moral claims of the aggressor, aspires to achieve a just reconciliation, and *therefore* attests the fact of a grave injustice and opposes it. As we should distinguish between appropriate anger and immoderate anger, so we should distinguish between, on the one hand, retaliation governed by a certain care for the aggressor and a desire for genuine peace, and on the other hand, retaliation that is driven by a self-regarding indignation. Or, to put the matter more succinctly, we should distinguish between retaliation that is directed by love and that which is not.

Notwithstanding this, it might be protested that loving retaliation cannot be violent, and *a fortiori* it cannot be lethally violent. According to Hays, the practice of loving enemies is, *pace* Augustine and Reinhold Niebuhr, 'incompatible with killing them'.[147] This is not so, however. I might deliberately kill an aggressor, not at all because I hate him, nor because I reckon his life worth less than anyone else's, nor because I want him dead, but because, tragically, I know of no other way to prevent him from perpetrating a serious injury on an innocent neighbour. My deliberate killing is loving, therefore, in two respects: first, its overriding aim is to protect the innocent from serious harm; and second, it acknowledges the aggressor's equal dignity, it wishes him no evil, and it would gladly spare him if it could.

One of my main complaints against Richard Hays's pacifist reading of the New Testament is that it generalizes too much and distinguishes too little. The New Testament does forbid certain kinds of violence: that which is disproportionate because motivated by contemptuous or hateful or vengeful anger; that which retaliates in response to trivial or tolerable personal injury; that which lacks public authorization; and that which is inspired by religious nationalism. But its prohibition of violence is specific, not absolute. Therefore it is not accurate to summarize the New Testament's position in terms of a commitment to 'non-violence' *simpliciter*.

---

146. Hays, *Moral Vision*, p. 326.   147. Ibid., p. 329.

The Christian's vocation: not to suffer-in-general

The specification or delimitation of the violence forbidden by the New Testament implies a corresponding delimitation of the patient suffering that it recommends as morally normative for Christian life and ethics. We should demur from saying, as Hays does, that all four evangelists present Jesus' choice of messianic career, epitomized in the symbol of the cross, as involving 'the vocation of suffering' rather than conquering Israel's enemies;[148] and that the Epistle to the Hebrews and the Catholic Epistles prescribe the suffering of violence as the pattern of Christian life.[149] To talk of 'the vocation of suffering' is to make the negative practice of suffering in general the central and defining feature of Jesus' life and teaching. However, Jesus' vocation would be better—because more fully and more positively—characterized as that of wooing sinners and enemies and gentiles into a generous, compassionate, if not undemanding, kingdom of God. Such a vocation did entail the abjuring of hatred, unloving anger and retaliation, knee-jerk recourse to private violence in self-defence, and religious nationalism. And it therefore entailed a patient endurance of the *correlative* suffering. But suffering is not the first thing to say about the character or pattern of Christian life, and *suffering-in-general* should not be said about it at all.[150]

Paul's theology of the Atonement: why it includes killing

The final element of Hays's interpretation of the New Testament with which we take issue is his reading of St Paul's theology of the Atonement in the Epistle to the Romans. This, too, falls prey to a lack of moral analysis. As Hays presents it, Paul infers from the death of Christ that God deals with his enemies, not by killing them, but by seeking peace through 'self-giving' or

---

148. Ibid., p. 329.
149. Ibid., pp. 331–2: 'in Hebrews and the catholic Epistles we encounter a consistent portrayal of the community as called to suffer without anger or retaliation ... [T]he author of I Peter holds up the suffering of Christ as a paradigm for Christian faithfulness'. To his credit, Hays reports the qualifications that these texts make on the suffering to which Christians are called—the suffering *of Christ*, and suffering *without anger or retaliation*—as he reports the qualification that the Gospels make on the suffering to which Jesus himself was called—suffering *rather than the conquest of Israel's enemies*. His mistake, however, is that he does not notice the strict implication of these qualifications—namely that they only require the enduring of some kinds of violence under certain circumstances, rather than all kinds of violence everywhere.
150. I have argued this point more fully in *Aiming to Kill: The Ethics of Suicide and Euthanasia* (London: Darton, Longman, and Todd, 2004), pp. 49–55.

'self-emptying service'; and that those whose lives are reshaped in Christ must treat their enemies likewise.[151] In textual substantiation of this interpretation Hays quotes Romans 5:8–10:

> But God shows his love for us in that while we were yet sinners Christ died for us. Since, therefore, we are now justified by his blood, much more shall we be saved by him from the wrath of God. For if while we were enemies we were reconciled to God by the death of his Son, much more now that we are reconciled, shall we be saved by his life.

This clearly affirms that God regards sinners with love, that he has taken gracious initiative toward sparing them his wrath by being reconciled with them, and that this initiative has expressed itself in the death of his Son, Jesus Christ. What ethical implications may Christians draw from this theology? Certainly, that they should respond with love to those who do them wrong, that they should therefore desire reconciliation above punishment (or wrath), and that this predominant desire should express itself in the taking of appropriate initiatives. Can we go further and, with Hays, infer an absolute prohibition of the use of lethal force? I think not. While the text clearly implies that God wants to save sinners from his wrath and that those who are 'in Christ' shall be saved, it does not imply that salvation will embrace all the rest. It follows that, if (with Hays) we take death to be the effect of divine wrath on sinners, then, notwithstanding God's active desire that they should be saved, he nevertheless ends up 'killing' those who do not participate 'in Christ'.

Paul's talk here of being 'justified' or 'acquitted' ($\delta\iota\kappa\alpha\iota\omega\theta\acute{\epsilon}\nu\tau\epsilon\varsigma$) and being saved from God's 'wrath' ($\tau\eta\varsigma$ $\acute{o}\rho\gamma\eta\varsigma$)—the execution of which, he later tells us, is the task of governing authorities (Romans 13:4)—makes metaphorical use of the administration of criminal justice. God is being likened to a civil magistrate, and his wrath to the execution of capital punishment. The notion that God 'kills' sinners as a magistrate authorizes the capital penalty is, of course, one to which many contemporary Christians strongly object. The reasons for their objection bear reflection. The first carries little weight: namely the fact that in Western societies—or at least among their liberal elites—capital punishment is widely assumed to be a premodern, 'medieval' barbarity. There is ground for this view, of course, in the (to us) shocking and brutal readiness with which regimes in previous centuries

151. Hays, *Moral Vision*, p. 330.

meted out the death penalty for (to us) trivial crimes. On the other hand, there is ample room for 21st-century Western liberals to become more mindful of the extent to which they enjoy the luxury of historically unprecedented public order and social peace; of the horrors and terrors into which a society can very quickly plunge when that order breaks down; and of the immense difficulty of hauling that society back into a condition of civilization. There is an argument—and to my mind it is a good one—that the infliction of capital punishment may be warranted *in extremis*, when a society cannot afford other effective means of containing violent crime.[152] The death penalty is always severe and terrible; but it need not be gratuitously cruel.

A second objection assumes that anyone authorizing the death penalty must be motivated by a sadistic or vengeful ill will and *wants* to see the criminal or sinner dead. But this need not be so. The condemning judge might have no such desire. What he might desire is the safety of innocent citizens; and if this could be secured by any means other than the tragic death of the criminal, he would gladly choose it. But because there is no alternative, he reluctantly accepts the death of the criminal as an unavoidable and proportionate side effect of ensuring public security.

A third reason for declining to think of God killing sinners as magistrates kill capital criminals is that human magistrates are warranted in so doing by the exigencies of history, whereas almighty God is presumably not subject to these. The rationale for capital punishment that I have articulated above is that it might be the only effective way for a society to contain grave violence: that is, it might be warranted *in extremis socialibus*.[153] While it might be justified, the death penalty is nevertheless tragic. It involves causing at least two evils—the cutting off of the possibility of a criminal human being's (earthly) repentance and reformation and reconciliation, as well as his

---

152. See Oliver O'Donovan, *Measure for Measure: Justice in Punishment and the Sentence of Death*, Grove booklet on Ethics no. 19 (Bramcote: Grove Books, 1977), pp. 21–2. As my former colleague, Dr John Perry, pointed out to me, this is also the view of the Roman Catholic Church (*Catechism of the Catholic Church* (London: Geoffrey Chapman, 1994), sections 2266–7.

153. This, of course, is a non-Kantian rationale, for it is not the intrinsic nature of the criminal's crime alone that makes him worthy of the death penalty, but also the capacity of his society to contain violence. The consideration here is prudential, but it does not render our rationale consequentialist or utilitarian: the death penalty may only be inflicted on someone who has committed a crime by a public body that has a duty to protect citizens from criminal violence. It may not be inflicted on an innocent by a public body that aspires to achieve the greatest happiness of the greatest number of people.

physical death. Were there an alternative way of securing innocent neighbours against the threat of violence, the execution of the criminal would not be justified; but sometimes history constrains us into a tragic set of circumstances where we cannot do our primary duty to our innocent neighbours without bringing grave evil (albeit justifiably) upon the heads of those who threaten them. Presumably in his dealings with sinners and their moral and spiritual wrongdoing, almighty God is never so constrained.

On the contrary, he might be. Whatever the radically different conditions of the Next World, the ultimate well-being of creation will require the eradication of sin and the threat it poses; and if some sinners should persist in cordial commitment to their sin, then the ultimate well-being of creation would require their destruction too. It might prove to be the case that God's love is sufficiently powerful to woo every last sinner away from their sin— that his Yes will exhaust all our No's. But with Karl Barth, we can only hope and pray so; we cannot know so for sure.[154] And it has to be said that, in the face of some notorious cases of persistent and atrocious wickedness, repentance looks most unlikely.[155] As the dignity of free will makes possible the voluntary growth of human beings into virtuous maturity, so it necessarily also makes possible the voluntary degeneration of human beings into terminal corruption. We must entertain the possibility, then, that the ultimate salvation of creation will require the permanent removal of some sinners along with the sin to which they are inextricably attached; and unless we can conceive of a form of permanent removal short of final destruction, then we must entertain the possibility that ultimate death will be the destiny of some sinners.

It is true, of course, that St Paul's use of the terms of criminal justice to talk about God's dealing with sinners is metaphorical, and that there might be other ways of talking that have certain advantages over this one. Paul Fiddes, for example, recommends that we think of the ultimate death of sinners in naturalistic, rather than judicial, terms: as the natural, automatic

---

154. See, for example, Karl Barth, *Church Dogmatics*, Vol. II, Part 2, 'The Doctrine of God', ed. G.W. Bromiley and T.F. Torrance (Edinburgh: T. & T. Clark, 1957), pp. 417–18; and Vol. IV, Part 3.1, 'The Doctrine of Reconciliation', ed. G.W. Bromiley and T.F. Torrance (Edinburgh: T. & T. Clark, 1962), p. 477.

155. I write this with Andrzej Wajda's film, *Katyń* (2007)—about the meticulous murder in cold blood of 22,000 Polish prisoners by the Soviets in 1940—fresh in my mind. After my first viewing I exited the cinema with the overriding thought that there *must* be a hell for Stalin and his like. What it would mean for a Stalin to repent, I just cannot imagine. Nevertheless, I concede that God's imagination is greater than mine.

consequence of persistent spiritual alienation from God, rather than the result of an act that God decides to perform.[156] This has the advantage of making clear that the immediate responsibility for a sinner's death belongs to the sinner. However, insofar as it is designed to dissociate God from all responsibility for the death of sinners, it both fails and misleads. It fails because God, having deliberately created the world as it is, remains indirectly responsible for death being the natural end of intractable sinners. Therefore, the ultimate death of sinners remains the result of a deliberate decision of God, by which God presumably still stands.

This naturalistic conception of the death of sinners also misleads in that it assumes that if God is (at all) responsible for the death of sinners, then he must be culpable. But God's responsibility here is not that of one who malevolently *wants* the sinner dead (which would be morally culpable). Rather, it is the responsibility of one who, for the sake of the possibility of the voluntary growth of virtuous persons into human fulfilment, is willing to risk the possibility of the voluntary degeneration of vicious persons to the point of ultimate death—and is ready to accept its realization.[157]

Whither has this extended discussion brought us? How does it help us to answer the question of whether Richard Hays is correct to claim that St Paul's theology of the Atonement conceives of God responding to sinners by serving rather than killing them; and that therefore Christians are forbidden to kill their enemies? First, Paul does not say that all sinners will escape God's 'wrath'. Second, it is not inappropriate for Christians to think of God dealing with incorrigible sinners as magistrates deal *in extremis* with criminals who continue to pose a grave threat—since the authorization of the death penalty need not be malevolent or wanton; since its execution need not be cruel or barbarous; since the dignity of free will requires that sinners

---

156. Paul Fiddes, *Past Event and Present Salvation: The Christian Idea of Atonement* (London: Darton, Longman, and Todd, 1989), pp. 91–3.

157. At this point some atheist philosophers might enter the objection that God (if we suppose that he exists) would have been culpably rash in risking the possibility of ultimate death for the sake of the possibility of virtuous growth. That might be. But, frankly, what human being has the competence to say so? Who among us can judge that the terrible annihilation of incorrigible sinners 'outweighs' the shining beauty of fulfilled humanity? (And is the ultimate bringing to nought of a Hitler or Stalin or Pol Pot really so terrible?) How do we begin to compare the relative 'weights' of annihilation and fulfilment? Who has the numbers and proportions of saved and damned to hand? It is not manifestly unreasonable to trust that a world in which some sinners might perish beyond hope is worth a world where other sinners might grow into glory. Nor is it unreasonable, therefore, to trust that God was not being culpably rash when he made it so.

be allowed to become inextricably attached to their sin; since the ultimate fulfilment of creation requires the permanent removal of sin; and since in the case of incorrigible sinners this must amount to their death.

I conclude, then, that we should think of God as being prepared to respond to incorrigible sinners (should there be any) by authorizing their deaths, not at all because he wants them dead, but because he wants to secure the fulfilment of creation, and because he cannot have the latter without the former. In this sense we may say that God kills incorrigible sinners. And we may say so without in any way detracting from God's driving desire to save sinners from their sin, and from the costly, gracious initiatives that he has taken to do so. Accordingly, I think Hays mistaken to infer from St Paul's theology of the Atonement that Christians may never kill their enemies.

Taking methodological stock

I have tested Richard Hays's pacifist reading of the New Testament against what the text itself says. What I have taken the text to say has been determined by three factors. The first is what it consistently and significantly fails to say—namely that soldiers should abandon their immoral profession. The second is a relevant feature of the social context of its main subject, Jesus— that is, the option of revolutionary violence inspired by religious nationalism. The third factor comprises the logical limits of what we may take the text strictly to imply—namely that we may not infer an absolute prohibition of the use of lethal violence from the prohibition of vengeance, anger, hatred, and retaliation, or from the injunction of love for one's enemies, or from St Paul's theology of the Atonement. According to this interpretation of the text, we may say that the New Testament abjures vengeance, hatred, unloving anger and retaliation, knee-jerk recourse to private violence in self-defence, and violence inspired by religious nationalism. We may say that it enjoins whatever faithful suffering is involved by forbearance from these. We may say that, beyond the passive suffering of frustration, insult, and tolerable injustice, it also enjoins the active, generous, and enterprising desire for reconciliation. From this, however, it does not follow that the New Testament absolutely forbids the publicly authorized use of lethal violence by Christians, nor even their use of private violence *in extremis*. My concluding verdict, therefore, is that the New Testament does not bear Richard Hays's pacifist reading.

I am aware of three objections that this interpretation might attract. One objects to its use of argument from silence with regard to the soldiers who appear in the New Testament. An argument from what is *not* said is obviously weaker than an argument from what *is* said. Still, an argument from what is not said can have force. Some silences are simply empty and ambiguous, and they can be read in opposite ways with equal justification. Other silences, however, are loaded. Were the pacifist reading of the New Testament correct, there is strong reason to expect that soldiers whose faith was approved by Jesus or his disciples would be shown to distance themselves from their fundamentally incompatible profession. But they are not so shown. The New Testament's silence on this matter is, therefore, loud with significance. And when set within hearing of St Paul's affirmation of the public use of force in Romans 13, it becomes even louder.

A second objection to my interpretation might be that I distinguish too much, meaning either that I use moral distinctions that are spurious or that I import moral distinctions that are 'unbiblical'. One of these distinctions that many consider to be spurious is that between on the one hand a deliberate act that it is foreseen will likely or certainly cause an evil (such as death), where that evil effect is reluctantly accepted, and on the other hand a deliberate act that it is foreseen will likely or certainly cause an evil, where that evil is intended or wanted. Whether this doctrine of double effect is or is not spurious is the subject of long-standing controversy and it remains controversial. Those who think that it is spurious tend to be utilitarian philosophers; and I have explained elsewhere why I think that they are wrong.[158]

Another distinction that is held to be spurious is that between loving and hateful violence. Here it is assumed that violence is always driven by hatred. But that assumption is empirically false, for it is widely recognized that soldiers in battle are usually motivated by loyalty to their comrades and by fear of shame, rather than by hatred for the enemy. Moreover, there is also the phenomenon of soldiers regarding and treating their enemies with a certain 'amiability'.[159]

---

158. Biggar, *Aiming to Kill*, ch. 3, 'The Morality of Acts of Killing'.
159. See, for example, Joanna Bourke, *An Intimate History of Killing: Face-to-Face Killing in Twentieth Century Warfare* (London: Granta, 1999), chapter 5, 'Love and Hate', especially pp. 141–8. A reader of an earlier version of this chapter judged that my view of military motivation smacks of an armchair perspective. In case readers of the present version should think likewise, let me say that my armchair has afforded me the opportunity to read copious amounts of military history, which furnishes plenty of cases where soldiers have regarded their enemy

As for the charge that I use moral distinctions that are 'unbiblical', that is either untrue or beside the point. The distinction between what is permitted public officials and what is permitted private subjects or citizens is implied in Romans 12–13, where Paul makes plain that only the governing authorities may mediate the wrath of God on wrongdoers. And the distinction between anger that is sinful and anger that is not is implied in Ephesians 4:6. However, whether or not a moral distinction is actually to be found, explicitly or implicitly, in the Bible is not important. One does not have to hold as true *only* what the Bible states or implies, in order to regard it as authoritative. I am not aware that the Bible states or uses the doctrine of double effect; but I still have good reason to think it valid. And even if the Bible does not distinguish between murder and manslaughter, we would, I suggest, still have good reason to do so. Obviously, it would be problematic for a Christian theologian to espouse things that the Bible unequivocally denies. But 'non-biblical' distinctions are not necessarily 'anti-biblical'. They might be, of course, but that remains to be shown.

This brings us to a third possible objection. When I say that there is 'good reason' to hold something that the Bible does not affirm, what kind of good reason am I talking about? I am talking about reasons furnished by human experience of the world and reflection upon it. The idea that the moral quality of an act depends not primarily on its good or evil effects, but upon the intention or circumspection of the agent is, in my view, correct. It is not one, however, that I am aware of having first learned from the Bible. As for the idea that soldiers might not be motivated by hatred, I am aware that it came to me from military witnesses belonging to the twentieth and twenty-first centuries. Some might find it suspect that I presume to take these fruits of experience into my reading of the New Testament. My own view is that there is no such thing as pure interpretation or even pure exegesis. It is surely a truism that no exegete or interpreter comes to the text as a *tabula rasa*. Richard Hays agrees. He acknowledges that experience is involved in interpretation,[160] and that the hermeneutical, synthetic, and descriptive tasks

---

with respect rather than hatred. I present some of them in Chapter Two. Moreover, on one occasion I managed to struggle out of my armchair to speak with a colonel in the Royal Marines, who confirmed my bookish view by testifying that military training with which he is familiar positively discourages 'hot' violence in favour of 'cool'. This is because violence that is motivated by intemperate anger or hatred lacks self-control, and therefore makes mistakes, jeopardizes plans, and endangers comrades. Violence that would be efficient and effective cannot afford such distractions. If you doubt it, ask a boxer.

160. Hays, *Moral Vision*, p. 209.

'inevitably interpenetrate and overlap'.[161] He appears, however, to think of experience in curiously narrow, religious terms; and he confines its primary role to that of confirming the truth of the teaching of Scripture. As an example, he cites the experience of God's love confirming that eschatological hope is not futile.[162] I think, however, that a far wider range of human experience of the world that God has created should come into play. I also think that one of its main roles should be to help determine the meaning of Scripture, and not merely to confirm its truth. I agree with Hays that we cannot take the apparent deliverances of experience at face value. These can deceive, and we must test them. I also agree that the data of experience must find their place 'within the world narrated by the New Testament witnesses'.[163] Therefore if what the text clearly, recurrently, and predominantly says simply will not wear the moral distinctions and empirical data that I bring to it, then as a Christian ethicist I must reconsider and perhaps abandon them. But if the text will wear them, then I may infer that its meaning includes them. As it happens, Hays himself brings more empirical data—and brings it more deeply—into his exegetical and synthetic work than he himself recognizes. It seems to me that the reason why he reads Jesus' death on the cross as meaning the absolute repudiation of all violence everywhere is that he has imported empirical assumptions about anger and violence as necessarily vengeful and malevolent. I do not complain at all about the importation. I merely dissent from the assumptions.

Concluding judgement

In spite of these three objections, then, I persist in judging that the New Testament does not bear Richard Hays's pacifist reading. What is more, I think that Hays is wrong to claim that '[i]t is not possible to use the just war tradition as a hermeneutical device for illuminating the New Testament'.[164] It is not only possible, but preferable; for the doctrine of just war can make better sense than pacifism of all that the New Testament text does and does not say. On the one hand, of course, this doctrine does not prohibit the publicly legitimate use of violent force by police or soldiers. On the other hand, it insists that lethal violence may only ever be used with the intention of securing a just peace (or reconciliation). This intention is

161. Ibid., p. 199.   162. Ibid., p. 297.
163. Ibid., p. 296.   164. Ibid., p. 341.

incompatible with motives such as unloving anger or vengeance or hatred. And it is all the more incompatible with a religious nationalist view of the enemy, which sees them as infidels to be ruthlessly destroyed by the righteous, rather than as one set of fellow sinners whose evil actions must, alas, be curtailed by another set. Given the basic requirement of an intention of just peace, it follows that recourse to lethal violence cannot be justified unless its inevitable evils are made sufficiently proportionate by the serious prospect of actually ending grave and intolerable injustice. This implies that injustices that are less than grave should be suffered rather than used as a pretext for impatient violence; but it also implies that they should be suffered in a creative manner that extends compassion to the oppressor in the hope of wooing repentance and making peace. Just war doctrine encompasses, therefore, not only moments of the use of lethal violence that intends peace and is disciplined by it, but also moments of forbearance, suffering, and compassion.

IV. Conclusion

My analysis of the leading contemporary expressions of Christian pacifism has exposed, I believe, a number of major flaws. One of these is a lack of moral analysis and discrimination. Each of the pacifists under consideration assumes that violence is all of one piece. They do not distinguish violence that is well motivated, rightly intentioned, and proportionate from that which is not. Nor do they distinguish anger from vengeance or hatred. As a consequence it never occurs to them that love and forgiveness might be compatible with certain kinds of anger and violence. I think that this is a mistake; and I think so on empirical grounds.

This mistake then generates another one. When our conceptually indiscriminate Christian pacifists turn to the New Testament and read that Jesus repudiated some kinds of anger and violence, they assume that he must have repudiated all kinds. Their assumptions about violence do not allow them to accord Jesus' political context any specifying significance. If he rejected messianic violence, then because violence is all of a piece, he must have rejected violence in general.

Such an understanding of Jesus' social ethic stands *prima facie* in contradiction of Paul's affirmation of the divine authorization of sword bearing in the 13th chapter of his Epistle to the Romans. Our pacifists seek to manoeuvre around this by importing the 'Anabaptist distinction': namely that sword bearing is indeed authorized by God, but not for Christians. While importation in principle is acceptable—indeed, inevitable—this particular import is theologically incoherent and morally hypocritical. So it constitutes a third mistake.

Finally, since violence is all of a piece, since Jesus repudiated it, and since his followers are forbidden to use it even in defence of the innocent, just war thought is obviously sub-Christian. Therefore, our pacifists reason, there is no need to read its classic texts and engage with it at close quarters. Nor have they: their fourth mistake.

Nevertheless, as I have admitted, there is one point where the pacifist case presses hard on just war reasoning: namely on the requirement of proportion. This deserves further discussion, which I will give it in Chapters Four and Seven and in the Conclusion.

Immediately, however, I need to explicate one claim that I have made in this chapter, and I need to substantiate another. I need to explicate the claim that love and forgiveness can, and sometimes should, incorporate anger and retribution; and I need to substantiate the claim that the use of violence—and by extension, the waging of war—can, in fact, be qualified by love, and even by forgiveness of the enemy. This will be the task of the following chapter.

2

Love in war

I. 'Kind harshness': forgiveness and the qualification of violence

The New Testament does not generate an absolute prohibition of violence, but it does generate an absolute injunction of love. Accordingly, just war doctrine's claim to belong to a *Christian* ethic rests on its conception of the right use of violence as an expression of love for the neighbour. This makes obvious sense when the neighbour in view is the innocent victim of unjust aggression, on whose behalf the just warrior takes up arms. However, the innocent victim is not the only neighbour on site. Since love is an absolute injunction, applying always and everywhere, the just warrior is also bound to love the unjust aggressor. His love—as Jesus made plain—must extend itself to the enemy. But in what plausible senses can it do that?

According to the leading patriarch of Christian just war doctrine, St Augustine, the just warrior loves the unjust aggressor insofar as he withholds himself from vengeance, commits himself to benevolence, and so uses violence to punish him 'with a sort of kind harshness', doing him the service of constraining him from further wrongdoing and encouraging him to repent and embrace peace.[1] What this amounts to is the qualification of the use of violence by forgiveness. Such a claim will seem strongly counterintuitive to many Christians and non-Christians alike, for surely punishment and forgiveness are mutually exclusive alternatives? Surely one forgives *instead of* punishing? As I see it, that is not quite so; and in order to show

---

1. Augustine, Letter 138 (to Marcellinus), in *Political Writings*, ss.9,11, 14 (pp. 35, 36, 38).

why, I must set out here the theory of the process of reconciliation that I have developed elsewhere.[2]

It seems to me that discussion of the process of reconciliation and of forgiveness is generally vitiated by a tendency to conflate two moments that ought to be distinguished. On the one hand, this leads some to hold on biblical and theological grounds that victims are bound to forgive their oppressors unilaterally and unconditionally—that is, without waiting for any sign of repentance.[3] On the other hand, it leads others to hold on philosophical and psychological grounds that the victim's forgiveness must be conditional upon the perpetrator's repentance, if it is to be morally responsible.[4] It seems to me that both sides are half-correct, for each champions a different moment of forgiveness, one of them unilateral and initial and the other conditional and final. I call these, respectively, 'compassion'[5] and

2. See Nigel Biggar, 'Forgiveness in the Twentieth Century: A Review of the Literature, 1901–2001' in *Forgiveness and Truth*, ed. Alistair McFadyen and Marcel Sarot (Edinburgh: T. & T. Clark, 2001), pp. 215–17; 'Making Peace and Doing Justice: Must We Choose?', in *Burying the Past: Making Peace and Doing Justice after Civil Conflict*, ed. Nigel Biggar (Washington, DC: Georgetown University Press, 2003), pp. 7–13; 'Conclusion', in ibid., pp. 314–17; 'Epilogue: Burying the Past after September 11', in ibid., pp. 328–9; 'The Ethics of Forgiveness and the Doctrine of Just War: A Religious View of Righting Atrocious Wrongs', in Thomas Brudholm and Thomas Cushman, eds, *The Religious in Responses to Mass Atrocity: Interdisciplinary Perspectives* (Cambridge: Cambridge University Press, 2009), pp, 105–23; 'Forgiving Enemies in Ireland', *Journal of Religious Ethics*, 36/4 (December 2008), pp. 559–79; and 'Melting the Icepacks of Enmity: Forgiveness and Reconciliation in Northern Ireland', *Studies in Christian Ethics*, 24/2 (May 2011), pp. 199–209. Much of what follows immediately here has been taken from 'The Ethics of Forgiveness and the Doctrine of Just War' and 'Forgiving Enemies in Ireland'.

3. E.g. Paul Fiddes, *Past Event and Present Salvation*, pp. 176–7; and L. Gregory Jones, *Embodying Forgiveness: A Theological Analysis* (Grand Rapids: Eerdmans, 1995), pp. 21, 102, 121, 144, 146, 160–1. Fiddes appeals to the cases of Zacchaeus (Luke 19:1–10) and the prostitute who anointed Jesus' feet with ointment (Luke 7:36–50) in support of his view that, according to a Christian understanding, forgiveness should precede repentance: 'When Jesus asks for hospitality from Zacchaeus, the notorious tax collector of the Jericho area, he does not first require him to return what he has gained through fraud and extortion, though this is the happy outcome. He accepts from a prostitute the intimate act of her anointing his feet and wiping them with her hair, without first establishing whether she has given up her trade, and pronounces the forgiveness of God without further enquiry' (Fiddes 1989, p. 177). Alternatively, according to my own view, Jesus' asking for hospitality amounted to an act of compassionate forbearance rather than one of absolving forgiveness; and he did not need to ask first whether the prostitute had repented, since her tears made it implicitly clear that she had.

4. E.g. Richard Swinburne, *Responsibility and Atonement* (Oxford: Clarendon Press, 1989), pp. 81–6, 148–9.

5. It might be thought odd, even inappropriate, to use the word 'forgiveness' to refer to compassion. Why not speak simply of an initial moment of compassion, and reserve 'forgiveness' for the concluding moment of absolution? The reason is that in colloquial speech we do not so reserve it. It is not uncommon to hear victims say that they have 'forgiven' their oppressors, when what is meant is not at all that they have been reconciled with them, but rather that, in spite of the absence of any apology or reparation, they have nevertheless managed to tame or transcend

'absolution'. Yet both sides are also half-wrong, since each champions one moment to the exclusion of the other; whereas in fact a Christian theory of reconciliation should incorporate them both.

The first moment of forgiveness—compassion—is where the victim allows her feelings of resentment to be moderated by a measure of sympathy for the perpetrator. Moderated by what? Partly by the acknowledgement of the authority of certain truths. These truths are: that she herself is no stranger to the psychic powers that drive human beings to abuse each other; that some individuals, for reasons that remain hidden in the mysterious inter-penetration of history and the human will, are less well equipped than others to resist common pressures; and that some are fated to find themselves trapped in situations where only an extraordinary moral heroism could save them from doing terrible evil.[6] Even victims have responsibilities; and one of them is to acknowledge truths like these, even in the midst of the mael-strom of pain and resentment.

Openness to the truth, however, is not the only matrix of sympathy and the only force for moderation. There is also the commitment to rebuild rather than destroy—to reconciliation rather than vengeance. Now, 'recon-ciliation' should mean different things according to the nature of the rela-tionship between victim and perpetrator. In the paradigmatic case of relationships between family members or friends it will mean the restora-tion of intimacy, signalled typically by the act of embrace. In the case of relationships between political dissidents and their informers or of génocid-aires and surviving victims, however, it will usually mean something analo-gous and weaker—say a readiness to coexist in the same city or neighbourhood

their anger toward them. It means that the victims' lives are no longer possessed by rage and hatred. This does not quite amount to the growth of compassion, although it is a major step in that direction. The main point, however, is that the victims' taming of anger and growth of compassion are both entirely subjective processes, which proceed independently of what the perpetrators do or do not do, and which do not change the objective relationship between them. To refer to such processes as 'forgiveness' is appropriate, partly because it describes what actually happens and partly because it is good that it does so. Were it otherwise, the deliverance of victims from all-consuming rage would have to wait upon the perpetrators to repent; and in some cases, that would condemn them to vengeful obsession forever.

6. I allude here to the Christian concept of original sin, which refers to the fated dimension of human wrongdoing. This does not displace the individual's responsibility for his choices; but it does refer to the fact that every individual makes his choices under the weight of history's socio-psychological legacy. If we are free, we are free only within bounds; and the bounds are unequal, for history has dealt more kindly with some than with others. This freedom-under-fate is something that victims share with perpetrators.

or street.[7] But whatever kind of reconciliation is appropriate, victims should prefer it to the sheer wreaking of vengeance—that is to say, action whose overriding intention is to inflict harm and which takes no care to moderate the harm inflicted.

Why should victims prefer reconciliation? They should prefer it at least because of a proper care for their own souls—or, if you like, for the shaping of their moral and spiritual characters; for to devote oneself to vengeance is to drink a poison that embitters and tyrannizes. The point is arrestingly made in Peter Shaffer's play, *The Gift of the Gorgon*. Here, Edward Damson, hot-blooded playwright of Slavo-Celtic parents, champions the cleansing, cathartic virtue of the passion for revenge. Liberal forbearance and toler-ance, in his eyes, are 'just giving up with a shrug—as if you never really cared about the wrong in the first place... *Avoidance*, that's all it is!'[8] But to this, Helen, his wife and cool English daughter of a classics don, retorts:

> You go on about passion, Edward. But have you never realised that there are many, many kinds—including a passion to kill our own passion when it's wrong?... The truest, hardest most adult passion isn't just stamping and geeing ourselves up. It's refusing to be led by rage when we most want to be... No other being in the universe can change itself by conscious will: it is *our privilege alone*. To take out inch by inch this spear in our sides that goads us on and on to bloodshed—and still make sure it doesn't take our guts with it.[9]

At the very end of the play Helen wins the argument by showing that it is forgiveness, not revenge, that requires the greater strength and realizes humanity. But there is one cliff-hanging moment when, enraged by a maca-bre trick that Edward has played on her, Helen sways on the brink of plung-ing into vengeance. What pulls her back are the bald words of her stepson,

---

7. For further discussion of the relationship between political 'reconciliation' and its interpersonal paradigm, see Nigel Biggar, 'Conclusion', in *Burying the Past*, pp. 314–17. Why do I suppose that the paradigm of forgiveness is interpersonal? One immediate reason is the paradigmatic status in Christianized culture of the Parable of the Prodigal Son. Another reason is that when, refer-ring to an injustice that I have done to you, I say that I repent, you forgive, and we are recon-ciled, none of the verbs needs to be qualified. However, when I say that Prime Minister Tony Blair has 'repented' on behalf of the British people for the Irish Famine, or that paramilitary prisoners released early from prison in Northern Ireland have been 'forgiven', or that support-ers of the apartheid state in South Africa and members of the ANC have been 'reconciled', then qualification is needed.
8. Peter Shaffer, *The Gift of the Gorgon* (London: Viking, 1993), p. 16.
9. Ibid., pp. 60–1.

Philip: 'The truth is,' he says, 'you must forgive him or die.'[10] That is to say, she must forgive or forever be possessed by bitterness.

Another, real-life, expression of this prudential wisdom comes from the lips of the daughter of one of three women taken from the Spanish village of Poyales del Hoyo on the night of 29 December 1936 and murdered by Fallangists at the roadside. Interviewed sixty-six years later, she said: 'This thing has stayed in my mind all my life. I've never forgotten. I am reliving it now, as we stand here. All the killers were from the village... I can pardon, but I cannot forget. We have to pardon them or it makes us just like them.'[11]

Vengeance does grave moral and spiritual damage to the one who wreaks it. That's one good reason why victims should steer clear of it. Another is that vengeance is—by common definition—excessive.[12] It does not strive to proportion its retribution to the wrong done. Its driving ambition is to make the wrongdoer—together with his family or his village or his race or his country—*suffer*. As a consequence, vengeance has the effect of multiplying injustice, as wrongdoers are made to suffer more than they deserve and suffering is inflicted on innocents who do not deserve it at all.

There is yet a third motive for preferring reconciliation to vengeance: the knowledge that vengeance upon the murderer will not raise the innocent dead to life again. This is, of course, common sense. But some common sense is just too desolate to constrain the vital, throbbing pain of loss and indignation from spiralling into an ecstatic, destructive rage. Theological hope for the resurrection of the innocent dead, resting as it must on faith in a more-than-human power, can so infuse desiccated common sense as to strengthen its moral arm.

---

10. Ibid., p. 92.
11. Giles Tremlett, *Ghosts of Spain: Travels Through a Country's Hidden Past* (London: Faber and Faber, 2006), pp. 13–14.
12. I am being careful here because I am aware that some argue for the moral rehabilitation of vengeance as an appropriate response to grave and malicious injury (e.g. Willa Boesak, *God's Wrathful Children: Political Oppression and Christian Ethics* [Grand Rapids: Eerdmans, 1995]; Willa Boesak, 'Truth, Justice, and Reconciliation', in H. Russel Botman and Robin M. Petersen, eds, *To Remember and to Heal: Theological and Psychological Reflections on Truth and Reconciliation* [Cape Town: Hutman and Rousseau, 1996]; and Martha Minow, *Between Vengeance and Forgiveness: Facing History after Genocide and Mass Violence* [Boston: Beacon, 1998], pp. 9–24). One may, of course, choose to use the word 'vengeance' to refer to proportionate retribution. My own sense, however, is that in common English usage 'vengeance' tends to connote something excessive and out of control; and that therefore to talk of 'vengeance' when one means something moderated and proportionate is to risk at least confusion and perhaps even serious misunderstanding.

However it moderates resentment—whether through the confession of human solidarity in sin-as-moral-weakness or through the intention of reconciliation—forgiveness-as-compassion is unilateral and unconditional. It does not need the green light of the perpetrator's repentance in order to proceed. It is entirely the responsibility of the victim to acknowledge the truths of solidarity-in-sin and to commit herself to reconciliation rather than revenge.

Compassion, however, is just the first moment of forgiveness. The second is absolution. This is the moment when, paradigmatically, the victim addresses the perpetrator and says, 'I forgive you. The trust that was broken is now restored. Our future will no longer be haunted by our past.' Forgiveness-as-absolution should not be granted unilaterally and unconditionally. To proffer trust to someone who has shown himself to be untrustworthy and who is unrepentant about it is foolish. But it is also careless of the wrongdoer, for it robs him of the salutary stimulus to reflect, to learn, and to grow, which the punitive withholding of trust constitutes. Even worse, it degrades him by implying that what he does is of no consequence.[13] Out of respect and care for the wrongdoer, then, forgiveness-as-absolution should wait for signs of his genuine repentance—all the while looking upon him with the eyes of forgiveness-as-compassion.

As I understand it, then, the process of reconciliation involves two moments of forgiveness, one inaugural and one conclusive. In between those moments, as I have implied, there is room for both resentment and retribution of certain kinds. Again, to many contemporary Christians—and to many contemporary post-Christians—this will sound counter-intuitive; for surely love for the wrongdoer must exclude any hostile attitude or feelings toward him? Not so, according to the Anglican moral philosopher-cum-bishop, Joseph Butler, for whom resentment is a 'natural passion' that may be virtuous or vicious according to circumstances, but which in itself is indifferent.[14] Not so, even according to St Paul, who in his epistle to the

---

13. My thinking here follows Richard Swinburne (e.g. *Responsibility and Atonement*, pp. 81–6, 148–9), except that what he takes to be the whole of forgiveness I take to be just the second moment.

14. Joseph Butler, 'Upon Resentment', *Fifteen Sermons*, ed. W.R. Matthews (London: G. Bell & Sons, 1953), p. 123 (section 3). As I (and Butler, as it happens) understand common English usage, resentment is a constant form of anger. 'Anger' tends to refer to an explosive moment or passing mood, 'resentment' to a more settled attitude. 'Resentment', however, sometimes carries the connotation of meanness, lack of generosity, or egotism. When I use the word, I do not mean such a connotation, since I obviously do not think that resentment against injustice need carry any of those qualities.

Ephesian Christians enjoined them, 'Be angry, but do not sin' (Eph. 4:6). Not to resent an injustice is akin to not grieving the death of a beloved. Something—someone—of great value has been damaged, perhaps destroyed. Not to react negatively is pathological—a failure to care for something that deserves to be cared for. And in cases where another person is culpably responsible[15] for the damage, proportionate anger or resentment against that person is an appropriate expression of care for what has been damaged. Resentment can, of course, be inappropriate (because the wrongdoer should not be blamed for what he did) or disproportionate (because the damage done was not *so* great); and, given the pejorative connotation of the word, common English usage assumes that it is vicious in one of these two ways. Maybe here the language bears the imprint of fifteen centuries of Christianization—or, as I see it, mis-Christianization. After all, St Paul made a distinction between anger and sin. And Jesus himself showed no compunction about addressing 'the scribes and Pharisees' in stinging language that is replete with righteous resentment.

If a certain form of resentment is a morally fitting response to injustice, then so is a certain form of retribution. This is because resentment is the opprobrium for the wrongdoing and against the wrongdoer that naturally expresses itself in retributive punishment. The concept of retributive punishment is very controversial in contemporary Western societies, and in certain circles—not excluding the Christian churches—it is very unpopular. The main reason why many repudiate retribution (and war along with it) as an appropriate response to wrongdoing is their assumption that retribution is vindictive or vengeful, aiming at very best to achieve a barren equality of suffering. To this many Christians add the further assumption that the duty of forgiveness by definition logically excludes retribution. Let me deal with each of these in turn.

First, retribution need not be vengeful. Basically it comprises a negative 'giving back' or response to a wrongdoer on account of the wrong done. This response need not comprise a vindictive attempt to inflict pain on the one who first caused it *for the sake of seeing him suffer*. Rather, liberated from the temptations of rage, it can take the form of a disciplined reaction

---

15. One can be responsible for an effect without being culpable for it. I can choose to perform an act that I foresee will probably or certainly have an evil effect, without intending (or wanting) that effect, provided that my choosing is sufficiently reluctant and its reasons sufficiently strong. Hereby, of course, I endorse the doctrine of double effect. For further discussion, see my *Aiming to Kill*, pp.71–88; and Chapter Three below.

designed to spare the victims further injury and prevent the perpetrator from further wrongdoing. Moreover, it can take the form of responsible communication to the wrongdoer, whether in words or gestures, which recognizes his dignity as a moral agent, and which tells him that his action is not acceptable and that he must show a genuine willingness to change before a relationship of trust can be restored. Whether in fact it will take these forms depends, of course, upon how the victim sees the perpetrator and upon what ultimate outcome she seeks. If she is free to view him with the eyes of forgiveness-as-compassion, and to commit herself to keeping open the door of forgiveness-as-absolution, then her retribution will be proportioned accordingly and preserved from the demons of vengeance.

This brings us to the second questionable assumption: that forgiveness logically excludes retribution. It is clear from what I have just said that I do not believe this. Rather, I think that forgiveness should qualify, not supplant, retribution. Retribution remains vitally important as an attestation of the importance of the wrong done and thereby of the one who has been wronged. If qualified both by forgiveness-as-compassion and by a desire for forgiveness-as-absolution, retribution can also be an act of fraternal responsibility toward the wrongdoer, caring that he should learn and change, so that reconciliation might be possible. Forgiveness that supposes itself to be sufficient without retribution amounts to premature absolution, implying that neither the wrong, nor the victim, nor the wrongdoer matters—truly, a shrug of avoidance.

Let me bring to a conclusion this discussion of forgiveness, and its relation to resentment and retribution, with a summary. As I see it, the process of reconciliation consists of the following sequence of moments:

1. Victim: forgiveness (i) as compassion: unilateral, unconditional, abjuring vengeance, and intentionally conciliatory.

2. Victim: proportionate expression of resentment in retribution. In addition to preventing the wrongdoer from further injury of the innocent, proportionate retribution seeks to uphold before him the value of what has been damaged and to communicate to him the wrongness of damaging it, in the hope of eliciting his repentance and so enabling reconciliation. (If, however, the wrongdoer were already penitent, then the expression of resentment in retribution would be unnecessary and therefore disproportionate.)

3. Wrongdoer: repentance.

4. Victim: forgiveness (ii) as absolution: conditional upon 3, and ushers in . . .

5. mutual reconciliation.

II. How Christian a theory?

Such is my theory of reconciliation and of twofold forgiveness; but is it Christian? Without doubt, forgiveness is *characteristically* Christian. It has a prominent place in the teaching and practice of the founder of the Christian religion and in its founding documents—the New Testament—and it often has a correspondingly prominent place in subsequent Christian ethics (even if many Christians are, I think, rather confused about what it requires). Perhaps less certainly, but still probably enough, forgiveness is *distinctively* Christian—as has been noted, not always with approval, by some informed and reflective non-Christian observers.[16] What is Christian, of course, is not necessarily theological. Christians are human beings as well as believers in God. Their ethics too are formed partly by common human experience. They too know the damage that vengeance can do to its devotees, and the injustices that it proliferates. Nevertheless, to call such knowledge 'common sense' is actually to indulge in a complacency only open to those who have managed to avoid noticing how often human societies dissolve into vicious

---

16. This is a very grand claim, and counter-evidence can certainly be brought against it. Historical religions are complex entities, finding different—and sometimes contradictory—expressions at different times and in different places. On the one hand, there are instantiations of Christianity, for example, where retributive (even vindictive) punishment appears to be the norm. And forgiveness is by no means absent from, say, Judaism and Islam. Indeed, it might even be more present in certain versions of them than in certain versions of Christianity. Nevertheless, it was the Jewish philosopher, Hannah Arendt, who accredited Jesus with being '[t]he discoverer of the role of forgiveness in the realm of human affairs' (*The Human Condition* [Chicago: University of Chicago, 1958], p. 238). It was Jewish commentators on *The Sunflower* who rebuked Christian ones for judging that the concentration camp inmate should have granted forgiveness to the dying SS officer (Simon Wiesenthal, *The Sunflower: On the possibilities and limits of forgiveness*, rev. edn [New York: Schocken, 1997], pp. 164–6 [Abraham Joshua Heschel], 216–20 [Dennis Prager]). And it was Christian influence on South Africa's Truth and Reconciliation Commission that is blamed by some critics for using forgiveness to buy reconciliation at the price of justice (e.g. Richard A. Wilson, *The Politics of Truth and Reconciliation: Legitimizing the Post-Apartheid State* [Cambridge: Cambridge University Press, 2001]; 'Reconciliation and Revenge in Post-Apartheid South Africa: Rethinking Legal Pluralism and Human Rights', *Current Anthropology*, 41 [2000]). According to the testimony of *outsiders*, then, it seems that Christianity and forgiveness have a close association that is not only characteristic but distinctive.

cycles of increasingly atrocious vendettas. Take as witnesses Ireland in the 1920s, Spain in the 1930s, Bosnia and Rwanda in the 1990s, and Iraq after March 2003. What passes for common sense in social circles privileged with a long history of peace is far from universal. Experiences may be common and yet give rise to seriously different lessons. Not everyone experiences vengeance like Shaffer's Helen. Arguably, most people experience it like Edward: 'There's only one real moral imperative: don't piss on true rage—it can be the fire of sanity.'[17] It may be, then, that the counterproductiveness and futility of vengeance only appear obvious (or rational) in the light of a particular set of beliefs—or, more modestly, that a particular set of beliefs helps them to appear obvious. One such set of beliefs is provided by Christian theology. The belief that there is a more-than-human agent, who is able and intends to do justice beyond this world of space and time, frees theists to accept the limits of such justice as can be done here and now without compounding injustice. The belief that human creatures are responsible to their Creator for the growth of their lives *as a whole* endows theists with a greater sense of participation in spiritual weakness and moral shortcoming—and so with a disposition to compassion for fellow sinners—than is possessed by those who measure themselves moralistically in terms of their avoidance of bad conduct in discrete relationships with other humans. The belief that Jesus was God Incarnate imbues his teaching and example of forgiveness with an unusual moral authority—for this, after all, is how the Creator and Redeemer seeks to right wrongs. And the belief that Jesus rose from the dead transforms forgiveness from being a symptom of moral weakness—the feeble shrug of avoidance—into the salvific route to glorious vitality beyond death.

It is arguable, then, that the norm of forgiveness is distinctively, as well as characteristically, Christian; and that its distinctiveness is rooted in Christian theology. But what about a theory of forgiveness that finds place for resentment? How Christian is that? Of course, the notion that resentment is a fitting response to wrongdoing has not been given to the world by Christian theology. On the contrary, it is, as Joseph Butler admits, a natural passion. No one needs to be taught to resent injustice—although one might need to be taught what it is that truly deserves resentment. However, not everyone supposes that resentment *should* be moderated by forgiveness-as-compassion and by the desire to achieve forgiveness-as-absolution; and not everyone

17. Shaffer, *Gorgon*, pp. 16–17.

supposes that it *can* be so moderated. As I understand it, a properly Christian ethic holds that such moderation is both possible and obligatory; and, as I have explained above, some of the reasons for taking such a position are theological. This does not mean, of course, that one must own those theological reasons—that one must be a Christian theist—in order to take this particular ethical position. Nevertheless, it might still be the case that Christian theism provides stronger reasons or, more boldly, the only fully adequate ones. Whatever the truth of this moot point, it is clear that Christian theology makes a difference: it supports a particular, finely balanced position that commends resentment while requiring its moderation—and this is a position that not everyone takes. It is not a conclusion of natural reason. It is not common sense.

So much for resentment; now for retribution. Given its high esteem for the vocation of human beings and given its deep concern for their salvation, Christian theology is bound to treat injury to innocent victims very seriously. Therefore, provided that forgiveness-as-compassion has exorcised vengeance, theology will endorse a benevolent form of retribution that aims to uphold the dignity of the injured and contradict the offence of the perpetrator. Except for the fact, some might object, that Jesus himself did not. But is that a fact? His reaction to those whom he saw as lacking in compassion or as exploitative was often verbally explosive: 'You brood of vipers' (Matthew 3:7, 12:34, 23:33); 'Woe to you . . . hypocrites!' (Matthew 23:13, 15, 23, 25, 27, 29); 'You blind fools!' (Matthew 23:16, 17, 19). To describe such language as 'critical' is to tame and civilize it. Surely it is also violent language, designed to wound and sting. Is it vindictive? Not necessarily. Not if it aimed to sting into new awareness and a change of mind. Not if it aimed to provoke repentance. Not if, governed by forgiveness, it was benevolently retributive. The notion that retribution is an appropriate response to atrocious wrongdoing is, of course, not peculiarly Christian. The notion, however, that such a response should take the form of forgiving retribution is as peculiar to Christianity as is its emphasis on forgiveness. As we have argued above, that is *quite* peculiar and strongly formed by theological considerations.

It is my view, therefore, that a genuinely Christian understanding of reconciliation and forgiveness includes space for resentment and retribution. It was for that reason that I dared to say of St Augustine's explanation of the love that the just warrior bears toward the unjust aggressor that it amounts to forgiveness. On the one hand, insofar as the doctrine of just war insists that just belligerents understand what they are doing as a policing action of one set of sinful creatures to limit and repair the wrongdoing of another set—and *not* as the crusading action of the righteous upon the unrighteous, or the godly upon the infidel—it enjoins a constitutive element of forgiveness-as-compassion. This in turn serves to moderate the use of violence, so that it is proportioned both retrospectively to the nature of the wrongdoing and prospectively to the goal of reconciliation or a more just peace.[18] Thus it is saved from the vengeful temptation to answer injustice with atrocity. On the other hand, since just war makes a punitive, retributive response to wrongdoing, it withholds the political analogue of forgiveness-as-absolution until the offender has demonstrated the political analogue of repentance. However, the fact that just war is looking for repentance at all means that its goal is reconciliation, not vengeful annihilation—peace with the living, not peace among the dead.

III. The coercive justice within forgiveness

Forgiveness, properly understood, includes the proportionate expression of resentment and retribution. Resentment and retribution are hostile forces: they seek to coerce the wrongdoer—to stop him, to make him conscious of the evils he causes, to urge repentance onto him. Therefore forgiveness qualifies, rather than excludes, coercion; and coercion sometimes takes physical form. In asserting this, I am relaxing a tension—even dismantling a contradiction—that is often supposed to exist between love and justice. This common supposition is attributable above all to the influence of the thought of Reinhold Niebuhr.[19] On the one hand, Niebuhr writes of Christian love[20] as rising in 'sublime naïvete'[21] above the mean calculations of prudence[22] and in 'sublime madness' above immediate enmities.[23] Here he refers specifically to

18. The observation that the proportionality of just warfare is constituted by both a backward and a forward reference is Oliver O'Donovan's (*The Just War Revisited* [Oxford: Oxford University Press, 2003], pp. 48–63).
19. What follows in this section is a modified version of part of my chapter, 'Reinhold Niebuhr and the Political Possibility of Forgiveness', in Richard Harries and Stephen Platten, eds, *Reinhold Niebuhr and Contemporary Politics: God and Power* (Oxford: Oxford University Press, 2010).
20. Throughout *Moral Man and Immoral Society* Niebuhr talks about 'religious love' when he means primarily Christian love.
21. Reinhold Niebuhr, *Moral Man and Immoral Society* (New York: Scribner's, 1960), p. 53.
22. Ibid., pp. 57, 257, 263, 265–6.
23. Ibid., p. 255.

what he sees as the crown of the ideal of love[24]—forgiveness, self-sacrificially transcending the claims of remedial justice by absolving injustice unilaterally and unconditionally. Niebuhr thinks it both unrealistic and inappropriate to expect such forgiveness to find expression in relations between large social bodies at the level of national or international politics. This is because social injustice *deserves* coercive opposition, perhaps punishment:

> The victim of injustice cannot cease from contending against his oppressors, even if he has a religious sense of the relativity of all social positions and a contrite recognition of the sin in his own heart. Only a religion full of romantic illusions could seek to persuade the Negro to gain justice from the white man merely by forgiving him. As long as men are involved in the conflicts of nature and sin they must seek according to best available moral insights to contend for what they believe to be right. And that will mean that they will contend against other men. Short of the transmutation of the world into the Kingdom of God, men will always confront enemies...[25]

Nevertheless, Niebuhr does recognize that justice—and the coercion it inevitably involves—needs to be leavened by love: '[a]ny justice which is only justice soon degenerates into something less than justice. It must be saved by something which is more than justice.'[26] In a rare allusion to just war thinking, he acknowledges that violent coercion can be governed by benevolence,[27] in which case 'its terror must have the tempo of a surgeon's skill and healing must follow quickly upon its wounds'.[28] He thinks that love can qualify coercive justice in several ways. It can curb the element of vengeance, increase the intention of reform,[29] and restrain the use of violence. This it achieves partly through an appreciation of the transcendent and equal worth of the life of the enemy;[30] and partly through the spiritual disciplining of resentment[31] by placing the moral agent 'under the scrutiny of [God's] omniscient eye',[32] thus generating contrite acknowledgement that the enemy's moral frailty is also his own.[33] This latter element of the disciplining of resentment I ascribe to

24. Reinhold Niebuhr, *An Interpretation of Christian Ethics* (New York: Seabury, 1979), p. 137.
25. Ibid., pp. 140–1.
26. Niebuhr, *Moral Man*, p. 258.
27. Ibid., pp. 170, 172.
28. Ibid., p. 220.
29. Niebuhr, *Interpretation*, p. 67.
30. Niebuhr, *Moral Man*, p. 255; *Interpretation*, p. 65.
31. Niebuhr, *Moral Man*, pp. 248–9.
32. Ibid., pp. 51, 60.
33. Ibid., pp. 254–5.

forgiveness (as compassion); and indeed at one point so does Niebuhr, when he explicitly identifies with forgiveness 'the demand that the evil in the other shall be borne without vindictiveness because the evil in the self is known'.[34] What this implies is that even Niebuhr sometimes acknowledged that love-as-forgiveness *can* shape coercive justice.[35]

The reason for Niebuhr's inconsistency over the relationship between forgiveness and coercion lies, I think, in his failure to distinguish clearly between vengeance and retribution; and in his mistaken tendency to *identify* forgiveness with the self-sacrificial abandonment of all claims to justice. While I do think that forgiveness always involves the absolute self-sacrifice involved in swallowing one's impulses to vengeance and in suffering disci-pline by the motive of compassion and the intention of peace, I do not think that it must or should involve the bypassing of justice, appropriate resentment, and proportionate punishment.

The analysis of forgiveness into the two components of compassion and absolution affords the advantage of enabling it to incorporate coercive justice. According to this conception, the process of reconciliation contains not only initial compassion and final absolution, but between them also the coercive contradiction of injustice by the expression of proportionate resentment and the meting out of proportionate punishment. Forgiveness-as-compassion qualifies but does not replace coercive resentment; and it qualifies but need not replace coercive retribution.[36] It makes them both media of communica-tion intended to persuade the wrongdoer of the wrong he has done, to elicit his repentance, and so to enable forgiveness-as-absolution and consequent reconciliation. By ordering resentment and retribution toward reconciliation, it saves them from vengeance.

However, there is coercion and there is coercion. Emotional coercion that takes the form of furrowed brows or pursed lips and physical coercion in the form of a refusal to shake hands or of forcible confinement are one thing. Physical coercion that wounds or kills is surely another. How on

34. Niebuhr, *Interpretation*, p. 137.
35. Where Niebuhr differs from me is in thinking that the contrite recognition of one's own sinfulness and the acceptance of mutual responsibility for the sin of the accused are com-pletely beyond the capacities of collective man (*Interpretation*, p. 67).
36. Insofar as the resentment of injustice finds any external expression—say, in the victim's mistrustful attitude and behaviour toward his wrongdoer—it is itself a kind of informal retribution. Forgiveness-as-compassion should not replace the retributive expression of proportionate resentment. However, were the expression of this resentment to succeed in communicating to the wrongdoer that he has done wrong, and in eliciting from him sufficient apology and reparation as to restore trust, then further, formal retribution would be rendered unnecessary and so disproportionate.

earth can that be an expression of forgiveness-as-compassion? I believe that it can be. Even wounding or lethal coercion can be compassionate at least insofar as it refuses vengeance, intends to stop the wrongdoer doing wrong, intends that he should not resume it, would be content to achieve that by persuading him to surrender, and restrains its use of violence according to its intentions.

This integration of forgiveness with the hostile, coercive expression of resentment and meting out of retribution, sometimes wounding and lethal, confers a further advantage; for it enables us to discern how forgiveness could find fitting political expression in circumstances where simple absolution would be breathtakingly naïve and inappropriate—that is, in circumstances of hostility born of atrocious injustice from which there has been no repentance. And insofar as forgiveness is a defining feature of a Christian ethic of response to wrongdoing, this conception spares such an ethic from having to choose between relevance and plausibility.

For example, I take it for granted that, in response to the attacks of 11 September 2001, it would not have been heroic but ludicrous for the US government to have addressed al-Qaeda and said, 'We forgive you. We will not let what you have done sour our regard for you. We will continue to treat you as friends.' If such absolution were the sum of forgiveness, then it could have had no plausible place in America's reaction. If, however, forgiveness can take the form of compassion as well as absolution, then it could have had two plausible roles. First, it could have ordered the use of force toward the end of peace, and disciplined it away from vindictiveness. And second, it could have moved the US government to entertain the possibility that, though al-Qaeda's ill-disciplined resentment had festered out of all proportion, not all of its roots were simply malevolent and irrational, and that in the rank growth of its malice and falsehood there lay genuine grievances that deserved sympathetic attention—for example, the plight of the Palestinian people. Thus conceived, forgiveness could have had plausible political purchase even where violently coercive retribution is appropriate.

IV. Love, hope, and modesty

So far I have considered at length the relationship between love-as-forgiveness on the one hand, and coercive resentment and retribution on the other. I have done this because forgiveness is widely reckoned to be the epitome of Christian love and because it is widely assumed to exclude coercion. If this is true, then, since war is a form of coercion, it cannot be compatible with forgiveness, and the concept of just war has no good claim to the title 'Christian'. Against this conclusion, I have argued that forgiveness should be understood to include and qualify coercion, rather than displace it, where repentance is not forthcoming. In the next section, I shall take this argument one stage further and seek to show that love, even in the specific form of forgiveness, can find expression on the battlefield. Here I want to pause briefly and observe that, in its pursuit of just peace and in its use of coercive, perhaps belligerent, means, Christian love is qualified by religious hope and therefore by realistic modesty in its secular expectations.

The doctrine of just war understands it to be a retributive act, motivated in part by a proper resentment at a grave injustice. The resentment and the retribution that it fuels, however, should be qualified by forgiveness-as-compassion and disciplined by the intention of the reconciliation or peace that forgiveness-as-absolution ushers in. Ideally this peace should involve the repair of the damage done to the victim, the healing of the moral corruption of the perpetrator through his coming to own and repudiate his deed *as wrong*, and the consequent restoration of trust between the perpetrator and his neighbours. In fact, justice as rectification usually falls far short of the ideal. Some kinds of damage are simply beyond human repair: the death of victims, the apparently irreversible moral corruption of some wrongdoers. One of the distinguishing features of *atrocious* wrongs is that their combination of extension (the massive number of victims) and intensity (the high degree of indiscrimination, mercilessness, and cruelty) exposes the limits that almost invariably attend human attempts at justice, but which are usually not so shockingly obvious. Just war doctrine is wisely Augustinian in the modesty of its end:[37] the stopping

---

37. I say 'Augustinian' here because it was St Augustine who characterized our historical situation as 'secular'. By this he meant that we belong to the *saeculum* or age that runs between the token of the glorious transformation of the world, which is the Resurrection of Jesus from the dead, and its fulfilment. As a consequence, our moral and political endeavours are fraught with tragic tension, aspiring to ideals that can only be realized partially, ambiguously, and fleetingly under the conditions of secular history. In *The City of God* Augustine offers an arresting judicial example of the tragic character of secular endeavour (*City of* God, trans. Henry Bettenson [London: Penguin, 1972], Book XIX, chapter 6, pp. 859–61): the need perchance to torture someone who might be innocent, in order to find out the truth about a crime. And at one point in a letter to Paulinus of Nola in AD 408, he gives moving voice to the spiritual agony that the exercise of judicial office produces in the judge: 'On the subject of punishing and refraining from punishment, what am I to say? It is our desire that when we decide

of the wrongdoing by the disabling of those who are perpetrating it, and the building of a new political order that is at least *sufficiently* just and stable not to return to the old ways. The building of a just future will require that there is sufficient public repudiation of the past; but the building of a stable future may well require something less than comprehensive retribution. Some wrongdoers will not be punished at all; others will not be punished enough. Some may learn the errors of their ways; others will not. And, when all is said and done, their murdered victims will remain dead. No 'infinite justice' here, then.

Such Augustinian modesty is partly inspired by the prudence that cumulative common experience teaches: to insist on too much justice is to risk propagating further injustice. However, what experience would teach and what humans are prepared to learn are often discrepant— especially when those humans are disturbed and driven by inordinate resentment at terrible wrongs. So prudence alone may not be a sufficient matrix of patience. Augustinian modesty, however, also has the fuel of religious, eschatological hope. This is the hope that the justice that we humans cannot do here and now—the raising from the dead of innocent victims, the meting out of retribution upon those perpetrators who have escaped earthly punishment, the maturing of penitence and reconciliation that history has cut short—will yet be done by God at the end of history. While such hope can be construed in such a way as to undermine moral effort, equally it can be construed so as to inspire it. And while such hope can be dismissed as nothing but wishful thinking, it can also be proposed as a reasonable wager upon the truth of the value of the good of human beings: if that value is not an illusion, if our commitment to defend and promote it is not a noble absurdity, and if eschatological hope is necessary to make such commitment maximally intelligible, then adhering to such hope is both morally serious and rational.

whether or not to punish people, in either case it should contribute wholly to their security. These are indeed deep and obscure matters: what limit ought to be set to punishment with regard to both the nature and extent of guilt, and also the strength of spirit the wrongdoers possess? What ought each one to suffer? . . . What do we do when, as often happens, punishing someone will lead to his destruction, but leaving him unpunished will lead to someone else being destroyed? . . . What trembling, what darkness! . . . 'Trembling and fear have come upon me and darkness has covered me, and I said, Who will give me wings like a dove's? Then I will fly away and be at rest'. . . . [Psalm 55 (54):5–8] (Augustine, *Political Writings*, Letter 95, pp. 23–4)

V. Can love walk the battlefield?

In this chapter so far, I have sought to explain how Christian love might qualify coercion. But can it really? It might be possible in theory, but is it possible in practice? And even if it is possible in the case of certain limited kinds of coercion, what about physical violence? What about war? Surely soldiers in the heat of battle are driven by hatred and vengeance, not love? As the non-religious pacifist, Robert Holmes, puts it: '[O]ne cannot help but wonder... whether it is humanly possible amidst the chaos of slaughter and gore that marks... combat to remain free of those things Augustine identifies as evil in war, the cruelty, enmity, and the like...'[38]

I do not doubt that soldiers are sometimes motivated by vengeance and hatred. That, however, does not count against my thesis. What would count against it is evidence that it is psychologically necessary that war-fighting be motivated by malevolence; for then the shaping of violence by love would indeed be a mere academic fantasy. In support of my thesis, however, I can offer empirical evidence that malevolence does not necessarily motivate soldiers, even in the front line, and that various forms of love do.

Battlefield motivation varies enormously. Sometimes what prevails is a clinical professionalism. 'In the heat of battle,' writes the eminent military historian Richard Holmes, 'most soldiers regard their adversaries as ciphers: anonymous figures to be dealt with as expeditiously as possible... Most soldiers in contact killed to stay alive, and some went further, gaining professional satisfaction from outmanoeuvring or outshooting their adversaries, even if the consequence of this success was the death of another human being.'[39] Such cool professionalism is evident in Ernst Jünger's classic memoir of the First World War. 'Throughout the war,' Jünger wrote, 'it was always my endeavour to view my opponent without animus, and to form an opinion of him as a man on the basis of the courage he showed. I would always try and seek him out in combat and kill him, and I expected nothing else from him. But never did I entertain mean thoughts of him. When prisoners fell into my hands, later on, I felt responsible for their safety, and would always do everything in my power for them.'[40] Karl Marlantes, a veteran of

---

38. Robert L. Holmes, *On War and Morality* (Princeton: Princeton University Press, 1989), pp. 133–4, 135.
39. Richard Holmes, *Dusty Warriors: Modern Soldiers at War* (London: HarperPress, 2006), p. 317.
40. Ernst Jünger, *Storm of Steel*, trans. Michael Hoffman (London: Allen Lane, 2003), p. 58.

jungle combat in Vietnam, concurs: 'Contrary to the popular conception, when one is in the fury of battle I don't think one is very often in an irrational frenzy...I was usually in a white heat of total rationality, completely devoid of passion, to get the job done with minimal casualties to my side and stay alive doing it.'[41]

Another motive, especially among soldiers entering battle for the first time, is to prove oneself by meeting an inner, almost spiritual challenge. Thus Private Bosch of 7 Platoon, C Company, 1 Prince of Wales's Royal Regiment, describes his first experience of combat in Iraq:

> And then it happens, your first contact. You come face to face with the demon inside you. Fear and anxiety grips [sic] you and squeezes [sic] the very life out of you. This is life and death. This is where a man stands up and faces his destiny...This is what you were born for...You were born to be strong and courageous; to be a man. And with that the demon turns and runs. The fear and anxiety disappears [sic] and your senses sharpen into a knife's edge with which you take control of yourself and lunge forward...[42]

Perhaps the predominant military motive is love for one's comrades, which is one of the forms of love that the Johannine literature in the New Testament endorses in Jesus' name: 'Greater love has no man than this, that a man lay down his life for his friends' (John 15:13). In her analysis of face-to-face killing in 20th-century warfare, Joanna Bourke observes the predominant extent to which soldiers are motivated to kill by love for their comrades and their families, rather than by vengefulness against the enemy. Quoting a 1949 study, she writes:

> In a survey of 568 American infantrymen who had seen combat in Sicily and North Africa in 1944, men were asked what was the most important factor enabling them to continue fighting...[V]indictiveness...and self-preservation ('kill or be killed') were scarcely mentioned. Rather (after simply desiring to 'end the task'), combatants cited solidarity with the group and thoughts of home and loved ones as their main incentives.[43]

---

41. Karl Marlantes, *What it is Like to Go to War* (New York: Atlantic Monthly Press, 2011), p. 96.
42. Holmes, *Dusty Warriors*, p. 316.
43. Joanna Bourke, *An Intimate History of Killing. Face-to-face killing in twentieth century warfare* (London: Granta, 1999), p. 142; quoting from Samuel A. Stouffer et al., *The American Soldier: Combat and its Aftermath*, 2 vols., Vol. II (Princeton, NJ: Princeton University Press, 1949), p. 109. In his 1995 study Lieutenant-Colonel Dave Grossman confirms this point and extends its significance. 'Numerous studies have concluded,' he writes, 'that men in combat are usually motivated to fight, *not* by ideology or hate or fear, but by group pressures and processes' (Dave Grossman, *On Killing: The Psychological Cost of Learning to Kill in War and Society* [Boston: Little Brown, 1995], p. 89; quoted by Coady in *Morality and Political Violence*, p. 175).

One form that this sense of solidarity—this love—can take is a resolve to be worthy of one's predecessors in an historic regiment with a gallant reputation. As Patrick Bishop writes of the men of 3rd Battalion, the Parachute Regiment, during their tour in Helmand Province in the summer of 2006: 'They were fighting not just to hold their position but for the reputation of a regiment that was as dear to them as were their families.'[44] However, more frequently what mattered was less the esteem of long-dead ancestors than the trust of still-living comrades: '[T]he ideals that motivated every proper soldier... were nothing to do with queen or country, religion or political ideology. What sustained them was the determination not to let themselves down, and above all, not to let down their friends.'[45] Writing about his own experience in Helmand two years later, Lt Patrick Bury of 1st Battalion, the Royal Irish Regiment, puts flesh on this abstract point as he reflects on an exchange with his corporal:

> 'Corporal McCord, I'm sorry for shouting at you in front of the...'
>
> He interrupts and speaks hurriedly, passionately. '... I love you, boss. I'd do anything for you... I'd take a bullet for you.' He looks at me. It is not often that a man tells another he loves him. Especially in front of other men. I think of... the effort I have made to... respect and protect the boys, to build this team. To earn their trust and respect. And we call it respect because it's easy to say. It's not soft and it's not embarrassing. But Matt has called it by its true name, love. Simple, platonic love. This love that motivates men to do the most touching, brave, selfless things for their brothers. A love so deep it burns and tingles in you when it flickers, reminding you there are things greater than you, more important than you, things that last longer than you... And sometimes, out here, you get a glimpse and you understand. You understand why soldiers charge machine guns or hold out to the death while others escape. Love. For love melts fear like butter on a furnace; it transcends it.[46]

Later, an eighteen-year-old private, earlier found sobbing uncontrollably after a Taliban attack, steels himself to go out on night patrol. Bury comments: '[Mark] has refused... to leave the platoon, and has forced himself to come out with us tonight, despite all his fear, his terror... I watch him

---

44. Patrick Bishop, 3 *Para* (London: Harper Press, 2007), p. 188.
45. Bishop, 3 *Para*, p. 268.
46. Patrick Bury, *Callsign Hades* (London: Simon & Schuster, 2011), p. 136. The publishers ascribe Mr Bury's account to 2006; he himself has told me that it relates to 2008.

nervously twitch and scan, but endure. It was pure courage, the very essence of it. The triumph of will over fear... *Greater love hath no man.*[47] Sebastian Junger writes along the same lines of a US infantry unit in eastern Afghanistan in 2007–8, observing that the attraction of combat had more to do with protecting comrades than killing the enemy.[48] In a nutshell, 'Courage was love.'[49] To civilians this might seem a counter-intuitive, eccentric, even perverse interpretation. Nevertheless, it is confirmed by the commandant of the Royal Military Academy, Sandhurst, who, in a BBC documentary first broadcast in 2011, concluded his eve-of-commissioning address to the officer cadets: 'I'm often asked, "Is there one Golden Rule for leadership?" As officers you are serving your soldiers. Some day you may have to lead men into battle. This is an extraordinary thing to do. You are their servants and you do that through leading them. That's how it works. If you don't understand that, *you ain't got it!* That's "serve to lead". Go out and *love* your soldiers.'[50]

Self-sacrificial love for one's friends is admirable, but he that would follow Jesus must extend love to his enemies, too. Is this possible in the heat of combat? Many will suppose not, assuming that soldiers typically hate their opponents. But this is not so. In his acclaimed history of the Spanish Civil War, Antony Beevor makes this remarkable report: 'There was said to have been a sweet-natured youth among Moscardó's [nationalist] defenders at Toledo [in 1936], who was called the Angel of the Alcázar because before firing his rifle he used to cry, "Kill without hate!"'[51] This is remarkable presumably because it is so unusual. What is unusual about it, however, is the pious, adolescent scrupulousness with which the absence of hatred is expressed, not the absence as such; for hatred of the enemy is not at all a constant motive of soldiers in the field, or even a usual one. Indeed, it seems that hatred is more common among civilians than combat troops. In his extraordinarily wise meditation on the psychology and spirituality of combat, informed by his own experience of military service in the Second World War, Glenn Gray writes: 'A civilian far removed from the battle is nearly certain to be more bloodthirsty than the front-line soldier whose

47. Bury, *Callsign Hades*, pp. 231–2, 261–2. The italics are the author's.
48. Sebastian Junger, *War* (London: Fourth Estate, 2010), pp. 214, 234. See also pp. 120, 123–4, 210, 239–40, 243.
49. Junger, *War*, p. 239.
50. Major-General Marriott, Commandant, Royal Military Academy, Sandhurst at the end of Episode 3 of BBC 4's documentary, 'Sandhurst', first broadcast on 3 October 2011.
51. Antony Beevor, *The Battle for Spain: The Spanish Civil War, 1936–9* (London: Weidenfeld and Nicholson, 2006), p. 425.

hatred has to be responsible, meaning that he has to respond to it, to answer it with action.'[52] This view is substantiated by R.H. Tawney, the Anglican economic historian, who fought in the early stages of the battle of the Somme in July 1916 before he was severely wounded and invalided back to England. The following October he published an article in the press, where he reflected on the bewildering gulf in understanding that, he felt, had opened up between the men at the front and their families and friends back home. At one point he protests against the view of the soldier that has come to prevail in many civilian minds:

> And this 'Tommy' is a creature at once ridiculous and disgusting. He is repre-
> sented as...finding 'sport' in killing other men, as 'hunting Germans out of
> dug-outs as a terrier hunts rats', as overwhelming with kindness the captives
> of his bow and spear. The last detail is true to life, but the emphasis which you
> lay upon it is both unintelligent and insulting. Do you expect us to hurt them
> or starve them? Do you not see that we regard these men who have sat oppo-
> site us in mud—'square-headed bastards', as we called them—as the victims of
> the same catastrophe as ourselves, as our comrades in misery much more truly
> than you are? Do you think that we are like some of you in accumulating on
> the head of every wretched antagonist the indignation felt for the wickedness
> of a government, of a social system, or (if you will) of a nation?...Hatred of
> the enemy is not common, I think, among those who have encountered him.
> It is incompatible with the proper discharge of our duty. For to kill in hatred
> is murder; and soldiers, whatever their nationality, are not murderers, but
> executioners.[53]

Tawney's experience was by no means unique. It was shared by Charles Barberon of the 121 *Régiment d'artillerie*: 'It's surprising, but the soldier who has suffered the enemy's fire does not show the same hatred for the enemy as civilians.'[54] Further confirmation, if it is needed, is available from the next world war. RAF pilot Michael Constable Maxwell reports in his diary an encounter he and some colleagues had had with a local lawyer, who was friendly with his squadron. The lawyer was told of the Dornier [the German plane that Maxwell had just shot down]. 'Oh how absolutely splendid of you, I do hope they were all killed!' he remarked. Maxwell found this, he

52. J. Glenn Gray, *The Warrior: Reflections on Men in Battle*, intro. Hannah Arendt (Lincoln, Nebraska:
University of Nebraska Press, 1998), p. 135.
53. R.H. Tawney, 'Some Reflections of a Soldier', in *'The Attack' and Other Papers* (London:
George, Allen, Unwin, 1953), pp. 25, 27.
54. William Philpott, *Bloody Victory: The Sacrifice on the Somme and the Making of the Twentieth
Century* (London: Little, Brown, 2009), p. 177.

wrote, 'the filthiest remark I have ever heard and I was staggered by its bloody sadism...it is this loathsome attitude which allows papers to print pictures of wounded Germans. They must be killed and I hope to kill many myself...but the act is the unpleasant duty of the executioner which must be done ruthless and merciless [sic]—but it can be done silently.'[55]

Front-line servicemen do not necessarily hate the enemy. Sometimes they even feel a sense of solidarity or kinship with him. Thus Gerald Dennis, who fought on the Western Front, confessed that at Christmas 1916 he would:

> not have minded fraternizing as had been done the previous two years for in a way, [sic] the opponents on each side of No Man's Land were kindred spirit. We did not hate one another. We were both P.B.I. [poor bloody infantry], we should have liked to have stood up between our respective barbed wire, without danger and shaken hands with our counterparts [sic].[56]

Thus, too, Ernest Raymond, a British veteran of the Gallipoli campaign in 1915, recalled that the Turk 'became popular with us, and everything suggested that our amiability toward him was reciprocated'.[57]

An absence of hatred for the enemy, even a certain sense of kinship with him, are not at all uncommon in the experience of front-line troops. But what about compassion? I put this question to a British veteran of the Falklands War in 1982. Chris Keeble, then a major in the Parachute Regiment, found himself in command of a battalion during the Battle of Goose Green after its colonel had been killed in action. The paratroops, he told me, were very ferocious as long as the battle continued, but once it was over he witnessed many instances of his men cradling wounded Argentine soldiers in their arms.[58] Compassion for the enemy—after combat—was not foreign to that battlefield. And if Glenn Gray is to be believed, it is commonly found elsewhere.[59]

This is all true, but it is not the whole truth. It would surely strain credibilty to pretend that pleasure in destruction, anger, and hatred are all stran-

55. Patrick Bishop, *Fighter Boys: Saving Britain 1940* (London: HarperCollins, 2003), p. 336.
56. Bourke, *An Intimate History*, p. 148, quoting Gerald V. Dennis, 'A Kitchener Man's Bit (1916–1918)', 1928, p. 129, Imperial War Museum.
57. Ernest Raymond, *The Story of My Days: An Autobiography 1882–1922* (London: Cassell, 1968), p. 120, quoted by Richard Harries in 'The De-romanticisation of War and the Struggle for Faith', in *The Straits of War: Gallipoli Remembered*, introduced by Martin Gilbert (Stroud: Sutton, 2000), pp. 190–1.
58. Chris Keeble, in conversation with the author, June 2009.
59. Gray, *Warriors*, pp. 83–4.

gers to the battlefield. Of course, they are not. 'The least acknowledged aspect of war, today,' writes Karl Marlantes, 'is how exhilarating it is.'[60] This exhilaration, however, is not always malicious. It is not always the destruction that pleases, so much as the thrill, even the ecstasy, of danger. A month before he was killed at the very end of the First World War, the poet Wilfred Owen—yes, he of the pity-of-war fame—wrote to his mother:

> I have been in action for some days. I can find no word to qualify my experiences except the word SHEER... It passed the limits of my Abhorrence. I lost all my earthly faculties, and fought like an angel... With this corporal who stuck to me and shadowed me like your prayers I captured a German Machine Gun and scores of prisoners... I only shot one man with my revolver (at about 30 yards!); The rest I took with a smile.[61]

More recently, and less angelically, Patrick Hennessey has written of his first experience of battle in Afghanistan in May 2007: 'But what I couldn't say in an email because maybe at the time I didn't know it or didn't want to believe it in case it ran out or wasn't true, was just how easy it all was, how natural it all felt and how much fun.'[62] And describing a later engagement, he says:

> I want to sit with him [the major] in the ditch and try and explain, try and piece together what it is about the contact battle that ramps the heartbeat up so high and pumps adrenalin and euphoria through the veins in such a heady rapid mix. I want to sit with him... and wonder what compares; the winning and scoring punch, the first kiss, the triumphant knicker-peeling moment? Nowhere else sells bliss like this, surely? Not in freefall jumps or crisp blue waves, not on dance floors in pills or white lines—I want to discuss with him whether it's sexually charged because it's the ultimate affirmation of being alive.[63]

A British veteran of the Iraq invasion in 2003, explaining his eagerness to go to Helmand, agrees: 'There's no better buzz than having a bullet flying past your face.'[64] Here, the exhilaration, the ecstasy of war seem akin to that of extreme sports—adolescent perhaps, but not exactly malicious.

60. Marlantes, *What it is Like to Go to War*, p. 62.
61. Wilfred Owen, Letter 662, to Susan Owen, 4 or 5 October 1918, in *Collected Letters*, ed. Harold Owen and John Bell (London: Oxford University Press, 1967), p. 580. The irregular capitalization is Owen's.
62. Patrick Hennessey, *The Junior Officers' Reading Club: Killing Time and Fighting Wars* (London: Penguin, 2010), p. 179.
63. Ibid., p. 211.
64. A soldier from the 2nd Battalion, The Royal Welsh, in Episode 1 of the BBC Radio 4 documentary, 'While the Boys Are Away', first broadcast on Wednesday 16 March 2011.

On other occasions, however, the ecstasy that impels soldiers is that of rage, which is more morally complex, perhaps dubious. Sometimes what inspires it is the death of comrades. In the Battle for Normandy in 1944, according to Antony Beevor, a member of the US 30th Infantry Division noticed that '[r]eal hatred of the enemy came to soldiers . . . when a buddy was killed. "And this was often a total hatred; any German they encountered after that would be killed."'[65] Sixty-three years later, their counterparts in eastern Afghanistan reacted in the same way. After the death of a popular comrade, Sebastian Junger tells us, 'Second Platoon fought like animals . . .'[66] And after a similar incident, one of its members commented, 'I just wanted to kill everything that came up that wasn't American.'[67] Fierce anger in response to the violent killing of a comrade seems to me quite natural, not merely in the sense of 'predictable', but also in the sense of 'appropriate'. Anger at the deliberate destruction of anything valuable is appropriate. Not to resent its loss is to fail in love for it. If it was valuable, then its violent destruction *deserves* resentment. Still, it deserves only *proportionate and discriminate* resentment. It deserves anger that is not sinful. This raises the important psychological question: Is it actually possible to control anger under battlefield conditions? It seems so. Describing a unit's reaction to the death of a popular colleague in Afghanistan, Sergeant Dan Jarvie of the Parachute Regiment observed: 'There wasn't a feeling that they [the dead man's section] were going to go out and do anything for revenge. That's not what we were there for. We weren't going to hand out any punishment to anyone who wasn't Taliban. But we had a resolution . . . we will go out there and fight harder, fight more aggressively . . .'[68]

What appears to anger combat soldiers most, however, is not the death of a comrade, but enemy conduct that breaks the rules, be they formal or informal: treachery, gratuitous sacrilege, wanton cruelty. So Michael Burleigh comments on the behaviour of troops in the Second World War: 'Anything that seemed sneaky . . . were [sic] liable to elicit a vicious response.'[69] During the battle for Sicily in 1943, American troops of the

---

65. Antony Beevor, *D-Day: The Battle for Normandy* (London: Viking, 2009), p. 260.
66. Junger, *War*, p. 60.
67. Ibid., p. 106.
68. Bishop, 3 *Para*, p. 144.
69. Michael Burleigh, *Moral Combat: A History of World War II* (London: HarperPress, 2010), p. 380.

45th Division responded to cases of treacherous surrender by German troops by adopting a policy of taking no prisoners.[70] In South-East Asia, '[a]s they pursued the Japanese, the Australians encountered countless examples of sadism: the body of a native boy, his head incinerated with a flamethrower and a bayonet protruding from his anus; a woman whose left breast had been cut off before she died; the body of a militiaman tied to a tree with a bayonet left rammed into his stomach. By the time the Australians found evidence of cannibalism, they had come to regard the enemy as something other than human.'[71] Similarly, US Marine Eugene Sledge told of 'an incident where he happened upon Marine dead, one of whom had been decapitated and had his hands cut off at the wrist—his head was posed on his chest—while his penis had been cut off and stuffed in his mouth. Another man had been "butchered" into neat pieces... "From that moment on I never felt the least pity or compassion for [the Japanese] no matter what the circumstances."'[72]

Again, it seems to me that deep anger is the only morally fitting response to such appalling, sadistic cruelty; and that fitting anger here may require the intensity of a certain kind of hatred. Confronted with such atrocity, soldiers have cogent reason not to extend to those responsible any benefit of doubt; and if such conduct is typical of the enemy, or unless and until they can find a way of discriminating between the guilty and the innocent among them, they have sufficient reason to withhold doubt's benefit from anyone wearing the enemy's uniform in the relevant arena. Such fitting hatred and mercilessness need not last forever, however: 'During the assault on Longstop Hill in Tunisia in April 1943 a captured German drew a concealed pistol and shot several of his Argyll and Sutherland Highlander captors. The latter were "roused to a state of berserk fury—We just had a hate—at the Germans, the hill, everything." For a few days they accepted no surrenders, but by the time they had stormed the hill, losing a third of their own men in the action, they had taken three hundred prisoners.'[73] Nor need hatred be universal and indiscriminate. An American infantryman, Sidney Stewart, leapt into a bomb crater and found himself face to face with a Japanese soldier who had done the same thing: '"I knew I couldn't take him prisoner. We didn't have time... He said something in

---

70. Carlo D'Este, *Bitter Victory: The Battle for Sicily 1943* (Glasgow: Collins, 1988), p. 317.
71. Burleigh, *Moral Combat*, p. 382.
72. Ibid., p. 365.   73. Ibid., p. 379.

Japanese...I knew it was surrender...He didn't cringe or sneer, nor did he show any hatred. Why, I don't hate this guy. I can't hate him...This man was like a friend."' Nonetheless, when ordered to move out, Stewart ignored the prayer board the Japanese was tugging from his pocket and shot him dead. He did this, however, neither out of hatred nor without necessity.[74]

Writing of his experience in Helmand Province in 2008, Patrick Bury tells a very revealing tale about what happened when a Talib blew himself up while laying a roadside bomb:

> I was glad he was dead. It was funny. He had tried to blow us up, and the stupid fucker had blown himself up. That was gratifying, warming, pleasant. But later I see photos of his body and I feel sick. Somewhere within me, under the hardening crust, compassion still pervades my thoughts. *What about his mother, his family? What a waste of a life.*
>
> My compassion lasts less than twenty-four hours. As we debate whether to return his body to a mosque before sundown, like the soft, moral, Geneva-bound men we are, the Taliban prepare to ambush us at the mosque. Luckily, we don't have the manpower. The family can collect him later. Then we find out about the ambush. Rage.
>
> *Fuck them, the dirty despicable bastards. Is nothing sacred? Ambush your enemy as he returns your dead? Honour? You bastards. YOU FUCKING BASTARDS. I WILL KILL EVERY LAST ONE OF YOU.*
>
> ...I am struggling with this war...Struggling with our enemy. An enemy that says it is strictly Islamic yet runs harems and makes and takes drugs, an enemy that uses handicapped kids as mules for suicide bombs, that executes children for going to school. I start to hate them. Hate them for what they are doing to me. Hate them and their terrifying suicide bombs that separate us from the locals. Hate them for eroding me.
>
> *Do they hate us in the same way?*
>
> *Yes.*
>
> And I hate the locals for not standing up to them. For harbouring them, sheltering them. For not returning our smiles. For not being human. For hating us. For watching us walk over IEDs [improvised explosive devices].
>
> *Not all of them...Not all of them.*[75]

In the first place what this reveals is the emotional maelstrom within Bury: on the one hand, a sense of satisfaction that an enemy had got his come-uppance, sharpened by righteous indignation against the Taliban's

---

74. Ibid., p. 367.
75. Bury, *Callsign Hades,* pp. 218–19. The italics and the block capitals are all Bury's.

outrageous unscrupulousness,[76] and on the other hand the constraining voice of compassion ('*What about his mother, his family? What a waste of a life... Do they hate us in the same way? Yes... Not all of them... Not all of them*'). In the second place it displays the struggle that Bury undergoes to retain his compassion, which he articulates elsewhere: 'Faced with the poor chances of our own survival, with death permeating everything, with the cheapness of life and the Afghan disregard for it, our morality, our compassion, diminishes within us. We try to keep our empathy. Our humanity. But it is getting harder.'[77] Finally, Bury's experience implies that the enraged hatred of the enemy, powerful though it may be, need not get its own way, need not take over, because in his case it did not. The voice of compassion was able to speak, to push back.

It seems to me that anger, even with the intensity of rage and hatred, can sometimes be a morally fitting motive on the battlefield. Despicable deeds deserve no less of a reaction. For sure, even morally justified rage and hatred are dangerous emotions, not easily governed; but the empirical evidence is that they can be governed. If it is love of justice that grounds and inspires them, then perhaps that same love is well placed to restrain them.

It has to be admitted, however, that rage is not always inspired by care for goods and love for justice. Sometimes, it is fuelled by the sheer joy—the ecstasy—of destruction. Ernst Jünger bears witness from the First World War:

> As we advanced, we were in the grip of a berserk rage. The overwhelming desire to kill lent wings to my stride. Rage squeezed bitter tears from my eyes. The immense desire to destroy that overhung the battlefield precipitated a red mist in our brains. We called out sobbing and stammering fragments of sentences to one another, and an impartial observer might have concluded that we were all ecstatically happy... The fighter, who sees a bloody mist in front of his eyes as he attacks, doesn't want prisoners; he wants to kill.[78]

76. Bury's view of the Taliban is not just an expression of partisan prejudice. Michael Semple, an Irish expert on Afghanistan and deputy to the European Union's special representative to Afghanistan in 2004–7, has written: 'In terms of the insurgents' operating methods, most sections of the insurgency have developed ruthlessness as an in-house style, even more so now than pre-2001. In fact the insurgents have developed a reputation for using extreme and arbitrary violence... In the post-2001 insurgency, the Taliban have been even more dependent on tactics that by any definition constitute acts of terrorism, including targeted assassinations of civilian figures and bomb attacks on civilian targets or on military targets without due precautions to prevent civilian casualties' (*Reconciliation in Afghanistan* [Washington, DC: United States Institute of Peace Press, 2009], pp. 36–7, 46).

77. Bury, *Callsign Hades*, p. 210.

78. Jünger, *Storm of Steel*, pp. 232, 239.

Looking back at his experience in Vietnam, Karl Marlantes recognizes the same phenomenon: 'This was blood lust. I was moving from white heat to red heat. The assigned objective, winning the hill, was ensured. I was no longer thinking how to accomplish my objective with the lowest loss of life to my side. I just wanted to keep killing gooks.'[79] Marlantes is acutely aware of 'the danger of opening up to the rapture of violent transcendence', of 'falling in love with the power and thrill of destruction and death dealing... There is a deep savage joy in destruction... I loved this power. I love it still. And it scares the hell out of me.'[80] Nevertheless, he is quite adamant that it is 'simply not true' 'that all is fair in love and war, that having rules in war is total nonsense'.[81] Appealing to incidents of German and British generosity towards the enemy during the North African campaign in the Second World War,[82] Marlantes comments, 'They remembered their common humanity and controlled the beast that lies within us all.'[83]

Anger, hatred, rage, the sheer pleasure of destruction: these are all powerful emotions on the battlefield, but they can be governed. The last one can be refused; the first three can be rendered discriminate and disproportionate. Whether or not they *will* be governed depends crucially upon the military discipline instilled by training, and especially upon the quality of leadership in the field. This last point is underscored by Patrick Bury's testimony:

> Most soldiers do not want to kill per se. Almost all of us have an inherent belief that killing is wrong. However, the situations we find ourselves in often mean we are forced to consider the use of lethal force. Our training helps us differentiate between threat and appropriate use of force, but also, by its very nature, makes it easier for us to kill...
>
> Killing, whatever its form, can be morally corrosive. Mid-intensity counter insurgency, with its myriad of complex situations, an enemy who won't play fair and the constant, enduring feeling of being under threat, compound such corrosiveness. A good tactical leader must recognise this and constantly maintain the morality of those he commands.

79. Marlantes, *What it is Like to Go to War*, p. 103.
80. Ibid., pp. 61, 63, 67, 160.
81. Ibid., p. 228.
82. It must be admitted that the fighting in North Africa during the Second World War was unusually civilized.
83. Marlantes, *What it is Like to Go to War*, p. 232.

...[A]t the beginning of the tour, it was relatively easy to maintain a sense of morality amongst the platoon. But when the threat to our lives increased, as the Taliban began fighting increasingly dirty, as the civilians became indifferent and as we were either nearly killed or took casualties, this became increasingly difficult. Soldiers who did not want to kill for no reason began to become unconcerned.

There is a balance to be struck between morality and operational effectiveness, between softness and hardness. It is a fine line to walk, but one which must be walked nonetheless. My platoon sergeant would always strive to keep the soldiers sharp, aggressive and ready to fight their way out of any situation...

However, as a junior officer I felt the need to morally temper what the platoon sergeant had said to the men. His could not be the final word on the subject... In the morphing, grey conflict we found ourselves in I pointed out that the civilians, even if they were untrustworthy and indifferent, were still our best form of force protection. They told us where the IEDs were. If we lost them, we lost everything... We had to treat captured Taliban correctly. Otherwise we might as well not bother coming out here.

I think, in hindsight, this unacknowledged agreement I had with my platoon sergeant worked well. He kept the platoon sharp and ready, 'loaded' as it were, and I just made sure the gun didn't go off at the wrong place at the wrong people... The platoon was so well drilled it barely needed me for my tactical acumen. But they did need me for that morality.

Sometimes I felt my own morality begin to slip, that hardness creeping in. Sometimes I thought that I was soft, that my platoon sergeant was right and I should shut up and get on with it. Sometimes I'm sure the platoon felt like that! I was unsure. And at these times my memory would flit back to Sandhurst, to the basics, and I would find renewed vigour that what I was saying was indeed right. My moral compass, for all its wavering, was still pointing North. And that was the most important lesson I was taught in Sandhurst, and that I learnt in Afghanistan.[84]

VI. Conclusion

The testimony that I have adduced is first-hand and comes from front-line soldiers in six wars, spanning almost a century from 1914 to 2012.

---

84. Lt Paddy Bury, 'Pointing North', unpublished paper, May 2009. Bury instances the demoralization that poor leadership allows to develop in *Callsign Hades*, pp. 117, 233: 'I can't trust some of that platoon to make the right decisions. Some of them are fully aware that down here they are indeed deities of their own little universes... Much of it is down to leadership... It feels like the platoon commander lost the respect of his platoon months ago. It was the little things that added up, the little things he didn't do.'

It contradicts the charge that military violence is mainly and necessarily motivated by hatred. It disturbs the assumption that battlefield hatred is always morally unfitting and ungovernable. It confirms the thesis that soldiers are usually motivated primarily by love for their comrades. And it supports the claim that they can regard their enemies with respect, solidarity, and even compassion—all of which are forms of love. Therefore, the notion that love can govern the use of violence is no mere academic fantasy. Love can be active in the making of war. Augustine was right: belligerent harshness can be kind.

3

The principle of double effect

Can it survive combat?

With due respect to pacifists, killing comes in different kinds. To kill a person is always to cause an evil. It is to cause the death of someone with an equal calling to discern, interpret, embody, and represent what is good in the world. Even when the victim is one who has let himself grow monstrously corrupt—think Hitler, Stalin, or Pol Pot—and whose death involves the loss of nothing good, a tragic quality still attaches to it. The tragedy is that someone should have so misdirected their lives that their death amounts to a moral gain and not a loss.

To kill a person is always to cause an evil, but it is not always to do a wrong. History is sometimes very unkind to us and forces us into the position of not being able to do anything without becoming responsible—in some sense— for causing evil. I can kill you out of contemptuous hatred, intending nothing less than your annihilation, constrained by no necessity, and with no proportionate reason to prefer another's life to yours. Or I can kill you without malice, with respectful and manifest reluctance, necessitated by love for others, and with sufficient reason to prefer their lives to yours. Not all killing is murder. Morally speaking, there are different ways of causing death. Some are culpable, some are innocent, and some (tragically) are commendable. One factor that is important in making the difference is the intention of the killer.

I. The principle of double effect: an interpretation

The Christian doctrine of just war comes from the same Thomist stable as the principle of double effect; and insofar as it remains Thomist, the former involves the latter. The distinction of an act's effects into those that are intended and those that are foreseen but unintended is, of course, famously controversial; and elsewhere I have sought to negotiate my way through the swirling waters of the controversy and to emerge with a version of the distinction intact.[1]

Against consequentialist analyses, which reckon an act's rightness or wrongness simply in terms of its consequences, the principle of double effect makes the agent's intention (or his negligence) an important criterion. The reasons for this are several and good. First, it articulates the common intuition that, though their effects are the same, accidental homicide and murder should be distinguished in terms of intention. Next, the subjective, reflexive impact upon the agent himself of his intending harm is an important effect that consequentialist reasoning usually ignores. When we intend harm, we identify ourselves with evil and thereby corrupt ourselves.[2] Further, while the human agent has relatively little control over the objective effects of his actions, he has complete control over their subjective effects: while the effects upon others of an act of infidelity, for example, run down the generations far beyond the agent's sight, and through the actions of innumerable other responsible agents, the effect that consists in the agent himself becoming unfaithful depends entirely on *his* decision. This is one reason why intention should have priority over consequences in deciding the moral quality of an act. Another reason is, fourth, that the growth of virtuous persons is itself a great good in the world. This is partly because as I make myself today, so I dispose myself to act tomorrow. If today I act out of malice or undue carelessness and intend an injustice in one situation, then tomorrow I will be more inclined to do so in others. But virtuous character has more than instrumental or consequential value; it also has an intrinsic beauty that exhilarates the human heart. Finally, for Christians and some other religious believers, virtue is a very great good indeed, since it is a condition of participation in the fullness of life beyond death.

Given the importance of intention in determining the moral quality of an act, the principle of double effect is able to make a crucial moral distinction between the effects of an act that I intend and those that I accept with reluctance. Good effects (e.g. justice) I may intend, but evil effects (e.g.

---

1. Biggar, *Aiming to Kill*. The version that I emerged with is a modified form of Germain Grisez's and differs in important respects from that espoused by Thomas Aquinas, as I explain later in this chapter.
2. Norvin Richards is a rare consequentialist who appreciates this point: 'As causes actions affect the likelihood of various consequences. As symptoms of personality, they do the same, but in a different way: by making it more likely the person will act in ways which have those consequences' ('Double Effect and Moral Character', *Mind*, XCIII [1984], p. 386).

death) I may accept only as side effects. The upshot of this is to permit some actions whose effects are ambiguous—for example, the shooting of a gun that protects one person and kills another at the same time. I may shoot the gun, provided that I intend protection and only accept the killing. Thus I avoid identifying myself with the evil that my act causes.

The meaning of 'intention', however, is susceptible of several interpretations, and it is important for us to be clear about what we mean here. What exactly is it to intend something, and how can we tell an effect that is intended from one that is merely foreseen and accepted? One option is to say that we intend whatever it is that we choose to do. According to this reading, an intention involves a deliberate choice of a purposive course of action. The problem with this, however, is that a single deliberate course of action might be foreseen to involve several effects, and the agent's will might relate to each of those effects in significantly different ways. Take the following case from the film version of Patrick O'Brien's novel, *Master and Commander*, set in the 18th century aboard a warship of the Royal Navy.[3] At one point in the story, the ship is engulfed in a severe Atlantic storm. One of her masts is broken and crashes into the sea—sails, rigging, and all. The midshipman warns the captain that unless the ship is cut free from the fallen mast, it will drag her over and cause her to sink. But there is a dilemma; for clinging to the wrecked mast is a sailor who was blown over with it. If the ship is cut free from the wrecked mast, the sailor will—with a practical certainty—drown. The captain makes his decision. He calls for axes and orders another sailor standing nearby to help him cut the ropes binding the ship to the fallen wreckage. This sailor happens to be the best friend of the fellow clinging to the wreckage; and as he lifts his axe and brings it down on the ropes, tears stream down his cheeks. The sailor with the axe knew what he was doing. He knew that he was performing an act that would help to cause his friend to drown. He could have disobeyed orders and refused to cut the ropes. But he did not refuse; he chose to obey. Did he therefore intend to kill his friend? To give an affirmative answer would, I think, imply that the sailor was *intent* upon killing his friend—that that is what he *wanted*. Such an implication would be entirely inappropriate. What he was intent upon, what he wanted, was to save the ship and its crew by the only means possible. The death of his friend was entirely *un*wanted, as his streaming tears bear witness. In this case, then, it seems appropriate to say that in choosing

3. *Master and Commander*, directed by Peter Weir (2003).

to cut the ropes, the sailor intended the effect of saving the ship, but that he only accepted with the deepest reluctance the effect of causing his friend to drown. His friend's death was quite beside his intention—even though he *chose* it. What this analysis reveals is that intention is not just about deliberate choice, but also about desire; not just about willing, but also about wanting. An effect that I intend, therefore, is one that I both choose and want; and an effect that I accept is one that I choose but do not want.

However, there are different kinds of wanting. Sometimes I intend to do something that (in a certain sense) I do not want to do. Sometimes I commit myself to doing something only through gritted teeth, fearing the costs and flinching at the pain that my commitment incurs. In a sense, what I do here I do not want. This phenomenon inspires us to distinguish at least two kinds of wanting, two kinds of desire. On the one hand, there is the desire for what one knows to be good, the desire to align oneself with it, and so the desire to do what is right. On the other hand, there is the desire to be in a state of physical and emotional satisfaction and to avoid what is painful. Let us call the first kind 'rational', and the second kind 'sensual'. What matters is that I should want rationally what is good and right, even if at the same time I do not want sensually what is painful.[4]

It matters that an agent should not want to cause evil simply and as such, for so to want to cause evil is to desire it, and to desire evil is to desire

---

4. At a conference in 2010 my proposal to identify what one intends with what one wants met with objections from several quarters. One critic made the point that one can intend something but not want it. This has moved me here to distinguish different kinds of wanting. In addition I appeal to the authority of Elizabeth Anscombe, as reported by Christopher Kaczor: 'The fundamental sign of intention, says Anscombe, is desire. We cannot be said to intend those effects of our action which, however closely connected with the desired effects, we do not desire' (*Proportionalism and the Natural Law* [Washington, DC: Catholic University of America Press, 2002], p. 63). I also note that my distinction concurs with John Finnis's observation that 'desire' is equivocal between one's rational response to an intelligible good and one's response to what appeals to one's feelings. Accordingly, an intention is the agent's volitional commitment to achieving a goal that the agent grasps as good, and not 'mere desire' ('Intention and Side-Effects', in R. Frey and C. Morris, eds, *Liability and Responsibility* [Cambridge: Cambridge University Press, 1991], p. 35; cited by T.A. Cavanaugh in *Double-Effect Reasoning: Doing Good and Avoiding Evil* [Oxford: Clarendon Press, 2006], pp. 92–3). The only qualification that I would make to this account is to say that the necessary distinction is not sharply between the will and desire. Certainly, in intending something I commit myself to it in an act of volition. However, if my intention is morally right, then what I will is what I know to be good. But not everything that I know moves me to act in accordance with it—not everything known is a motive. What is good does move me, because it is intrinsically attractive and desirable. Therefore I do not merely will what is good. I will it because, in knowing it, I desire it and am drawn to it. The distinction that we need, therefore, is between 'rational desire' and 'sensual desire', not between the will and 'mere desire'.

damage to something of intrinsic value. Certainly, that is unjust: good things do not deserve harm from responsible agents. However, to desire evil is not only unjust to someone else, but also corrupting of the one who desires. What we love, we become; where our treasure is, there lie our hearts. To desire evil stunts an agent's growth into virtue and robs him of fitness for life beyond death. Further, it disposes him to cause further harm, for one who chooses to desire evil today will the more easily choose it tomorrow.

Nevertheless, what the agent intends is not the only determinant of the moral quality of his act. Insofar as he chooses to embark on a course of action that is foreseen to involve an evil effect as well as a good one, he is responsible for what he accepts as well as for what he intends. But to be responsible is not yet to be culpable. To be responsible for causing evil is to be required to give a justifying account for causing it—to show that it was not caused needlessly, in the sense that it could have been avoided; or in vain, in the sense that it undermined the good effect for whose sake it is being tolerated; or disproportionately, in the sense that it did not 'outweigh' the good achieved.[5] If an agent accepts needless, vain, or disproportionate evil, then at very least he has been culpably negligent or careless; and at very worst he actually wanted the evil that he only pretended to accept reluctantly. Either way, his irresponsible acceptance of evil could be such as to render his act immoral. Good intentions are not enough.

So to say of the sailor who brought down his axe on the rope that he did not intend the death of his friend is not to say that he was not responsible for it. He was responsible for it: he knew with a practical certainty that cutting the rope would result in his friend's death, and yet he chose to cut the rope anyway. One is responsible for everything that one knowingly chooses. But to be responsible is not yet to be blameworthy. So was the sailor blameworthy? No. First, he did not want his friend's death and he helped to cause it only with manifest and appropriate reluctance. And second, he accepted his friend's death as necessary and proportionate: that is, as the only way of saving the whole of the ship's company from drowning. The sailor with the axe did not intend death, but accepted it with due reluctance and for sufficient reasons. He was therefore right in what he did and in why he did it.

---

5. That is, 'outweigh' in senses other than 'undermine'. For further discussion of this, see Chapter Four.

However, even if an agent intends only what is good and merely accepts with reluctance a concomitant evil effect, and even if his acceptance is necessary, non-subversive, and proportionate, what he does might still not be morally right. For his acceptance of a particular evil might yet be unfair to other people or in breach of an obligation. Take an example I have used before elsewhere.[6] Suppose a professor not long in his current post is offered a more attractive position in another university. Suppose that on balance he has sufficiently good reasons for accepting it. Suppose also, however, that his leaving would damage the morale of his current department (although at the same time it would considerably relieve its chronic financial deficit). If his decision to take the new post is to be morally justified, it is certainly important that he should genuinely not want to cause damage, that he should take all reasonable steps to avoid or minimize it, and that it should be proportionate in some sense. But that is not enough; for it is also important that he should not be bound by any clear moral obligation to stay—for example, a promise made to see his department through a particular set of difficulties.

If an act that causes foreseen evil (such as death) is to be morally justified, it is important that what is intended by it is something else, something good. However, while right intention is important, it is not sufficient. In addition, the evil must be accepted with an appropriate reluctance that manifests itself in serious attempts to avoid or minimize it—serious attempts to render its acceptance proportionate. But that, too, is not sufficient. In addition, the acceptance of proportionate evil must not offend against any strict obligations.

II. A philosophical pacifist's objection

Some philosophers, however, argue that intention is relevant only to the moral quality of the agent, *not* to that of his action. One such is Robert Holmes, whose non-religious argument for pacifism is reckoned by the non-pacifist philosopher David Luban to be 'as powerful as any I know'.[7] A major plank in Holmes's critique of just war theory is his objection to

---

6. In *Aiming to Kill*, p. 78.
7. David Luban, 'Preventive War and Human Rights', in Henry Shue and David Rodin, eds, *Preemption. Military Action and Moral Justification* (Oxford: Oxford University Press, 2007), pp. 179–80.

Augustine's turning Christianity 'inward, emphasizing not so much outward action as purity of heart and motivation'.[8] As a consequence, 'nothing we *do* in terms of outward conduct can by itself constitute sin'.[9] This
Augustinian interiorization of morality finds expression in the principle
of double effect, which prohibits 'no [outward] action whatsoever'.[10]
Opposing this view, Holmes argues that intention is not integral to an
act, because we often know and identify the latter apart from the former:
an act can be at once objectively right and subjectively wrong.[11] Since
the principle of double effect 'lends itself to the justification of virtually
any action its user wants...from a practical standpoint it is vacuous'.[12]
Instead, Holmes prefers to think about acts of killing in terms of subjective rights:

> everyone has a right not to be harmed or killed by others...We have a
> strong prima facie obligation to refrain from [deliberately causing
> death]...The killing of innocents by an aggressor is no worse *as such* than
> the killing of innocents by those who would oppose him by waging war.
> Human beings have as much right to be spared destruction by good people
> as by bad...If I choose to kill innocent persons in order to prevent the
> deaths of others at the hands of an aggressor, I, no less than and perhaps even
> more than he...am using innocent persons as a means to an end...modern
> war inevitably kills innocent persons. And this...makes modern war pre-
> sumptively wrong.[13]

What Holmes says about the principle of double effect is not true in general, since some versions do hold that the deliberate killing of the innocent
involves intrinsic moral evil. However, my own preferred version does not
hold this view. As I see it, the deliberate killing of the innocent is not wrong
as such. Whether it is so depends on the motive and intention of the killer,
and on whether the killing is proportionate. Why do I see things this way?
One reason is that to suppose otherwise is to assume a pacifist position in
practice. For if the deliberate killing of the innocent is absolutely forbidden,
then the successful waging of war would very probably be impossible in
practice; and a war whose success is impossible is very probably unjust.
Of course, unless one is already a convinced proponent of just war, such a

8. Holmes, *On War and Morality*, p. 118.
9. Ibid., p. 141. The emphasis is Holmes's.
10. Ibid., p. 196.   11. Ibid., p. 198.
12. Ibid., p. 199.   13. Ibid., pp. 210–11.

reason will carry little weight. Another, more cogent one is that common moral and legal sense distinguishes different kinds of homicide. It tells accidental from negligent from deliberate kinds; it proceeds to differentiate deliberate self-defence from deliberate aggression; and, when considering mercy killing, it even tells malevolent from benevolent aggression. Holmes appears to say that *any* kind of deliberate killing of the innocent is wrong. Inadvertently, however, he equivocates and gestures in the opposite direction. He tells us that we have an obligation not to harm the innocent deliberately—and by implication that the innocent have a right not to be harmed deliberately—'*prima facie*'. What this last phrase implies is that the right and the obligation are not absolute, holding always and everywhere, but that closer inspection of the circumstances—that is, *secunda facie*—might show them to be lacking. What circumstances might correct first impressions? Holmes does not tell us. Indeed, he cannot afford to tell us, because to do so would be to surrender his pacifist position. If he were to name consequences—for example, where the failure to kill one innocent will result in the deaths of ten others—he would concede a consequentialist justification of killing. And if he were to name motive and intention, he would concede a Thomist justification.

Holmes is wrong to try and separate intention and action. Intention is what makes an action human and voluntary, distinguishing it from a mere event. A human action comprises ends and means, and is unintelligible apart from its intentional structure. Holmes concedes this, when he writes that '[a]cts are the means by which we try to realize the purposes our intentions embody'.[14] But then he adds, puzzlingly, 'acts do not themselves include the intentions'.[15] He says this because, he claims, '[w]e can often know and identify acts apart from their intentions; indeed, we often do not know what those intentions are'.[16] In support he cites proponents of the principle of double effect, who talk of withholding intention or directing it appropriately, implying that 'one and the same act' can be accompanied by different intentions.[17] Whatever some proponents of double effect say, this does not make sense. Suppose an act of firing a missile that kills a dozen civilians. The act does not remain one and the same, regardless of whether the civilian deaths were intended or whether they were accepted with appropriate reluctance. Had they been intended, the

---

14. Ibid., p. 197.   15. Ibid..
16. Ibid.   17. Ibid., p. 198.

act would be one where the civilian casualties were integral to the agent's plan, where no attempt to avoid or minimize them had been made, where their number was (depending on circumstances) greater than military necessity required, where the agent expressed and confirmed his vindictiveness, and where he thereby disposed himself to perform further acts of indiscriminate vengeance on the morrow. On the other hand, had the casualties been accepted with reluctance, the act would be one where the civilian casualties were incidental to the agent's plan, where an attempt to reduce them had been made, where (depending on circumstances) they were minimal, where the agent restrained his frustration and anger, and where he had thereby disposed himself to be capable of discriminate conduct in the future.

Such subtle, but morally important, considerations obtain even in cases where an act seems at once objectively right and subjectively wrong. Let us suppose, for the sake of argument, that it is right deliberately to kill a soldier mortally wounded on the battlefield, in agonizing pain, and for whom no other relief is available. Suppose, then, a case where a soldier comes upon an enemy in such a condition, and that this soldier is generally moved by vindictive hatred to annihilate his opponents. With such motivation and with such an intention he cuts the throat of his wounded enemy. Subjectively, his action was morally wrong. But was it objectively right? No, not simply. It is true that his act relieved the wounded man of his physical agony. However, since physical pain is in part socially constructed, it is also true that the vindictive soldier intensified his victim's agony and despair by the hateful contempt he communicated as he killed him. What is more, the vindictive soldier confirmed his own vindictiveness, so strengthening his subjective disposition to commit thoroughly objective atrocities later on. The subjective and objective aspects of moral action—its inwardness and outwardness—may be distinguishable, but they are not separable.

III. Operating the principle in the field

I have explained my understanding of the principle of double effect, and I have defended it against one philosophical pacifist's objection. Now let me bring it to bear on the doctrine of just war. Insofar as the life of any human being is a good and his death an evil,[18] it is wrong to intend (or choose to want) to kill anyone. The life of the human individual is precious because it is constituted and dignified by a unique vocation by God to affirm, defend, and promote what is valuable in the world, at very least by bearing witness to it. No one should *choose to want* or *intend* to damage or destroy such precious life, for to do so would be to vitiate the agent's heart and will, to corrupt his moral character, to jeopardize his fitness for life beyond death, and to increase the likelihood of his committing further malevolent harm in the world. Nevertheless, it may be permissible to choose to act in such a way as to cause the death of a human being, provided that what is intended is something other than his death (e.g. defending the innocent), that the possibility (or even certainty) of his death is accepted with an appropriate and manifest reluctance, and that this acceptance is necessary, non-subversive, and proportionate. Morally speaking, deliberately to cause death in this fashion is not the same as intending to kill.

Conceptually, this is all very neat and tidy. It is coherent and consistent, and coherence and consistency are necessary qualities of intelligibility. Sometimes, however, we can buy intelligibility at the expense of reality. So the question that arises here is: Can this theory of double effect really get up and walk on the battlefield? Does this kind of moral analysis do justice to the empirical reality of war, or does it do violence instead?

Some certainly doubt its viability. Among them is the eminent theological ethicist, James Gustafson.[19] After reading my defence of a version of the principle of double effect in *Aiming to Kill*, he wrote to me as follows:

> I hope that you and other refiners of the principle of double effect know that in the course of critical events there is no way to think through the distinctions that are made and argued about. I knew the double-effect literature and its applications up and through the writings of... [Paul] Ramsey and [Richard] McCormick, and only once lost my temper with them orally. It was when they and an older Jesuit insisted that soldiers are justified in killing only if they

18. Strictly speaking, I think that the life of a human being is a good, and his death an evil, except where that human being has become irrevocably incapable of responding to other goods in the world—that is, where he has been irreparably bereft of what I have called 'responsibility' (*Aiming to Kill*, pp. 42–7), but would perhaps better be called 'responsiveness'. This qualification was developed with an eye to the medical treatment of those patients the cortical part of whose brain has been permanently destroyed. Since the treatment of such cases is not the usual focus when killing in war is under consideration, I have not entered the qualification here.

19. I was privileged to have Jim Gustafson as my doctoral supervisor at the University of Chicago in the early 1980s.

intend to maim.[20] ... [A]ll my life of studying and teaching ethics, including the principle of double effect, [I] have been wary of the rationality that is assumed of agents in times of crisis.

Gustafson then proceeded to explain why he has long been sceptical of casuistry, while nevertheless recognizing the importance of something like it. His explanation came in the form of a story from his own experience in Central Burma during the Second World War, when, as a nineteen-year-old soldier on midnight guard duty in the summer of 1945, he suddenly came under attack by a drunken comrade. 'I fired my rifle into the air, and held it against Pancho's stomach. He kept swinging his knife at me, and kept saying that I was chicken and did not have the guts to shoot him.' Fortunately, an officer intervened quickly, so in the event Gustafson did not have to pull his trigger. But the point of the story is this: when you suddenly find yourself under terrifying life-threatening assault, you do not have the leisure or the presence of mind to examine your motives, sift your intentions, weigh up alternatives—and consider whether wounding rather than killing would be proportionate, and whether a shot in the stomach delivered in the middle of wartime Burma in 1945 would or would not be lethal.

Gustafson is surely right. Life often demands a response from us without granting time for reflection. Often we have to react viscerally rather than cerebrally. And if, with the advantage of hindsight, it seems that we made an understandable error in the heat of the extraordinary moment, then judgement should not stint on forgiveness. Nevertheless, it is also true that instincts can be trained to become more virtuous and educated to become wiser, so that in reacting we do not overreact. Surely that is exactly what many modern armies are doing when they train their soldiers to conduct themselves in counter-insurgency operations in such a way as to be discriminate and proportionate in the use of violent force. One cannot reasonably expect squaddies to plough their way through the mind-bending literature on the principle of double effect, but one can expect those who instruct their officers to do so—or at least those who instruct their instructors. Out of

20. So, for example, in his commentary, 'Robert W. Tucker's *Bellum Contra Bellum Justum*', Paul Ramsey writes:

The objective of combat is the incapacitation of a combatant from doing what he is doing because he is this particular combatant in this particular war; it is *not* the killing of a man because he is a man or because he is this particular man. The latter and only the latter would be 'murder'. This is the indestructible difference between murder and killing in war; and the difference is to be found in the intention and direction of the action that kills. (*The Just War: Force and Political Responsibility* [Savage, Maryland: Littlefield Adams, 1969, 1983], p. 397)

dialogue between instructors and officers one can expect rules of conduct to emerge that are practicable in the field. And one can expect those rules to be—literally—incorporated into military training, especially into the training of junior officers, and so into military leadership in the field. Indeed, these things not only can be expected; they already happen.[21]

IV. Can soldiers *really* not intend to kill?

James Gustafson's response raises a more difficult question against my read-ing of the principle of double effect, however. As he wrote above, the expression of the principle that once provoked him to an angry outburst was the claim that soldiers should intend never to kill but only to maim. My reading leads me to make an even more irritating claim: that soldiers should not intend either to wound or to kill, but only to accept maiming or killing with due reluctance as the necessary, non-subversive, and propor-tionate side effects of intending something good—say, the protection of the innocent. I have no difficulty understanding why such a view tests the patience of those who have first-hand experience of war-fighting, or even those inexperts who have given more than a passing thought to what is actually involved in it. I can quite see how morally fastidious—how dis-tastefully precious—my view might look. If soldiers in battle may not intend to wound or kill their armed enemies, how on earth may they pull their triggers at all? How can they be *soldiers*?

Part of what is at issue here is the meaning of 'intention'. To say that sol-diers should not intend to wound or kill might be taken to mean that they are being required to adopt a rationale for pulling their triggers that makes wounding or killing accidental; and that is surely sophistical, for wounding or killing is surely integral, not accidental, to what they are choosing to do. According to my broader understanding, however, to say that soldiers should not intend wounding or killing does not mean that they should not choose to cause such things; nor does it mean that they are not responsible for so choosing. In the limited sense of choosing to embark on a course of action with certain foreseeable effects, of course it is true that soldiers must intend to wound and kill, if they wish to conduct themselves as soldiers in battle. However, as I explained above in the light of the *Master and Commander* case

21. See Patrick Bury's remarks in Chapter Two, pp. 89–90.

of the sailor who obeyed the order to cut the ropes tying his precarious ship to the wrecked mast, knowing with a practical certainty that this would cause his friend to drown, to intend something is not just to *choose* it, but also to *want* it. So in saying that soldiers ought not to intend wounding or killing, I am saying that they ought to choose and *accept* such things with reluctance, rather than choose and *want* them.

Is *that* realistic? I think so. I would not dare to deny that war loosens the reins on lethal malevolence, nor that in any given war there is likely to be malevolence on the battlefield. I would not deny that soldiers sometimes regard their enemy as vermin to be exterminated at every possible opportunity. Nor would I deny that, when soldiers are killed—or worse, tortured and mutilated—by the enemy, their comrades will probably be animated by fierce anger against them. (Whether and how far this is malevolent is not immediately clear, however, since atrocity actually warrants and deserves fierce resentment. Love for what has been atrociously harmed demands no less.) What I do deny is that soldiers necessarily or as a rule *want* their enemy maimed or dead. There is considerable evidence that many soldiers are reluctant to harm. Brigadier S.L.A. Marshall's argument that only 15 to 25 per cent of US riflemen in certain combat theatres during the Second World War actually shot at the enemy[22] might be methodologically flawed, but his general conclusion about a widespread reluctance to kill finds corroboration elsewhere. A British analysis of killing rates in more than one hundred battles in the 19th and 20th centuries has shown that the killing potential of the weapons in the hands of soldiers with the opportunity to kill far exceeded the actual number of casualties inflicted.[23] Besides, as Tony Coady points out, 'the widespread acceptance of Marshall's claims for so long in the military and elsewhere suggests that there is something in the "reluctance to kill" thesis'.[24] There is indeed. We have it on record that some soldiers do actually make a deliberate decision to wound the enemy, rather than kill him. Take Harry Patch, advancing with his unit against the Germans in the Third Battle of Ypres in 1917: 'Patch's Lewis gun team was struggling towards an enemy second-line trench when three German soldiers climbed out of it, one advancing on them with bayonet fixed. Guessing correctly that the man had used all his ammunition, Patch drew the Colt

---

22. As reported by Grossman in *On Killing*, p. 3; quoted by Coady in *Morality and Political Violence*, p. 50.
23. Grossman, *On Killing*, p. 16; quoted by Coady in *Morality and Political Violence*, p. 50.
24. Coady, *Morality and Political Violence*, p. 50.

revolver the Number 2 carried and shot the man in the shoulder [and] then, as he still came on, in the leg. As a good shot with the Colt, he could easily have killed him, but he chose to spare his life.'[25]

While reluctance sometimes prevents killing, at other times it qualifies it. The twenty-one-year-old First World War flying ace, Albert Ball, was quite resolved to shoot his enemies out of the sky, but not because he took any pleasure in their deaths. As a fellow pilot wrote of him: 'He had but one idea: that was to kill as many Huns as possible, and he gave effect to it with a swiftness and certainty that seemed to most of us uncanny.' Nevertheless, 'almost from the beginning the mild bragging in [his] letters home is matched by disgust at what duty led him into..."I do so want to leave all this beastly killing for a time," he sighed...'[26] In 1939 the British went to war with markedly less enthusiasm than in 1914, responding to it with 'a grim determination to shoulder the unwelcome task that history had thrust upon them';[27] and this reluctance *ad bellum* often survived *in bello*. As one RAF fighter pilot wrote in the midst of the Battle of Britain in the summer of 1940, 'We carry on here you know, hating it rather, but continuing to shoot down our quota of [Messerschmidt] 109s...I can't write. The war comes between me and my words, and I can't find them.'[28]

All this is true. But it is also true that when soldiers are themselves under fire, (unlike Harry Patch) they cannot be expected to be too particular about exactly where they aim to hit the enemy. Their overriding concern will be to make sure that he falls down and does not get up again, and one way to ensure that is to shoot him in the head. Such a wound will very probably be lethal. Does it follow that, in fact, soldiers in combat must intend to kill? No, it does not. When a soldier intends to kill, in the sense of having as his primary aim the death of his enemy, then, having shot and felled him, should he draw near in the aftermath of battle and find him still breathing, he would shoot him again until his breathing stopped. If he does not shoot his incapacitated and non-threatening enemy, then that implies that it was not his death—as such—that he wanted. Take the case narrated by Patrick Bury in his account of soldiering as a junior officer in Afghanistan in 2008. His platoon is in combat with the Taliban. A small Afghan boy is

25. 'Harry Patch', obituary, *The Times*, 27 July 2009.
26. Bishop, *Fighter Boys*, pp. 14–15.
27. Kenneth Pinnock, 'November Thoughts', *The Oriel Record 2002* (Oxford: Oriel College, 2002), p. 38.
28. Ibid.

spotted repeatedly popping his head over the lip of a roof in the enemy's vicinity to watch the soldiers. The British strongly suspect that he is scouting for the enemy. Bury fires at the lip of the roof directly in front of the boy, to warn him away. He then says to the man next to him, 'If he does that again, kill him.'[29] Did Bury intend that that the boy should be killed? I think not. I doubt very much that, had he come across the boy's still breathing body after the fight was over, he would have shot him dead. If the boy's death had really been his aim, that is what he would have done. So his conditional order to kill was actually efficient shorthand for something more complicated: namely, 'Shoot him, so as to be sure that he does not raise his head over that wall again. Since only his head is visible, that is where you should shoot him. It is very probable that you will kill him. Do it anyway.' Strictly speaking, what Bury wanted or intended was absolutely assured incapacitation. Under the circumstances, that would very probably amount to death. Nevertheless, the boy's death would have been accepted rather than strictly intended. Had the boy actually been killed, I have no doubt that Bury would have regretted it—after the battle. Regret, however, is retrospective reluctance, sorrow for tragic necessity. It is not the same as guilt.

Notwithstanding a certain *prima facie* implausibility, therefore, I still think that it makes sense to say that military personnel ought not to intend to kill their enemy—insofar as 'intend' means 'choose and want as a goal' rather than 'choose and accept with reluctance'. Nevertheless, there is an alternative moral analysis of killing that avoids testing the patience of realists and straining credibility; and I need to explain why I have not adopted it, in spite of that advantage. The analysis that I have in mind is one offered by Thomas Aquinas.

V. Reckoning with Aquinas

Aquinas's ethic of killing is complex to the point of inconsistency. He holds it wrong to intend to kill not just any human being, but specifically the innocent, since these are not a threat to a community (being 'innocent' or non-harming) and, indeed, are a support to it ('the life of righteous men preserves and forwards the common good').[30] It is also wrong

---

29. Bury, *Callsign Hades*, p. 263–4.
30. Aquinas, *Summa Theologiae*, 2a 2ae, q. 64, a.6.

for a private citizen to intend to kill an unjust aggressor in self-defence. He may nevertheless kill him, however, provided that the aggressor's death is 'beside the intention', that the natural end or good of self-preservation is what is intended, and that the violence employed is proportioned to the latter.[31]

In Aquinas's view, however, not all intentional killing of human beings is wrong. When he argues that members of a community who are 'dangerous or infectious' to others may be killed by those with public authority 'in order to safeguard the common good',[32] he makes no distinction between killing that is intended and that which is unintended.[33] This is because it is not 'an evil in itself' to kill sinners, since in sinning a man 'falls away from the dignity of his manhood... and falls into the slavish state of the beasts'; and to kill a sinner is therefore no more evil than to kill a beast.[34]

There are two problems with this analysis. First, the dangers of justifying killing on the ground that one's victim is a mere beast are obvious to those of us who live in the aftermath of the 20th century's several genocides, and who recall that the machete-wielding Hutu used to refer to their Tutsi prey in Rwanda as 'cockroaches'. To view the enemy as subhuman loosens all restraint and invites atrocity. And if that consequential consideration does not tip the scales, then one might add the weight of Christian theological anthropology and its endowment of all other human beings with the status of fellow creatures and fellow sinners. For sure, we ought not to be sentimental here. There are human beings who have so persisted in choosing and wanting gross evil that they seem to be one with it; and in such cases we might well wonder what *exactly* would be lost to the world by their summary annihilation. I think here of Hitler or Stalin or Pol Pot, or of any battlefield sadist who wantonly perpetrates grotesque cruelty. It might well be that some humans are so identified with evil as to be inextricable from it, with the consequence that to intend to kill them is to intend harm to nothing valuable at all, but rather something simply bad. I am quite prepared to believe this. Nevertheless, the history of a person's spiritual and moral corruption is largely opaque to human view; and his

31. Ibid., a.7.
32. Ibid., a.2; a.3, r. obj. 2, 3.
33. Ibid., a.7: 'But as it is unlawful to take a man's life, except for the public authority acting for the common good... it is not lawful for a man to intend killing a man in self-defence, except for such as have public authority, who while intending to kill a man in self-defence, refer this to the public good, as in the case of a soldier fighting against the foe...' (ibid., a.7).
34. Ibid., a.2, r. obj. 3.

fellows would be wise to refrain from claiming the competence to judge it irreversible.

To his credit, Aquinas himself was not at all consistent in arguing (as he does in the *Summa Theologiae*, 2a 2ae, question 64, article 2, reply to objection 3) that one may intend to kill sinners on the grounds that they have forfeited human dignity, and that there is therefore no evil in their deaths. In the very next article, where he addresses the question 'Whether it is lawful for a private individual to kill a man who has sinned?' he rows back in asserting that public authorization is needed, because sinners are not 'by nature' distinct from good men and so equivalent to beasts;[35] and three articles further on he confirms this by saying that 'in every man, though he be sinful, we ought to love the nature which God has made, and which is destroyed by slaying him'.[36]

The second problem with Aquinas's analysis is a certain equivocation over the meaning of 'intention'. In the case of the private individual we are told that he may kill a wrongful assailant only if he intends self-preservation and not the other's death, and if his violence is proportioned to the former. How does Aquinas explain this? First, he implies that the assailant's life deserves a certain care and therefore has a certain value (that is to say, is a good), when he says that 'one is bound to take more care of one's own life than of another's'.[37] This is confirmed by his statement that 'it is unlawful to kill any man, since in every man though he be sinful, we ought to love the nature which God has made, and which is destroyed by slaying him'.[38] Second, the private individual has not been entrusted with care for the common good and therefore lacks the public authority 'to decide what is to be taken from the parts for the welfare of the whole'.[39] Third, since public authorities are wrong to kill 'if they be moved by private animosity',[40] then presumably so are private citizens. What Aquinas's rationale implies is that even the life of a wrongful aggressor is a good that deserves care and not hostility. If one may nevertheless take such a life, as he allows, then in what sense may one not *intend* to do so? Clearly one may choose to perform an act that in fact causes death. If we go further and assume what Aquinas does not make clear here—that the possible effect of death is foreseen—then we may take him to say that one may intend death in the narrow, simply

---

35. Ibid., a.3, r. obj. 2.   36. Ibid., a.6.
37. Ibid., a.7.   38. Ibid., a.6.
39. Ibid., a.3 and r. obj. 3.   40. Ibid., a.7.

voluntary sense of 'choose to perform an act that is foreseen to involve the possibility, more or less probable, of death'. In what alternative sense, then, is he saying that one may *not* intend death? In the sense that one may not be moved by animosity against the good of another's life so as to *want* his death. Thus far Aquinas's rationale is entirely in line with my own.

Thereafter, however, it begins to diverge. Aquinas proceeds to tell us that one who has public authorization—for example, a soldier or someone commissioned to enforce judicial decisions[41]—may intend to kill in self-defence. What explanation does he offer? He gives (or implies) three alternatives. One is that the wrongful assailant, being a sinner,[42] has forfeited his human dignity and no longer has a life whose loss would be an evil; in which case to choose *and want* to take it—to intend to take it, in my broader sense—would involve no failure of due care. As I have pointed out above, Aquinas is ambivalent about this dangerous rationale—to his credit.

The second explanation is that public officers 'refer this [their self-defence] to the public good' and are not motivated by private animosity (or by any other kind of animosity).[43] That is to say, what moves them is public spiritedness, not a desire to hurt; and what they intend is to serve the common good, not to maim or kill the wrongdoer. According to this analysis, however, the public officer does not intend (in the broader sense) the wrongdoer's death, but only accepts it.

The third explanation is a modification of the second: that public officers intend (that is, choose and want) to serve the common good, that they are motivated not by private but by *public* animosity against the wrongdoer, and that therefore they also intend (that is, choose and want) to kill him instrumentally. This reading does enjoy the advantage of recognizing that resentment is an entirely appropriate response to a seriously wrongful injury (provided that it is proportionate), as I explained in the previous chapter; and that soldiers who believe that they are defending their country against injustice will probably and rightly view the enemy with some such resentment. It might also be supposed to enjoy the advantage of having moral analysis recognize the allegedly necessary fact of hatred on the battlefield:

41. I take it that this is what Aquinas means by 'the minister of the judge' (ibid.).
42. I am applying what Aquinas says about the killing of sinners in the *Summa Theologiae*, 2a 2ae, q. 64, article 2 to what he says about self-defence in article 6. In so doing, I am assuming that this self-defence is against a wrongful aggressor (as is implied by Aquinas's reference to 'robbers'), and that a wrongful aggressor is a species of sinner. If Aquinas means by 'sinner' something more specific, then my interpretation would need to be revised.
43. Ibid., q. 64, a. 7.

the soldier may hate the wrongdoer, although not because of some wrongful injury to himself, but only because of his offence against the common good. I do not think, however, that resenting the enemy's invasion is quite the same as hating his troops—RAF pilots were quite capable of bitterly resenting German attempts to bomb their homeland without turning their machine guns onto Luftwaffe pilots who had baled out of their burning aircraft.[44] Besides, I have already cast doubt on whether hatred *is* a necessary battlefield fact that must be taken into account by any realistic moral analysis.[45] That is one, empirical problem with this interpretation. Another is exegetical: Aquinas makes no mention whatsoever of any kind of animosity other than the private one.

We are left, then, with the first two rationales. The second one is tantamount to the analysis that I espouse: the soldier does not intend (in the broader sense of 'choose and want') his unjust enemy's death, but merely accepts it as the necessary and proportionate side effect of intending service of the common good. The first rationale is Aquinas's alternative to my preferred analysis: the soldier *does* intend (choose and want) the death of his unjust enemy, because in doing wrong the latter has forfeited his human dignity and no longer has a life whose loss would constitute an evil. I have explained why I think this view both dangerous and contrary to Christian anthropology; and I have noted that Aquinas himself contradicted it on anthropological grounds.

VI. Conclusion

I continue to hold, therefore, that military personnel ought not to intend to wound or kill their enemy—insofar as 'intend' means 'choose and want as a goal' rather than 'choose and accept with reluctance'. This view is, I think, more Christian and better calculated to restrain violence. And although it may seem empirically implausible at first glance, further reflection shows it sufficiently realistic about military psychology as to be able to get up and walk on the battlefield.

---

44. See Patrick Bishop, *Fighter Boys*, p. 335: 'Most pilots told themselves and the outside world that, when they shot at a German aeroplane, they were aiming at the machine not the man. George Bennions "was relieved when they baled out".'
45. See Chapter Two, pp. 78–90.

4
Proportionality
Lessons from the Somme and the
First World War[*]

I. Is it worth it? The principle of proportionality

> We attacked, I think, about 820 strong. I've no official figures of casualties. A
> friend, an officer in 'C' Company, which was in support and shelled to pieces
> before it could start, told me in hospital that we lost 450 men that day, and
> that, after being put in again a day or two later, we had 54 left. I suppose it's
> worth it.[1]

Thus wrote R.H. Tawney—then a sergeant, later the famous Anglican
socialist—of the action on the Somme on 1 July 1916 in which he himself
was shot in the stomach and lay wounded in no man's land for thirty hours.
The Battle of the Somme has since become a byword for criminally disproportionate military slaughter. In their assault on the German trenches, the
British (which at that time and in that place included the southern Irish and
the Newfoundlanders) suffered 57,470 casualties *on the first day*, of which
19,240 were fatalities. The battle, which began in July, carried on for over
four months into November. At its end, British losses amounted to 419,654
killed, wounded, missing, and taken prisoner. The French lost an additional

[*] I owe Professor Hew Strachan a particular debt of thanks for commenting in some detail on an
early draft of this chapter. The final product, of course, is my responsibility alone.
[1]. R.H. Tawney, 'The Attack', in *The Attack and Other Papers*, p. 20. 'The Attack' was originally
published in *The Westminster Gazette* in August 1916.

202,567.[2] And the gain for this appalling cost? An advance of about six miles.[3]

One requirement of just war doctrine is, loosely speaking, that the use of violent force be 'proportionate'. However, since the doctrine is in the business of judging the moral quality of military decisions made by human creatures of naturally limited vision in the fog of war, we actually need to speak less loosely and more exactly. What is required is only that the use of violent force *appear* proportionate according to a judgement that was reasonable at the time—not that it actually *was* proportionate in Olympian hindsight.[4] So, for example, after losing 6,500 officers and men out of the 20,000 who were deployed in a vain attempt to overwhelm the Turkish trenches at Krithia on the Gallipoli peninsula in June 1915, the British and French commanders should be forgiven for judging it profligate, and so disproportionate, to renew the attack on the following day. The fact that, after the war, their German and Turkish counterparts revealed that a further attack would probably have succeeded in breaking through[5]—and the possibility that this might have led to Allied victory in the field, Turkey being

2. Consensus about the numbers of British and French casualties in the Battle of the Somme settles around those given by Captain Wilfrid Miles in his contribution to the British official history of the war, which are the ones cited here (Philpott, *Bloody Victory*, p. 600). Estimates of the German figures, however, range from 400,000 to 680,000 killed, wounded, missing, and prisoners and are the subject of vigorous dispute, since what is at stake is the identity of the victor in the battle of attrition (Philpott, *Bloody Victory*, pp. 600–1; Gary Sheffield, *The Somme* [London: Cassell, 2003], pp. 68, 151).

3. Martin Gilbert reckons that during the whole of the battle 'the deepest Anglo-French penetration of the German lines was less than six miles' (*Somme: The Heroism and Horror of War* [London: John Murray, 2006]), p. 243.

4. David Rodin asserts that it is insufficient 'to honestly believe' that an action is necessary and proportionate, and that such a belief also has to be 'objectively reasonable' (*War and Self-Defense* [Oxford: Clarendon Press, 2002], p. 42). This stipulation is attended by ambiguity, however. It might mean one of three things: either that an action must be objectively proportionate, in order to be morally right; or that it must seem proportionate according to a reasonable apprehension of the available data, in order to be non-culpable, should it turn out to be objectively wrong; or that it must be objectively proportionate, in order to be non-culpable. I endorse the first two options, but not the third.

5. Hans Kannengiesser, *The Campaign in Gallipoli*, intro. Liman von Sanders, trans. C.J.P. Ball (London: Hutchinson, 1927), p. 178: 'I felt that a similar energetic attack of the English could have the worst results'; Mehmed Nehad Bey, 'Les Opérations de Sedd ul Bahr Campagne des Dardanelles, 25 avril au 13 juillet 1915', trans. by M. Larcher from a lecture given in Turkish in 1919, *Revue d'histoire de la guerre mondiale*, vol. 3 (Paris: A. Costes, 1925), p. 248: 'Le groupe sud avait dépensé ses dernières réserves; il eût été probablement détruit, si l'ennemi avait continuer à attaquer le...5 juin avec le même violence' ['The southern group had exhausted its last reserves; it would probably have been destroyed, if the enemy had continued to attack on 5 June with the same violence'].

knocked out of the war, Russia being supported and stabilized, the Bolshevik revolution prevented, communism nipped in the bud, and the 'anti-Bolshevism' that engendered Nazism aborted[6]—does not render that judgement any less reasonable and morally right.

So, according to the doctrine of just war, a political decision to embark on a war and to keep on prosecuting it, and a military decision to launch and continue an operation, are both required to appear proportionate, according to what one may reasonably expect the decision-makers to have known at the time. Whether *ad bellum* or *in bello*, *ius* requires proportionality. But why is it important, and what does it mean in practice? The purpose of the criterion is to have the use of violence governed by the rightly intended moral ends, partly to limit the damage caused, and partly to provide a way of measuring the sincerity of intention. If the violence used is *not* proportionate to one's purported end, then there is *prima facie* reason to doubt what is purported.[7] Accordingly, one is only justified in embarking upon a war or continuing to fight it if the terrible evils that it entails are 'worth it'—that is, if, according to a reasonable estimate, they seem to be made worthwhile (in some sense) by the just peace intended. And one is only justified in launching a military operation or persisting in it if the losses to one's own side (and to non-combatants) seem, according to a reasonable estimate, necessary to gain and efficient in gaining the military advantages aimed at. The criterion of proportionality, therefore, rules against the resort to violence that is less governed by the constructive intention of just peace than driven by the annihilating motives of revenge or hatred. And it also rules against military operations that appear to be imprudently expensive of human lives. Its purpose is to keep declared intention honest and to subject the use of violence to the service of moral ends, thereby reining in its destructiveness.

As for what the criterion of proportionality means in practice, there are two interpretations. First, an evil can be said to be disproportionate if it is such as to subvert or destroy the very good that one hopes to gain by it. One clear example of this would be a case where a nation's use of nuclear weapons in self-defence would probably provoke a counter-strike that would not only devastate its own territory but would render it uninhabitable for

---

6. As speculates Philip Orr in *Field of Bones: An Irish Division at Gallipoli* (Dublin: Lilliput Press, 2006), p. 235.
7. The reasonable doubt, however, is only *prima facie*, since further examination might reveal that the disproportion was due to culpable negligence rather than culpable intention.

generations. Another example would be where counter-insurgency tactics so alienate the civilian population as to generate fresh recruits for the insurgency. Second, an evil may be said to be disproportionate where it is unnecessary. Clear examples of this would be a case where a state goes to war to achieve an end that diplomacy could have secured, or where a field commander takes risks with the lives of civilians that his military purposes do not require, or where soldiers kill enemy combatants after they have ceased to pose any threat.

II. Permissive proportionality

The criterion of proportionality, therefore, does rule against the use of certain kinds of violence in certain circumstances; and insofar as it is applied, it might serve to save many human lives. Nevertheless, it still permits killing on a very grand scale indeed. Let us return to the Somme. The expense of 622,221 Allied casualties seems a grossly disproportionate price to pay for an advance of six miles or so. That, however, was not the only gain. The attack on the Somme had been launched in part to relieve the severe pressure to which the French were being subjected at Verdun, by forcing the enemy to redeploy troops northwards. This it succeeded in doing. It had also been undertaken by the initially reluctant British at the urgent insistence of the French, thus serving to confirm the alliance upon which successful resistance to the German invasion depended. Its main and original military aim, however, was to contribute to a concerted effort on both the Western and Eastern fronts to exhaust Germany's reserves.[8] This it also achieved. If the Somme cost the Allies dearly, it also drained the Germans who, though defending, probably suffered more than 500,000 but less than 600,000 casualties.[9] One German officer described the Somme as 'the muddy grave of

---

8. Hew Strachan, 'The Battle of the Somme and British Strategy', *Journal of Strategic Studies*, 21/1 (1998), p. 91: 'The Allies' conference at Chantilly in December 1915 set as the target for their strategy of 1916 the exhaustion of Germany's reserves by the mounting of simultaneous attacks on all fronts.'

9. J.P. Harris tells us that '[t]he best German sources' estimate their casualties at 500,000 (*Douglas Haig and the First World War* [Cambridge: Cambridge University Press, 2008], p. 271). Gary Sheffield notes that this figure does not include the losses incurred in the seven-day preliminary bombardment, and he quotes Richard Holmes as saying that 'it is hard to place them lower than 600,000' (*The Somme*, p. 151). Hew Strachan, however, has observed that the figure of 600,000 'is a fiction as it puts the lightly wounded back in' (personal communication). See note 2 above.

the German Army', and Crown Prince Rupprecht of Bavaria observed that '[w]hat remained of the old first-class peace-trained German infantry had been expended on the battlefield'.[10] It was the first time on the Western Front that the Allies had seized the initiative, and the experience of the Somme left the Germans considerably more shaken than the British.[11] At the end of 1916, according to his memoirs, General Erich Ludendorff, who was in effect deputy of the Chief of the General Staff, warned the German High Command to:

> bear in mind that the enemy's great superiority in men and material would be even more painfully felt in 1917 than in 1916. They had to face the danger that 'Somme fighting' would soon break out at various points on our fronts, and that even our troops would not be able to withstand such attacks indefinitely, especially if the enemy gave us no time for rest and for the accumulation of material. Our position was uncommonly difficult, and a way out hard to find. We could not contemplate an offensive ourselves, having to keep our reserves available for defence... If the war lasted our defeat seemed inevitable.[12]

The following February the Germans abandoned their positions on the Somme and retreated up to twenty miles backwards to the Siegfried Stellung or 'Hindenburg Line'.

Richard Tawney can be forgiven for wondering whether the 93 per cent casualties sustained by his battalion, and the sudden, violent destruction of so many friends and colleagues were 'worth it'. On the first day of the Battle of the Somme, the British army achieved very, very few of its tactical objectives at a very, very high cost. Nevertheless, over the next four months it won valuable strategic gains. Many contemporary historians would agree with the judgement of Charles E.W. Bean, the famous Australian war correspondent and historian, that:

> [i]t is true that the Somme offensive relieved Verdun; prevented the transfer of more than a few divisions to the Eastern Front...; and strained—more by its dreadful bombardment than by infantry action—the morale of German divisions. It is beyond doubt that in this battle a considerable part of the German forces reached and passed their zenith of endurance; a decline of morale was evident to all its opponents in the last stage of the offensive, and is admitted by German historians. On the other hand the new British army... acquired

---

10. Sheffield, *Somme*, pp. 155–6.
11. Harris, *Haig*, pp. 270–1.
12. E. Ludendorff, *My War Memories, 1914–1918*, 2 vols. (London: Hutchinson, n.d.), vol. 1, p. 307.

confidence and experience. To this extent the battle marked a definite step towards the winning of the war.[13]

III. Disproportion as profligacy

Nevertheless, there remains the question of whether the Somme's gains were 'outweighed' by its dreadful losses. As Bean continues:

> But the cost was dangerously high...The question must arise whether so disproportionate an expenditure of manpower was necessary, and whether the same ends could not have been better attained by different means.[14]

This has long been controversial and it still is. A common perception is that the British Commander-in-Chief, General Sir Douglas Haig, was callously profligate with the lives of his own troops. Certainly, this is the view of some contemporary moral and political philosophers who have commented on the subject. A.J. Coates, for example, writes that '[i]n the end it is the suspicion not so much of military incompetence...as of callous indifference that lies behind the moral criticism of Haig's leadership: the suspicion that he was able to take the decisions he did only because he had lost sight of their human cost'.[15] And although he does not refer to anyone in particular, Tony Coady gives no reason to suppose that he would exempt Haig from his general indictment of military leadership in the First World War:

> Part of the widespread moral revulsion from the dreadful conflict of World War I is produced by the perception that there was a callous disregard by the general staff of both armies for the well-being of their own troops. I lack the expertise to be confident about the validity of this perception, though I suspect that it is accurate. Certainly, the generals seldom got close enough to the

---

13. C.E.W. Bean, *The Official History of Australia in the War of 1914–18*, vol. III: 'The A.I.F. [Australian Imperial Force] in France, 1916' (Sydney: Angus and Robertson, 1929), pp. 946–7. William Philpott is one contemporary expert who largely corroborates Bean's claims. While the Battle of the Somme did not exactly prevent Germany's transfer of divisions to the Eastern front, it reduced those resources that it did transfer (*Bloody Victory*, p. 336). Of the eleven German divisions that went from the West to the East during the second half of 1916, nine had been 'eviscerated' on the Somme or at Verdun (*Bloody Victory*, p. 447). More generally, '[t]he Battle of the Somme had relieved the pressure on Verdun, restored the initiative of the allies, worn down the enemy's manpower and morale and, as part of the General Allied Offensive, stretched German resources dangerously thin' (*Bloody Victory*, p. 384).

14. Bean, *Official History*, pp. 946–7.

15. Coates, *The Ethics of War*, pp. 219 and 230 n.14.

conflict to gain any sense of what their policies were inflicting upon the men, and they displayed an attitude toward the wastage of human life that suggested they viewed the troops as mere cannon fodder. It has been claimed...that the frightful stalemate of trench warfare...was forced upon them by circumstance and that no other tactics were available to fight the war. I doubt that this is so...Had the general staff viewed the wastage of life as the moral enormity it has subsequently come to seem, they would have exercised more imagination in trying to find other ways of fighting...On the other hand, if no other methods were available or devisable, this surely constituted a reason to make urgent efforts to negotiate a settlement.[16]

My first response to these charges is to distinguish callousness from indifference or carelessness. There is a sense in which any military commander who is going to do his job has to be able to callous himself—to thicken his skin. He has to be emotionally capable of ordering his troops to risk their lives, and in some cases he must be capable of ordering them to their probable or certain deaths. Moreover, the doctrine of just war requires the prospect of success; and history suggests that successful military commanders are those who are calloused enough to be ruthless in what they demand of their own troops. Take this example from the battle of El Alamein in October 1942, which was the first (and last) major land success that British imperial troops, alone, achieved against German forces in the Second World War. In the middle of the battle, the New Zealander Major General Freyberg held a briefing conference at which he communicated General Bernard Montgomery's orders to Brigadier John Currie, commander of the 9th Armoured Brigade:

[T]he task for 9th Armoured Brigade—to advance past the infantry objective, break through the enemy defences and immediately beyond the Rahman Track and then hold open the gap against enemy counter-attacks until the heavy brigades of the 1st Armoured Division had gone through—was so obviously one of difficulty and danger that when Currie's time came to make comment,

16. Coady, *Morality and Political Violence*, pp. 184–5 and 185 n.8. By 'both armies' I take Coady to mean the British and the German, neglecting the French. Shortly before this passage he explicitly connects the Battle of the Somme with his indictment of military leadership: 'Images of the Somme...fuelled antiwar sentiment as very little before had done; and much of the revulsion and moral outrage sprang from the futility of the trench warfare and the sense that the generals on both sides had too little concern for the human lives committed to their responsibility...Many believed at the time that this war was unjustified, and with the benefit of hindsight, many more believe it now...[M]uch of the rejection of World War I as unjust stems from the wholly intelligible belief that the costs were so disproportionate' (ibid., p. 181).

he rather diffidently suggested that by the end of the day his brigade might well
have suffered 50 per cent casualties. To this Freyberg had replied with studied
nonchalance, "Perhaps more than that. The Army Commander [Montgomery]
says that he is prepared to accept a hundred per cent."[17]

Was Montgomery callous? In a certain, militarily necessary sense, yes, he
was. Was he careless of the lives of his troops? Not at all. On the contrary,
Montgomery was a highly popular commander because, while he was willing to spend his soldiers' lives, he was careful not to waste them;[18] and he
was also careful to make sure that his men understood what was being asked
of them and why.[19]

To be just, a war must have the prospect of success. To be successful, a
military commander must be sufficiently callous to spend the lives of his
troops. Such callousness can accompany carefulness. But can it also accompany compassion, as Anthony Coates would require?[20] In one, colloquial
sense, the answer has to be negative; for 'compassion' connotes a certain
emotional identification, an entering into the suffering of others, which is
exactly what a commander must callous himself against, if he is to order his
troops to risk or spend their lives. In the midst of battle, he cannot afford
compassion of this sort, if he is to make a success of his job. This callousness,
however, is perfectly compatible with having such sympathy for the plight
of front-line troops before battle, or for the plight of the wounded afterwards, as to make sure that they have what they need. In sum, then: carefulness before battle, callousness in it, and compassion after it.[21]

Let us return to the Somme. Was Haig callous? Did he treat his own
soldiers 'as the merest cannon fodder'?[22] Haig was characteristically taci-

17. Barrie Pitt, The Crucible of War, 2 vols., Vol. 1: 'Year of Alamein 1942' (London: Jonathan Cape,
    1982), pp. 396–7.
18. Ibid., pp. 190, 192: 'Montgomery's view was the staff were the servants of the troops, and that
    it was the staff's job to see that whatever objective was given to fighting troops, it was within
    their capability and that they were provided with everything necessary to achieve it'.
19. At El Alamein Montgomery instructed his officers to explain to every one of their men, on
    the eve of battle, the overall plan and the part he was to play in it (ibid., pp. 282–3).
20. Coates, The Ethics of War, pp. 221, 227.
21. As it happens, A.J. Coates means by 'compassion' largely what I mean by 'carefulness': 'the
    principle of proportionality applies in the first place to the economical and compassionate
    deployment of one's own troops . . . It demands economy in the use of force: that commanders
    should not waste the lives of their own soldiers in the pursuit of unattainable or relatively
    unimportant military objectives . . . Compassion is a military as well as a civilian virtue' (ibid.,
    pp. 221, 227). My reservation is not over what Coates means by 'compassion', but over what
    the word generally connotes.
22. Coady, Morality and Political Violence, p. 95.

turn and outwardly impassive, as Edwardian gentlemen were wont to be. He also displayed exactly the kind of professional callousness that I have just defended. Winston Churchill, who knew him 'slightly',[23] wrote that '[h]e presents to me in those red years the same mental picture as a great surgeon before the days of anaesthetics:... intent upon the operation, entirely removed in his professional capacity from the agony of the patient... He would operate without excitement... and if the patient died, he would not reproach himself.' But then Churchill adds: 'It must be understood that I speak only of his professional actions. Once out of the theatre, his heart was as warm as any man's.'[24] Haig was a very professional soldier, but he was not insensible of the plight of his men. Contrary to popular myth (and to Tony Coady), he did get close enough to the front line to witness the effects of his decisions upon the men required to carry them out. He visited the trenches, was appalled by what he saw, and took steps to improve his troops' lot by ordering the construction of 'a vast infrastructure of canteens, baths, and the like'.[25] In the early days of the Battle of the Somme he paid visits to the wounded in field hospitals,[26] which made him so 'physically sick' that his staff officers had to persuade him to stop.[27] In 1918 he was badly upset at the death of Captain George Black, muttering repeatedly, 'Poor lad, poor lad' upon hearing the news.[28] After the war, he devoted the better part of his time to working for the cause of war veterans through the British Legion.[29] Douglas Haig did not view his men as mere cannon fodder.

23. Winston Churchill, *Great Contemporaries* (London: Thornton Butterworth, 1937), p. 226.
24. Ibid., p. 227.
25. Niall Barr and Gary Sheffield, 'Douglas Haig, the Common Soldier, and the British Legion', in Brian Bond and Nigel Cave, *Haig: A Reappraisal Seventy Years On* (London: Leo Cooper, 1999), p. 226.
26. Douglas Haig, *War Diaries and Letters, 1914–1918*, ed. Gary Sheffield and John Bourne (London: Weidenfeld & Nicolson, 2005), pp. 197 (1 July) and 199 (4 July).
27. Robin Neillands, *The Great War Generals on the Western Front, 1914–18* (London: Robinson, 1999), p. 170; Gordon Corrigan, *Mud, Blood, and Poppycock: Britain and the First World War* (London: Cassell, 2003), p. 205. The report that his hospital visits made Haig 'physically sick' Neillands attributes to Haig's own son, whose witness is, arguably, not disinterested; and Corrigan's report of Haig's staff officers persuading him to cease visiting I have not been able to corroborate. Nevertheless, what they claim is consistent with my reading of Haig's diaries (as edited by Gary Sheffield and John Bourne), where I found mention of visits to field hospitals and a main dressing station in the entries for 1 and 4 July 1916, but none thereafter.
28. Gary Sheffield, *The Chief: Douglas Haig and the British Army* (London: Aurum, 2011), p. 134.
29. Barr and Sheffield, 'Douglas Haig', p. 230.

IV. Is attrition 'morally bankrupt'?

The British commander was not lacking in sympathy or compassion for his men's plight. Was he, nevertheless, careless in the spending of their lives? This brings us to the issue of attrition. For Coady it is precisely its attritional character that makes the First World War so morally revolting.[30] And what is it about attrition that he finds so repulsive? Its expression of a dullness of strategic imagination that only a criminal indifference to the loss of human life could allow: 'Had the general staff viewed the wastage of life as the moral enormity it has subsequently come to seem, they would have exercised more imagination in trying to find other ways of fighting,' he writes; and in a footnote he adds that '[i]n fact, there were other strategies and tactics available, most notably tank warfare, which was introduced at Cambrai but used inappropriately'.[31] Wittingly or not, Coady stands downstream from his Australian compatriot, Charles Bean. To the question of whether the same ends could not have been better attained by different, less expensive means, Bean answered in 1929:

> It is impossible to believe that they could not. Britain was not ill-served in the matter of technical invention: by the adoption of the Lewis gun, for example, she had already far more than counterbalanced the former German preponderance in machine guns. The tank—a British invention—was to become one of the deciding factors in the war. In technical invention the British artillery staff, in contrast to the general leaders, applied its imagination to the situation of opposing infantry, and constantly furnished the sole element of surprise to be observed in this battle. That vital element appears to be almost entirely absent from Haig's strategy of this period; nor was ingenuity devoted to the invention of suitable methods for 'wearing down' the enemy.[32]

---

30. Coady, *Morality and Political Violence*, p. 181.
31. Ibid., p. 185 and n.8.
32. Bean, 'The A.I.F. in France, 1916', p. 947. It is only fair to Haig that we should take note of Bean's judicious overall assessment of him: 'Haig's leadership of his partly trained army in 1916 has been bitterly and not always unjustly criticized; in two important qualities—quick imagination and sure judgement of subordinates—he was deficient. But nations are all too prone to require of their military leaders only qualities of brilliance, neglecting those attributes which, for the attainment of the common aim, are perhaps more essential and equally rare . . . [Haig] had the capacity of learning by his mistakes and the moral courage to change his attitude when the need became clear to him. Terrible as was to be the fighting of 1917, his conduct of the Third Battle of Ypres was marked by a coordination almost unknown on the Somme. In 1918 his greatest blow was at last accompanied by the vital element of surprise; and it is probable that history . . . will assign him a greater share than is yet recognized in the responsibility for the victories with which the war ended. It is difficult to conceive any factor more ominous to the Germans than the continued presence among their opponents of this resolute, unwavering soldier, deeply skilled in technique, but prevailing by qualities of character more than of intellect' (ibid., p. 948).

If contemporary historiography is to be believed, however, Bean and Coady are almost wholly wrong here. For example, William Philpott, author of a highly praised history of the Battle of the Somme, writes that '[i]t is overly simplistic to judge that the British army was too rigid or conservative in its tactics and command. It was keen to learn, engaging with its task thought-fully and professionally'.[33] Generals and government ministers were shocked by the numbers of casualties, and strove to find ways of breaking the stale-mate on the Western front and avoiding the need for attritional warfare. That is mainly why the ill-fated Gallipoli campaign was launched in 1915—to try and open up a new, more mobile front in south-east Europe. That is why Haig was so quick to champion the development of the tank.[34] (Indeed, he had hoped that tanks would be available for the beginning of the Somme campaign, and was frustrated that they were not.[35] He deployed them eleven weeks later.[36]) And that was also why Haig persisted in planning for a dra-matic breakthrough on the Western front in July 1916, long after others had concluded that it could not be achieved. It was not lack of human feeling or military imagination that led the British (and the French) to adopt an attritional strategy; it was the lack of alternatives during a fateful period of history that favoured defence by coming after the mass production of machine guns but before the mass production of tanks and, more impor-tantly, the development of the 'creeping barrage', of sound-ranging tech-niques in counter-battery fire,[37] and of wireless communications.[38] According

33. Philpott, Bloody Victory, p. 151.
34. Harris, Haig, p. 197: 'As we shall see, [Haig] would seize on the idea of the tank as soon as it was put to him and must be given the credit for the British army's assuming the lead in the whole field of armoured, "mechanical warfare".' See also ibid., p. 259. It is noteworthy that such affirmation comes from an author who generally does not flatter his subject.
35. Harris, Haig, p. 259.
36. Philpott, Bloody Victory, pp. 361–3.
37. According to Hew Strachan, artillery was 'the true artisan of victory' (The First World War [London: Pocket Books, 2006], p. 307). By November 1917 the Royal Artillery had 'perfected the techniques of predicted fire' and could locate an enemy battery by using microphones to sound-range. Consequently, they could register their guns in advance of an attack without warning the enemy by preliminary bombardment (ibid., pp. 307–8). They had also learnt to isolate second and third lines of defence from each other by moving curtains of fire backwards or forwards according to plan (ibid., p. 308).
38. Jeremy Black, Warfare in the Western World, 1882–1975 (Chesham: Acumen, 2002), p. 47: '[u]ntil wireless communications improved in late 1917, communications remained primitive, which stultified control of forward operations' and made it 'difficult to recognize, reinforce, and exploit success'. Philpott agrees, writing that the armies at the Somme 'combined the com-munication technology of the 19th century with the killing power of the 20th' (Bloody Victory, p. 606). Wireless sets were too large to be carried into battle, the buried network of telephone lines stopped at the front line, and new lines trailed across the surface of no man's land were vulnerable to rupture by enemy artillery. Consequently, '[i]nformation that reached the colo-

to Philpott, strategic attrition 'made sense in the dead-locked circumstances of 1916',[39] was necessary for any decisive defeat of the German army,[40] came very close to success [in September 1916],[41] and in the end 'it worked'.[42]

In addition, those who damn the generalship of the First World War for waging attritional war, and accepting casualties on a massive scale, must reckon with the fact that the undisputed turning point in the later war against Hitler—the Battle of Stalingrad—was horrifically attritional, its human cost rivalling that of the Great War battles.[43] They must also take on board the fact that on the mercifully few occasions in the Second World War when British troops found themselves bogged down in near-static fighting—hill to hill in Italy and hedge to hedge in Normandy—they reverted to the attritional tactics of 1917,[44] and that casualty rates in the 1944–5 campaign in north-west Europe equalled, and sometimes exceeded, those on the Western Front in 1914–18.[45]

The argument here, then, is that attrition, dreadful though it is, can sometimes be the only effective way of prosecuting a war; and that that was the case for much of 1914–18 (as it was for some of 1939–45). This undermines Jack Sheldon's view of the 'moral bankruptcy' of the strategy of attrition on the Somme, which assumes that its only possible justification consists in the lessons that it taught the British army, helping it to achieve victory in 1918. To this *ex post facto* rationalization Sheldon rightly retorts:

nels' dugouts or the generals' chateaux would often be inaccurate or out-of-date, if it reached them at all. Therefore, since orders could not be altered quickly once an attack had gone in, higher commanders and staff were relegated to a spectators' role...' (*Bloody Victory*, p. 156). John Keegan observes that '[t]he cloud of unknowing which descended on a First World War battlefield at zero hour was accepted as one of its hazards by contemporary generals' (*The Face of Battle: A Study of Agincourt, Waterloo, and the Somme* [London: Pimlico, 1976], p. 260).

39. Philpott, *Bloody Victory*, p. 130.
40. Ibid., p. 129.
41. Ibid., p. 346.
42. Ibid., p. 597.
43. Ibid., p. 628.
44. G.D. Sheffield, 'The Shadow of the Somme: The Influence of the First World War on British Soldiers' Perceptions and Behaviour in the Second World War', in Paul Addison and Angus Calder, eds, *Time to Kill: the Soldier's Experience of War in the West 1939–1945* (London: Pimlico, 1997), p. 36.
45. Ibid., p. 35: 'British and Canadian battalions suffered about 100 casualties per month on average on the Western Front in the First World War. In the 1944–5 north-west European campaign, battalions suffered a minimum of 100 per month but 175 per month was not uncommon. The daily casualty rate of Allied ground forces in Normandy actually exceeded that of the BEF, including the RFC, at Passchendaele in 1917.'

Any gains in military efficiency were a consequence of the battle and not the reason for fighting it. It was never a stated, or implied, aim beforehand . . . The Battle of the Somme had to be fought, but to attempt to justify it on the grounds that the British army was all the better for it and that that somehow makes the cost in blood and treasure a price worth paying, is to stretch a point, to put it no more strongly.

If it was just a matter of gaining experience, then there are other ways to obtain it than to commit all available forces to a long series of bludgeoning frontal attacks, which cause your army over 400,000 casualties. The cemeteries of the Somme stand in silent reproach.[46]

It is quite true that not every beneficial effect of a course of action may serve to augment its proportionality, as Thomas Hurka has argued.[47] If we take this principle and apply it to the justice of prosecuting a war at all—*ius ad bellum*—then, for example, the fact that fighting in 1941–5 lifted the United States out of the economic depression of the 1930s may not be used to contribute to its justification. This is because economic depression, though an evil, is not (usually) an injustice, and so cannot count as a just cause for embarking on war against a non-culpable people. Correlatively, the achievement of economic prosperity out of depression, though a good, cannot be set in the scales to weigh against a war's evils. Implicit here is a refusal of utilitarian justification in terms of an overall, objective predominance of benefits over costs. We refuse it, because the calculation of an overall 'utility' cannot be done rationally, the relevant goods and evils being too diverse in kind to be commensurable. What we attempt instead is the more modest and practicable judgement of the decisions of responsible human beings, asking whether they were justified in embarking upon certain voluntary courses of action and in persisting with them, given what we can reasonably expect them to have known. According to just war theory, war may not be waged simply in order to achieve a good, but only to rectify an injustice. The relevant goods and evils, therefore, are those that are foreseeable and either intended or accepted or wilfully ignored in the course of striving to rectify the injustice that constitutes a war's just cause.

When this principle of the specification of relevant effects is applied to the *in bello* circumstances of the battle of the Somme, what judgement does

46. Jack Sheldon, *The German Army on the Somme, 1914–1916* (Barnsley: Pen & Sword, 2005), pp. 397, 398.
47. Thomas Hurka, 'Proportionality and Necessity', in Larry May, *War: Essays in Political Philosophy* (New York: Cambridge University Press, 2008), pp. 130–5; and 'Proportionality in the Morality of War', *Philosophy and Public Affairs*, 33/1 (2005), pp. 39–45.

it produce? The fact that the Somme taught the British army some war-winning lessons was, of course, good. So why can this, by itself, not serve to justify its awful costs? Sheldon gestures toward the answer: not merely that this was not in fact the reason that Haig and his colleagues launched the Battle of the Somme in 1916, but more generally that military education as such is never a sufficient reason to send troops into battle. Why not? Because it is intrinsically profligate. To intend to teach a set of lessons presumes that one already knows what they are. If military commanders are morally responsible, they will strive not to waste the lives of their troops. If they know what the latter need to learn, they will incorporate the necessary lessons into military training, in which battlefield conditions are *simulated*, not replicated. Simulated conditions are not risk free—soldiers regularly lose their lives in training, sometimes in large numbers[48]—but they are designed at most to threaten, not to kill, the trainees. To send troops into battle primarily for the sake of their military education is—at least as a rule—insanely profligate. Sheldon, therefore, is entirely correct to reject the British army's steep learning curve as a stand-alone justification for the carnage of the Somme. He is wrong, however, to assume that no more sufficient justification is available, for, if Philpott and others are correct, there was no alternative to a strategy of attrition in 1916. Attrition on the Somme was a necessary military means toward the goal of reversing unjust aggression—as it would later prove at Stalingrad and in Normandy. If this is indeed the case, then the fact that the British army chose to learn war-winning lessons *in the course of waging unavoidably attritional warfare* may be permitted to supplement goods that are directly relevant to deliberation about proportionality. What it may not do is serve as a sufficient reason in itself.

It seems that the enormous number of casualties suffered by the British on the Somme cannot be blamed on Haig's lack of compassion for his men, or on his carelessness in spending their lives, or on his disdain for technical innovation. Can it nevertheless be attributed to his failure to adopt a more efficient strategy? This was Winston Churchill's view (on 1 August 1916):

> We could have held the Germans on our front just as well by threatening an offensive as by making one. By cutting the enemy's wire, by bombardments, raiding and general activity at many unexpected points begun earlier and kept

---

48. For example, according to Richard Holmes, 'German SS units took part in particularly realistic training with live ammunition, in which 5 per cent casualties were tolerated' (*Acts of War: The Behaviour of Men in Battle* [London: Cassell, 2003], p. 54).

up later we could have made it impossible for him to withdraw any appreciable force. If the French were pressed at Verdun we could have taken over more line and thus liberated reinforcements.[49]

The main aim of British action on the Somme, however, was not just to take pressure off the French at Verdun, but also to help wear down the German army. This a mere threat of attack would not have achieved. Nevertheless, some contemporary historians claim that alternative, more efficient means of waging war were indeed available to Haig, and that he failed to use them. As J.P. Harris writes:

> Mounting offensives under mature trench warfare conditions, with the limited resources the British army had, was naturally very difficult. But, in a staff paper of February 1915, even before the British army had mounted its first offensive under these conditions, [General Sir] William Robertson [then Chief of Staff of the British Expeditionary Force, and shortly to become Chief of the Imperial General Staff in December 1915] demonstrated that he had a fair intellectual grasp of the problem and could already suggest a reasonable approach: a series of limited attacks backed by concentrated artillery fire, designed to inflict loss on the enemy rather than to gain ground...By mid-1916 a substantial proportion of the army's most senior officers came to favour this kind of step-by-step approach. But Haig thought that he had failed to achieve complete break-through at Neuve Chapelle [in March 1915] only because of insufficient vigour on the part of subordinate commanders. Complete breakthrough was what he continued to aim for in most of his major operations, at least until the middle of 1917...Haig...became fixated on the achievement of dramatic breakthrough and achieving serious strategic results.[50]

In planning for the offensive on the Somme,

> Robertson, [General Sir Henry] Rawlinson, and [Major-General Archibald] Montgomery all wanted to adopt a cautious step-by-step approach and all the Fourth Army corps commanders agreed with them. But Haig still aimed at making deep penetration into the German defences on the first day and achieving complete rupture soon after...Haig proceeded with an approach that practically all the sources of advice available to him indicated to be dangerously overambitious.[51]

---

49. In Martin Gilbert, *Winston S. Churchill*, Vol. III, Companion, Part 2, Documents, May 1915–December 1916 (London: Heinemann, 1972), p. 1538.
50. Harris, *Haig*, p. 537.
51. Ibid., pp. 539–40. See also pp. 545–6: 'The systematic application of step-by-step methods (short advances backed by massive firepower) would almost certainly have been the best approach to offensive operations 1915–17. That a number of generals had conceived this

Harris's account has not gone unchallenged, however. Gary Sheffield has marshalled evidence that Haig's plans included *both* the launching of an attritional offensive *and* readiness for the contingency of a breakthrough,[52] and that breakthrough was not a fantasy but a possibility that could have been realized, had his immediate subordinate, Sir Henry Rawlinson, been willing to grasp it.[53] Whatever the historical evidence, this account is plausible a priori for two reasons. First, breakthrough is an end, not a means. The means is attrition. It follows that one cannot rationally plan for the former without also planning for the latter. Second, even if breakthrough on the Somme had been unlikely—even less likely than Haig supposed—it would still have made sense for him to plan for its contingency. However, what this amounts to is a qualification of Harris, rather than a contradiction. For Sheffield admits that Haig did tend to be over-optimistic and overambitious;[54] that there is 'some truth' in the claim that his record during the war shows 'a steady pattern of ambitious planning followed by disillusionment';[55] that his planning for the Somme suffered from 'ambiguities';[56] and that he did spread the opening artillery bombardment too thinly.[57]

It seems, then, that Haig's planning for the Battle of the Somme suffered, not from a lack of ingenuity or imagination, but from a measure of impatience and over-optimism. The irony—the dreadful irony—is that it was not his boneheaded commitment to a long attritional slogging match that made his battle strategy wasteful, but rather his refusal to settle for it. His eagerness for a breakthrough, while not just wishful thinking, nevertheless led him to compromise his attritional operations. Therefore on the first day of battle the British artillery bombardment was spread too deeply into enemy territory, with the result that its firepower was dissipated and too much of the German front line survived to entangle the attacking British infantry in barbed wire and mow them down with machine guns. And what was the alternative to this terribly wasteful, because overambitious plan? Even more prolonged attrition.

approach by the end of March 1915, and that a substantial proportion of the most important...were to adopt or endorse it by the middle of 1916, indicates that there was nothing wrong with the capacity of the British army as a whole to analyse and adapt. The biggest obstacle to its general adoption as the British army's *modus operandi* for much of the 1915–17 period was Douglas Haig, who, for most of it, remained obsessed with decisive breakthrough.'

52. Sheffield, *The Chief*, pp. 163, 164, 166, 374.
53. Ibid., pp. 171, 173, 175.   54. Ibid., pp. 174, 369.
55. Ibid., p. 374.   56. Ibid., p. 163.   57. Ibid., p. 175.

In the light of this, what are we to make of A.J. Coates's critique of the attritional character of the battle of the Somme,[58] and of attritional warfare as essentially disproportionate? He writes thus:

> The moral permissibility of the war of attrition (not merely a war with an attritional element, but a war in which attrition defines the entire strategy) must be in grave doubt. Here is a method of warfare that has as its deliberate aim the mass expenditure of men and material. It is a dehumanized view of war according to which war is seen as an industrial and mechanical process in which the distinction between the human and the material element is systematically suppressed. The problem with a war of attrition is that it is difficult to see how such a war can ever engage the criterion of proportionate *conduct* or means. The policy of attrition serves as a blank cheque, allowing commanders to prosecute the war without regard to those considerations that the principle of proportionality is meant to uphold: the policy is profligate and disproportionate by design. What the policy of attrition does is to throw the weight of the moral argument on to the proportionality of *ends* rather than means: is the cause grave enough to warrant the war of attrition?[59]

The first thing to say in response is that the distinction between a war with an attritional element and a war with an attritional strategy is not clear. Presumably any strategy of attrition will aim at breakthrough, for which plans will be made. In other words, attrition can never be anything but one element in a more complex plan. Second, the Somme seems not to fall within range of Coates's critical guns, since, as I read it, Haig's plan was designed to break the stalemate on the Western front and abbreviate prolonged attrition. Third, I do not think that a policy of attrition does necessarily express a dehumanized view of war, in which human beings are regarded merely as resources to be spent like artillery shells. As I have argued above, it is a necessary part of high military command in the field that a commander should callous himself against the human cost of his plans and orders—otherwise it would be emotionally impossible for him to do his job. This need not make him deficient in care before battle or in compassion after it, however. It need not make him inhumane, and in the case of Douglas Haig it did not. Fourth, a military strategy of attrition does not hand field commanders a blank cheque, allowing them to cast off all constraint by the principle of proportion. Some attritional operations and tactics are more efficient than others—either because they are more likely to be successful

58. Coates, *The Ethics of War*, p. 217.
59. Ibid., p. 220. The emphasis is Coates's.

and so less likely to waste lives, or because they are equally likely to reach the desired goals but are less costly in getting there.

Let us grant that no sane commander would ever opt for attritional operations or tactics that he knew to be inefficient. Nonetheless, he might choose them because he was avoidably ignorant; and he might be avoidably ignorant because he was culpably stubborn. In one sense, of course, military commanders are paid to be stubborn. They are expected to keep their nerve when everyone else is losing theirs, and to be resolute in the face of terrible adversity and fierce criticism. Nevertheless, a wise commander will not be so stubborn as to make himself impervious to cogent criticism. Rather he will seek out colleagues whose advice he can respect and he will listen to that advice even when its import is not welcome. Paul Harris argues that Haig was not so wise:

> [t]he evidence is overwhelming that Haig did not engender at GHQ [General Headquarters] an intellectually stimulating environment in which force structure, policy, plans and operational methods could be frankly debated in his presence...[H]e did not want some of his fundamental ideas and preconceptions disturbed...He seems to have chosen the staff officers with whom he had the most regular contact from people who would implement his will without trying fundamentally to change his thinking.[60]

Against this, Gary Sheffield contends that 'the idea that Haig did not allow debate does not square with the facts': 'On the Somme Haig commanded by issuing broad orders, which would result in plans being formulated by corps and armies, which were then criticized by Haig and GHQ until a synthesis emerged... The command culture was consensual, with the judgement of the man on the spot accorded much respect.'[61] Again, however, while Sheffield's account implies that Harris's criticism is overdrawn and argues for its softening, it does not contradict it: the permission of dialogue within broad limits is quite consistent with an aversion to having those limits challenged.

It seems that it was not the attritional character of the battle that Haig waged on the Somme that made it disproportionate. It was the fact that his attritional operations were weakened by his eagerness to achieve a breakthrough, resulting in a greater number of British casualties than a less ambitious plan would have entailed. There is some reason to suppose that,

60. Harris, *Haig*, pp. 538–9.
61. Sheffield, *The Chief*, pp. 180, 375.

had he heeded the advice of his senior colleagues, he could have avoided
this. (Had he done so, of course, he would have handed ammunition to
those who now charge him with careless and unimaginative complacency.)
However, whatever the degree of Haig's culpability, this truth remains: that
even more cautious and proportionate attritional operations would still have
been horrendously expensive of British lives.

We may say, then, that the losses incurred by the British on 1 July (and
sometimes subsequently) were disproportionate in the sense that they were
inefficient, since the same goals could have been attained by less costly
means. Nevertheless, something can still be worth doing even though it
could have been done more efficiently. Something can be worth buying
even when one pays over the odds for it. So may we say that the unnecessary loss of life rendered the Somme offensive not worth doing? Should we
respond to Richard Tawney's quizzical statement, 'I suppose it's worth it',
with the firm assertion, 'No, it was not'? If the offensive had failed in its
main aims, yes, we certainly should. But it did not fail in its main aims. True,
there was no dramatic breakthrough, but the French were saved at Verdun,
the pressure on the Russians was reduced, and the Germans were dealt such
a tremendous blow that they retreated twenty miles four months later. The
Somme was costly—excessively costly—but it was not futile, and nor were its
achievements trivial. It is not clear, then, that the Somme was not worth
622,000 Allied casualties. Indeed—though I tremble to say it—it is not clear
that it would not have been worth many more. In the real world there are
only imperfect wars prosecuted by imperfect generals—and if any real war is
to be just, then it will have to be just in spite of imperfections. It would have
been better if General Haig had possessed all the virtues equally. It would have
been better, perhaps, if he had been as strong in listening as he was in determination. It would have been better, perhaps, if he had been less ambitious
and settled for a strategy of simple attrition (in spite of what some contemporary moral philosophers think). Nevertheless, the fact that his plan could have
been better does not mean that it was either worthless or wicked.

V. Proportionality and just cause

There is one sense, however, in which it could make good sense to say that
the Somme was disproportionate in the sense of being worthless—namely,
if it was part of a war that should never have been fought in the first place.

Evils caused by the prosecution of an unjust war cannot be proportionate. If Britain's opposing the German invasion of Belgium and France was unjustified, then it was worth *no casualties at all*.

Nowadays it is common to see the First World War as a collective act of unmitigated folly. Jeff MacMahan expresses this sweeping view confidently: 'World War I is the paradigm of an utterly pointless war. There was, in effect, no reason for anyone to go to war. This war was a consequence of fatuous assertions of national pride together with a series of misjudgements about anticipatory mobilization, alliance commitments, and so on.'[62] Such a view is common in popular culture today, but not, as we shall see, among professional historians.

A more specific popular reading sees the war as a senseless clash of rival imperial powers—senseless because empires are assumed to be intrinsically evil enterprises that are worth neither expanding nor defending. As I see it, however, empires are not all of a single immoral piece. Like nations, they carry mixed moral records. The British empire, for example, presided over the massacre at Amritsar in 1919 and the brutal rampages of the Black and Tans in 1920s Ireland; but twenty or so years later that same empire offered the only effective opposition to the fascist domination of Europe from 1940–1 and was the only opponent to fight in the Second World War from the very beginning to the very end. And if the British empire did sometimes give rise to disgusting racial arrogance and racist contempt, it was also the first political body to abolish the slave trade and the institution of slavery and to enforce the ban internationally. Accordingly, it was the imperial British who baulked when asked by the US Army, upon its arrival in England in 1942, to endorse its policy of racial segregation.[63] Empires do not always

---

62. Jeff McMahan, *Killing in War* (Oxford: Clarendon Press, 2009), p. 2.
63. See Christopher Thorne, 'Britain and the Black GIs: Racial Issues and Anglo-American Relations in 1942', in *Border Crossings: Studies in International History* (Oxford: Blackwell, 1988), pp. 259–74; David Reynolds, 'The Churchill Government and the Black American Troops in Britain during World War II', in *Transactions of the Royal Historical Society*, Fifth Series, 35 (1985), pp. 113–33; and David Reynolds, *Rich Relations: The American Occupation of Britain, 1942–1945* (London: HarperCollins, 1995), chapters 14 and 18. The British reaction was not all of one kind, of course. Some cabinet ministers, for example, argued in favour of respecting, and even replicating, the American 'color-bar'. Significantly it was the Secretary of State for the Colonies who 'deplored the idea of seeking to guide British citizens into the ways of the Americans. Such a move, he felt, was likely to cause serious resentment among coloured people already in Britain, as well as those in the colonies; it could also lead to a reaction among the general public "gravely prejudicial to Anglo-American relations"' (Thorne, 'Britain and the Black GIs', p. 266).

live down to their stereotypes any more than republics always live up to their ideals.

The fact that the First World War was a war between rival empires, then, does not in itself establish that the causes of the warring parties were all equally worthless. Nor does it establish that imperial expansion was the reason for its being fought. Indeed, such a reading goes against the stream of contemporary historiography, of which the view of the American historian, David Fromkin, is typical:

> Lenin was wrong. [The First World War] was a war for control of continental Europe, not for empire in Asia or Africa... When the world war was over, it could be seen that one of the results, in 1919, had been the dramatic expansion of the British Empire... Some who observed these results drew the conclusion that it had been an imperialist war, a war for imperial expansion all along. That was an illusion. In August 1914, Grey and Asquith, in bringing Britain into the war, harbored no desire to expand and pursued no strategy designed to further imperial expansion; and they did not preside over their country's entrance into the war in the hope or expectation of acquiring more territory. The same was true of Germany... [I]t was not imperialism that caused the war.[64]

So what *did* cause it? From the late 1920s until recently it has been fashionable to attribute the First World War not to the decisions of individuals or governments but to the effects of impersonal systems or forces. Thus in 1928 Sidney B. Fay wrote that 'the War was caused by the system of international anarchy involved in alliances, armaments and secret diplomacy' and that 'all the powers were more or less responsible'.[65] This view too is no longer in favour among contemporary historians. Here we take Hew Strachan and David Stevenson as representative:

> [W]hat remains striking about those hot July weeks [in 1914] is the role, not of collective forces nor of long-range factors, but of the individual.[66]

> The European peace might have been a house of cards, but someone still had to topple it. It used to be argued that 1914 was a classic instance of a war begun

---

64. David Fromkin, *Europe's Last Summer: Why the World Went to War in 1914* (London: Heinemann, 2004), p. 278. Hew Strachan confirms Fromkin's reading of Germany: 'Germany did not in the end go to war in pursuit of its *Weltpolitik*. But the conduct of *Weltpolitik*, and the setbacks which it entailed, contributed to its sense of humiliation, beleaguerment, and fatalism in 1914' (*The First World War*, vol. I: *To Arms* [Oxford: Oxford University Press, 2001], p. 35).
65. Sidney B. Fay, *The Origins of the World War*, 2 vols (New York: Macmillan, 1928), vol. I, p. 2; cited by Strachan in *The First World War: To Arms*, p. 2.
66. Strachan, *The First World War: To Arms*, p. 101.

through accident and error: that no statesmen wanted it but all were over-borne by events. This view is now untenable.[67]

So *who* caused it, and why? It seems that a consensus has now settled around a modified version of Fritz Fischer's 1961 and 1969 interpretation,[68] which David Stevenson expresses thus: 'It is ultimately in Berlin that we must seek the keys to the destruction of peace... Germany willed a local war between Austria–Hungary and Serbia, deliberately risked a continental war against France and Russia, and finally actually started one.'[69] Whereas '[a]ll the

---

67. David Stevenson, *1914–1918. The History of the First World War* (London: Penguin, 2004), p. 41. The view that the war's decisive cause comprised the choices made by individuals has always had its advocates. James Joll, for example, wrote in 1984 that 'the question whether war was inevitable, or at least that particular war at that particular date, is not one which can be answered except in terms of individual responsibility' (*The Origins of the First World War* [London: Longman, 1984], p. 205); and in 1934 Pierre Renouvin argued that, when all is said and done, we must look for a sufficient explanation of the war's outbreak 'in the orientation of national politics, in the action of governments' (*La crise européene et la grande guerre, 1914–1918* [Paris: Félix Alcan, 1934], p. 180: 'Cette [suffisante] explication, c'est dans l'orientation des politiques nationales, dans l'action des gouvernements, qu'il faut en fin de compte la chercher').

68. Jay Winter and Antoine Prost describe this as 'an interpretation of great moral power, unsurprising in a man who had trained in theology' (*Great War in History: Debates and Controversies, 1914 to the Present* [Cambridge: Cambridge University Press, 2005], p. 47). Nevertheless, Winter and Prost (ibid., p. 38) see the contemporary consensus as a return to the position taken by the French historian, Pierre Renouvin, when he wrote in 1925 that '[Germany and Austria] did not agree to accept any solution other than the resort to force; they decided on their plan deliberately and after coolly considering all the possible consequences. With regard to the *immediate* origins of the conflict, this is the fact that dominates all the others' (*Les origines immédiates de la guerre [28 juin–4 août 1914]* [Paris: A. Costes, 1925]: p. 268: 'Mais elles n'ont pas consenti à accepter d'autre solution que l'acte de force; elles ont fixé le programme en pleine conscience, après avoir envisagé de sang-froid toute [sic] les conséquences possibles de leur décision. Dans le cadre des origines *immédiates* du conflit, voilà le fait qui domine tous les autres'). '[S]eventy years after Renouvin examined this question,' comment Winter and Prost, 'we have come full circle back to his position, published only five years after the end of the conflict. One can only admire how scholarly and cautious he was, and how well his conclusions have stood the test of time' (*Great War in History*, p. 40).

69. Stevenson, *1914–1918*, pp. 16, 590. According to Keir Lieber, this is also the current consensus among scholars in the field of international security: '[T]he current consensus among international security scholars is that a simple "blind blunder" explanation for the origins of World War I is incorrect. Most scholars acknowledge Germany's key role in the outbreak of the war and assign Germany a greater share of the blame, though almost always in qualified terms' (Keir A. Lieber, 'The New History of World War I and What It Means for International Relations Theory', *International Security*, 32/2 [Fall 2007], pp. 155–6). Lieber proceeds to argue that many of the qualifications should now be dropped: 'Newly available primary source material... suggests that German leaders went to war in 1914 with eyes wide open. They provoked a war to achieve their goal of dominating the European continent, and did so aware that the coming conflict would almost certainly be long and bloody. They neither misjudged the nature of modern military technology nor attacked out of fear of Germany's enemies moving first' (Lieber, 'The New History', p. 156).

European powers contributed to the growth of tension in the pre-1914 decade...the fundamental contention of the Versailles "war-guilt" article was
justified'.[70] While it is untrue that Kaiser Wilhelm II and his chancellor,
Theobold von Bethmann Hollweg, were intent upon a continental war in
July 1914, they were nevertheless prepared to risk it in giving Germany's full
support to Austro-Hungary's invasion of Serbia, with a view to isolating
Russia diplomatically.[71] Britain, France, and Russia had all made it quite clear
that a local Balkan war would escalate into a major continental conflict; but
it was only after hostilities against Serbia had begun that Bethmann Hollweg,
finally persuaded that Russia would not stay out, sought to prevent escalation
by restraining Austro-Hungary.[72]

German responsibility was not limited to imprudence on the part of the
Kaiser, his chancellor, and their foreign policy, however. It also involved
generals who were actually looking for war against Russia (and therefore
against its ally, France). Since 1908 the Kaiser and his entourage had become
dominated by the military,[73] among which social Darwinism was 'a prevailing

70. Stevenson, *1914–1918*, p. 596. See Fritz Fischer, *Germany's Aims in the First World War* (London:
    Chatto & Windus, 1967), and *War of Illusions: German Policies from 1911 to 1914* (London: Chatto
    & Windus, 1975. The contemporary consensus modifies Fischer's position in two respects: first,
    Germany did not actually make the decision to go to war in 1914 at the so-called 'War
    Council' of 8 December 1912; and second, her motive for going to war in the summer of 1914
    was not imperial expansion and world domination—as the original, German title of Fischer's
    earlier book implies: *Griff nach der Weltmacht: die Kriegszielpolitik des kaiserlichen Deutschland
    1914/18* ('Grasp for World Power: the War Aims Policy of Imperial Germany, 1914–18')—but
    rather the maintenance of her leading position in Europe. While all of the expressions of the
    contemporary consensus to which I will appeal are either British (Stevenson) or American
    (Fromkin), it is also shared (according to Stevenson) by the majority of their German peers:
    'Even though [Fischer's] first book has better withstood criticism, it overstated the unanimity
    within the Berlin elite and understated the resemblances between Germany's war aims and
    those of the Allies. None the less, most German historians came round to its more nuanced
    assessment of Germany's role in the July crisis, and (despite some important qualifications by
    subsequent writers) much of its analysis of German wartime ambitions has survived unchal-
    lenged' (Stevenson, *1914–1918*, p. 591).
71. Strachan, *First World War: To Arms*, pp. 73–4; Hew Strachan, 'Preemption and Prevention in
    Historical Perspective', in Henry Shue and David Rodin, eds, *Preemption: Military Action and
    Moral Justification* (Oxford: Oxford University Press, 2007), pp. 32–3.
72. Strachan, *First World War: To Arms*, pp. 86–8. Whereas Fischer and others believe that Bethmann
    Hollweg accepted the possibility of a European war from the outset of the crisis, Strachan sees
    him first as hoping against all the evidence that it could be avoided by a policy of localization,
    and then when that policy had evidently failed, acting in vain to stop Austria's war against
    Serbia. Stevenson's view is closer to Fischer's: 'both Wilhelm and Bethmann reasoned that an
    Austro-Serb conflict was likely to stay localized...But they accepted squarely the prospect of
    a European conflagration if it did not...Moltke having stated repeatedly that it was better to
    act now than to wait' (Stevenson, *1914–1918*, p. 25).
73. Strachan, *First World War: To Arms*, p. 21.

orthodoxy'.[74] For the German general staff and its chief, Helmuth von Moltke (the younger), international relations were about the struggle for survival—and so the dominance—of ethnic nations, and war was the natural way of deciding it.[75] At the 'War Council'[76] of 8 December 1912 Moltke pressed the view that a European war was inevitable and that, as far as Germany was concerned, the sooner it happened the better.[77] His advocacy of preventive war prevailed, with the result that 'the decision for peace or war was made conditional not on the objectives of policy but on the state of military readiness'.[78] Twenty months later, then, when both the Kaiser and Bethmann Hollweg got cold feet over the prospect of a continental war and called on Austro-Hungary to halt its invasion and seek terms with Serbia, Moltke bypassed the chancellor and urged the chief of the Austrian general staff, Conrad von Hötzendorff,[79] to mobilize against Russia, promising him that Germany would follow suit.[80] Later that evening Moltke

74. Ibid., p. 54. One expression of social Darwinism that was 'widely celebrated' at its publication in 1912 (Winter and Prost, Great War in History, p. 54) was Friedrich von Bernhardi's Deutschland und der nächste Krieg. In it Bernhardi writes thus: 'War is a biological necessity of the first importance... Without war, inferior or decaying races would easily choke the growth of healthy budding elements, and a universal decadence would follow... Might is at once the supreme right, and the dispute as to what is right is decided by the arbitrament of war. War gives a biologically just decision, since its decisions rest on the very nature of things' (Germany and the Next War, trans. A.H. Powles [London: Edward Arnold, 1912], pp. 10, 12, 15).

75. It seems that Bethmann Hollweg was an independent convert to Darwinist fatalism. As a young man his reading of Ernst Haeckel, Charles Darwin, and David Strauss had undermined his religious-humanist, Aristotelian confidence in basic cosmic harmony and replaced it with a vision of the universe as subject to the eternal struggle of blind forces (Thomas Lindemann, Les doctrines darwiniennes et la guerre de 1914, Hautes Études Militaires [Paris: Institut de stratégie comparée & Economica, 2001], pp. 203–4).

76. So named by Fischer, who in War of Illusions (1969) claimed that it resulted in a decision to go to war in 1914. Fischer himself later retracted this claim (Stevenson, 1914–1918, p. 591).

77. Strachan, First World War: To Arms, p. 52.

78. Ibid., p. 54.

79. Hötzendorff was also a social Darwinist, writing that the struggle for existence is 'the basic principle behind all the events on this earth' and 'the only real and rational basis for policy making' (ibid., p. 68); and that '[w]hat follows is the need to recognise an unavoidable enemy at the right time and to defend against him at the right time' (Strachan, 'Preemption and Prevention', p. 31).

80. Strachan, First World War: To Arms, pp. 87–8. To be fair, at the eleventh hour Moltke himself seems to have blinked at the prospect of a continental war. The minister of war, Erich von Falkenhayn, was appalled at the lack of resolution being shown by both the Kaiser and Moltke, and on 29 July called for the preliminary steps of mobilization to be taken. Moltke, aware that this would commit Germany to general war, refused to endorse the call, instead supporting Bethmann Hollweg's policy of letting Russia initiate hostilities. The following day, however, Moltke changed his mind and persuaded the chancellor to decide on general mobilization by noon on 31 July—regardless of Russian conduct. Preliminary mobilization began on that day, followed by general mobilization on 1 August (ibid., p. 89).

persuaded Bethmann Hollweg to decide on general mobilization, regardless of Russian equivocation.[81] Two days later Germany declared war on Russia.[82]

It was the German government, and especially its military leadership, that first risked and then caused continental war in August 1914. Why did they do it? Because they took it for granted that war is the natural and inevitable way by which the balance of international power is decided; because they foresaw that the longer the next war was delayed, the longer would be the odds against Germany's victory—especially in the light of the growth of Russia's power;[83] because they were determined at least to maintain Germany's ability to back its wishes by credible military force and therefore its status as a Great Power;[84] and because 'the memory of 1870 [the Franco–Prussian War], still nurtured through annual commemorations and the cult of Bismarck, had addicted the German leaders to sabre-rattling and to military gambles, which had paid off before and might do so again'.[85] In addition to this—and indeed generated by it—was paranoia: 'Convinced that France wanted revenge for the loss of Alsace-Lorraine, determined that Britain would be challenged by the naval programme, and terrified by the strategic dilemma of a war on both its western and eastern fronts simultaneously, Germany projected its fears onto its putative opponents and in due course gave its imaginings a reality which in origin they need not have had.'[86]

It is natural for a nation not to want to see diminished its power to realize its intentions in the world. But if social Darwinism thinks it natural for a nation to launch a war simply to prevent the loss of military and diplomatic dominance, just war doctrine does not think it right. Just cause must consist of an injury; and Germany had suffered none. Nor was it about to: 'no evidence exists that Russia, France, or Britain intended to attack'.[87] On the contrary, as we have seen, Russia mobilized only after Berlin had already flirted with general war and then decided upon it. As for France, she had

---

81. In the event, Russia did decide on general mobilization before Germany; but Moltke and Bethmann Hollweg had already decided to mobilize and go to war before they learnt of Russia's decision (ibid. See also Fromkin, *Europe's Last* Summer, p. 274).
82. Strachan, *First World War: To Arms,* p. 89.
83. Fromkin, *Europe's Last Summer,* p. 260.
84. Stevenson, *1914–1918,* p. 42.
85. Ibid., p. 596.
86. Strachan, *First World War: To Arms,* p. 15. 'To use epithets like "paranoid" and "fatalistic" of Germany after 1905 ... does not seem so misplaced' (ibid., p. 20).
87. Stevenson, *1914–1918,* p. 596.

deliberately kept one step behind Germany in her military preparations so as to make her defensive posture unmistakeable, and as late as 1 August she reaffirmed the order for her troops to stay ten kilometres back from the Franco–Belgian border.[88] Notwithstanding this, Germany declared war on France on 3 August 'on the basis of trumped-up allegations that French troops had crossed the border and French aircraft had bombed Nuremberg'.[89]

In Britain a majority of the government's cabinet was against entering the fray until 2 August. Notwithstanding the Entente Cordiale, an exchange of letters in 1912 had spelt out that if the peace of Europe were threatened, the British were obliged only to consult with the French and not to activate their joint military contingency plans and to go to war.[90] What eventually decided the cabinet in favour of declaring war on 4 August was Germany's violation of Belgian neutrality. In British minds Belgium conjured up a variety of altruistic just causes: honouring a treaty to guarantee Belgian independence,[91] punishing a violator of the treaty, and defending the rights of small nations. It also involved British national security, however, since the Belgian coast faced London and the Thames estuary, and it had therefore long been British policy to keep that coastline free from hostile control, both to prevent invasion and to preserve command of the sea.[92] It is true that if France, rather than Germany, had invaded Belgium, it is unlikely that Britain would have gone to war; and that in rising to the defence of Belgium the British also sought to forestall a German domination of Europe that they found menacing. Nevertheless, Britain did not initiate a war to maintain a favourable balance of power, nor would she have intervened to maintain it without the invasion of Belgium.[93]

Germany had suffered no injury, nor was she under any immediate or actually emergent threat of suffering one. Unprovoked, she launched a

---

88. Strachan, *The First World War: To Arms*, p. 91. See also Stevenson, *1914–1918*, p. 30.
89. Stevenson, *1914–1918*, p. 29.
90. Ibid., p. 35.
91. Britain was a guarantor of the 1839 treaty between all the great powers to maintain Belgian independence and integrity.
92. British anxiety about the Belgian coast was not paranoid: during the Great War the Germans used Belgium as a U-boat base (ibid., p. 147).
93. I cannot quite agree with David Stevenson's inference that '[t]he vital point was not the invasion, but that Germany was the invader' (ibid., p. 33). Surely it was both, as Stevenson later implies: 'For Asquith, Grey, and Bonar Law...German domination of the continent likewise appeared menacing, even if *Realpolitik* considerations would not, without the invasion of Belgium, have secured prompt British intervention' (ibid., p. 42).

European war in order to assert and establish her own military and diplomatic dominance. In response, Britain went to war against Germany primarily to maintain international order by upholding the treaty guaranteeing Belgian independence and by resisting its violator, and to fend off a serious threat to its own national security. In so doing she sought, secondarily, to prevent the domination of Europe by a power that had shown itself willing to unleash war on its innocent neighbours.

Given what we now know of the terrible cost of resistance, however, it is reasonable to wonder whether it would not have been prudent—whether it would not have been proportionate—for Belgium, France, Russia, and Britain to suffer domination by Germany instead. How bad would that really have been?

Judging by the 'Peace Programme' of war aims framed by Bethmann Hollweg in September 1914, and by the terms of the Treaty of Brest-Litovsk in 1917, German domination would have been seriously oppressive. According to the Programme, Germany would annex Luxembourg; Liège and Antwerp in Belgium; and the Briey-Longwy iron ore field, the fortresses of the Hauts-de-Meuse, the western Vosges mountains, and possibly the Channel coast from Dunkirk to Boulogne in France. In addition, France was to be subjected to a crippling indemnity that would prevent rearmament for twenty years, and to a commercial treaty that would make it 'economically dependent on Germany'. Belgium was to become a 'vassal state' under military occupation and 'economically a German province'. Although the Programme of September 1914 was not an authoritative policy statement, David Stevenson implies that it was moderate in comparison with the 'more extreme annexationism' of the military and the circles around the Kaiser;[94] and he says that '[s]imilar (if less sweeping) proposals for western Europe appeared in war documents for the rest of the conflict, and planning for...the Belgian "vassal state" began without delay'.[95] Certainly, the peace terms that the Programme envisaged for France were actually *less harsh* than those actually imposed on Russia in 1917: at Brest-Litovsk Russia was made

94. Ibid., p. 130.
95. Ibid., p. 130. Jay Winter and Antoine Prost confirm Stevenson's estimation of the significance of the September Programme: 'As a whole, despite some adjustments according to circumstances, this programme corresponded to the desires of the Ruhr magnates and the Prussian Junkers. It was supported by the General Staff and informed German policy until 1918' (*Great War in History*, p. 47).

to sign away over a third of her population, much of her heavy industry and coal production, and her best agricultural land.[96]

In addition, we may take the atrocious behaviour of the German military toward civilians in 1914 as expressive of a brutal ruthlessness that would have characterized post-war German domination, especially in those regions subjected to military occupation. William Philpott provides an example: on 27 August 1914 '[w]hen the mayor [of Péronne] refused to take down the tricolour flying over the *mairie* it was torn down by the furious enemy. In pique, and to deter resistance, the passing Prussians burned fifty-eight houses to the ground and looted the rest of the town, casually shooting passers-by who got in the way.'[97] As John Horne and Alan Kramer have recently confirmed, it was German military policy to use civilians as human shields in combat, to burn villages in collective reprisal for resistance, and to shoot local irregulars who were caught bearing arms.[98] Between August and October 1914, German troops deliberately killed 6,427 civilians in Belgium and France;[99] and a further 10,000 French civilians and 13,000 Belgians were forcibly deported to prison camps across Germany.[100] This ruthlessness was not always unprincipled: it was sometimes generated by the moral outrage naturally felt by regular troops who believe themselves to be under attack by 'partisans' who, eschewing military uniforms, exploit their indistinguishability from the civilian population. Nevertheless, paranoia reigned here too: the fear of partisan warfare in 1914 far outstripped the fact of it. Indeed, Horne and Kramer go so far as to describe the German belief that enemy civilians were engaged in large-scale *franc-tireur* resistance as 'a collective delusion'.[101] 'We can state categorically,' they write, 'that there was neither collective civilian resistance nor military action by franc-tireur units as in 1870–1. There were a few isolated cases of individual civilians firing on Germans, but none of these incidents provoked mass executions such as those of Dinant, Louvain, or Liège in Belgium, and NoD, Longuyon, and Haybes in France.'[102] Horne and Kramer also observe that the Germans'

---

96. Stevenson, *1914–1918*, p. 394.
97. Philpott, *Bloody Victory*, p. 15.
98. John Horne and Alan Kramer, *German Atrocities, 1914: A History of Denial* (New Haven: Yale, 2001), pp. 424 and 76–7: '[F]or whatever motive... the Germans from start to finish used civilians for cover when attacking and... this measure was not the result of maverick orders. Hostage-taking and deportation were equally integral to German behaviour.'
99. Ibid., pp. 74, 420.
100. Ibid., p. 166.
101. Ibid., p. 419.
102. Ibid.

brutal, indiscriminate, disproportionate response was also generated by anti-democratic hostility toward—and fear of—'the politicized citizen'.[103]

The ruthless character of post-war German domination may also be foreseen in the plans that Ludendorff and others drafted for the German colonization of a large strip of Poland and the forcible resettlement of Polish and Jewish populations further east. Since the plans were never implemented, Alan Kramer is quite correct to say that 'for all the harshness of the occupation of 1914–18, the German state did not carry out brutal mass population expulsions which were the order of the day from 1939 to 1945'.[104] Nevertheless, Ludendorff's proposals were entertained by the highest level of government and by the German High Command; and the reason for their eventual rejection was not moral scruple but military concern about the disadvantageous consequences of offending international public opinion.[105]

Had Russia, France, and Britain not resisted in 1914, therefore, there is good reason to suppose that Germany would have dominated Western and Eastern Europe in such a rapacious and ruthless manner as to have stoked widespread resentment among its newly subject peoples and high alarm among the newly menaced British. Domination of this kind would have ushered in an era of civil unrest and even more acute international tension. Moreover, given the cult of Bismarck and the crushing success of the victories of 1866 (against Austro-Hungary) and 1870 (against France), 'if Germany had again won quickly [in 1914] (as it probably would have done if Britain had stayed out) the temptation for further gambles would have been stronger than ever'.[106] In short, non-resistance in 1914 would have produced neither a just peace nor a stable one.

Still, one might argue, as pacifists would, that no matter how unjust and unstable, peace is always better than war; that there is no injustice so great as to warrant its belligerent opposition; that war is *always* disproportionate. This is most plausible if one thinks only in terms of the number of lives saved. In the case of the First World War, it seems unlikely that Prussian hegemony over Europe would have been so oppressive as to result in the

---

103. Ibid., p. 421.
104. Alan Kramer, *Dynamics of Destruction. Culture and Mass Killing in the First World War* (Oxford: Oxford University Press, 2007), p. 336. However, the Germans did forcibly deport 120,000 Belgian workers to Germany in the summer of 1916 (Stevenson, *1914–1918*, p. 133; Strachan, *The First World War* (Pocket Books), p. 322).
105. Kramer, *Dynamics of Destruction*, pp. 335–6.
106. Stevenson, *1914–1918*, p. 596.

violent deaths of many millions. This appearance rests, however, on the dubious assumption that such hegemony would have been no more aggressive or ruthless than the German invasion of 1914–18. It is dubious because our counterfactual speculation requires us to suppose that German hegemony discovers that its already somewhat ruthless aggression provokes no armed opposition. We must suppose that it finds itself without serious rival in armed force. Then we must imagine how it would have dealt subsequently with non-violent opponents; or with workers who refused to be deported; or with Slavs who stood in the way of the colonization of the east; or with any of its subject peoples who, too feeble even for self-defence, now deserved contempt as servile losers in the Darwinist struggle for national survival. Long experience and history tell us that wickedness unchecked tends to wax. That is why punishment is so important. Therefore, it is probable that, had German aggression and ruthlessness been unopposed, it would have grown and shed blood more liberally. And over the ensuing decades and generations the number of lives unjustly taken might have climbed into the millions.

The truth is, however, that the justification or otherwise of war is not usually—and should not be—articulated simply or primarily in terms of the number of lives saved or lost.[107] There is also the consideration of justice and of upholding it. The British decision to go to war against Germany in 1914 was partly a decision to uphold an international treaty—and thereby international order—against its wilful violation. It was therefore both an act of faithfulness and an act of retributive punishment, which combines a naming and contradiction of wrongdoing with action to stop and reverse it.[108] As soon as considerations of faithfulness and justice enter into the calculation of proportion, however, it becomes quite clear that the 'calculation' is nothing of the sort. While we can count the number of lives lost and can guess at the number of lives that might have been saved, the value of promises kept and justice upheld will not render itself in numerical terms. So, when considering questions of proportion we are in fact not calculating at all; we

---

107. Thus A.J. Coates, who approvingly quotes Michael Walzer: 'the gains of war and peace cannot be measured simply in lives saved' (Michael Walzer, 'World War Two: Why was this War Different?', in *War and Moral Responsibility*, ed. Marshall Cohen, Thomas Nagel, and Thomas Scanlon [Princeton: Princeton University Press, 1974], p. 91; quoted by Coates in *The Ethics of War*, p. 174). For a fuller discussion of this issue, see Chapter Five, sections IX and X.

108. As I explain in Chapter Five, I understand 'retribution' to refer, basically and broadly, to a hostile response to wrongdoing that need not be vengeful and that may intend the repentance of the wrongdoer rather than his annihilation.

are judging. The process of this judgement is, if not mysterious, then certainly complex, and I shall have more to say about it in Chapter Seven. For now, let it suffice to say that many people, probably most, have thought and do think that it can be right to defend justice at the cost of sacrificing human life. Jesus did, and so do those of his followers who, trusting in God, hope for life beyond death.[109] Even pacifists do not dissent on this point. They do not deny that it can be right to sacrifice one's own life for justice, and to allow the sacrifice of *someone else's* life. They only deny that it is right deliberately to inflict such sacrifice.

VI. Proportionality and right intention

A good case can be made, then, that Britain was right to go to war against Germany in 1914. But was she right to keep on waging war for so long? Could she not have sought and secured decent peace terms long before November 1918? Was not Siegfried Sassoon correct to protest in 1917 that the war was being unnecessarily prolonged and that Britain's original war aims of self-defence and Belgian and French liberation could have been achieved by negotiation?[110] The answer appears to be 'No'. Germany showed

---

109. The rise of materialism and the decline of religious faith and hope, in at least certain parts of the Western world, have corroded the rationale for sacrificing one's life for the sake of justice. Hegel observed how, through bourgeois worship of material peace and prosperity, 'freedom has died from the fear of dying' (*Elements of the Philosophy of Right*, trans. H.B. Nisbet [Cambridge University Press, 1991], p. 362). And Paul Ramsey ('The Uses of Power', in *The Just War*, pp. 14–18) observed that, in a post-national age the 'immortality' of the nation no longer provides a secular substitute for belief in the individual's resurrection to supernatural life; and in an age menaced by nuclear annihilation the 'immortality' of the human race no longer does so either. 'Secular man,' he writes, '...has...lost the conviction that there is an ultimate non-temporal resolution of the problem of historical action and sacrifice...Letting go the heavenly city, he held on to the earthly city with infinite passion. He began to make infinite demands of political action. Such action must be worth the sacrifice of a man's life. So modern secular man is unable any longer to look into the heart of the tragic ambiguity of all earthly sacrifice...This is the ultimate source of the modern persuasion that all war is murder.' (ibid., p. 17).

110. In June 1917 Sassoon, serving as an officer in the British army, published his famous protest against the continuation of the war, which included the following: 'I believe that the War is being deliberately prolonged by those who have the power to end it...I believe that this War, upon which I entered as a war of defence and liberation, has now become a war of aggression and conquest. I believe that the purposes for which I and my fellow-soldiers entered this war should have been...clearly stated...and that, had this been done, the objects which actuated us would now be attainable by negotiation' (Max Egremont, *Siegfried Sassoon. A Biography* [London: Picador, 2005], p. 143).

no sign of being willing to return Belgium (or France) to the status quo
ante until October 1918. In the winter of 1915–16, when it was clear that the
war was not going to end any time soon, there was an informal diplomatic
exchange between Germany and Belgium, in which Germany demanded
Belgian alignment with German foreign policy, Belgian disarmament,
German occupation and transit rights, a coastal naval base, and German
majority shareholding in Belgian railways. As David Stevenson comments,
'The consensus among Germany's leaders was more or less as the September
programme envisaged.'[111] By late 1916 '[b]oth unofficial opinion and gov-
ernmental planning were becoming harsher. The military emergency of
summer 1916 might have been expected to cause a reconsideration, as had
the defeat on the Marne, but in fact German aims became more draconian
than ever.'[112] By the end of December 1916, 'with Germany's armies under
unprecedented pressure and the economy beginning a downward spiral,
Hindenburg and Ludendorff sought more sweeping annexationist claims,
not fewer'.[113] In April 1917 the Kaiser and the German High Command
endorsed the secret statement of German war aims known as the Kreuznach
Programme, according to which Germany 'would annex Longwy-Briey
and Luxembourg, hold Liège and the Flanders coast for at least a century,
and run Belgium's railways'.[114] When in August 1917 Pope Benedict XV
published proposals for a return to pre-1914 European boundaries without
annexations and indemnities, and for the full independence of Belgium
(with an eye to meeting German objections to British or French predominance there), 'the Germans and Austrians tried to kill the initiative by delay-
ing their response'.[115] While Woodrow Wilson rejected a return to the status
quo ante, Britain decided to feel the Germans out by inviting them to spell
out their intentions regarding Belgium. In preparing their response
Hindenburg and Ludendorff, who now dominated Germany's government,
aimed to divide Paris and London by making concessions to Britain and
suspending the German navy's demand for bases on the Flanders coast.
Nevertheless, they continued to insist upon strategic control of Belgium by
annexing Liège and through military guarantees.[116] However, when Britain

111. Stevenson, *1914–1918*, p. 131.
112. Ibid., p. 136.
113. Ibid., p. 137.
114. Ibid., p, 345. While Bethmann Hollweg initialled the Programme only under protest, 'he
      accepted it as a guideline in the event of Germany's being able to dictate peace' (ibid.).
115. Ibid., p. 355.
116. Ibid.

eventually replied that she would only consider the German proposals in consultation with her Allies, '[t]he Germans never responded'.[117] Even as late as September 1918, judging by the speech of vice-chancellor Payer, Germany still resisted abandoning Belgium. '[T]he turn of military fortunes had failed to soften the Germans' war aims.'[118] Only on the night of 4 and 5 October 1918 did Germany offer to enter peace negotiations on the basis of Woodrow Wilson's Fourteen Points,[119] Point VII of which required Belgium to be evacuated and restored.[120] In sum, then, there is no evidence that Britain could have secured satisfactory peace terms before November 1918. Siegfried Sassoon himself admitted in 1945 that 'in the light of subsequent events it is difficult to believe that a Peace negotiated in 1917 would have been permanent'.[121] It is even more difficult to believe that acceptable peace terms were actually on offer.

A good case can be made, I think, that Britain had sufficient moral grounds to go to war against Germany in 1914; and that peace terms satisfying those grounds were not on offer until the autumn of 1918. If there was good enough reason to start fighting and to carry on fighting, then resistance to German aggression and domination was worth *some* casualties. But how many? We have seen that at the Somme in 1916 more casualties were suffered than were necessary to achieve the desired goals—and as there and then, so elsewhere and at other times (e.g. Loos and Neuve Chapelle in 1915, and Arras and Ypres in 1917). Because of deficiencies in Haig and in his planning, the war was prosecuted less efficiently than it could have been. In that limited sense, therefore, Britain's war against Germany in much of 1914–17 was disproportionate. But all actual warriors have vices as well as virtues, and all actual wars are less than optimally efficient and are therefore disproportionate. If war is ever actually to deserve the title of 'just', then imperfection as such cannot disqualify it. Of course, it would have been better if fighting Germany had cost Britain and its empire less than the 1,114,914 military deaths (and 2,090,212 military wounded) it did. But can we say that such a cost was disproportionate in the sense that it was not worth it? Can we say that, once the casualties had got to a certain point, Britain should have sued for peace on whatever terms she could get? I believe that we can. That decisive point, however, is not absolute and

117. Ibid., p. 357.   118. Ibid., p. 467.
119. Ibid., p. 471.   120. Ibid., p. 391.
121. Siegfried Sassoon, *Siegfried's Journey* (London: Faber & Faber, 1945), p. 57.

numerical but pragmatic and circumstantial: either where the rate of casualties outran the supply of replacements, or where it demoralized sufficient troops to the point of mutiny, or where it undermined domestic political support for the war. To have carried on fighting in such circumstances, when the writing was already on the wall, would indeed have been an exercise in futility, and further loss of life would have been sheer waste. Before October 1918, however, Britain was not at that point. Indeed, she was not at it even in October 1918. What this implies—though, again, I tremble to say it—is that it would not have been manifestly disproportionate for Britain to have chosen to suffer *even more* casualties than she did, had Germany continued to fight.

In case this should seem just too outlandish, we should call to mind that the main brunt of defeating Hitler in the Second World War was borne neither by the British, who suffered 382,600 military deaths; nor by members of the British empire, who lost 185,600; nor by the United States of America with her 407,300 dead. The main cost was borne by the Soviets on the Eastern Front, where they lost 10,700,000 troops (and a further 11,500,000 civilians). Notwithstanding this appalling cost—many times greater, both numerically and proportionally, than that borne by Britain in 1914–18—it is widely agreed that the war against Nazi Germany was justified. In retrospect, of course, the Nazi regime proved to be of an order of wickedness significantly greater than the Wilhelmine one; but neither Britain in 1939 nor the Soviet Union or the United States in 1941 went to war against Germany to bring an end to the death camps. The Final Solution was not even decided upon until 1942. Britain went to war against Hitler for reasons very similar to those that had propelled it against Wilhelm II: the clear violation of international order through the unleashing of war on an innocent Poland by a Germany which, absent any immediate threat, had built its armed forces into the strongest in Europe and had then used the menace of its military dominance to annex Austria and Czechoslovakia.

VII. Conclusion

All things considered, then, it seems to me that Britain's war against Germany in 1914–18 was not disproportionate as a whole, in the sense that its terrible costs undermined its basic justification, so that it should never have been embarked upon in the first place or that it should have been brought to a halt earlier than it was. The assertion of this overall proportionality—or, to be more exact, this overall lack of manifest disproportionality—is quite consistent with the admission of moments of culpable operational inefficiency in the expenditure of troops' lives and limbs. Only if culpable operational profligacy had exposed morally wrong strategic intentions, and only if the expenditure of troops had reached materially or politically unsustainable proportions, would they have undermined the basic justification of British belligerency. To the best of my knowledge, no immoral intentions were exposed and no point of unsustainability had been reached by November 1918.[122]

Those who doubt that Britain should ever have entered the war in the first place need to surrender the benefit of hindsight, suspend the attribution of cynical motives, enter charitably into the shoes of those burdened with decision-making, and ask themselves what honourable, responsible, realistic, and preferable alternatives were available at the time. Those who hold that Britain should have made peace earlier than she did need to consider what terms were actually on offer before October 1918. Those who attribute the enormous number of casualties simply to the gross indifference and incompetence of the staff officers need to extend some sympathy to men who, trained to command small colonial forces, suddenly found themselves carrying responsibility for millions;[123] who were compelled to take the offensive against an invader at a time when technological development smiled upon defence; and whose professional responsibilities precisely required them *not* to lose their nerve in the face of the shocking costs. They also need to ask themselves why none of the other belligerents was more successful in transcending attritional warfare. Britain's war against Germany

---

122. I note that my ethical conclusion contradicts those of at least two eminent historians of the First World War, David Stevenson ('Intrinsic to all military undertakings, however legitimate their motives, is the risk that they will violate the principle of proportionality between ends and means, and that they too will lead to a bad war and a bad peace. The 1914–18 conflict and the settlement that followed it remain archetypes of both' [Stevenson, *1914–1918*, p. 600]) and John Keegan ('Principle perhaps was at stake; but the principle of the sanctity of international treaty, which brought Britain into the war, scarcely merited the price eventually paid for its protection' [Keegan, *The First World War* [London: Pimlico, 1999], p. 456]). How, exactly, do Stevenson and Keegan *know* this? If it is true, it remains to be *shown* so.
123. Philpott, *Bloody Victory*, p. 51: 'When an army expands tenfold it necessarily becomes temporarily deskilled, and has to relearn its trade. When that trade is also changing, such a process of adjustment is doubly difficult; especially when, after the heavy casualties amongst its pre-war cadres, the bulk of its junior field command, senior ranks and staff appointments were filled by officers promoted rapidly and with limited responsibilities of command.'

was terribly and tragically expensive. It was also imperfectly managed by imperfect generals. But it was not criminally careless; nor was it futile.

So much for the moral assessment of British belligerency in 1914–18. What general light does it throw on the concept of proportionality in war? Its most important revelation is critical: namely that all talk of judging proportionality in terms of making an arithmetical 'calculation' or a quantitative 'weighing' and reaching a precise and certain conclusion is nothing but a modernist technocrat's fantasy. It ignores the obvious fact that the many goods and evils involved—on the one hand, the vindication of the innocent, the maintenance of international order, and freedom from serious oppression; on the other hand, the deaths of individuals, social breakdown, economic destruction, and long-standing resentments—are incommensurable. There is no common currency in terms of which they can all be measured and weighed against each other to produce a reliable answer. Incommensurability, however, is not the only problem. There is also the unpredictability of the future. Our control over the effects of what we ourselves do is disconcertingly limited. Too often other agents interfere or natural events obstruct. Sometimes benevolence, meticulous planning, and painstaking execution are all of no avail in preventing the opposite of what we intend. Moreover, if we have limited control over the effects of our own action, we have even less over those of many and uncoordinated other agents. And what is difficult to control is difficult to predict.

I do not mean to say that conscientious estimates of the probable consequences of going to war or of a particular military operation should not be made. Of course they should. What I mean to say is that we cannot expect of them a high degree of accuracy. What is more, however accurate our predictions of good and evil consequences may be, they cannot comprise a judgement of proportionality until they have been ordered according to a particular hierarchy of goods, and until conflicts between equal goods have been resolved by appeal to particular moral rules.[124] Charles Guthrie and

---

124. Thomas Hurka oscillates rather violently on this matter. On the one hand, he writes of 'calculations' yielding 'net good or bad effects' ('Proportionality and Necessity', p. 129; and 'Proportionality in the Morality of War', p. 38). On the other, he admits that 'the task of weighing is complex' and concludes that the irreducible diversity of goods 'leaves their comparison to direct intuition' ('Proportionality in the Morality of War', pp. 51, 57). 'Calculation' is too precise; 'direct intuition' too vague. What we need, at least, is intuition that is tacitly informed by a hierarchy of goods and by moral rules that can resolve conflicts between goods of the same kind.

Michael Quinlan, both of whom have had experience of manning the front line of military decision-making, agree:

> There underlies all the evaluations [about proportionate cause]...a difficulty that is uncomfortable but inescapable: they entail taking very serious decisions on the basis of estimates of complex futures, with wide margins of uncertainty and as a result much scope...for different perceptions and judgements about where justice and prudence point.[125]

This general, critical point about the *non*-arithmetical and *non*-quantitative nature of judgements of proportionality, and therefore about their necessary lack of accuracy and certainty, implies another general point, but this time a constructive one. This is that, whereas it is often impossible to demonstrate that a military action is positively proportionate (in the sense of producing a greater quantity of benefit than cost), it is usually possible to determine whether or not such an action is clearly *dis*proportionate (in the sense of being provoked by an obviously trivial cause, or serving an obviously trivial end, or being self-subverting, or being unsustainable and futile).[126]

Other, more specific lessons about the consideration of proportionality, which our moral analysis of British belligerency in 1914–18 has taught us, are the following. First, that a war that lacks just cause or right intention cannot be proportionate, since none of the evils that it causes is justified.

Second, one cannot expect any real war, run by real human beings, to be maximally efficient. Even a just war, therefore, is going to be somewhat inefficient, and a measure of inefficiency need not amount to culpable disproportion.

Third, attritional warfare is not necessarily disproportionate. Sometimes it can be the only available way of fighting; and it can be more, rather than less, efficient.

---

125. Charles Guthrie and Michael Quinlan, *Just War. The Just War Tradition: Ethics in Modern Warfare* (London: Bloomsbury, 2007), p. 23. General Lord Guthrie of Craigiebank was the UK's Chief of the Defence Staff, 1997–2001; and Sir Michael Quinlan was for thirty years a British civil servant in posts concerned with defence, including those of Policy Director in the Ministry of Defence, 1977–81, and of Permanent Under-Secretary of State, 1988–92.

126. I note that David Rodin reaches a similar conclusion. He writes that whether or not good consequences exceed bad ones is impossible to determine. Nevertheless, he thinks that a negative and minimal judgement of proportionality remains possible: namely, whether or not the moral costs are 'grossly disproportionate to' or 'significantly greater than' the expected benefits ('The Problem with Prevention', p. 155).

Fourth, a certain kind of callousness is a military virtue, and the fact that a commander's chosen plan involves the foreseeable annihilation of whole bodies of his troops need not be culpably disproportionate.

Nor, fifth, need the foreseeable destruction of tens—or even hundreds—of thousands of his troops, since virtuous callousness can go hand in hand with careful planning.

Sixth, the fact that a certain operation was less than maximally efficient, and culpably so, does not mean that it was not worth undertaking. It can therefore be culpably disproportionate (in the sense of inefficient) at one level while at another level not being disproportionate (in the sense of futile) at all.

Finally, granted sufficiently just cause, the only quantity of military casualties at which belligerence as a whole becomes disproportionate is that which is unsustainable—whether in terms of human resources, military morale, or political support. Such a quantity has no fixed number: it can range from a few hundreds all the way up to multiples of millions.

In sum, then, the principle of proportionality in its various senses does serve to limit the evils of war. Without its constraints, the number of lives lost and the extent of political, social, and economic damage done would be far greater. Nevertheless, given the objective vicissitudes of history and the severe limitations of human foresight, the deployment of the principle is bound to be speculative, even when it is careful.[127] And however elaborate the analysis of proportionality into its elements, and however broad the consensus that such analysis attracts, its deployment will ultimately depend upon human judgement, morally controversial and more or less wise.[128] Moreover, the constraints that the principle of proportionality imposes can still permit costs that are very, very high indeed. For those of us who adhere to the doctrine of justified war, that is a mightily sobering thought. Yet why would we suppose that the price of doing what is right should never be enormous, indeed dreadful? For sure, dreadful costs rightly raise the question of worthwhileness. The question, however, does not amount to a negative answer.

---

127. *Pace* Tony Coady, who insists that the estimate of costs and benefits should not be 'speculative' (*Morality and Political Violence*, p. 97).

128. Although it concurs with the managerialist *Zeitgeist*, which aspires to abolish the need for the exercise of individual conscience and discretion, I consider utterly utopian and impracticable Janina Dill's desire to have 'professional experience and personal morality' replaced with 'a transparent and stable set of criteria' that are susceptible to impersonal, objective, uncontroversial application ('Applying the Principle of Proportionality in Combat Operations', Policy Briefing [Oxford: Oxford Institute for Ethics, Law, and Armed Conflict, 2010], p. 4).

5

Against legal positivism and liberal individualism

I. Rodin's challenge

Opposition to just war reasoning comes not only from pacifism but also from contemporary liberal, analytical philosophy. In particular, David Rodin has written an outstandingly lucid, logically careful, analytically searching, and argumentatively circumspect critique, which, when still in unpublished form, won a prize from the American Philosophical Association,[1] and when published, sported a Foreword by Bernard Williams. Rodin's thesis is 'that our traditional conceptions of international law and international ethics need to be fundamentally rethought',[2] because just war theory, 'one of the few basic fixtures of medieval philosophy to remain substantially unchallenged in the modern world',[3] fails both theoretically and practically. This is a challenge that any advocate of just war must meet.

Rodin's argument runs as follows. Just war theory makes national self-defence (henceforth, 'national defence') 'the central "just cause"'[4] and therefore paradigmatic of just war. It supposes that the justification of national defence lies in its analogous relationship with individual self-defence.[5] Individual self-defence is best justified in terms of rights, and the most coherent rights-based justification operates in terms of a normative account of the relationship between the innocent defender and the morally guilty aggressor. However, national defence is disanalogous to individual

---

1. The 1997 American Philosophical Association's Frank Chapman Sharp Memorial Prize.
2. David Rodin, *War and Self-Defense* (Oxford: Clarendon Press, 2002), p. 199.
3. Rodin, *War and Self-Defense*, p. 189.
4. Ibid., p. 162.   5. Ibid., p. 107.

self-defence in that its end is not simply the protection of individuals' right to life. What is more, the various accounts that just war theory gives of the alternative, common ends of national defence are incoherent. Further still, national defence cannot give an adequate account of why enemy soldiers are liable to be killed. Finally, while military action could be justified as law enforcement instead of self-defence, it cannot be so in the absence of a global state. For all these reasons just war theory is found wanting theoretically. But it is also found wanting practically. This is because it 'has failed to provide a robust set of principles for effective operation in the political realm',[6] since the moral contrast between culpable aggressor and innocent defender is subverted both by the historicity of international conflicts and by the background conditions of mutual distrust and readiness for conflict.

David Rodin's argument is very impressive, but the scope of its cogency is much more limited than he appears to know. This is because he tends to identify just war theory either with positive international law governing war or with Michael Walzer's classic liberal version. Against both of these much of his criticism tells. At the same time, however, much of it tells in favour of the earlier tradition of just war thinking that runs from Augustine, through Aquinas, Vitoria, and Suarez, to Grotius; and of this Rodin (like Walzer) seems largely oblivious.[7] He certainly knows that it exists, for he quotes from it occasionally, but he tends to acknowledge it only in the course of passing it by.

In this chapter I hope to show how, in his criticism of legal-positivist and Walzerian just war theory, Rodin is often the unwitting mouthpiece of an earlier tradition; and that in damning the former, he implicitly vindicates the latter. Further, where Rodin's argument does press against the older tradition or against just war theory in general, I shall endeavour to rebut it.

First of all, however, I must address a terminological question: How best to refer to the tradition of just war thinking that runs from Augustine to Grotius? We could refer to it as 'premodern'. The problem there, however, is the connotation of obsolescence. The words 'modern' and 'premodern' are

---

6. Ibid., p. 189.
7. According to James Turner Johnson, Walzer took his cue from international law and relations, not the just war tradition (*The War to Oust Saddam Hussein. Just War and the New Face of Conflict* [Lanham, Maryland: Rowman & Littlefield, 2005], p. 33). Johnson finds this typical of contemporary philosophers—but also of Paul Ramsey and Roman Catholic thinking since at least 1983.

not just innocently descriptive, but insidiously evaluative. What is 'modern' purports to stand at the forefront of inexorable progress; so what is 'premodern' is, by definition, *passé*. To complain, therefore, that Rodin neglects 'premodern' just war thinking sounds odd to modernized minds; for why *should* he attend to what has been surpassed? Therefore, if we are to refuse modern smugness and show due respect to voices from the past, we must find another epithet.

The most obvious alternative is 'Christian'. The tradition of just war thinking that spans the 5th to the 17th centuries AD was developed within a predominantly Christian civilization, and operated within a Christian, sometimes theological intellectual framework. It is true that some think that this tradition became steadily less Christian, so that by the time it reached Grotius it was substantially 'secular'.[8] Rodin shares this view, writing of '[t]he great transformation of the law of war from theological code to secular international law' during the 15th, 16th, and 17th centuries.[9] However, formidable scholars of intellectual history dissent from this secularization thesis;[10] and so do I.

Take Grotius, for example. For sure, he was the one who famously wrote that natural right, stemming from a combination of natural human sociability and prudential judgement, 'would take place, though we should grant... that there is no God [*etiamsi daremus Deus non esse*], or that he takes no care of human affairs'.[11] Brian Tierney observes, however, that this 'was a rather common topos of late scholastic discourse'.[12] Grotius was merely giving expression to the idea, voiced at least as far back as Thomas Aquinas,

---

8. E.g. Frederick J. Russell: 'Hugo Grotius ushered in modern just war theory when he secularised the just war by removing medieval religious considerations from it' ('Just War', in *The Cambridge History of Medieval Philosophy*, vol. 2, ed. Robert Pasnau and Christina Van Dyke [Cambridge: Cambridge University Press, 2010], p. 605).

9. Rodin, *War and Self-Defense*, p. 169.

10. See, for eminent examples, Brian Tierney, Oliver O'Donovan, and Joan Lockwood O'Donovan: Brian Tierney, *The Idea of Natural Rights: Studies in Natural Rights, Natural Law, and Church Law, 1150–1625*, Emory Studies in Law and Religion (Grand Rapids: Eerdmans, 1997), pp. 317–24; Oliver O'Donovan and Joan Lockwood O'Donovan, eds, *From Irenaeus to Grotius: A Sourcebook in Christian Political Thought* (Grand Rapids: Eerdmans, 1999), esp. p. 787 ('Grotius, for all his embrace of the program of a humanist science, was a true heir of the theological tradition'); and Oliver O'Donovan, 'The Justice of Assignment and Subjective Rights in Grotius', in Oliver O'Donovan and Joan Lockwood O'Donovan, *Bonds of Imperfection: Christian Politics, Past and Present* (Grand Rapids: Eerdmans, 2004), pp. 172–4, 190–1.

11. Hugo Grotius, *The Rights of War and Peace*, 3 vols, ed. Richard Tuck (Indianapolis: Liberty Fund, 2005), 'The Preliminary Discourse', XI, p. 89.

12. Tierney, *Idea of Natural Right*, pp. 319–20.

that the principles of morality are rooted in human nature, and being natural are constant and accessible in principle to human reason.[13] Yet, in the very next section of 'The Preliminary Discourse' in his *De iure belli ac pacis*, Grotius proceeds to tell us that besides nature, there is another 'original of right', namely the free will of God.[14] This has made itself known in the moral laws articulated in the course of the sacred history that is recorded in the Old and New Testaments, and which finds its climax in the latter. While these 'divine' laws never contradict the principles of natural right,[15] they do serve to make them 'more clear and evident'[16] and they can enjoin 'a greater sanctity... than the meer [sic] law of nature'.[17] What is more, according to Grotius, God's role in human moral life is not confined to that of lawgiver. Immediately after his notorious *etiamsi daremus* clause, he tells us that 'God, as being our Creator, and to whom we owe our being, and all that we have, ought to be obeyed by us in all things without exception', and 'we have room to conclude that he is able to bestow, upon those that obey him, the greatest rewards, and those eternal', and that he is willing to do so.[18] That is to say, God's benevolence can and should inspire in us both gratitude and hope of ultimate fulfilment, and that these can and should motivate us to resist 'those impetuous passions, which, contrary to our own interest, and that of others, divert us from following the rules of reason and nature'.[19] The implication is clear: the principles and rules of natural right are not the sum of moral life, and religious faith and hope have an important role in aiding human reason in its struggle to be truly *rational* in the face of the pressures of 'exceeding unruly' passions.[20]

---

13. In so doing, Grotius was reacting strongly against late scholastic voluntarism, which held that natural right is determined by ad hoc commands of God. Accordingly, he makes a point of stating that the moral quality of acts is determined by their 'suitableness or unsuitableness to a reasonable nature' (*Rights of War and Peace*, Book I, chapter I.X.1, p. 151), that actions are '*in themselves* either obligatory or unlawful, and must, *consequently*, be understood to be either commanded or forbid by God himself' (ibid., I.I.X.2, pp. 151–2; my emphasis); that God's power does not extend to making what is intrinsically evil not so (ibid., I.I.X.5, 6, p. 155); and that once they exist, the being and essence of things—and the moral properties that follow from them—'depend not upon any other', and that '[t]herefore God suffers himself to be judged according to this rule' (ibid., I.I.X.5, p. 156).
14. Ibid., 'The Preliminary Discourse', XII, p. 90.
15. Ibid., 'The Preliminary Discourse', XLIX, p. 124; Book I.I.XVII, p. 175.
16. Ibid., 'The Preliminary Discourse', XIII, p. 91.
17. Ibid., 'The Preliminary Discourse', LI, p. 126.
18. Ibid., 'The Preliminary Discourse', XI, pp. 89–90.
19. Ibid., 'The Preliminary Discourse', XIII, pp. 91–2.
20. Ibid., 'The Preliminary Discourse', XIII, p. 92.

The point of this brief diversion into intellectual history has been to confirm the propriety of referring to the tradition of just war theory spanning Augustine and Grotius as 'Christian'. However, because Christian thinking about such matters has continued since, especially after the Second World War, we must add a further qualification and refer to the Augustine–Grotius stretch as '*early* Christian'.

II. The paradigm: defence of the self or defence against natural injustice?

The most basic flaw in Rodin's critique is its tendency to confuse the whole of just war theory with only the late modern part. While showing some awareness of early Christian thinking, his critical focus lies mainly on modern legal-positivist and Walzerian versions. To be fair, he has some good, rhetorically tactical reasons for doing this: namely, international law has 'a certain privileged status possessed by no philosophical treatise, in that it represents a form of consensus among the world's states', and 'it is increasingly international law which furnishes the context for debate amongst policy-makers on the justice of war and military action'.[21] Nevertheless, such a reading of just war theory is problematic. First, international law is considerably political, and international institutions fall a long way short of their impartial ideal. The laws governing war are the product of political negotiation and compromise, and so they incorporate pragmatic considerations as well as—and sometimes to the detriment of—moral ones. Thus a nation-state has a right to use armed force to repel aggression, regardless of its own moral character and that of its aggressor. Moreover, the laws of war make optimal sense in the context of the effective operation of an ideal set of international institutions—which we do not have. Thus it would make sense to cede authorization of military intervention in enforcement of international law to the United Nations Security Council (UNSC) if there were universal agreement about how the law should be interpreted, and if the Council could be relied upon to interpret it impartially. Since neither of those conditions obtains, however, we cannot rely simply on the laws of war, but have to appeal beyond them to just war morality. While Rodin is candid

21. Rodin, *War and Self-Defense*, p. 104.

about the politically compromised nature of international law and the imperfection of international institutions,[22] and while he is aware of early Christian tradition, he nevertheless proceeds as if there were no independent, moral tradition of thinking about just war—or at least none worth appealing to. The reason for this oversight is that he is intent, not upon rescuing just war thinking, but upon burying it.

Second, Rodin tells us that national defence 'is central to modern international law'[23] and is 'one of the lynchpins' of international law's intellectual progenitor, the just war theory.[24] Neither of these assertions is true. International law recognizes as just *two* forms of the use of armed force—in national defence against attack *and* as authorized by the UNSC to enforce its Resolutions. Rodin does not explain why he thinks that the first is more central than the second. More importantly, throughout its first millennium and beyond, Christian just war thinking has taken as the paradigm of just military action the defence of the innocent neighbour against injustice. Accordingly, it approves the state's self-defence only insofar as it comprises the defence of the common good against unjust aggression. In other words, the Christian understanding of just national defence is moral, and subjects its justification to moral conditions.

Since this last point is fundamentally important to my argument, it warrants extensive demonstration. The practical norm that immediately generates Christian just war thinking is Jesus' command that we should love our

---

22. Ibid., pp. x–xi.   23. Ibid., p.1.

24. Ibid., p. 2. Rodin might have been misled here by Jonathan Barnes. Barnes's essay, 'The Just War' (in *The Cambridge History of Later Medieval Philosophy*, ed. Norman Kretzman, Anthony Kenny, Jan Pinborg, Eleonore Stump [Cambridge: Cambridge University Press, 1982]), is one of the few histories of the medieval just war tradition that Rodin cites in his bibliography. Barnes writes that medieval theorists grounded the right to national self-defence 'on the domestic analogy: as a private person may violently defend himself against an assailant, so a state may repel an invader by force of arms' (p. 780). He then refers us to a footnote, which contains this quotation from Aquinas, *Summa Theologiae*, 2a 2ae, q. 40, a.1, resp.:'gladio bellico ad eos [i.e. principes] pertinet rempublicam tueri ab exterioribus hostibus' ('so they lawfully use the sword of war to protect the commonwealth from foreign attacks' [Blackfriars edition, p. 83]). However, Barnes omits to re-present the passage immediately preceding this, where Aquinas quotes St Paul, Romans 13:4:'He beareth not the sword in vain for he is God's minister, an avenger to execute wrath upon him that doth evil' (ibid.). The 'he' to whom St Paul refers is not a 'private person': the analogy is with police action, not domestic self-defence.

Explicit quotations of Aquinas's *Summa Theologiae* in Latin or English are taken from the Blackfriars edition (ed. Thomas Gilby [London: Blackfriars with Eyre & Spottiswoode, 1964–81]). While my own English paraphrasing usually follows this edition, it sometimes takes its cue directly from the Latin original.

neighbours, whom he then specifies as including our enemies.[25] Sometimes Augustine explicitly cites Jesus' love command when justifying war. He does so in his letter, *Ad Bonifacem* (189), before proceeding shortly afterwards to discuss the propriety of a Christian serving as a soldier[26] and to prescribe peace as the proper end of a just war;[27] and he does it again in *Ad Bonifacem* (220), when enjoining 'single-minded love' toward the enemy, even while treating them with 'an unpleasant severity'.[28] But even when he makes no overt reference to the dominical injunction, he affirms it implicitly by consistently describing just war as a benevolent response to injustice, which intends just peace. So in his letter, *Ad Marcellinum* (138), after initially arguing that Christians should eschew the passion for revenge and intend to persuade the wrongdoer to repent and embrace peace,[29] he then articulates what this implies: namely, that just war is waged out of a benevolent concern for the interests of the unjust enemy.[30] And in the *City of God*, he defines just war as a necessary response to injustice,[31] which intends just peace.[32]

---

25. E.g. Matthew 5:43–4, 19:19b; Mark 12:31a; Luke 6:27–8, 6:35, 10:27. Lest analytical philosophers infer from this the confirmation of their usual prejudice that religious ethics invariably depend on an arbitrary divine command, let me hasten to point out that Jesus' practical norm has a eudaimonist hinterland. (Eudaimonism holds that moral obligations and duties find their ultimate rationale in the service of human well-being or, to use Aristotle's word, *eudaimonia*.) We should love our neighbours, Jesus tells us, because it is good for us to do so—because it profits us (Matthew 16:24–6). The relevant profit, however, is not extrinsic but intrinsic, and its currency is not money but virtue. It is good that we should grow in the virtues of benevolence and justice; it belongs to our own good or flourishing that we should become benevolent and just. And that will remain true, even if it should cost us our very lives; for God will recover the righteous (or, better, the faithful) from death (Matthew 16:27–8).
26. Augustine, *Political Writings*, p. 215, s.2; p. 216, s.4.
27. Ibid., p. 217, s.6.
28. Ibid., p. 222, s.8.
29. Ibid., p. 35, s.9, p. 36, s.11.
30. Ibid., p. 38, s.14.
31. Augustine, *City of God*, Book XIX.7, p. 862.
32. Ibid., XIX.12, p. 866. With reference to *On the Free Choice of the Will*, Robert Holmes has argued against Paul Ramsey and James Turner Johnson that Augustine did not justify publicly authorized killing in defence of innocent third parties (*On War and Morality*, pp. 118–27, 137–8). Whatever he meant to say in this particular treatise, which Holmes admits is 'an early discussion' (ibid., p. 120), Augustine makes clear in the *City of God* that it is the injustice of the enemy that creates a duty to wage war against him (XIX.7, p. 862). It is natural to infer from this that just war is basically about vindicating those neighbours who are the victims of injustice. It is true that Augustine's attention is largely focused on arguing that the use of violent force can be an expression of love for the unjust enemy neighbour, but that is because such a case is less obvious and harder to sustain. It is surely bizarre to suppose that he affirmed resort to war out of love for the hostile neighbour, while denying it out of love for the innocent one.

This same definition is the one that, just over eight centuries later, Aquinas endorsed.[33]

Initially the justification of the use of force in terms of the obligation of neighbour love told *against* the justification of self-defence. In his early work, *On Free Choice of the Will*, Augustine regards temporal life as a perishable good that, compared with the eternal good of union with God, should be despised.[34] Consequently he thinks that an individual's act of self-defence must be motivated by inordinate desire or lust.[35] In contrast, the soldier as an agent of the law, acting in defence of the innocent and to keep the peace, 'can easily avoid lust in performing his duty'.[36] Ten years later in his letter, *Ad Publicolam* (47), Augustine clarifies his position, when he writes that self-defence is permissible, but not for one's own sake, only for others' or for the state's.[37] In other words, one may defend oneself, provided that the end is public, not private.

Aquinas both agrees and disagrees with Augustine. He agrees that killing by public authorities 'charged with the care of the whole community' is straightforwardly legitimate.[38] However, he disagrees in holding that 'it is natural for anything to want to preserve itself in being as far as it can', that 'a man is under a greater obligation to care for his own life than for another's', and therefore that a private person may kill another if in so doing he intends to save his own life rather than to kill his assailant.[39] Nonetheless, Aquinas does not seek to justify belligerency by analogy with individual self-defence (as does Rodin's 'just war theory'). Rather, following St Paul's Epistle to the Romans 13:3–4, he justifies it by analogy with the police action of civil authorities in defending the vulnerable by punishing criminals: 'And just as they use the sword in lawful defence against domestic disturbance when

---

Moreover, there is clear evidence that he did not. In his letter *Ad Bonifacem* (189) Augustine writes that if one must keep faith with an enemy against whom one wages war, '[h]ow much more so with a friend, *for whose sake* one is fighting!' (*Political Writings*, p. 217, s.6. The emphasis is mine).

33. Aquinas, *Summa Theologiae*, 2a 2ae, q. 40, a.1, pp. 81–93.
34. Augustine, *On Free Choice of the Will*, in *Augustine: Earlier Writings*, ed. and trans. J.H.S. Burleigh, Library of Christian Classics (Philadelphia: Westminster Press, 1953), Book I.5.11, 13, pp. 118, 119–20.
35. Ibid., I.5.11, p. 118.
36. Ibid., I.5.12, p. 118.
37. Augustine, *Letters*, Vol. I (1–82), trans. Wilfrid Parsons, the Fathers of the Church, vol. 12 (Washington, DC: Catholic University of America Press, 1951), p. 230.
38. Aquinas, *Summa Theologiae*, 2a 2ae, q. 64, a.3, resp., p. 27.
39. Ibid., a.7, resp., p. 43. Since our bodily nature is created by God, it deserves our love (ibid., 2a 2ae, q. 25, a.5, resp., pp. 94–5).

they punish criminals . . . so they lawfully use the sword of war to protect the commonwealth from foreign attacks. Thus it is said to those in authority, "Rescue the weak and the needy, save them from the clutches of the wicked" ' [Psalm 81, v.4].[40]

Over three hundred years later, the reasoning of Francisco de Vitoria, Francisco de Suárez, and Hugo Grotius remains essentially the same. Thus Vitoria tells us that the prince bears the sword 'for the defence of the state', which, he implies, amounts to the defence of the people against aggressors.[41] That the relevant aggressors are not mere aggressors, but unjust ones, he also implies by specifying the state's self-defence as an act of punishment for an injury suffered.[42] Suárez writes similarly:

> just as within a state some lawful power to punish crimes is necessary to the preservation of domestic peace; so in the world as a whole, there must exist, in order that the various states may dwell in concord, some power for the punishment of injuries inflicted by one state upon another; and this power is not to be found in any superior, for we assume that these states have no commonly acknowledged superior; therefore, the power in question must reside in the sovereign prince of the injured state, to whom, by reason of that injury, the opposing prince is made subject.[43]

Grotius's route is by far the most elaborate, but he arrives at the same destination. Contradicting cynical 'realists' and echoing Aquinas, Grotius denies that nature inclines human beings simply to seek their own private advantage, and that the law is simply instituted for the sake of self-interest.[44] 'Man is indeed an animal,' he writes, 'but one of a very high order, and that excels all the other species of animals much more than they differ from one another . . . Now amongst things peculiar to man, is his desire of society';[45]

---

40. Ibid., q. 40, a.1, resp., p. 83.
41. Francisco de Vitoria, 'De Bello: On St Thomas Aquinas, *Summa Theologiae*, 2a 2ae, Question 40', trans. Gwladys L. Williams, in James Brown Scott, *The Spanish Origin of International Law: Francisco de Vitoria and his Law of Nations*, Appendix F (Oxford: Clarendon Press, 1934), Art. I.2, p. cxvi.
42. Vitoria, 'De Bello', I.3, p. cxvii; 'On the Law of War', in Vitoria, *Political Writings*, ed. Anthony Pagden and Jeremy Lawrance, Cambridge Texts in the History of Political Thought (Cambridge: Cambridge University Press, 1991), Question I, Art. 2.2, p. 300.
43. Francisco de Suárez, 'On Charity: Disputation XIII', *A Work on the Three Theological Virtues, Faith, Hope, and Charity* (1621) in Francisco Suárez, S.J., *Selections from Three Works*, 2 vols, Vol. II: 'The Translation', ed. Gwladys L. Williams et al., The Classics of International Law (Oxford: Clarendon Press, 1944), Section IV.5, p. 818.
44. Grotius, *The Rights of War and Peace*, 'The Preliminary Discourse', V, VI, p. 79.
45. Ibid., 'The Preliminary Discourse', VI, p. 79.

and '[t]his sociability... or this care of maintaining society... is the fountain of right, properly so called'.[46] Accordingly, while the animal instinct for self-preservation finds 'nothing repugnant to war',[47] 'right reason, and the nature of society' prohibit violence that is 'repugnant to society, that is, which invades another's right'.[48] Further, if we bring to bear the light of the Evangelical law (that is, the law of the Christian Gospel), 'we are to prefer the good of the innocent to that of the guilty, and a public good before a private one... Now out of love to the innocent, arise capital punishments and pious wars.'[49] Therefore, Grotius concludes, citing Augustine, '[t]here is no other reasonable cause of making war, but an injury received';[50] and all just wars 'avenge' injuries in the sense of stopping and repairing them.[51]

Further, Grotius is quite clear that the positive law of nations is one thing, and the rules of morality another. According to the former, it is lawful for one enemy to hurt another, be he just or unjust;[52] the right of licence to kill reaches beyond those who are combatants to all who reside in the enemy's territories,[53] including infants, women,[54] and prisoners;[55] and prisoners of war are slaves,[56] to whom anything may be done with impunity, unless restrained by civil law.[57] However, 'many things are said to be of right and lawful, because they escape punishment, and partly because courts of justice have given them their authority, tho' they are contrary to the rules, either of justice properly so called, or of other vertues [sic]'.[58] Seneca rightly 'puts a difference between *ius* and *iustitia*, right and justice. He means by right, that which is actionable in courts of judicature.' What is lawful 'in itself' is distinct

---

46. Ibid., 'The Preliminary Discourse', VIII, pp. 85–6. Grotius does not deny that profit or advantage is 'annexed' to the law of nature, 'to the end that we might more eagerly affect society' (ibid., XVII, pp. 93–4). Nevertheless, he holds that 'human nature itself, which, though even the necessity of our circumstances should not require it, would of itself create in us a mutual desire of society (ibid., XVII. p. 93). The 'most judicious philosophers' are correct, he tells us, to claim that friendship is not only founded on indigence, 'for it is evident we are prompted to it by natural inclination' (ibid., II.I.IX.3, p. 405).
47. Ibid., I.II.3, pp. 182–3.
48. Ibid., I.II.3, p. 184.
49. Ibid., I.II.VIII.3, p. 215.
50. Ibid., II.I.I.4, p. 393.
51. Ibid., II.I.II.2, p. 396.
52. Ibid., III.IV.III, p. 1275.
53. Ibid., III.IV.VI, p. 1280.
54. Ibid., III.IV.IX.1, p. 1283.
55. Ibid., III.IV.X.1, p. 1284.
56. Ibid., III.VII.I.2, pp. 1360–1.
57. Ibid., III.VII.III.1, p. 1362.
58. Ibid., III.X.I.1, p. 1411.

from what is only lawful 'externally'.[59] So, for example, there is 'a vast difference between what may be done to a slave by the law of nations, and
what by natural right'.[60] 'Internal justice'—'equity and humanity'—require
us to moderate our right over prisoners, and to discriminate between innocent and guilty.[61]

In sum, just war theory in its early Christian form took its bearings primarily from morality, natural and revealed, and not from positive law. Its
paradigm was the defence of the innocent against injustice, not the defence
of the (national) self simply. Consequently it did not consider state sovereignty to be a morality-free zone. When it discussed the state's self-defence,
it assumed *unjust* aggression. And when (as we shall see in Chapter Six) it
sanctioned humanitarian intervention, it implied that the state's right to
resist invasion is morally conditional.

That was the religious past. But what about the secular present? Surely in
a modern, 'globalized' world, where the full plurality of moral understandings is laid out in plain view, belief in a single, universal morality that transcends individuals and states and cultures, and which is somehow given in
the nature of things, is untenable? And while morality that is alleged to be
divinely revealed may hold religious believers in the blinding glare of its
authoritarian headlights, surely it has no claim on the attention of others?

To the first rhetorical question, I would respond by saying that belief in
a single, universal moral reality is entirely compatible with the acknowledgement of moral plurality. It is perfectly consistent to affirm universal
moral principles, while acknowledging that there is a variety of ways in
which these may be specified, that various circumstances require various
instantiations, and that interpretations of them vary according to the wisdom and virtue of the interpreter. Unity at a high, generic level is quite
consistent with plurality at lower, specific and concrete levels.[62]

Further, the concept of natural moral law should not be identified with
the particular version expressed in the Roman Catholic church's magisterial
prohibition of contraception and homosexual practice. There is a variety of
concepts of natural law, not all of which concur with the church's official

59. Ibid., III.X.I.3, p. 1414.
60. Ibid., III.XIV.II.3, p. 1483.
61. Ibid., III.XIV.I.1,2, p. 1481.
62. Aquinas himself says this (*Summa Theologiae*, 1a 2ae, q. 94, aa.4, 5, pp. 86–95; q. 95, a.2, pp. 102–7).
    For a modern discussion, see Morris Ginsberg, 'On the Diversity of Morals', in *On the Diversity
    of Morals* (London: Mercury, 1962), pp. 97–129.

doctrine. And belief in natural moral law is not, and has not been, confined to Roman Catholics. Grotius, for example, was an Arminian Calvinist.

Further still, in its broadest sense, 'natural law' thinking means the same as ontological 'moral realism'. It refers to a body of moral principles that are given in the nature of reality and that constitute the universal, necessary, and objective ground and framework of all subjective moral thinking. In this broad sense, natural law thinking in recent years has been enjoying a revival, not only in Christian theological circles but also in moral philosophical ones. After two generations of scepticism and subjectivism, moral realism is now resurgent in philosophy. One major symptom of this is Derek Parfit's recent affirmation of moral truth and objective moral value in his magisterial *On What Matters*.[63] Another symptom, not so major but more germane to the argument of this chapter, is that David Rodin himself can be found to affirm 'objective, trans-cultural goods', even if only the liberal ones of freedom, autonomy, and self-determination.[64]

Finally, if there is no natural moral law or basic moral reality, then the now widely popular rhetoric of universal human rights is just that: rhetoric.

To the second question about revealed morality, my briefer response is that there is no moral view from nowhere. Human beings cannot help but grasp universal moral reality in terms of their own particular intellectual contexts. In that sense, all ethical views are historical; all of them belong to one tradition or another. Human beings are bound to discern the universal through the particular, and some particular discernments are better (more reasonable, more comprehensive, more beautiful) than others. Therefore, the fact that a morality is alleged to be divinely revealed to a particular religious tradition is no good reason for dismissing it without a hearing. Moral wisdom is only ever to be found in particular viewpoints, and it might lie in this one too. Whether or not it actually does, we can only ever find out by looking and seeing.

III. Is just war punitive?

Early Christian just war theory regarded the use of coercion, sometimes lethal, as justified if it is necessary to protect the innocent from injustice.

---

63. Derek Parfit, *On What Matters*, 2 vols (Oxford: Oxford University Press, 2011).
64. Rodin, *War and Self-Defense*, p. 155.

Note that the posture is basically reactive and defensive, not beneficent—or, more exactly, it is defensive before it is beneficent. It might be, for example, that the natives of the 16th-century Caribbean would have been better off with the Christian religion, and that the inhabitants of 19th-century China would have benefited from the free trade of opium. Nevertheless, the conferring of such benefits could not have amounted to a sufficient just cause for waging war on them (as did the Spanish and British, respectively). Why not? One reason is that some benefits can only be enjoyed when held sincerely, and sincerity cannot be coerced. Another is that no one is likely to appreciate a benefit that has been forced on them at gunpoint and over the corpses of their kith and kin.

Note also that the hostile reaction is not simply defensive, but defensive *against injustice*. For this reason it is broadly 'punitive', punishing the wrongdoer by forcing him to stop, by deterring him from resuming, and ideally by provoking him to think again and change his aggressive ways forever. The idea that war is basically a form of punishment was present right at the beginning of Christian thinking about the justified use of force, and it remained influential thereafter. Writing in *Contra Faustum Manichaeum*, Augustine said that 'it is generally to punish these things [love of violence, revengeful cruelty, fierce and implacable enmity, wild resistance, and the lust of power], when force is required to inflict the punishment, that...good men undertake wars'.[65] Eight hundred years later Aquinas followed suit when he justified war by analogy with the use of force by civil authorities to 'punish criminals'.[66]

Before Aquinas, however, more refined views of the relationship between war and punishment had been developed. In the previous century, for example, Gratian had analysed war into different kinds. Although he described just war in general terms as avenging injustice,[67] he also specified it according to its various ends: resisting injury by repelling attack, recovering stolen property, and inflicting vengeance for the sake of correction.[68] Only to this

65. Augustine, *Reply to Faustus the Manichaean*, trans. R. Stothert, in *A Select Library of the Nicene and Post-Nicene Fathers of the Christian Church*, ed. Philip Schaff, Vol. IV (Grand Rapids: Eerdmans, 1956), Book 22, s.74, p. 301.
66. Aquinas, *Summa Theologiae*, 2a 2ae, q. 40, a.1, resp., p. 83.
67. Gratian, *Decretum*, in Gregory M. Reichberg, Henrik Syse, and Endre Begby, eds, *The Ethics of War: Classic and Contemporary Readings* (Malden, MA: Blackwell, 2006), Part II, causa 23, question II, canon 3, p. 113.
68. Ibid., question I, canon 1, p. 109, canon 4, p. 112; question II, canon 1, p. 113; question IV, canon 51, p. 115.

last species did he attach the title 'punishment', which he makes conditional upon public authorization.[69]

In the early 16th century the seminal Cajetan also reserved the word 'punitive' to denote war in its offensive, invasive mode, where it pursues 'vindicative justice' beyond mere satisfaction, where it therefore requires public authorization, and where the just warrior assumes the role of a judge in criminal proceedings.[70]

Vitoria, too, distinguished defensive war, which defends or reclaims property, from offensive war, which seeks vengeance in order to deter future aggression.[71] However, he also implied that this conceptual distinction of modes and ends does not amount to an actual, practical separation. So he described offensive war as '*not only* war in which property is defended or reclaimed, *but also* war in which vengeance for an injury is sought'; and he writes that 'even defensive war could not conveniently be waged unless there were also vengeance inflicted on the enemy for the injury they have done, or tried to do. Otherwise, without the fear of punishment to deter them from injustice, the enemy would simply grow more bold about invading a second time.'[72]

Later in the 16th century Suárez rolled out the standard Thomist analogy between the punishment of crime within a state and the prosecution of war by one state against another (which we quoted in the previous section). He followed Cajetan and Vitoria in distinguishing between defensive and offensive war, and doing so in terms of public authorization—the latter requiring it, the former not.[73] But he deviated in *not* telling the two modes of war apart in terms of their ends, but rather in terms of the maturity of the injustice to which they are responding. So he described offensive war as necessary for a state to ward off acts of injustice and hold its enemies in check[74]—which corresponds more to the defensive than the punitive conception of his predecessors; and he argued instead that war is defensive when injustice is in progress, but offensive when injustice is complete.[75]

69. Ibid., question I, canon 1 (p. 109); question IV, canon 51, p. 115.
70. Cajetan, *Commentary on Summa Theologiae, 2a 2ae, q. 40, a.1*, in Reichberg, *The Ethics of War*, pp. 242, 247, 248.
71. Vitoria, 'On the Law of War', 1.1, 2, pp. 298, 300.
72. Ibid., 1.1, p. 297–8. My emphasis.
73. Suárez, 'On Charity: Disputation XIII', Section I.4, pp. 802–3.
74. Ibid., I.5, pp. 803–4.
75. Ibid., I.6, pp. 804.

Suárez's contemporary, Luis de Molina, self-consciously qualified the line of thinking that ran from Augustine through Aquinas to Vitoria by introducing a further distinction, which might actually correspond to different instances of war. Sometimes the injustice to which just war responds is culpable, but sometimes, where the wrongdoer is invincibly or unavoidably ignorant of the wrong he is doing, it is merely material.[76] Accordingly, offensive war can take two different forms according to two different ends. First, it can aim to avenge an injury against a guilty party, whether or not at the same time it intends to recover stolen property and claim damages. But, second, it can aim simply to recover property that is wrongfully held in invincible, non-culpable ignorance.[77] Here the implication would seem to be that, in this last case, war is not punitive at all.

In the following century, Grotius refined the specification of war further by ranking punishment as but one of four just causes of war, the others being defence, the recovery of property, and the exaction of debt.[78] On the other hand, he also cited Augustine in defining all just cause for war as the suffering of injury,[79] devoted more of his treatise on *The Rights of War and Peace* to a discussion of punishment than to any other topic,[80] and wrote that 'the desire of inflicting punishment is often the occasion of war… And this reason of war is generally joined with that of reparation of damage, since the same fact is generally both vitious [sic] in itself, and injurious to others.'[81] In other words, just war usually intends several ends at once, and punishment is often among them.

The early Christian tradition, then, displays quite some variety in its view of the punitive nature of just war. Many of its later representatives regard its offensive phase as specifically punitive, when it intends, not (only) defence or recovery, but vindication or correction (of the guilty) or deterrence. Molina uniquely implies that some war, whose just cause is material but non-culpable, should not be punitive at all. Others take it for granted that just war will usually involve a specifically punitive element, which will not be separable from defence and reparation. However, all of the major repre-

76. Luis de Molina, *De iustitia et iure*, Tract II, Disputation 102.2, in Reichberg, *The Ethics of War*, pp. 334–5; 102.4, p. 336.
77. Ibid., 102.4, 5, p. 336.
78. Grotius, *The Rights of War and Peace* II.I.II.2, p. 395.
79. Ibid., II.I.I.4, p. 393.
80. Grotius's discussion of punishment runs over two chapters (ibid., II.XX, XXI), comprising seventy-one sections and, in the Liberty Fund edition, covering over 150 pages.
81. Ibid., II.XX.XXXVIII, p. 1018.

sentatives of early Christian tradition agree that just war is punitive in the broad sense of being a hostile response—whether defensive or offensive—not merely to damage, but to injustice.[82]

David Rodin is aware of this early tradition of viewing just war as punitive, but he rejects it. He takes John Locke's social contract rationale as typical of the tradition. According to this, while in the state of nature each person has the 'natural executive right' to punish breaches of the natural law, the problems arising from each person being judge in his own case furnish reasons for entering into a commonwealth.[83] However, insofar as the sovereign and his citizens have entered into no social contract with the sovereigns and citizens of foreign states, they retain the rights of nature with respect to them, including that of punishing breaches of natural law.[84] To this Rodin responds that in the state of nature neither individuals nor states may punish each other. When one person claims he has been wronged by another and inflicts harm on him, he tells us, 'we are disinclined to call this punishment precisely because we feel that he would not have the authority to punish'.[85] By 'authority' here Rodin means a special kind of inequality or superiority in the agent of punishment, which consists of neutrality or impartiality—a single-minded devotion to 'reasons of justice itself'—and which therefore elicits the consensual submission of disputants. Although he concedes that 'it is not inconceivable' that interested parties will act impartially, he considers that 'it is far from likely and cannot be relied upon. More importantly, their involvement in the dispute alters the character of their action, giving it the quality of revenge or reprisal rather than punishment.'[86]

82. This is a view that contemporary Christian just war theorists have resumed. Jean Bethke Elshtain, for example, writes that '[t]he presupposition of just war thinking is that war can sometimes be an instrument of justice . . . by using force to stop wrongdoing and to punish wrongdoers' (*Just War against Terror: The Burden of American Power in a Violent World* [New York: Basic Books, 2003], pp. 50, 52). And although Oliver O'Donovan differentiates punishment from defence and reparation, he affirms all three as necessary elements of justified armed force: 'while these forms of judgement can be distinguished, they cannot be separated. Any concrete act of armed force will depend in some measure upon each of the three, and will combine defensive, reparative, and punitive objectives' (*The Just War Revisited*, p. 53).

83. Rodin, *War and Self-Defense*, pp. 174–5.

84. John Locke, *Two Treatises of Government*, Book II, chapter VII, paras 90, 91; cited in Rodin, *War and Self-Defense*, pp. 174–5.

85. Rodin, *War and Self-Defense*, p. 176.

86. Ibid., pp. 176–7.

An alternative conception of punishment that Rodin considers is that to which parents are supposed to have a right over children. Parents' authority stems from their natural superiority in knowledge, wisdom, power; their natural love toward their child; and the reciprocity between their duty of protection and the child's duty of obedience. However, in Rodin's eyes,

> [t]he parents' principal responsibility is not to ensure that their administration of punishment is impartial and just, but rather that it is beneficial to the overall welfare and development of the child; impartiality enters only as an instrumental value to this broader end. For this reason the notion of punishment explicated by the parental model should perhaps not be seen as part of an account of *justice* at all.[87]

Partly for this reason, but mainly because a fundamental assumption of international law and just war theory is the equality of sovereign states, the parental model cannot explain the right of one state to punish another.[88]

If Christian just war theory—and, indeed, if *just* war theory of any kind—is to maintain a grip on plausibility, then Rodin's objections here must be dismantled. I believe that they can be. First of all, however, we should concede what ought to be conceded, namely that the parental model of punishment should be laid aside. This is not because, as Rodin supposes, it has nothing to do with justice. Children lie, steal, and physically abuse their peers, and when a child does so, he deserves to be contradicted, and to have that contradiction impressed upon him by proportionate punishment. That is, he deserves retributive punishment—*but not for its own sake.* He deserves it in order to achieve the various benefits of protecting, vindicating, and reassuring his innocent peers, as well as of encouraging him to repent and reform. Retributive punishment and beneficence should not be seen as alternatives. All forms of criminal justice should aim, as far as possible, to benefit the wrongdoer—to punish with a sort of *kind* harshness, as Augustine put it. No, the reason why we should put aside the parental model of punishment is not that it is retributive, but that it does not generally suit relations between states, since states do not usually relate to one another as superior to inferior in a structured hierarchy. (The obvious exception to this rule would be the relationship between a 'mother' country and her colonies in a formal empire.)

---

87. Ibid., p. 178. The emphasis is Rodin's.
88. Ibid., pp. 178–79.

What we need is a fraternal model of punishment, not a paternal one; and it is this that Christian just war theory gives us. While Rodin is correct to say that just war theory (along with international law) regards all nations as equals, he is wrong to imply that every version of the theory views all nations as moral equivalents. Christian just war theory does not follow Hobbes in regarding individuals basically as lone wolves fighting for survival in original anarchy, nor in regarding social contracts as the only source of moral obligation. On the contrary, it holds that individuals are originally sociable, originally subject to the natural law, and originally their brother's keeper. Therefore equals may and should judge one another in the exercise of fraternal correction. Rodin objects to this, claiming that no private individual has the authority to judge another, since as an interested party he lacks due neutrality and impartiality. Here I think him mistaken. In prescribing 'neutrality' and 'impartiality' as the qualities requisite for the moral authority to punish, he makes it a contradiction in terms to claim that an interested party may punish; for by definition such a party cannot be *neutral*. If, however, we were to prescribe a different, less typically liberal, more traditional set of virtues—fairness, charity, self-control, and prudence—then the unthinkable becomes thinkable again. We *can* imagine a victim so controlling her resentment as to be fair, charitable, and prudent in punishing her oppressor. She might not be 'neutral', but she could be 'impartial' in the sense of 'fair'. That is not 'far from likely'—as is shown by reflection on human experience in general, and on the scrupulousness of victors' justice at Nuremberg in 1946 in particular. Therefore Rodin's claim that the involvement of an interested party necessarily changes an act of punishment into one of vengeance simply is not true.[89] For sure, there is no guarantee that

---

89. It is true that, when early Christian theorists write about punishment, they often use the language of vengeance. Yet, at the same time, they often talk about the use of just force as an expression of love for one's enemies. Thus Augustine in his letter, *ad Marcellinum*: 'For people are often to be helped, against their will, by being punished with a sort of kind harshness' (*Political Writings*, p. 38, s.14); and wars should be waged 'in a spirit of benevolence' (ibid.). Thus also Suárez: 'war is not opposed to the love of one's enemies; for whoever wages war honourably hates, not individuals, but the actions which he justly punishes' ('On Charity: Disputation XIII', I.3, p. 802). What this implies is that insofar as 'vengeance' means measured aggressiveness, it is permissible; but insofar as it means vindictiveness, it is forbidden. Grotius makes this clear, sometimes by implicitly qualifying the meaning of 'vengeance', but more often by repudiating intemperate vengeance altogether. So on the one hand, he tells us that, where Augustine says that just wars revenge injuries, 'he took the word revenge in a general sense, which implies all removal, cessation, abolition, and reparation of injuries' (*Rights of War and Peace* II.I.II.2, p. 396); and that 'the design of an avenger in punishing, ought not to terminate in the sufferings of the criminal' (ibid., II.XX.IV.3, p. 958). However, on the other hand, he writes that the desire for revenge 'is so void of reason in itself, that it often mistakes its object, and is hurried on with

self-control, etc. will govern the use of punishment by one individual against another, and it follows that its virtue cannot be presumed. But in what sphere of human affairs *can* it be presumed? Even publicly appointed judges can be imprudent, unfair, vindictive, and corrupt. *Pace* the starry-eyed children of the Enlightenment, social institutions cannot be made so structurally and procedurally perfect as to relieve their human inhabitants of the responsibility to grow and exercise virtue.

Of course, Rodin is quite correct to hold that the justice of punishment is generally safer in the hands of public judges bound by public law and judicial procedures. But he is wrong to imply that just punishment cannot occur outside courts. Grotius tells a subtle story here. According to the natural law, it is not absolutely necessary that punishment be carried out by a superior, 'unless by superior we mean him who is innocent':[90] 'It is lawful for any one who is judicious and prudent, and not guilty of the same, or of like a fault, himself, to inflict punishment.'[91] However, in the case of corporal punishment, reason and human law have reserved it to 'our nearest relations only, by whom we are most tenderly loved'.[92] Further, 'because we are apt to be partial in our own cases or of those that belong to us, and to be hurried on too far by passion, therefore as soon as many families came and lived together in the same place, that liberty which nature indulged them in of vindicating every man his own quarrel, was then taken away, and judges appointed to determine all controversies between man and man'.[93] Nonetheless 'the antient [sic] liberty, which the law of nature at first gave us, remains still in force where there are no courts of justice', or when they malfunction—for example, 'when complaint having been made to the judge, he does not render justice in a certain time'.[94] In the absence of well-functioning courts, fraternal punishment—and war as a form of it—might be justified.

violence, even against those that have done us no harm' (ibid., II.XX.V.1, p. 959); that 'revenge is condemned' alike by Christian teachers and philosophers (ibid., II.XX.V.2, p. 960); and that '[i]t is...contrary to nature, for one man to be pleased and satisfied with the pain and trouble he brings upon another, barely as it is pain or trouble' (ibid., II.XX.V.3, p. 960).

90. Ibid., II.XX.III.1, p. 955.
91. Ibid., II.XX.VII.2, pp. 963–4. It is notable that Grotius refers the reader here to Aquinas's *Summa Theologiae*, IaIIae, q. 33, whose topic is 'fraternal correction'.
92. Grotius, *The Rights of War and Peace*, II.XX.VII.2, p. 964.
93. Ibid., II.XX.VIII.4, p. 968.
94. Ibid., II.XX.VIII.5, p. 970; see also II.XX.IX.5, p. 975: 'even in this punishment [for the satisfaction of the offended party]...there remain some footsteps of the antient [sic] right in those places, and among those persons, who are not subject to any established courts of judicature; and even among those too who are so subject, in some particular cases'.

David Rodin's objections to a punitive conception of just war can be met; but Rodin's are not the only objections. Other critics accuse it of fostering moral self-righteousness and loosening the reins of war.[95] Clearly, to think of war in terms of punishment is to think of it in terms of justice and so to characterize it as a *moral* enterprise. As we shall see, this moralized conception of war does encourage intervention and therefore conflict, where amoral *Realpolitiker* decry the naïve, messianic moralism that would disturb the peace. But their own distinction between war and peace is not lacking naïvete of it own. The fact that the West turned its back on Rwanda in 1994 meant that we spared ourselves war and left the Hutus in peace—to slaughter the Tutsis. And the fact that Europe spared itself war in Bosnia until August 1995 left Ratko Mladić at peace to supervise the July massacre at Srebrenica. Less conflict was good for us, of course, but not so good for those whom we declined to defend. If peace were always simple, then war could never be preferable. But peace is seldom simple.

It is true that those who make moral judgements against others risk becoming 'judgemental'. They risk buying into a Manichaean vision of things where the basically good (the judges) battle against the basically bad (the judged), and where the bad, being basically so, deserve to be fought without restraint. Just wars do stand in danger of becoming holy wars. Nevertheless, just wars need not become holy wars where divine sanction bars no holds; and if they remain faithful to the logic of Christian just war thinking, they will not. As a Christian the just warrior cannot stand to the unjust perpetrator as clean to unclean, righteous to unrighteous, good to evil. He can only stand as one sinful creature to another. Even the enemy partakes of an equal dignity that deserves respect. According to the Christian view, therefore, cleansing the world of wickedness cannot be an aim of just war, since wickedness lies within as well as without, *here* as well as *there*. Just war is only ever a police action, never a crusade—always proximate, never ultimate.

Some critics would draw a strict distinction between the police or humanitarian action of stopping crime and the judicial one of punishing it,

---

95. See, e.g. Ian Clark, *Waging War: A Philosophical Introduction* (Oxford: Clarendon Press, 1988), p. 37; Russell, 'Just War', p. 596; Anthony F. Lang, 'Punitive Intervention: Enforcing Justice or Generating Conflict?', in *Just War Theory: A Reappraisal*, ed. Mark Evans (Edinburgh: University of Edinburgh Press, 2005), pp. 52, 69 n.2; and Cian O'Driscoll, *The Renegotiation of the Just War Tradition and the Right to War in the Twenty-First Century* (New York: Palgrave MacMillan, 2008), pp. 57–60, 63–5, 135–6.

arguing that military action should be confined to the former.[96] Where most of their early Christian counterparts drew a conceptual distinction, these modern theorists want to create an actual separation. Jeff McMahan explains the reason for their proposal, namely that war is too blunt an instrument for meting out discriminate and proportionate retribution.[97] However, he points out, correctly, that there is more to punishment than retribution—namely defence and deterrence—and he argues that while war should not be retributive, it should still be defensive and deterrent.[98] Such war would punish, not according to desert, but according to liability:

> If a person deserves to be harmed, there is a reason for harming him that is independent of the further consequences of harming him. Giving him what he deserves—retribution—is an end in itself. But a person is liable to be harmed only if harming him will serve some further purpose—for example, if it will prevent him from unjustly harming someone, deter him from further wrongdoing, or compensate a victim of his prior wrongdoing... 'Pure retribution' [is]...the infliction of harm on a person for the sole purpose of causing him to suffer what he deserves to suffer as a result of having committed a completed offense.[99]

I both agree and disagree. I agree, of course, that just war is punitive; but I disagree that it is never retributive. Just war is a hostile response to injustice directed against the agents who cause it. Within this basic, punitive form, however, a variety of ends are sought: to fend off and stop the injustice, to vindicate actual victims and reassure potential ones, to deter other potential wrongdoers, and to bring home to these wrongdoers the significance of what they have done for the sake of their own moral and spiritual health. The punitive response is a means to all of these ends—defensive, vindicative, deterrent, and reformative—and so long as the means are proportionate to the ends, the wrongdoers deserve whatever harms they impose. After all, without their misdeeds such corrective measures would not be necessary in the first place. This applies paradigmatically to agents of injustice whose culpability is clear, and less paradigmatically to those whose culpability may be presumed. However, it even applies to those who are known to be non-

---

96. Lang, 'Punitive Intervention', p. 59; Anthony F. Lang, *Punishment, Justice, and International Relations: Ethics and Order after the Cold War* (London: Routledge, 2008), p. 61.
97. Jeff McMahan, 'Aggression and Punishment', in Larry May, ed., *War: Essays in Political Philosophy* (Cambridge: Cambridge University Press, 2008), p. 84.
98. Ibid., p. 84.   99. Ibid., p. 81.

culpably ignorant, although the kind of reformation sought from them will differ from that sought from the morally corrupt.

Where is retribution in this picture? It cannot reside in the very meting out of desert, for disproportionate or excessive retribution is *un*deserved, and the notion of *dis*proportionate retribution is not a contradiction in terms. Nor should it enter the picture as another specific mode intending a peculiar end, which stands alongside and in addition to defence, vindication, deterrence, and reformation. *Pace* Kant, retribution is not about restoring an abstract, quasi-aesthetic balance of harms, by making the wrongdoer suffer penalties somehow equal to the injuries he has caused. Such a balance has no intrinsic value, because there is nothing worthwhile to be found in an equal wasteland of suffering. Retribution is neither the meting out of desert nor a specific mode of punishment. Rather, it refers to the common, basic form of all the several modes: namely that of a hostile, corrective response to injustice. It picks out what makes something *punishment*. Defence, for example, need not be punitive. When an atrocious tyrant defends his borders against invasion by an aggressor justly intent upon liberating his oppressed people, his self-defence is not punitive, because there is no injustice in the invasion for him to retribute. Similarly, reformation need not be punitive. When a utilitarian tyrant forcibly detains unemployed graduates, in order to retrain them for redeployment in undermanned coalmines, his reformation is not punitive, since in the graduates' failure to volunteer for coalmining there is no injustice to retribute. Retribution is not a specific mode of punishment alongside others, but rather the basic form of its several modes. Therefore, whenever war is punitive, it must also be retributive.[100]

This, however, is 'retribution' in a general sense. There remains another, narrower sense in which war should not be retributive. As a hostile response to injustice, just war is directed at those who are responsible for causing it. How far those responsible are also culpable will usually be impossible to ascertain with any certainty in the course of war-fighting. Under those circumstances just warriors may presume that the enemy are culpable and deserve the harms that proportionate punitive (and so generally retributive) defence, vindication, deterrence, and reformation impose on them. However, after victory has been won and the end of defence achieved, more might still remain to be done to complete the work of vindication, deterrence, and

---

100. If punishment *is* retribution, why do I persist in using two words to refer to the same thing? I persist, because many believe that punishment should *not* be retributive.

especially reformation. Then it might be possible to make punishment more discriminate—to single out the masterminds of injustice from the minions, to determine their guilt, and to impose fitting penalties. While the ends would still be vindicative, deterrent, and reformative, the form would remain retributive. This discriminate kind of *post bellum* retribution is not something that just warriors *as warriors* are fit to dispense. It belongs in considerate courts of law, not in the maelstrom of the battlefield.[101]

IV. The justification of killing (i): subjective guilt or objective harm?

David Rodin holds that just war cannot be about the punishment of wrongdoing. He also holds that culpability for wrongdoing is the only justification for killing someone. Therefore he concludes that just war reasoning is unable to furnish a coherent justification for the killing of enemy combatants. If I have succeeded in breaking the grip of his first premise, then this conclusion falls.

However, Rodin's conclusion also rests on a second ground: namely, his identification of just war reasoning with the thought of Michael Walzer and his claims that *ius ad bellum* considerations are logically independent of *ius in bello* ones, and that opposing combatants are morally equal with regard to the former.[102] In Walzer's thought, soldiers cannot be held responsible for

101. Since I argue that all punishment has a generally retributive form, and that war is always retributive, the question arises as to how preventative or pre-emptive military action can be war. The question presumes, as does McMahan, that retribution must always be a response to wrongdoing that is already complete. That is not quite correct. Since it is responsive, retribution can only address something that precedes it. What precedes it need not be complete, however: it might still be in process. This implies that the wrongdoing must only have *begun*. If pre-emptive military action is defined as a response to a threat that is in the process of being actualized, then it is a retributive response to an injury that has begun, even if it is not yet mature. By contrast, if preventative military action is defined as aiming to prevent a possible threat from being actualized at all, then it is not a response to an actual threat, but only to a speculative one. Preventative military action, therefore, is a non-retributive form of war, but it is not a just form.

102. Michael Walzer, *Just and Unjust Wars: A Moral Argument with Historical Illustrations* (London: Allen Lane, 1978), p. 127: 'In our judgments of the fighting, we abstract from all considerations of the justice of the cause. We do this because the moral status of individual soldiers on both sides is very much the same: they are led to fight by their loyalty to their own states and by their lawful obedience. They are most likely to believe that their wars are just, and while the basis of that belief is not necessarily rational enquiry but, more often, a kind of unquestioning acceptance of official propaganda, nevertheless they are not criminals; they face one another as moral equals'.

the launching of an unjust war, because they fight without consent, either because they are coerced by conscription or because they are constrained by their own conscience and sense of loyalty.[103] What this amounts to, in Rodin's view, is that soldiers may offer a plea of duress against the charge that they have wrongfully killed the innocent. Duress, however, is not generally thought to provide a moral or legal excuse for wrongful killing.[104] Walzer also proposes an alternative argument, namely that soldiers on both sides of a war have an equal entitlement to kill the enemy. Rodin observes that this moves in a 'radically different' direction to the first argument; for whereas that sought to excuse on the ground of a lack of responsibility, this seeks to justify and so implies possession of responsibility.[105] He also argues that Walzer's mutual entitlement of soldiers to kill cannot be grounded in the mutual consent and acceptance of risk, like boxers; nor in common compulsion, like gladiator slaves.[106] Why does Walzer espouse these inadequate and incompatible arguments? Because, according to Rodin, he allows his secular treatment to remain trammelled by a position foisted on just war theory by Augustine and Aquinas, which is only sustainable within their theistic framework.[107] Rodin concludes that just war theory's long-standing tenet—that soldiers not be held responsible for the justice of the wars in which they fight—must be abandoned, since 'soldiers fighting an unjust war have no permission to kill, and there is no "moral equality" between soldiers'.[108]

However cogent against Walzer, Rodin's critique does not tell against just war reasoning as a whole. Since Christian tradition regards just war as basically punitive, it cannot logically espouse a general doctrine of the moral equality of combatants. There might be particular cases where both parties to a conflict are equally unjust and neither has moral licence to kill. Otherwise, just warriors are justified in killing insofar as that is a proportionate means of punishing wrongdoing, and unjust warriors deserve to be killed on account of the wrong that they do. But perhaps early Christian theorists were logically inconsistent: perhaps they affirmed both the punitive nature of just war and the moral equality of combatants. Did they?

---

103. Rodin, *War and Self-Defense*, p. 171.
104. Ibid., p. 171.   105. Ibid., p. 172.   106. Ibid., pp. 172–3.
107. Ibid., pp. 171, 173.   108. Ibid., p. 173.

Certainly, Augustine and Aquinas did not. They assumed the paradigmatic case where belligerent harm is justified in order to punish a culpable aggressor. As we have already shown, Augustine writes that 'it is the injustice of the opposing side that lays on the wise man the duty of waging wars';[109] and while he does not distinguish between injustice that is merely objective and that which is subjectively culpable, his depiction of the agent of injustice as being worthy of moral correction implies culpability. As for Aquinas, it is true that he holds that an individual may be killed if he endangers the community to such an extent that the community's well-being requires his excision;[110] but it is clear that the individual under consideration is a sinner, that is, not merely a material cause of injustice but also culpably responsible for it. In Aquinas's view, the sinner, by deviating from the rational order through his sin, loses his human dignity and thereby becomes the target of justified killing.[111]

Later, however, the tradition begins to take into account the fact that not all warriors in an unjust cause are equally culpable; some might not be culpable at all, and under the conditions of warfare it is usually impossible to discriminate between gradations of culpability. On the battlefield whether and how far a combatant is culpable will usually be invisible. One might be able to point confident fingers at the enemy's dictatorial political and military leadership; but who can claim to measure the proportions of collusive malice and invincible ignorance in the participation of middle-ranking officers and teenage privates? What can be *seen*, however, is that a soldier fighting in an unjust cause is threatening harm. Practically speaking, therefore, it is objectively unjust harmfulness, rather than subjective moral guilt, that will usually serve as the criterion of liability to lethal punishment.

Vitoria represents this shift of practical attention from moral guilt to objective injustice when he writes that all who bear arms should be considered injurious and may be killed, 'unless it is manifest that they are not *injurious* [*extra noxam*]'.[112] At one point, he appears to retreat to moral ground, when he is translated as saying that 'the innocent may not be slain by [primary] intent, when it is possible to distinguish them from the *guilty*'.[113] This

109. Augustine, *City of God*, XIX.7, p. 862.
110. Aquinas, *Summa Theologiae*, 2a 2ae, q. 64, a.2, resp., p. 23.
111. Aquinas, *Summa Theologiae*, 2a 2ae, q. 64, a.2, ad 3, p. 25.
112. Vitoria, 'De Bello', I.11, pp. cxx–cxxi. My emphasis. Latin references here and in the following note are to *Comentarios a la Secunda secundae de Santo Tomás*, ed. Vicente Beltrán de Heredia, Vol. II: 'De Caritate et Prudentia (qq. 23–56)' (Salamanca: Apartado 17, 1932).
113. Ibid., I.11, p. cxxi. My emphasis.

appearance might deceive, however, since the Latin word here translated into English as 'guilty' is actually '*nocentes*', which can also mean simply 'harming'.

Whereas in Vitoria the ambiguity might be merely linguistic, in Suárez it is evidently real. First, he asserts that 'no one may be deprived of his life save by reason of his own guilt [*propter culpam propriam*]', and 'the natural law demands that, generally speaking, no one who is actually known to be free from guilt [*non esse in culpa*], shall be slain'.[114] Then, however, writing of killing in the course of war, he says that those who should not be killed are not the guiltless, but the harmless—that is, women, children, and all unable to bear arms,[115] as well as those 'who are able to bear arms, if it is evident that, in other respects, they have not shared in the crime nor in the unjust war [*non fuisse participes criminis, neque belli iniusti*].[116] Yet the latter distinction between participating 'in the crime' and participating in 'the unjust war' hints at a distinction between moral guilt and objective injustice, and suggests that evident moral guilt still remains a criterion for justified killing. This moral criterion then unambiguously reasserts itself after victory, when, Suárez tells us, 'only those who are clearly guilty [*nocentes*] may be slain'.[117] Here '*nocentes*' must imply moral guilt, since by definition victory involves the disarming of the enemy, who consequently cannot threaten harm.

Grotius is less ambiguous than Suárez, distinguishing more sharply between the justifications of killing *in bello* and *post bellum*. He agrees upon the need to distinguish between 'the unfortunate and culpable' and 'the principal Authors of a War, and those who have been drawn into it'—*post bellum*.[118] *In bello*, however, the justification for killing is self-defence against objective injustice simply:

> [the] right of self-defence, arises immediately from the care of our own pres-
> ervation, which nature recommends to every one, and not from the injustice
> or crime of the aggressor; for if the person be no ways to blame, as for instance,
> a soldier who carries arms with good intentions; or a man that should mistake

114. Suárez, 'On Charity: Disputation XIII', VII.15, pp. 845–6. Latin references here and subse-
     quently are to *Opus de triplici virtute theologica, fide, spe, et charitate* (Paris: Edmundus Martin,
     1621).
115. Ibid., VII.10, p. 843.
116. Ibid., VII.15, p. 846.
117. Ibid., VII.16, p. 847; VII.7, p. 841.
118. Grotius, *Rights of War and Peace*, III. XI.II.1; III.XI.V, pp. 1423, 1431. Grotius implies that
     discriminate moral reckoning should occur *post bellum*, insofar as all the ancient historical
     examples of 'retribution', to which he appeals, occur in the wake of victory.

me for another; or one distracted or delirious (which may possibly happen), I don't [sic] therefore lose that right that I have of self-defence: for it is sufficient that I am not obliged to suffer the wrong that he threatens to do me, no more than if it was a man's beast that came to set upon me.[119]

The evidence does not suggest, I think, that in the 16th and 17th centuries early Christian just war theorists came to espouse the moral equality of combatants. With Augustine (and Rodin) they agree that culpability for wrongdoing is the paradigmatic justification of killing in just, punitive war; and where culpability can be discerned and its degrees discriminated—especially *post bellum*—it should be the sole criterion. *In bello*, however, such discrimination is not practicable and an alternative criterion must be found, namely the objective threat or performance of unjust harm. If the practical criterion for justifying killing were the threat or performance of harm simply, that would imply the moral equality of combatants. However, according to Vitoria implicitly and Suárez and Grotius explicitly, the relevant harm is criminal, wrongful, *unjust*. Unjust warriors are distinguished morally from just ones, therefore, by their participation in objective injustice. This need not imply that the paradigmatic criterion of culpability has simply been jettisoned; and both the ambiguity of some of the discussion and the fact that the paradigm reasserts itself *post bellum* suggest that it has not. In the epistemic uncertainty of war's fog, objective injustice serves as a proxy for guilt rather than a substitute for it.

This is not the whole story, however, for Grotius does argue in favour of the justified killing, sometimes, even of those who are *known* to be innocent of the wrong that they do. Here early Christian tradition collides head-on with Rodin; for Rodin is uncompromising in his assertion of a 'right to life' that can be forfeit on one condition only: moral guilt for wrongdoing. That, at least, is how things seem at first sight.

V. The justification of killing (ii): the 'right to life' and its contingency

David Rodin wisely acknowledges a plurality of sources of moral normativity—not only rights and duties, but also virtues and consequences.[120]

---

119. Ibid., II.I.III, p. 397; see also III.I.II.1, p. 1186.
120. Rodin, *War and Self-Defense*, pp. 9–10.

Rights are not the whole of morality: having a right and being in the right are not logical equivalents.[121] Instead he aspires to 'an all-things-considered moral judgement',[122] holding it as 'absolutely certain that consequentialist considerations sometimes override rights and duties'—for example, that one should deceive a murderer about the location of his would-be victim[123]—and that 'rights may be violated and a right-bearer wronged by an action which, all-things-considered, is the right thing to do'.[124] In taking this position, Rodin distances himself from the common view that rights are absolute, famously expressed by Ronald Dworkin in his notion of rights as trumps, which 'suggests that rights are absolute ethical considerations which always override competing considerations'.[125] More particularly, Rodin dissents from the widely held belief that the right to life is 'inalienable' and possessed 'unconditionally'.[126] Nevertheless, notwithstanding these major qualifications, he insists that rights have 'a distinctive stringency' such that they generally override competing moral considerations, especially consequential ones that appeal to the interests of society as a whole over and against those of individual agents.[127] If rights are not trumps, he tells us, they are still 'a strong "breakwater"'.[128]

This account of moral reasoning, and of the place of the concept of rights within it, is consistent as far as it goes. Rights considerations override others as a rule, although there are occasions when they do not. Their obliging force is stringent, but not absolute. Confirmation of conceptual coherence awaits a cogent explanation of when rights act as an effective breakwater and when they should be overwhelmed by other considerations, and of what circumstances make the difference and why. In the meantime, however, some signs of internal tension are already evident. For example, the notion that it can be morally right to *violate* a right and to *wrong* its bearer surely jars logically. How can it be morally *right* to *violate* anything—given that the very word 'violate' connotes not merely harm but *wrongful* harm? And if, in these circumstances and all things considered, it is morally right for me to harm you, how far does it make sense to say that *in those circumstances* you *still* possess a right to life—or, more exactly, a right not to be harmed? The fact that a right is

---

121. Ibid., p. 24.   122. Ibid., p. 24.
123. Ibid., p. 9.   124. Ibid., p. 24.
125. Ibid., p. 24.   126. Ibid., p. 71.
127. Ibid., pp. 24–5; see also p. 9.   128. Ibid., p. 25.

said to be 'violated' rather than 'suspended' when someone is rightly harmed implies that there is something about the very concept of a right that resists demotion from absolute status.

How does Rodin's concept of rights and its role in moral reasoning—especially about the taking of human life—compare with the views of early Christian just war theorists? Since the very notion of plural rights adhering to individual subjects—as distinct from an objective situation of what is right—excites controversy within the academic discipline of Christian ethics,[129] I shall lay out the evidence methodically.

In Augustine's consideration of the morality of the use of lethal force the concept of an individual's right to life is entirely absent. His concern focuses predominantly on the motive and intention of the killer, who must eschew 'love of violence, revengeful cruelty, fierce and implacable enmity, wild resistance, and the lust of power',[130] act 'in a spirit of benevolence',[131] and intend public peace.[132] Nonetheless, since Augustine defines just war as a form of punishment for injustice, he does recognize the moral importance of the wrong done to the innocent, even if he does not articulate this in terms of the violation of a subjective right. As for the unjust aggressor, the just warrior is obliged to show him benevolence, but there is no suggestion that the aggressor has a right to this. Indeed, in one passage concern about the death of the unjust—who 'will soon die in any case'[133]—is brushed aside as 'mere cowardly dislike, not any religious feeling'.[134]

Aquinas resumes Augustine's concern with motive and intention, refining the latter in terms of an incipient theory of double effect.[135] On the other hand, he gives greater consideration to what human life obliges and

129. See, for example, Nicholas Wolterstorff, *Justice: Rights and Wrongs* (Princeton: Princeton University Press, 2008); Oliver O'Donovan, 'The Language of Rights and Conceptual History', *Journal of Religious Ethics*, 37/2 (June 2009); *Studies in Christian Ethics*, 23/2 (May 2010: '*Justice: Rights and Wrongs*: Critical and Interdisciplinary Engagements with Nicholas Wolterstorff'.

130. Augustine, *Against Faustus*, 22.74, in Oliver O'Donovan and Joan Lockwood O'Donovan, eds, *From Irenaeus to Grotius: A Sourcebook in Christian Political Thought* (Grand Rapids: Eerdmans, 1999), p. 117.

131. Augustine, *ad Marcellinum* (138), in *Political Writings*, p. 38, s.14.

132. Augustine, *ad Bonifacem* (189), in *Political Writings*, p. 217, s.6.

133. Augustine, *Against Faustus*, 22.74, p. 117.

134. Ibid.

135. Aquinas, *Summa Theologiae*, 2a 2ae, q. 40, a.1, resp., p. 83; q. 43, a.3, resp., p. 119; q. 64, a.7, resp., pp. 41–2.

therefore deserves, and he implies thereby that it possesses a positive objective quality—a goodness—that generates obligation. Thus he writes that suicide is contrary to that charity which an individual owes (*debet*) himself;[136] that to kill a just man is more sinful than to kill a sinner, because it harms somebody who deserves the injury less (*est minus dignus:* 'is less worthy' of it);[137] that considered in isolation 'every man, even the sinner, has a nature which God made, and which as such we are bound to love, whereas we violate it [*quae corrumpitur:* "it is ruined"] by killing him';[138] and that to kill 'someone who retains his natural dignity [*hominem in sua dignitate manentem*] is intrinsically evil [*secundum se malum*]'.[139] However, while Aquinas does attribute to human life a certain objective goodness, he does not think that this is inalienable. For he tells us that a sinner may lose his 'human dignity' and lapse into the servitude of the beasts, so as to serve the purposes of others;[140] and that insofar as his sin corrodes the common good and endangers the community, the sinner may be justly killed.[141] Nowhere in his discussion of homicide or war does Aquinas talk of a right to life.[142]

Three centuries later, however, the idea of discrete subjective rights possessed by everyone in general or groups and individuals in particular has come to expression—although it still operates in, and is made contingent upon, the larger moral context of objective right. Vitoria considers just titles under which the Spanish could have brought the American Indians under their control. Among these is a natural 'right of travel' (*ius peregrinandi*),[143] combined with permission to exercise 'all rights of war' (*omnia belli iura*), should the Indians deny the Spanish 'their right' (*ius suum*).[144]

136. Ibid., q. 64, a.5, resp. & ad 1, pp. 32–3.
137. Ibid., a.6, ad 2, pp. 38–9.
138. Ibid., a.6, resp., pp. 36–7.
139. Ibid., a.2, ad 3, pp. 24–5. The Latin is less proprietorial: 'someone remaining in his dignity'.
140. Ibid., a.2, ad 3, p. 25.
141. Ibid., a.2, resp., p. 23; a.6, resp., pp. 37–8.
142. In the Blackfriars edition, there is one occasion when the translator has Aquinas say of the killing of malefactors that 'this right belongs only to those who are charged with the care of the whole community' (ibid., a.3, resp., p. 27). The Latin text does not quite say this: 'occidere malefactorem ... et ideo ad illum solum pertinet cui committitur cura communitatis conservendae' (ibid. p. 26: 'and so the killing of a malefactor belongs only to him, to whom is committed the care of preserving the community'). However, it seems reasonable to translate what belongs only to a certain class of persons in terms of their having a 'right' to it.
143. Vitoria, 'On the American Indians', in *Political Writings*, III.1, p. 278. Latin references here and in the following notes are to *Relectiones theologicae tredecim partibus per varias sectiones in duos libros divisae* (Lyon: Petrus Landry, 1587).
144. Ibid., III.1, pp. 282–3.

Suárez refers to 'the common rights of nations (*communia iura gentium*), such as the right of transit';[145] to particular rights possessed by a certain class of person—for example the right of the sovereign prince (*ius supremi Principis*) to declare war;[146] and to particular rights possessed by particular persons, for example a certain king's 'own right' (*ius suum*) to a certain city.[147] He makes it clear that rights are not the whole of morality when he refers to the possibility of someone sinning against charity in 'pursuing his right' (*tale ius*).[148] He implies that rights emerge and recede according to circumstances when he says that 'a wrong done to another does not give me the right [*ius*] to avenge him, unless he would be justified in avenging himself and actually proposed to do so'.[149] When he claims that 'no one may be deprived of his life save by reason of his own guilt',[150] and describes the killing of innocent persons as 'intrinsically evil' (*intrinsice malum*),[151] he implies a right not to be killed, but assigns it only to innocents. Yet subjective innocence is not in fact its only condition, for Suárez makes it contingent upon two further, objective circumstances: that 'the slaughter is not necessary for victory...and...the innocent can be distinguished from the guilty'.[152]

For Grotius, right 'properly so called'[153] comprises 'the abstaining from that which is another's, and the restitution of what we have of another's, or of the profit we have made by it, the obligation of fulfilling promises, the reparation of damage done through our own default, and the merit of punishment among men'.[154] While his primary conception of right places the bulk of its weight on the obligation to render what belongs to others, it nevertheless implies the notion of a subjective right, insofar as that which you are obliged to give me *is* that to which I have a right. So Grotius tells us that 'right' can be 'a moral quality annexed to the person, enabling him to have, or do, something'.[155] This latter can either be a perfect 'faculty' or

---

145. Suárez, 'On Charity: Disputation XIII', IV.3, p. 817.
146. Ibid., II.2, p. 806.
147. Ibid., VI.1, p. 828.
148. Ibid., IV.8, p. 821.
149. Ibid., IV.3, p. 817.
150. Ibid., VII.15, pp. 845–6.
151. Ibid., VII.6, p. 815; VII.15, p. 845.
152. Ibid., VII.15, p. 845.
153. Grotius, *The Rights of War and Peace*, I.I.IV, p. 138.
154. Ibid., 'The Preliminary Discourse', VIII, p. 86.
155. Ibid., I.I.IV, p. 138.

an imperfect 'aptitude'.[156] On the one hand, a faculty is 'a right properly, and strictly taken', which a man has to his own: a power or liberty over ourselves or others; property, complete or imperfect; or the faculty of demanding what is due, which answers to an obligation to render what is owing.[157] This amounts to a subjective right and is the subject of 'expletive justice', which, *pace* Aristotle, transcends socially constructed contracts.[158] An aptitude, on the other hand, is a merit or fitness,[159] which attends 'those virtues that are beneficial to others, as liberality, mercy, and prudent administration of government', and is the subject of 'attributive justice'.[160] Determining who is the owner of a coat is an act of expletive justice, for example, while determining who would fit it best is an act of attributive justice.[161]

Since expletive justice is based ultimately on natural law, which issues from original sociability, personal faculties (or subjective rights) are not absolute. So, for example, natural equity qualifies property rights, so that 'in a case of absolute necessity, that antient [sic] right of using things, as if they still remained common, must revive, and be in full force'.[162] Here Grotius invokes Aquinas, who affirms that whoever takes from another's surplus what is absolutely necessary for the preservation of his own life is not guilty of theft. This is so, not on the ground of the proprietor's obligation by charity to give to those who need, but on the ground that the right to property is subject in exceptional cases to 'the rights of primitive community'.[163] Accordingly, someone engaged in a just war may occupy part of a neutral country, to prevent 'a certain danger' of the enemy's occupation and being 'capable of doing irreparable injuries', provided that he takes nothing but what is necessary for his security and that he withdraws as soon as the danger passes: 'The first right therefore that remains of the antient [sic] community, since property was introduced, is this of necessity.'[164]

Among the personal faculties that Grotius identifies is one over 'our lives, limbs, and liberties', 'for even tho' what we call property had never been introduced', these 'had still been properly our own, and could not have

156. Ibid., I.I.IV, p. 138.
157. Ibid., I.I.V, pp. 138–9.
158. Ibid., I.I.VIII, p. 142.
159. Ibid., I.I.VII, p. 141.
160. Ibid., I.I.VIII.1, p. 143.
161. Ibid., I.I.VIII.2, pp. 146–7.
162. Ibid., II.II.VI.1, 2, p. 434.
163. Ibid., II.II.VI.4, pp. 434–5.
164. Ibid., II.II.X, p. 437.

been (without manifest injustice) invaded'.[165] We may call this a natural right of liberty from bodily interference or harm. Nevertheless, it seems that this too is subject to the overriding claims of the social good; for Grotius claims confidently, 'if one subject, tho' altogether innocent, be demanded by the enemy to be put to death, he may, *no doubt of it*, be abandoned, and left to their discretion, if it is manifest, that the state is not able to stand the shock of that enemy'.[166] Yet the reasoning here is not simply that the urgent requirements of the social good trump an individual's right, but also that virtues other than justice can sometimes encourage, even oblige, us to 'a greater piece of goodness' and 'to abate somewhat of our right, than rigorously to pursue it'.[167] Thus in general charity often advises and sometimes commands us 'to prefer the advantage of many persons to my own single interest',[168] and in this particular case it obliges the subject to surrender himself to the enemy.[169] What is more, if he will not volunteer surrender, his sovereign may force him, since sovereigns may generally force their subjects to do what charity obliges—for example, in time of great scarcity to bring out their corn.[170]

For Grotius an individual's right not to be harmed or killed is contingent not only upon his subjection to the obligations of natural equity and charity but also upon circumstances entirely external to him: the intentions of other agents, whether taking his life would be proportionate, and whether it would be a last resort. So, alluding to Aquinas's adumbration of the theory of double effect, he writes that 'a distinction should be made between an intended and direct damage, and what is only consequentially such';[171] that a defendant should not 'purpose' to kill his aggressor[172] and that if the danger presented 'can possibly be avoided any other way', it should be;[173] and that 'no man can be justly killed with [direct] design, unless for a capital crime, or because we cannot really secure our lives and estates without doing it'.[174] Nevertheless, 'if all other means prove ineffectual', it is lawful 'to

---

165. Ibid., I.II.I.3, p. 184.
166. Ibid., II.XXV.III.1, p. 1152. My emphasis.
167. Ibid., II.XXIV.I.1, p. 1133.
168. Ibid., II.I.IX.3, p. 405.
169. Ibid., II.XXV.III.2, p. 1153.
170. Ibid., II.XXV.III.4, pp. 1154–5.
171. Ibid., II.XXI.X.1, p. 1081.
172. Ibid., II.I.IV.2, p. 398.
173. Ibid., II.I.V.2, p. 401.
174. Ibid., III.XI.II.1, p. 1422.

do that purposely by which the aggressor may die; but we take this course, as the only means left to preserve ourselves, and not as the principal end proposed'.[175] In addition, Grotius also argues that where an innocent person happens to obstruct defence or escape, which is absolutely necessary for our self-preservation, the law of nature, according to which 'the engagement we lye [sic] under to maintain society, is of less moment than the preservation of ourselves', permits us to kill; but that 'the law of charity, especially the evangelical, *which has put our neighbour upon a level with our selves*', withdraws that permission.[176] In other words, we may not kill the innocent bystander, because we have no proportionate reason to prefer our own life to his.

There we have early Christian reasoning about subjective rights in general, and about a 'right not to be harmed' in particular. In agreement with Rodin, at least by the 17th century, it explicitly affirms a personal faculty or subjective right to freedom from bodily harm. This right is not absolute, and can be suspended under certain conditions, one of these being when the subject of the right is himself culpably responsible for causing or threatening grave harm, such as the death of another person. So far, so much agreement.

The points of divergence are several and significant. In terms that jar, Rodin affirms the possibility of it being morally right, all things considered, to violate a right.[177] The awkward choice of language not only creates the logical oddity of it being right to do something wrongful, but also implies that, notwithstanding overriding conditions, the right somehow endures. This might just be the accident of an unfortunate turn of phrase, but it does inadvertently suggest a resistance to demoting rights from absolute status. In contrast, the Christian tradition is less squeamish about admitting the circumstantial contingency of the subjective rights of individuals. So when Aquinas says that in the case of dire necessity, natural or divine right overrides human property rights, and the indigent may take what they need from the superabundant, he does not describe what they do as 'rightful theft', implying that the property rights of the superabundant were rightly violated. Rather, he says that what the indigent do 'is strictly speaking no theft or robbery', thereby implying that *in those circumstances* the superabun-

---

175. Ibid., II.I.IV.2, p. 398.
176. Ibid., II.I.IV.1, p. 398. My emphasis.
177. So does Jeff McMahan: 'Acts that are permissible, justified, or even morally required can all inflict *wrongful* harms' (*Killing in War*, p. 38. The emphasis is mine). 'Wrongful' harm is that which contravenes the victim's rights (*Killing in War*, p. 173).

dant *do not have a right* to their superabundance.[178] In the same way, Suárez tells us that the killing of innocents is 'intrinsically evil', but only so long as 'the slaughter is not necessary for victory… and… the innocent can be distinguished from the guilty'.[179] Now, it might seem that Suárez's phrasing is as jarring as Rodin's, for it implies that it could be right to do what is intrinsically evil. However, what is intrinsically evil is so by way of motive and intention (otherwise it would not be 'intrinsic'). So to kill the innocent unnecessarily, and when they can be distinguished from the guilty, implies that the motive is malicious and that the deaths of the innocent are integral to the agent's intended plan. Absent these circumstances, however, we lack reason to suppose malice of motive and intention, in which case the killing is not intrinsically evil.

A second point of divergence concerns the role of the urgent claims of the social good. Following Aquinas in his treatment of 'theft' in extremis, Grotius argues that '[t]he first right… that remains of the antient [sic] community, since property was introduced, is this of necessity'.[180] Therefore in cases of absolute necessity 'the rights of primitive community' override human property rights,[181] and if it is necessary to prevent irreparable injuries, one state may invade a neutral state's territory to defend itself against an unjust aggressor. Might this abrogation of property rights by the prior claims of the social good extend to the suspension of the innocent's right not to be harmed? If so, then we have a major point of conflict with Rodin, for whom a *right* against bodily harm is by definition 'unassailable by external contingencies'[182] and can only be forfeited on the subjective normative ground of guilt. In his discussion of the case of the subject whose surrender to death is demanded by an overwhelming enemy, Grotius can indeed be taken to imply forfeiture on the ground of an external contingency when he writes that 'he may, no doubt of it, be abandoned, and left to their discretion, if it is manifest, that the state is not able to stand the shock of that enemy'.[183]

However, Grotius's reasoning here is also that charity obliges the subject to surrender himself to the enemy,[184] and that his sovereign may force him

178. Aquinas, *Summa Theologiae*, 2a 2ae, q. 66, a.7, resp. & ad 2., p. 83.
179. Suárez, 'On Charity: Disputation XIII', VII.15, p. 845.
180. Grotius, *The Rights of War and Peace*, II.II.X, p. 437.
181. Ibid., II.II.VI.4, pp. 434–5.
182. Rodin, *War and Self-Defense*, p. 88.
183. Grotius, *The Rights of War and Peace*, II.XXV.III.1, p. 1152. My emphasis.
184. Ibid., II.XXV.III.2, p. 1153.

to do what charity obliges.[185] This gives us a third point of divergence from Rodin. Nowhere in the main body of his argument does Rodin consider that a person's right to freedom from bodily harm might be overridden— or, better, suspended—by the obligation, which is generated by the virtue of charity, to sacrifice himself for the good of others.

In sum, Rodin's account of subjective individual rights contains tensions. Some are superficial and are resolved implicitly; others are less tractable. On the one hand, he concedes that it is 'absolutely certain' that 'consequentialist' considerations sometimes override rights—for example, where a murderer's right to be told the truth is overridden by the consequence of telling him the location of his would-be victim. On the other hand, he asserts that rights 'generally override' competing moral considerations, especially 'con-sequentialist' ones that invoke the common good.[186] This appears to leave open the possibility that the common good may *sometimes* trump individual rights. If so, then the door is shut again when Rodin urges that '[t]he most basic function of a morality of rights is to locate certain extremely impor-tant normative considerations [i.e. innocence and guilt] *wholly within the sphere of the subject itself so as to make them unassailable by external contingencies* such as are appealed to by consequentialism'.[187] The apparent inconsistency is resolved by reference to an implicit differentiation of classes of case, and by the implicit identification of one class where consequential considera-tions do *not* override rights. What this is and why it possesses such an immunity are not stated. What it is can be inferred, namely the class com-prising cases involving the right to life. Why is this supposed to enjoy an immunity from external, consequential considerations, whereas the right to be told the truth does not? One answer might be that an individual's life is more valuable than knowledge of the truth—although, since the two values are incommensurable, their ranking is not obvious and requires argument. Another answer is that the history of the 20th century is replete with cases where appeals to the social goods of national cohesion or expansion or

185. Ibid., II.XXV.III.4, pp. 1154–5.
186. Rodin slightly muddies the waters here by speaking of 'consequentialist' considerations, rather than 'consequential' ones. By definition 'consequentialism' determines the moral qual-ity of acts exclusively by reference to their consequences, and therefore always runs rough-shod over rights—unless rule-consequential considerations dictate otherwise. Even for rule-consequentialism, however, consequences remain trumps.
187. Rodin, *War and Self-Defense*, p. 88. My emphasis.

industrial development were used to justify the brutal and indiscriminate killing of the innocent on a massive scale.

Given this history, it might well seem that we have good reason to be shy of early Christian appeals to the 'common good' or 'social necessity'. We should recall, however, that some such appeals are made only to suspend positive property rights to superabundance. Where the common good is invoked to justify the taking of an individual's life, it is usually because the victim poses a threat by his wrongdoing. In the one case where Grotius appeals to social necessity to justify the surrender of an innocent to an enemy demanding his death—which is not quite the same as a case of directly killing him—he also appeals to the innocent's social obligation to demonstrate charity. This brings into play a contingency that is not external in the same sense as are consequences. Depending upon prudential circumstances— such as the probability of the enemy keeping their side of the bargain—it could be that an innocent person is subject to an obligation to sacrifice his life for the sake of his community. An obligation is 'external' in the sense that it bears down on the reluctant, sinful individual subject with a certain alien force; but it is 'internal' in the eudaimonistic sense that its obligatory force is rooted in a certain (Christian) vision of the individual's moral and spiritual fulfilment.[188] That is to say the obligation urges the subject to invest himself in a costly act of love, and so to find his life by losing it. If an individual should find himself under such an obligation, then he does not possess a right to life; and in embracing the obligation, he neither violates that right nor surrenders it. The right to life is contingent upon normative factors that attach themselves to the subject. The early Christian tradition of just war and Rodin both agree on this. Where they differ is over the range of such factors that they recognize. In the main body of his argument, Rodin recognizes only the subject's innocence or guilt, whereas Christian tradition also recognizes social obligation.

Yet things are not quite what they seem, for in an extended endnote Rodin comes very close indeed to embracing the early Christian position. Here he conducts an instructive analysis of an agonizing historical case that is very similar to Grotius's hypothetical one. During the Rwandan genocide of 1994, Vénuste Hakizamungu, a Tutsi, was ordered by the Hutu Interahamwe to kill his older brother, Théoneste, in order to save his family. This he even-

---

188. For a definition of 'eudaimonism', see note 25 above.

tually did.[189] According to Rodin, notwithstanding the duress to which he was subject, Vénuste remained a responsible agent. However, since Théoneste eventually consented to his own death for the sake of his family, he not only dignified himself but spared Vénuste from committing murder. Thus far, early Christian moral reasoning would concur.

Suppose, however, that Théoneste had not consented. Could he be faulted? In other words, was his consent obligatory or merely supererogatory? Rodin does not commit himself, but he does entertain the possibility that Théoneste could be faulted (and was therefore obliged)—and he does not repudiate it. Does it follow from this that Vénuste would have been morally permitted or obliged to kill his brother without his consent? 'That Théoneste has a right to life militates against such a thought,' Rodin correctly observes. Then he muses: 'For surely if there are moral reasons directing him to sacrifice himself, then they are operative only at the internal level. He may feel compelled to do so, but we can never say to him that he is obliged to sacrifice himself and would be at fault for not doing so.'[190] But then he rejects this line of thinking on the ground that the internal feeling of moral compulsion 'can be accessed in the objective sphere when we ask ourselves the question: what would we (feel ourselves compelled to) do in the circumstances?'[191] While he confesses himself unsure, he nevertheless concludes by affirming that 'internally derived obligations of sacrifice' should enter into an account of right action in such a terrible case.[192] In the end, then, Rodin unwittingly takes up Grotius's position. Gingerly he concedes that social obligation can justify not only an innocent's self-sacrifice but another's killing the innocent, should he refuse to meet his obligation. Part of what unnerves Rodin in making this concession is the lingering notion that Théoneste still 'has a right to life'. The kind of moral reasoning that issues from Grotius and the early Christian theorists of just war is not so encumbered. If Théoneste really is obliged to sacrifice his life, then he has no right to it; and if Vénuste kills him, no such right is violated.

189. Ibid., pp. 59–60, 67–9.
190. Ibid., p. 68.
191. Ibid., p. 68. The cogency of this argumentative move depends—precariously—upon who 'we' are supposed to be.
192. Ibid., p. 68. The meaning of 'internally derived' is unclear. It could mean that only the individual subject is in a position to discern such an obligation—except that Rodin has admitted that it can be objectively confirmed by reference to some universal moral understanding. It could also betray a typically liberal reluctance to acknowledge the subjection of an individual to a moral obligation that he might not himself own. That is, it suggests a reluctance to acknowledge the possibility that a moral subject might be sinfully alienated from his obligation.

On the questions of whether individuals possess a right to life, and of the nature of its contingency, it turns out that the difference between Rodin and early Christian just war reasoning (as represented by Suárez and Grotius) is far less abysmal than first appeared. Both agree that individuals possess a 'right to life'—or, better, a 'right not to be harmed'. Both agree that this right is not absolute, but depends on innocence of subjective culpability for wrongdoing. However—if we bring Rodin's marginal musings to centre stage—both also agree that such innocence is not sufficient to guarantee the right, which lapses in cases not only of subjective guilt but also of overriding objective social obligation.

VI. The justification of killing (iii): can we kill the innocent with due respect?

Rodin's off-stage concession that it can be justifiable to kill those innocent of wrongdoing implies that such killing can be done without failing in due respect for the victims. This undermines the very heart of his centre-stage argument. For there he urges that it is extremely important that defensive force should represent 'an appropriate response, not just to the situation at large, but to *them* [the culpably aggressive agents]'[193] 'as moral subjects'.[194] That is, defensive force must pay due respect to its potential human targets by holding its fire until they themselves forfeit their immunity against harm through voluntary and culpable wrongdoing. However, if it can be justifiable to kill the innocent—as Rodin himself concedes off-stage—it follows that this cannot be the only way of showing due respect. What, then, are the alternatives?

Early Christian just war reasoning has an answer to this question, but only because it is morally realist, not individualist. It agrees with Rodin that there is something about persons—call it 'dignity' or 'nature'—that deserves respect or, better, love, even when killing them.[195] But it disagrees over what

---

193. Ibid., p. 92. The emphasis is Rodin's.
194. Ibid., p. 89; see also, p. 94.
195. It is true, as I have shown above, that Aquinas thinks that a sinner loses his 'human dignity' (*Summa Theologiae*, 2a 2ae, q. 64, a.2, ad 3, p. 25). Notwithstanding this, he also thinks that 'every man, even the sinner, has a nature which God made, and which as such we are bound to love' (ibid., a.6, resp., p. 37). Quite how Aquinas thinks of human dignity and human nature in relation to one another is not clear. What is clear is that something remains in the sinner that deserves love.

this dignity consists of. For Rodin it lies in the *individual's exercise* of moral responsibility. One may take another's life only on the basis of wrong that *he has freely chosen* to do. So someone threatened by a fat man, who is falling involuntarily from a great height, may not defend himself by killing the innocent threat, for '[t]o say that the falling fat man has the right to life is to say that he has an interest in his living which cannot be overridden except on the basis of his *own choosing, willing, or acting*'.[196] What this implies is that his right to life lies securely in his own hands, under his control, at his disposal. It can never be taken from him; he can only ever lose it. Rodin's main-text conception of human dignity, then, is liberal-individualist: it consists of inalienable, absolute autonomy. By contrast, the Christian view of human dignity is that it consists not only of the sheer making of moral decisions but also of being subject to objective obligations to spend oneself in the service of intrinsically worthwhile goods, which are given in and with the world before they are chosen. Rodin himself tends toward such a view in his Rwandan endnote, where he not only observes how Théoneste *dignified* himself by the courage and generosity with which he consented to death at his brother's hands, but tentatively admits that his brother would have been justified in killing Théoneste, had his consent not been forthcoming.[197] What this admission implies is that killing on a ground other than one created by the victim's own free choice need not offend against his dignity— provided that it is done on the authority of an objective moral obligation that binds *him*. Here dignity consists primarily not in the sheer exercise of free will but in being the responsible subject of a claim or calling by what is objectively good and right. This dignity is morally realist: it consists in responsibility before a given moral order.

In its understanding of human dignity, early Christian just war theory shows its superiority by avoiding two awkward implications of Rodin's individualist position. The first of these is that an innocent aggressor may not be harmed, *no matter how grave the damage he causes or how evil the cause he unwittingly serves*. For an example of the former, take a clinically insane man who arms himself to the hilt, walks into a school, and sets about shooting anyone in sight. For an example of the latter, take a Wehrmacht soldier advancing into Poland on 1 September 1939, who had no good reason to

---

196. Rodin, *War and Self-Defense*, p. 89. My emphasis.
197. Ibid., pp. 67–8: by consenting to be killed for the sake of saving his family, Théoneste makes his own death 'an act of dignity' and keeps it from being his brother's act of murder.

doubt the lies he had been told of unprovoked Polish aggression at Gleiwitz.

The second implication of Rodin's position is that just war is virtually impracticable. This is because, if one may never deliberately kill the morally innocent, then one may never choose to perform an act that will foreseeably kill innocent civilians. In that case, one may not attack any enemy position where there is a known risk of incurring civilian casualties. Without permission to take such risks, however, military success would in most cases be highly improbable; and without a reasonable prospect of success, engaging in war in the first place is unjust. Christian just war thinking avoids this pacifist conclusion by deploying the theory of double effect. One may attack the enemy, knowing that there is a risk of civilian casualties, provided that those casualties are beside one's intention, that one has done everything feasible to avoid and minimize them, and that a successful attack on the enemy here and now is important for the success of a just cause. As Vitoria puts it: 'it is occasionally lawful to kill the innocent not by mistake, but with full knowledge of what one is doing, if this is an accidental effect... This is proven, since it would otherwise be impossible to wage war against the guilty.'[198] Of course, were it Rodin's intention to argue for pacifism (as well as against just war theory), this objection would not count against him. But, given what he writes in the closing paragraphs of his book, this seems not to be the case:

> Aggression faces us with an immediate personal challenge; we must either fight or submit, and many will find the conclusion that one may not fight against an international aggressor morally unacceptable. This conviction may stem from a consequentialist concern for the costs of not resisting aggression... It may arise from the feeling that to fail to resist aggression is to somehow acquiesce morally to it in an unacceptable way... *I must acknowledge that I feel the force of these reservations.*[199]

In sum, then, early Christian just war reasoning reckons it justifiable to kill the enemy on any one of several grounds: actual guilt, presumed guilt, imputed social obligation, or objective injustice. Provided that the motive and intention of the killer are benevolent, and that the killing is a last resort

---

198. Vitoria, 'On the Law of War', q. 3, a.1.2, p. 315.
199. Rodin, *War and Self-Defense*, pp. 198–9. My emphasis. In his 'Foreword', Bernard Williams comments that Rodin 'might be expected to end up with a pacifist conclusion, but he does not do so' (ibid., p. vii).

and commands proportionate reason, the victim's dignity is shown due respect. For killing to be respectful, it is not necessary for the victim to have forfeited his right to life by an autonomously chosen act of culpable wrong-doing. Nor is such a forfeit sufficient to make killing respectful; for without right motive and intention, last resort and proportion, even killing on the ground of moral guilt would be an act of *dis*respect. The innocence of the victim, therefore, is neither necessary nor sufficient for respectful killing. This analysis is enabled, of course, by the doctrine of double effect. Why Rodin does not deploy it is not clear. He acknowledges it without repudiation, but he passes it by nonetheless.[200] One plausible explanation is that, mesmerized by liberal individualism, Rodin's attention naturally gravitates to rights-talk. And rights-talk does seem to have the curious habit of sucking the oxygen out of every other moral consideration.

VII. The justification of killing (iv): is just war always punitive?

We have argued that the victim's moral guilt is not necessary for killing to be duly respectful and therefore justified; and that his objective wrong-doing—together with right motive and intention, last resort and proportion—is sufficient. What does this imply for my earlier argument in favour of the basically punitive nature of just war?

If it were absolutely certain that none of the enemy were at all culpable for their wrongdoing, then just war could not be punitive in the narrow

---

200. Ibid., p. 4 and 4 n.1; 'I do not intend to deal directly with the double effect account of self-defense.' Rodin does briefly echo the doctrine's crucial concern about the morally trans-formative effects of action on the *character of the agent*, but he mistakenly attributes the power of transformation to the choice of a certain way of acting rather than the choice of a certain intention in acting (*War and Self-Defense*, p. 65). In contrast, Jeff McMahan's analysis of the ethics of killing in war makes liberal use of the distinction between intended and unintended effects, even if he dissents from certain of the doctrine's traditional analyses (*Killing in War*, *passim* and pp. 171–2). As a consequence he is willing to entertain the possibility that the deliberate harming of the innocent could be morally justified: 'if causing...harm to the innocent could be the means of achieving much *greater* good effects, it might be permissible to cause it—though only if the agent acts with an acceptable intention, such as the intention to achieve the greater good...According to common sense intuition, intention can have a role not only in making the killing of the innocent impermissible, but also in making it permissible'. To this he adds, however, 'I am not entirely confident that these view are defensible' (ibid., p. 29).

sense of punishment—that is, trying to reform a culpable wrongdoer by communicating the wrongness of his doing by the imposition of fitting penalties. It would, however, still remain punitive in the broad sense of punishment—that is, making a hostile response, defensive and corrective, to the agents of wrongdoing.

In the midst of war, however, the degree of the unjust enemy's culpability is very likely to be unclear. In that case, it would be reasonable for the just warrior to presume guilt, but to take objectively visible injustice as a proxy for it. After victory has been secured, more discriminate judgement can be made and punishment meted out.

Even if their guilt were somehow mitigated, and if that were known, unjust warriors could still be punished. Rodin effectively agrees, since he thinks it 'entirely permissible to defend oneself against an aggressor who is excused by reason of necessity, duress, or provocation', since, while the aggressor deserves compassion on account of his constraining predicament, his acts are fully intentional and only involuntary 'in some sense'.[201]

In rare cases it might become clear that particular elements of the unjust enemy's forces are entirely non-culpable. In that case, particular military operations against them would not be punitive, but the wider waging of war as a whole would remain so.

VIII. The justification of killing (v): how responsible are combatants?

I have argued that just war theory in its classic, early Christian expression regards just war as basically punitive, and takes culpable wrongdoing to be the paradigmatic ground for the justification of killing. However, Rodin claims that the theory views combatants as responsible only for *ius in bello*, and that their absolution from responsibility for *ius ad bellum* is a 'long-standing tenet' of just war theory.[202] Therefore, when opposing combatants encounter each other on the battlefield, they do so as moral equals. This view

---

201. Rodin, War and Self-Defense, pp. 92, 90. Jeff McMahan agrees, but extends liability to defensive harm to 'virtually all unjust combatants', since, while duress can absolve of all culpability, it cannot absolve of all responsibility for choosing to join or allowing themselves to be conscripted (Killing in War, p. 183).
202. Ibid., pp 166, 173.

Rodin first finds in Walzer, but then traces back into medieval tradition. If his reading is correct, then mine cannot be, for then the killing of the enemy could be neither justified by their guilt nor punitive in form.

Rodin traces Walzer's unhappy distinction of responsibility *ad bellum* from responsibility *in bello* to what he sees as 'a tension which goes to the very heart of the Just War Theory'. Whereas *ius ad bellum* thinking assumes that war is an 'illegal' activity whose legitimate use is limited to one party,[203] *ius in bello* thinking assumes that war is law-governed with entitlements and restrictions accruing equally to both sides.[204] These two halves of just war theory in fact represent the antagonistic views of medieval churchmen and lawyers on the one hand, and the warrior classes on the other, which were cobbled together in a pragmatic attempt to regulate and mitigate the evil of war.[205] The result is that just war theory 'is committed to the seemingly paradoxical position that... [an aggressive] war taken as a whole is a crime, yet that each of the individual acts which together constitute [it] are [sic] entirely lawful. Such a war... is both just and unjust at the same time.'[206] The solution proposed by the theory is to reserve responsibility for *ius ad bellum* exclusively to the monarch, while limiting soldiers' responsibility to *ius in bello*.[207] So, according to Augustine, it is just for a soldier to fight 'in obedience to God or some proper authority'.[208] So long as he is properly authorized, he is 'but the sword in the hand of him who uses it, is not responsible

---

203. Rodin tells us that '[t]he old medieval pun equating *militia* with *malitia* is the central attitude of *ius ad bellum*' (Ibid., p. 167). If he is referring to Augustine's statement that '[s]oldiering doesn't prevent you doing good [*non militia*], but hating does [*sed malitia*]' ('Sermon 302', s.15, in *Political Writings*, p. 115), then the meaning he attributes to it is the very opposite of Augustine's. Alternatively, he might be referring to St Bernard of Clairvaux, when he wrote, 'Quis igitur finis fructusve saecularis huius, non dico, militiae, sed malitiae...' ['So what is the end or result of this secular—I do not say, militia, but—malice'] (in 'Liber ad Milites Templi de laude novae militiae', *S. Bernardi Opera*, 8 vols, Vol. III, ed. J. Leclerq and H.M. Rochais [Rome: Editiones Cistercienses, 1963], 'II. De militia saeculari', p. 216). However, Bernard is not here referring to military service in general, but rather to the old, sinful, secular knighthood, which he contrasts with the true *militia Christi* represented by the new Order of the Knights Templar. This contrast was a major theme in commentators writing on the First Crusade in the period 1100–10. All that I know about St Bernard on this matter I owe to Dr Christopher Tyerman of Hertford College, Oxford.
204. Rodin, *War and Self-Defense*, p. 166.
205. Ibid., pp. 166–7.
206. Ibid., p. 167.
207. Ibid., p. 167.
208. Augustine, *Contra Faustum Manichaeum*, in *Nicene and Post-Nicene Fathers*, 1st series, vol. IV (1974), Bk. 22.74; quoted in Rodin, *War and Self-Defence*, p. 168.

for the death he deals'.[209] It belongs to the order of nature that monarchs have the authority to make war, and that 'the servant's duty is to obey'.[210] The duty of obedience becomes overriding for Augustine because monarchs are held to rule by divine authority; and should the king turn out to be ungodly, 'the iniquity of giving the orders will make the king guilty while the rank of a servant in the civil order will show the soldier to be innocent'.[211] However, according to Rodin, once Augustine's theistic premise is put aside, his position 'has little to recommend it'.[212] Since we now believe that rulers and political institutions derive authority from the morally legitimating features of their rule, the presumption in favour of obedience will only be as strong as those moral features.[213]

As Rodin reads the development of just war tradition, Augustine's early modern and 'increasingly secular' successors struggled to make sense of his moral division of labour. Thus Vitoria holds that, while common soldiers may not fight in a war they believe to be 'patently unjust', they are not required to examine the justice of a war in which they fight. Moreover, if they are merely doubtful, rather than certain, about that justice, they must give benefit of their doubt and fight—as an officer of the law is required to carry out the sentence of a judge whose justice he doubts.[214] Rodin responds to Vitoria as follows. An executioner who continues to work in a judicial system that he knows condemns innocent men at least 50 per cent of the time would be 'something like a murderer'.[215] So even if a soldier is in doubt about the justice of a particular war, he can know with certainty that there is at least a 50 per cent chance—and probably far higher[216]—that he is fighting on the unjust side. In that case to adopt Vitoria's policy of 'in case of doubt, fight', would be 'an act of the most extreme moral recklessness'.[217]

How accurate an account of early Christian just war tradition does Rodin give here? It is true that Augustine affirms an unqualified duty of soldiers to obey the commands of their political superiors. But this is not simply

---

209. Augustine, *De Civitate Dei*, in P. Schaff, ed., *Nicene and Post-Nicene Fathers*, 1st series, Vol. II (Grand Rapids:Eerdmans, 1974), 1.21, p. 15; quoted in Rodin, *War and Self-Defence*, p. 168.
210. Augustine, *Contra Faustum Manichaeum*, Bk 22.71; quoted in Rodin, *War and Self-Defence*, p. 168.
211. Ibid., Bk 22.75; quoted in Rodin, *War and Self-Defence*, p. 168.
212. Rodin, *War and Self-Defense*, p. 169.
213. Ibid., p. 169.
214. Francisco de Vitoria, *De Indis Relectio Posterior, Sive de Iure Belli (On the Law of War)*, in *Political Writings*, ed. Pagden and Lawrence, 2.2, ss.22, 25; 2.3, s.31; quoted in Rodin, *War and Self-Defense*, p. 169.
215. Rodin, *War and Self-Defense*, p. 169.
216. Ibid., p. 170 n.15.
217. Ibid., p. 170.

authoritarian, appealing to an arbitrary and indiscriminate command of God. Augustine's basic concern was with the social good of order, of which God is the ultimate source and guarantor. Thus he writes that obedience to a prince in going to war is justified on the grounds of 'the natural order which seeks the peace of mankind';[218] and that a righteous man, who happens to serve an ungodly ruler, can wage war at the latter's behest, 'preserving the order of civil peace' (*civicae pacis ordinem servans*), since the obligations of his post establish his innocence.[219] If modern liberals are not much impressed by such a concern for order, then that is only because they are privileged to take so much of it for granted.

However much benefit of doubt one does, or does not, cede to Augustine, subsequent Christian thinking about the responsibility of social inferiors became more nuanced—sometimes invoking the authority of God to justify *dis*obedience to the ruler. So we find Aquinas writing that an executioner is not bound to obey a court's order if it contains 'a blatant error' (*intolerabilem errorem*) or 'manifest injustice'.[220] Similarly, Vitoria holds that, if subjects are conscious that a war is unjust, they may not fight, since 'one must obey God rather than obey [the prince]'.[221] Still, the common people, 'who are not admitted to the council of the prince', are not obliged to ascertain the just cause of the war, 'because it would be impossible... to put arguments about difficult public business before every member of the common people'.[222] The magnates, on the other hand, who are admitted to the council (and so can ascertain just cause), are obliged. Where doubt exists, but the cause of war is not clearly unjust, it is licit for soldiers to fight; but crass and wilful ignorance do not excuse.[223] Suárez's position is the same: common soldiers are not bound

---

218. Augustine, *Reply to Faustus the Manichaean*, Book 22, s.75, p. 301.

219. Augustine, 'Contra Faustum Manichaeum', *Patrologia Cursus Completus*, Series Latina, ed. J.-P. Migne, 221 vols (Paris, 1844–65), Vol. 42, *Augustini Opera Omnia*, Vol. 8, column 448: 'Cum ergo vir justus, si forte sub rege homine etiam sacrilego militet, recte poscit [sic: this might be a misprint instead of "possit"] illo jubente bellare civicae pacis ordinem servans; cui quod jubetur, vel non esse contra Dei praeceptum certum est, vel utrum sit, certum non est, ita ut fortasse reum regem faciat iniquitas imperandi, innocentem autem militem ostendat ordo serviendi'. R. Stothert, in *A Select Library of the Nicene and Post-Nicene Fathers of the Christian Church*, ed. Philip Schaff, Vol. IV (Grand Rapids: Eerdmans, 1956), p. 301, makes the soldier's obedience appear pointless, formal, and irrational by obscuring its end—'civicae pacis ordinem servans'—when he translated the passage 'recte poscit [possit]... servans' as '[a righteous man] may do the duty belonging to his position in the State in fighting by the order of his sovereign'.

220. Aquinas, *Summa Theologiae*, 2a 2ae, q. 64, a.6, ad 3, pp. 38, 39.

221. Vitoria, 'De Bello', I.8, pp. cxviii; see also, 'On the Law of War', 2.2, s.22, p. 307.

222. Ibid., I.8, pp. cxviii–cxix; see also, 'On the Law of War', 2.2, s.25, p. 308.

223. Vitoria, 'De Bello', I.8, pp. cxviii–cxix.

to make diligent investigation of the justice of the cause of war, 'provided it is not clear to them that the war is unjust';[224] and only if arguments render the justice of a war 'extremely doubtful' are soldiers obliged 'to inquire into the truth in some way'—otherwise, 'it would be impossible for princes to defend their rights, and this would be a serious and general misfortune'.[225] Grotius agrees with his predecessors that '[i]f it plainly appears [to subjects] that the war is unlawful, it is their duty not to meddle in it'.[226] However, perhaps reflecting his membership of a territorially compact republic, he is more sanguine about the possibility of public scrutiny, urging that the justifying reasons for war, if not the motives, 'should be made plain and demonstrable, and consequently, such as should and ought to be laid before all the world';[227] and that an executioner who is to put a malefactor to death ought to be acquainted with the merits of the cause.[228] In cases of doubt, he is markedly less permissive than his predecessors, arguing that the safer, less evil option should be taken—that is, to disobey rather than kill.[229]

It is not true, therefore, that early Christian thinkers about just war simply absolve ordinary soldiers from responsibility for assessing *ius ad bellum*, although they vary in their estimation of how far the exercise of that responsibility is likely to be practicable (and therefore obligatory). Although Grotius comes closest to Rodin's position in cases of doubt, not even he loads the dice quite so heavily against giving doubt's benefit to war. Rodin argues that, since in any given case one of two sides must be unjust, there is at least a 50 per cent chance that a war to which one is invited is unjust. Indeed, since war is frequently unjust on both sides, the odds against a war being just are far less than 50 per cent.[230] This makes sense, however, only on condition that one considers all regimes to be morally equal, and that the chances of a racist dictatorship and a liberal democracy engaging in an unjust war are the same. However, if one has good reason to suppose that a given regime is more likely to be constrained by moral considerations—because of the culture of its society and the exposure of its policies to critical assessment—then the odds in favour of a war proposed by such a regime increase. A sceptic

---

224. Suárez, 'On Charity: Disputation XIII', VI.8, p. 832.
225. Ibid., VI.9, p. 833.
226. Grotius, *The Rights of War and Peace*, II.XXVI.III.1, p. 1167.
227. Ibid., II.XXVI.IV.5, p. 1178.
228. Ibid., II.XXVI.9, p. 1180.
229. Ibid., II.XXVI.IV.5, p. 1177.
230. Rodin, *War and Self-Defense*, pp. 169–70 and 170 n.15.

might retort: 'But what about Britain and France in 1914 and the United States and Britain in 2003? On each of these occasions liberal democracies engaged unjustly in a catastrophic war.' In response I would say that, while I do not doubt that liberal democracies can fight in an unjust cause, or that they have done so, I disagree with the sceptic's judgement in both of these cases. I will not argue the particular cases here, since I do so in Chapters Four and Seven, respectively. The general significance of this point is that one's reckoning of how much benefit of doubt to accord a proposal to go to war depends upon the extent to which one trusts the political environment—the constitutional structures and procedures, the integrity of civil servants and elected ministers. If one does trust it, and if one has good reason to trust it, then one has concomitant reason to accord greater benefit of doubt to a proposal to go to war in that context.

That said, the fact that Christian tradition maintains a basically moral, punitive justification of war and of killing does not preclude it logically from endorsing laws of war that accord equal *legal rights* to all combatants. The justification for this is at once practical and moral: namely to stop the conduct of war from spinning out of all moral control, and so to limit its evils. This does not imply the logical impossibility that the same belligerency can be both just and unjust at the same time. Or, to be more exact, it does not imply that the same belligerency can be at once just and unjust *in the same sense of 'justice'*. A war that is unjust because it lacks just cause, right intention, last resort, etc. should not be fought, and those who fight it are in the wrong, although not all of them need be equally culpable for so doing. Nevertheless, it is better—because less destructive—that warriors fighting on behalf of a basically unjust cause should observe just constraints in the manner of their fighting. It is better both for their own souls and for those with whom they have dealings. They are, therefore, unjust and just at the same time, *but in different respects and at different levels*. *Pace* Rodin, this occasions no untenable paradox.

IX. The rationale of national defence (i): the rights of individuals

We established in section II above that Christian thinking about war operates in terms of justice, and not merely in terms of the legal defence of the territorial status quo. In this it agrees with Rodin against modern accounts of just war, which take their cue from international law, that legal sovereignty cannot, by itself, provide a *moral* justification of national defence.[231] However, Rodin proceeds to examine two possible moral justifications for such defence, finds them both wanting, and concludes that he has uncovered yet another point of incoherence in just war theory. This poses a further challenge to Christian tradition, since it espouses the possibility of morally justified national defence.

The first moral justification which Rodin considers is that a nation-state's right to self-defence can be *reduced* to the personal rights to self-defence of its citizens. Against this, however, he counts the following differences between the two kinds of right. First, defending soldiers enjoy liberties in excess of those justified by personal right of self-defence—for example, they can use violence against those posing no imminent threat, such as a retreating aggressor.[232] Second, personal self-defence is subject to a condition of necessity, which requires the threatened person to retreat if possible, whereas a state is not required to appease aggression.[233] And third, according to just war theory, but not according to a proper justification of personal self-defence, the right to kill is held equally by soldiers on both sides.[234] Because of these differences, Rodin judges that the *narrowly* reductive account of national defence fails, and that any adequate conception must take into account the communal nature of the state.[235] Christian tradition agrees: national defence is not identical to private self-defence, but only analogous, displaying points of difference as well as similarity. The reason for the first two differences is that private citizens, unlike nation-states, can rely on the intervention of superior, public authority. The third point of difference, for reasons explained earlier in this chapter, Christian tradition does not admit at all.

A broader alternative is to think of national defence as a 'collective form' of self-defence, where the state has a right to defend its citizens as a parent has a right to defend his child.[236] Rodin finds this wanting, too. First, if the end of national defence were that of protecting the lives of individual citizens, then it would share an underlying moral structure with humanitarian intervention. On the contrary, however, 'common sense tells us' that the end

---

231. Ibid., p. 119.   232. Ibid., pp. 127–8.
233. Ibid., p. 128.   234. Ibid., pp. 128–9.
235. Ibid., p. 129.   236. Ibid., p. 129.

of national defence is the maintenance of state-sovereignty.[237] Well, common sense might say that, but Christian just war theory does not. Its justification of national defence *does* share an underlying moral structure with humanitarian intervention: the protection of the neighbour from grave injustice. Therefore this complaint fails.

Second, Rodin tells us, the right to national defence in international law and in just war theory holds even where a state's territorial integrity or political independence is being compromised 'bloodlessly', that is, without any violation of its citizens' right to life.[238] Perhaps a nation-state's defence of its sovereignty could be justified as a protection of its citizens' freedom from conditional and non-imminent threats to 'central rights' (against being killed, maimed, or enslaved). Not so, says Rodin; for while to use lethal force in defence of central rights would be proportionate, to use it against a conditional and non-imminent threat would not be necessary; and morally legitimate acts of self-defence require both.[239] But cannot some conditional threats be sufficiently serious as to warrant armed defence? For, as Locke says, 'I have no reason to suppose that he, who would take away my Liberty [sic], would not when he had me in his power, take away everything else;'[240] and as Walzer says, 'once the lines [borders] are crossed, safety is gone . . . there is no certainty this side of the border, any more than there is safety this side of the threshold, once a criminal has entered the house'.[241] Not so, says Rodin again. A conditional aggressor in effect makes an agreement, and there may be good reason in a given case to suppose that he will honour it: 'After all, the practice of making conditional threats would quickly break down and cease to have usefulness for assailants if they never kept their word in such situations.'[242] As empirical corroboration, Rodin finds a 'good example' in the Soviet Union's invasion of Finland during the Second World War. The USSR had demanded that Finland cede certain territories around St Petersburg, in order to strengthen the defences of the city against German attack, and they offered the Finns compensation amounting to roughly twice the territory they proposed to take. When Finland refused, the USSR

237. Ibid., pp. 130–1.
238. Ibid., pp. 131–2.
239. Ibid., p. 134.
240. John Locke, *Two Treatises of Government* (Cambridge: Cambridge University Press, 1960), Bk II, ch. III, p. 279.
241. Michael Walzer, *Just and Unjust Wars* (New York: Basic Books, 1977), pp. 55–8; cited in Rodin, *War and Self-Defense*, p. 135.
242. Rodin, *War and Self-Defense*, p. 136.

invaded, and after they had overcome Finnish resistance, they adhered roughly to their territorial demands. In Rodin's opinion 'there does not seem to be any question as to the genuinely limited nature of the Soviet Union's intentions. The demands were made on the basis of clear and obvious security concerns.'[243]

Once again, what is true of international law and of modern, liberal just war theory is not true of Christian tradition. According to the latter, just cause for war must comprise some *grave* injustice to human beings; and if it does not involve grave injustice (or a substantial threat of it), then the mere invasion of borders does not provide just cause. Grotius provides a speculative example of such a 'mere' invasion, which anticipates Rodin's historical one almost perfectly. He writes that a state engaged in a just war may occupy part of a neutral country, to prevent 'a certain danger' of the enemy's occupation and of his thereby being 'capable of doing irreparable injuries', on condition that the just state takes nothing but what is necessary for its security and that it withdraws as soon as the danger passes. This Grotius counts as yet another instance of the resurgence of '[t]he first right... of the antient [sic] community, since property was introduced... [namely] necessity'.[244]

Rodin concedes that if there is a very high risk that the invasion of territory will develop into encroachment on central rights, then there is a right to use lethal force in national defence.[245] What this implies, however, is that there may be a right to national defence where there is no right to personal self-defence; and so that the right of national defence cannot be grounded in the end of defending the lives of individuals. Therefore the reductive strategy, whether narrow or broad, fails.[246] In case this conclusion seems counter-intuitive, Rodin adduces further reasons to doubt that war is centrally concerned with defending citizens from external threat. One is

243. Ibid., p. 136n.22. Rodin relies on Basil Liddell Hart's account in his *History of the Second World War* (London: Cassell, 1970), pp. 43–8. Liddell Hart is unequivocal in his assessment: 'An objective examination of these terms [offered by the USSR to Finland] suggests that they were framed on a rational basis, to provide greater security to Russian territory without serious detriment to the security of Finland' (*History of the Second World War*, p. 44). Russia's demands were, however, being pressed on Finland in October and November 1940, long before German invasion was anticipated and seven months before it actually came. Quite whether neutral Finland could reasonably have been expected to yield to Soviet pressure *before* the Nazi threat had materialized, and to trust *Stalin's* Russia to honour its stated intentions, I rather doubt.

244. Grotius, *The Rights of War and Peace*, II.II.X, p. 437.

245. Rodin, *War and Self-Defense*, p. 137.

246. Ibid., p. 138.

that the stronger the resistance that national defence offers, the greater the loss of the lives of those citizens, which are the very point of the defence.[247] Another reason is that wars have an inherent tendency to escalate in ferocity, as von Clausewitz avers,[248] as well as to destabilize regions and leave legacies of resentment and instability that sow the seeds of future conflicts. In contrast, '[p]ersonal self-defense does not commonly lead to blood feuds'.[249] Rodin concedes that military action can sometimes be justified as a collective form of the exercise of personal defensive rights—for example, when resisting genocidal aggression, as in the Warsaw ghetto during the Second World War.[250] Nevertheless, most wars are not about fending off genocide. Therefore, he concludes, the right of national defence in international law and just war theory cannot be based on the assumption that its end is fundamentally that of defending the lives of citizens. A war of national defence is not a collection of individuals exercising the right of self-defence at the same time in a coordinated fashion; nor is the state exercising the right of self-defence on behalf of its own citizens, since it can claim the right to defend itself when none of its citizens is under imminent threat—and it can claim this right even if it thereby puts its citizens under greater threat.[251]

Rodin's argument here only tells against the proposition that the right to national defence *is the same as* the right to self-defence. It does not tell against the proposition that they are analogous. So the fact that a state has the right to defend its borders in reasonable anticipation of grave injustice, where individuals lack an equivalent right to anticipatory self-defence, does not show that national defence is not grounded in the rights of individuals. All it shows is that the right to national defence is not the same as the right to self-defence in a civil context, since the latter can usually assume effective public policing, while the former (still) cannot. Because of the different contexts, different means are permitted; but the ends remain the same.

Moreover, while personal self-defence might not commonly lead to blood feuds in 21st-century Oxford (where Rodin completed his book), they probably did so in the 15th century, and within Europe's living memory they have done so in the likes of Sicily and Crete. And even in contem-

---

247. Ibid., p. 138.
248. Carl von Clausewitz, *On War*, ed. M. Howard and P. Paret (Princeton: Princeton University Press, 1976), p. 77; cited in Rodin, *War and Self-Defense*, pp. 138–9.
249. Rodin, *War and Self-Defense*, p. 139.
250. Ibid., p. 139.   251. Ibid., p. 140.

porary Oxford, it is not at all inconceivable that the family of someone killed in self-defence—even justly killed—by a neighbour would carry their resentment for a lifetime, and even down the generations. Let it be granted that war leaves a legacy of resentment, and therefore of potential future conflict, on an altogether grander scale. But then the difference is merely one of degree, not of kind.

Nevertheless, Rodin is surely correct to argue that national defence often cannot be justified simply in terms of the collective defence of the *bare physical lives* of individuals against an imminent threat of harm. Oftentimes it would be less expensive of the physical lives of citizens, if their states were to surrender rather than resist invasion. It is quite likely that Britain could have spared the lives of several hundred thousand British and imperial citizens, if it had come to terms with Nazi Germany in 1940, as Hitler wanted and as many influential Britons thought that it should. And it is arguable that Soviet surrender to the German invaders in 1941 would have cost the USSR rather fewer lives than the twenty million or so it eventually expended in resistance.

In the end, however, Rodin does grant that military action actually *can* be a collective form of the exercise of personal defensive rights, and he cites as an example the case of the Warsaw ghetto. Thereby he concedes that *some* belligerency can be justified simply in terms of the collective defence of persons against the imminent threat of, as he puts it, 'genocide'. By implication his argument, now modified, holds only that *most* wars cannot justify themselves strictly in those terms; and that is undoubtedly true. However, the terms of Rodin's concession are rather meaner than they should be. Why limit the collective defence of personal rights to cases of fending off genocide? Why not extend it to fending off the imminent threat of mass murder? Indeed, why not extend it (as Rodin himself did earlier[252]) to fending off imminent threats to any 'central right' at all, including 'enslavement'? If that were conceded, then, depending on how narrowly or broadly we were to define 'imminent' and 'enslavement', membership of the class of wars able to justify themselves in terms of the collective defence of personal rights would increase quite considerably.

David Rodin is quite correct to argue that a moral justification for war is needed, and that the mere defence of national sovereignty—even *de iure*—does not provide it. He is wrong, however, to suppose that just war theory

252. Ibid., p. 134.

as a whole thinks otherwise. Christian tradition holds that a just war is one
that intends to stop and correct a grave injustice to human persons. Such
injustice includes wrongful physical harm to, and killing of, individuals, but
it is not reducible to them. It also includes wrongful harm to the social and
political matrices upon which the flourishing of individual persons also
depends. After all, enslavement harms individuals by imprisoning them in
an oppressive social environment; and genocide harms them by eradicating
their people and culture.

X. The rationale of national defence (ii): common life or common goods?

Since Rodin rightly judges that national defence (as a rule) cannot find
adequate justification simply in terms of the good of the bare lives of individual citizens, he moves on to consider whether it can do so in terms of
the analogous good of the nation's common life. If national defence is not
reducible to personal self-defence, maybe it is analogous to it. This, he tells
us, is just war theory's classic claim.[253]

How is such common life understood? On the one hand, Rodin flatly
rejects what he calls the 'strong organic view' of common life as having a
moral value that is prior to and independent of the value of the component
individuals. He endorses Joseph Raz's 'humanistic principle' that the explanation of the goodness and badness of anything derives ultimately from its
contribution to human life and its quality.[254] On the other hand, notwithstanding the symptoms of individualism already observed above, Rodin
accepts that the community plays an essential role in shaping the individual.[255] In sum: '[a]n adequate conception of the common life will see it as
something whose value is separate from, and irreducible to, the value of the
particular individuals that make it up, yet its worth must be seen as deriving
from the value it has for them'.[256]

253. Ibid., p. 120. Rodin cites in particular Grotius, *De Iure Belli ac Pacis*, trans. F. Kelsey (New York: Classics of International Law, 1964), Bk II, ch. 1, p. 184 (*War and Self-Defense*, p. 107).
254. Ibid., pp. 143–4.
255. Ibid., p. 143.
256. Ibid., p. 144. Rodin's view of the relationship between the individual and community—and so with a national community's organ of cohesion, the state—may be somewhat opaque, but

Given this, and within the perimeter of international law and 'the best interpretation' of just war theory, Rodin finds three conceptions of common life that are considered worthy of armed defence: state legitimacy, the embodiment of a particular cultural and historical heritage, and the arena of collective self-determination and autonomy.[257] According to the first conception, the state is a centre of moral value insofar as its power is legitimated as authority, which obliges obedience from subjects; and according to its Hobbesian species, the state's moral authority derives from its ability to replace the anarchic state of nature with the basic good of order.[258] Rodin astutely observes, however, that the logic of this Hobbesian view tends toward a universal political association, whose legitimate sovereign would rescue states from the anarchic condition of international nature.[259] It therefore militates against the right to national defence, which enshrines the right of particular communities to political sovereignty and so sustains the international state of nature.[260] What is more, international aggression typically does not seek to destroy the value of the order secured by political association *as such*, and the offering of national defence could exacerbate disorder.[261]

Maybe state legitimacy, and so the right to national defence, requires the achievement of more than mere order. Perhaps, for example, it requires *liberal democratic* order. However, in international law the right to national defence is not limited to morally superior sovereign states: 'The law is neutral between different forms of political constitution.'[262] Rodin concludes: 'To justify national-defense we require a moral reason not simply to defend order, but to defend a particular form of order; to defend *our* order.'[263]

---

it is nevertheless more reciprocal and satisfactory than Robert Holmes's consistent individualism. Holmes writes: 'States are simply abstractions; there exist only human beings organized in different ways... It is their lives, their well-being and happiness that is important, not the "lives" of states. The latter have value only insofar as they contribute to the former' (*On War and Morality*, p. 260); 'the state is not in fact a superperson [sic]. It does not have... interests independently of those projected onto it by individual persons. Nor as an imaginatively personified superbeing [sic] is it the fitting object of devotion, much less the sacrifice of human lives. Only individual persons feel and suffer, live and die' (ibid., p. 85).

257. Ibid., p. 142.   258. Ibid., pp. 144–5.
259. Ibid., pp. 145–6.   260. Ibid., p. 146.
261. Ibid., p. 147.   262. Ibid., p. 148.   263. Ibid., p. 149.

This brings us to the second conception of common life that might be worthy of armed defence: namely, common life of a particular character. While it is true that this is integral to many of the substantive goods that compose an individual's life,[264] Rodin tells us, its value is merely subjective.[265] What is more, the common lives of some nation-states are systematically and pervasively corrupt and brutal, and display a disregard for human rights, and as such cannot be objectively valuable and so worthy of national defence—even if international law confers the right.[266]

So we reach the third communal candidate for a sufficient grounding of national defence: namely, a common life that embodies freedom, autonomy, and self-determination. These are 'objective, trans-cultural goods', since in pursuing the good as she sees it, each individual implicitly affirms the universal good of the freedom necessary for such pursuit.[267] Suppose, then, that it is the good of the process of collective self-determination that aggression threatens, and that this is only realized with the establishment of democratic rights. It follows that non-democratic regimes would lack the right to national defence—which contradicts current international law and just war theory.[268] Walzer, however, does not identify collective self-determination with democracy, understanding it rather as the freedom (from foreign interference) to choose a culturally congenial political system, even an illiberal and authoritarian one. Such freedom could take the form of a balancing of power between competing interest groups, and *in extremis* civil war. Against this, Rodin complains that it reduces collective self-determination 'ultimately to coercion and the balance of force'.[269] The faction with the greatest normative legitimacy (that is, the best fit with the common life of the population) does not always prevail.[270] A more fundamental problem, however, is that national communities do not coincide with the boundaries of states.[271] So the defence of the autonomy of a national community cannot ground the defence of a nation-state. Indeed, sometimes the defence of one will conflict with the defence of the other.[272]

It seems, then, that national defence can neither be reduced to a collective application of personal rights of self-defence nor explained as a state

---

264. Ibid., pp. 149–50.   265. Ibid., p. 151.
266. Ibid., p. 152.   267. Ibid., p. 155.
268. Ibid., p. 156.   269. Ibid., p. 157.
270. Ibid., p. 157.   271. Ibid., pp. 158–9.
272. Ibid., pp. 159–60.

right analogous to personal self-defence. Since Rodin supposes that the right of national defence has always been the central just cause for war in just war theory, and that the analogy with self-defence has always been its central justification, he thinks that this conclusion poses a serious challenge to the traditional doctrine of international morality.[273]

In fact, Rodin's argument is far more consonant with Christian just war tradition—both early and late—than he realizes. Although early Christian thinkers appreciated the social good of order rather more than modern liberals, because they were used to enjoying rather less of it, they were still aware that order can take insufferably unjust forms. So, as we shall see in the following section, they were not willing to make the rights of state sovereignty morally unconditional and to justify national defence of any kind of order whatsoever—*pace* modern international law. Early Christian just war theory is *not* Hobbesian—indeed, in substance it is *anti*-Hobbesian.

As with order, so with common life and self-determination: their value is subject to moral criteria. Although a global ecology of distinctive national cultures is something to be prized—as, for example, Anglican just war thinkers from F.D. Maurice to Oliver O'Donovan have affirmed[274]—a distinctive culture's independence or survival *as such* does not amount to a just cause for defensive war. Not all cultures are morally equal; and some are intolerably unjust, deserving to be invaded, not defended. What constitutes 'intolerable injustice' is a contentious issue, of course, but Michael Walzer is surely right not to consign to it every political constitution short of liberal democracy. Tolerable political justice did not first grace the earth in the 1780s. If the medieval history of England is any guide, then monarchy need not be equated with tyranny, since monarchical power often depends on consultation and consent, and so becomes politically accountable and subject to law.

Rodin is right to say that the value of a national culture somehow derives from the human individuals who participate in it, while transcending them. This is because, as the Christian tradition has long affirmed against Hobbes, human beings are *originally* social, and many of the forms of their flourishing—their basic goods—are either intrinsically social or have social dimen-

---

273. Ibid., p. 162.
274. See Nigel Biggar, 'Anglican Theology of War and Peace', *Crucible* (October–December 2004), p. 10.

sions. As a consequence a nation's social institutions and customs can incarnate important human goods, and *for that reason* become worth defending. In that humans flourish as individuals by investing themselves in human goods, it can make sense for them—as it often has and does—to sacrifice their *bare lives* in defence of their national culture. Of the paradox that we find our lives in losing them, Christians make full sense by reference to the promise of resurrection from the dead. Others must make what sense of it they can.

XI. Just war as law enforcement

Having, as he thinks, disposed of the claim that war can be justified as national defence, Rodin turns finally to consider the main alternative: the justification of war as law enforcement. For this to be justified, as he sees it, military action against an international aggressor would have to be sanctioned by an impartial body with recognized authority.[275] As things now stand, the permanent members of the United Nations Security Council use their power and their veto in their own national interest, not impartially, which 'makes it difficult' to view the military action that it authorizes as legitimate forms of punishment or law enforcement.[276] Still, '[a] genuine form of justification is clearly operative here even it if is not perfectly realised'.[277]

In Rodin's view, perfect justification would comprise authorization by a United Nations upgraded to a universal sovereign state. Individual sovereign states have not yet found themselves compelled to covenant together to form a universal commonwealth, because they are able to preserve a tolerable degree of security within the state of nature.[278] Why is this? A realist explanation is that the current disparity in power means, on the one hand, that great powers can secure themselves and so lack incentive to enter into a universal commonwealth; and on the other hand, that lesser powers can only find their security as vassals and clients of the great ones.[279] Rodin notes, however, that the security of great powers is now compromised by

275. Rodin, *War and Self-Defense*, pp. 179–80.
276. Ibid., p. 180.   277. Ibid., p. 181.
278. Ibid., p. 183.   279. Ibid., p. 183.

small states' possession of nuclear weapons, by international terrorism, and by guerrilla warfare.[280]

In addition to a prudential case for a universal sovereign state, however, there is also a moral case. The contractarian basis of international morality is not whether the interests of sovereigns are best served by their binding themselves to a universal system of law, but whether the security of the individual members of their states—the original contractors—is so best served.[281] Rodin believes that there is a clear *prima facie* case that citizens would choose a universal state.[282] What about the risk of universal despotism? What about absence of any external check? He notes that the presence of external powers has not prevented repression in Iraq and China, and that sometimes an external threat can facilitate despotism.[283] He concedes that there is 'clearly some truth in the observation' that it would be extremely difficult to organize effective resistance in a universal state, but he reckons that the international state of nature could be brought to an end by 'an ultra-minimal universal state', consisting solely in a monopoly of military force and a minimal judicial mechanism for the resolution of disputes, structured according to the principle of subsidiarity.[284]

Christian just war thinking does not share Rodin's point of departure here. For Rodin, as for any Hobbesian social contractarian, where positive law and courts are lacking, there remains merely an amoral state of nature. Grotius, however, sees things differently: 'Let it be granted then, that laws must be silent in the midst of arms, provided they are only those laws that are civil and judicial, and proper for times of peace; but not those that are of perpetual obligation, and are equally suited to all times.'[285] Before international treaties—and in their absence—stands created, natural right. From this it follows that, even where there is no law to enforce, there may still be injustice to punish: 'right still subsists when the way to legal justice is not open'—for example, where there is no (global) civil government;[286] the power of punishing is not 'properly an effect of civil jurisdiction', but 'proceeds from the law of nature';[287] and 'it is not to be doubted, but that before the penal law be made, an offence may be punished'.[288] From this

---

280. Ibid., p. 184.   281. Ibid., pp. 184–5.
282. Ibid., pp. 185–6.   283. Ibid., p. 186.   284. Ibid., pp. 186–7.
285. Grotius, *The Rights of War and Peace*, 'The Preliminary Discourse', XXVII, p. 102.
286. Ibid., I.III.II, p. 241.
287. Ibid., II.XX.XL.4, p. 1024.
288. Ibid., II.XX.XXII.1, p. 996.

follows a natural right to intervene militarily for humanitarian purposes. Sovereigns, writes Grotius, 'have a right to exact punishments, not only for injuries committed against themselves, or their subjects, but likewise, for those which do not peculiarly concern them, but which are, in any persons whatsoever, grievous violations of the law of nature or nations'. Indeed, 'it is so much more honourable, to revenge other people's injuries rather than their own, by as much as it is more to be feared, lest out of a sense of their own sufferings, they either exceed the just measure of punishment, or, at least, prosecute their revenge with malice'.[289] As an example of a grievous violation of the law of nature worthy of military contradiction Grotius cites cannibalism[290]—as had Vitoria before him, together with human sacrifice.[291]

Nevertheless, early Christian just war thinkers acknowledge that it is not entirely satisfactory that a ruler should be the judge in his own case. Thus Suárez:

> it cannot be denied that in this matter [of public vengeance], one and the same person assumes, in a sense, the role of plaintiff and that of judge... But the cause... is simply that this act of punitive justice has been indispensable to mankind, and that no more fitting method for its performance could, in the order of nature and humanly speaking, be found... Neither is this case analogous to that of a private individual. For... such an individual is guided by his own [unaided] judgement, and therefore he will easily exceed the limits of vengeance; whereas public authority is guided by public counsel, to which heed must be paid.[292]

Grotius writes similarly: while 'it is much honester, and more conducive to the peace of mankind, that differences should be decided by a third person that is disinterested, than that every man should be allowed to do himself justice in his own cause, wherein the illusions of self-love are much to be apprehended',[293] outside civil government that option is not available.[294]

---

289. Ibid., II.XX.XL.1, p. 1021.
290. Ibid., II.XX.XL.3, p. 1022.
291. Vitoria, 'On Dietary Laws, or Self-Restraint', in *Political Writings*, I.5.5, p. 225. Vitoria, however, makes a point of saying that not *every* violation of the natural law deserves to be stopped by military means, only those that involve *iniuria* to others. Suárez agrees: military intervention can only be justified 'in circumstances in which the slaughter of innocent people, and similar wrongs take place' ('On Charity: Disputation XIII', V.5, p. 826).
292. Suárez, 'On Charity: Disputation XIII', IV.7, p. 819.
293. Grotius, *The Rights of War and Peace*, I.III.I, p. 241.
294. Ibid., I.III.II, p. 241.

What this line of thinking says is that, ideally (setting aside all concern about a propensity to tyranny), injustice should be fended off and punished in a universal sovereign state, according to universal laws, and by universal courts and police. In their absence, however, unilateral belligerency can be justified in response to proportionately grave injustice, whether unjust invasion by an aggressor or another sovereign's maltreatment of his people. Not all justice takes place within courts; and some must take place without them. The international state of nature is not a moral wasteland, bereft of moral law or conscience; and conscientious rulers can exercise the virtues of fairness and temperance in judging and punishing unjust enemies.

XII. Negligence of civil conflict?

Because he tends to think of it in terms of modern liberal versions and international law, Rodin complains that just war theory has been transfixed by notions of aggression and national defence, and has consequently failed to address the problems of civil war and internal oppression. This is simply not true of just war theory as a whole. Aquinas and Suárez both addressed the question of sedition.[295] In the 16th century Protestants had an obvious interest in reflecting on the right of armed resistance to established authority and many did so, including Luther, Calvin, and, most notably, John Knox.[296] Grotius considered the question, although his conclusions are almost absolutely conservative.[297] In the 20th century, the Lutheran ethicist Helmuth Thielicke, mindful of the recent experience of Germans under the Nazi regime, devoted a substantial section of his *Theological Ethics* to the topic of 'Resistance to State Authority'.[298] Thinking in terms of the war in Vietnam, Paul Ramsey wrote about counter-insurgency in the late 1960s.[299] The guerrilla campaigns against states in Latin America and Africa in the

---

295. Aquinas, *Summa Theologiae,* 2a 2ae, q. 42, pp. 102–7; Suárez, 'On Charity: Disputation XIII', VIII, pp. 854–5.
296. See Quentin Skinner, *The Foundations of Modern Political Thought*, 2 vols, Vol. 2: 'The Age of Reformation', chapters 7, 8, 9; John Knox, *On Rebellion*, ed. Roger A. Mason, Cambridge Texts in the History of Political Thought (Cambridge: Cambridge University Press, 1994).
297. Grotius, *The Rights of War and Peace*, I.III.VIII.1,2; I.IV; II.I.IX.2.
298. Helmuth Thielicke, *Theological Ethics*, 2 vols (Grand Rapids: Eerdmans, 1979), Vol. 2: 'Politics', pp. 321–419.
299. Ramsey, 'Vietnam and Insurgency Warfare', in *The Just War*.

1970s and 1980s provoked further reflection;[300] as did the 'Troubles' in Northern Ireland.[301] There is, of course, much more that needs to be done. Nonetheless, Christian just war theory has not been asleep on this front.

XIII. Practical failings?

Rodin's concluding charge against just war theory is that it has failed, not only in theory, but in practice. Its theoretical distinction between culpable aggressor and innocent defender is subverted practically, he says, in two ways. First, it is subverted by the fact that today's legal status quo was yesterday's injustice, and today's victim was yesterday's aggressor. As an example, he cites Britain's possession of the Falkland Islands.[302] However, a blurring of an absolute moral distinction between aggressor and victim obtains at the interpersonal level too—indeed it obtains everywhere, even in courts. The lives of human beings are often intertwined, so that the wrong you did me today was in part provoked by the wrong I did you last year. Victims are often not entirely blameless. But that does not mean that the categories of guilt and innocence are rendered otiose. The wrong I did you last week might mitigate your guilt for the wrong you did me today, but, provided you remain a responsible human being, you remain guilty. Thus, on the international stage, the fact that France was party to the Treaty of Versailles in 1919, whose harsh terms helped to foster the rise of Nazism, does not mean that Nazi Germany did no wrong in invading France (for the third time in seventy years) in 1940. The fact that the lives of victims and aggressors are often bound up with one another is a reason for temperate, perhaps compassionate, judgement, but not a reason for suspending judgement altogether.

300. E.g. Richard Harries, *Should a Christian Support Guerrillas?* (Guildford: Lutterworth, 1982); and Charles Villa-Vicencio, ed., *Theology & Violence: The South African Debate* (Grand Rapids: Eerdmans, 1988).

301. E.g. Peter Phillips Simpson, 'Just War Theory and the I.R.A.', in *Vices, Virtues, and Consequences. Essays in Moral and Political Philosophy* (Washington, DC: Catholic University of America Press, 2001); and O'Donovan, *The Just War Revisited,* chapter 2, 'Counter-Insurgency War'. The 'Troubles' provoked just war analysis not only of itself but also of earlier conflicts in Irish history: e.g. Séamus Murphy, 'Easter Ethics', in Gabriel Doherty and Dermot Keogh, eds, *1916: The Long Revolution* (Cork: Mercier Press, 2007).

302. Rodin, *War and Self-Defense*, pp. 189–90.

The second way in which Rodin thinks that the distinction between guilty and innocent parties is subverted is by the background conditions of mutual distrust and readiness for conflict, which dissolve the distinction between aggression and defence.[303] Thus, a change in balance of power can give defensive justification to an act of aggression, and make a defensive move appear aggressive. And insofar as conflicts are infected by the politics of brinkmanship—whose 20th-century *loci classici* are the eve of the First World War in 1914 and the Cuban Missile Crisis of 1962—the application of the categories of aggression and defence 'is often nothing more than an exercise in moral bad faith'.[304] The ambiguity between defensive and aggressive acts poses a major problem for international law and just war theory, '[f]or the entire moral weight of the *ius ad bellum* rests on the determination of a single decisive moment of unlawful aggression'.[305] To this I would respond, first of all, that not all conflicts involve brinkmanship. Further, there may well be occasions when the claims of both sides to innocent victimhood are equally spurious; but in that case *both* are unjust aggressors. Then there might be other occasions when it is difficult to tell a morally licit defensive move from a morally illicit aggressive one. Yet difficulty is not impossibility. Let us take one of the cases that Rodin cites: 1914. It is true that Germany launched war against France because it felt itself surrounded by enemies and believed that its very survival depended on fighting sooner than later. It saw its aggression as a form of anticipatory defence. However, whereas social Darwinism might sanction such a view, just war theory does not. Legitimate pre-emption requires good reason to suppose imminent, or at least certainly developing, attack. Not only is there no evidence whatsoever that France, Britain, or Russia were planning to initiate aggression against Germany, but also before the Germans attacked, French forces were ordered to keep ten kilometres behind the frontier, so as to avoid communicating offensive intentions. As for the British Expeditionary Force, its main units would not begin to cross the English Channel until eight days after German troops had marched into Belgium. Whatever the initial appearances, there was no evidence of imminent threat, and yet Germany invaded anyway. There we have our 'single moment of unlawful aggression'.

---

303. Ibid., p. 190.   304. Ibid., p. 193.   305. Ibid., pp. 190–1.

XIV. Conclusion

David Rodin's searching critique is very cogent against just war theory that takes its cue from positive international law and Michael Walzer's version. He is quite correct to complain that national sovereignty as such cannot justify national defence; and that the assertion of the moral equality of soldiers removes a large part of the moral rationale for killing. However, whereas he thinks that he has exposed the incoherence of just war theory in general, he has in fact only exposed particular modern versions of it. Moreover, and ironically, he has inadvertently vindicated the Christian tradition, both early and late.

That tradition does not take self-defence as the paradigm of just war, but rather the restraint and punishing of injustice by civil police and judges. Were there a universal state with universal law, courts, and effective police, then (all other considerations apart) prudence would not leave the responsibility for such restraint and punishment to nation-states. However, in the absence of a universal state, international relations are not a moral free-for-all—*pace* Hobbes (and Rodin). Original, natural sociability persists and the natural right that it generates reigns on, even in the absence of social contracts; and to this the consciences of national leaders remain responsible, upon pain of the loss of human flourishing in this world and in the next. So even in a judicial desert, fraternal justice can and should be done—albeit fairly, charitably, and with the compassion owed by one set of sinners to another.

The doing of justice by means of war can only be warranted if it aims to defend genuine and important human goods against grave and unjust threats—and to mete out that punishment which comprises long-term defence. National sovereignty alone does not count as such a good, since it might preside over atrocious domestic oppression; nor does distinctive common life, since that might include atrocious oppression. Among the goods that would suffice are at least the bare lives of the innocent, but also national institutions and customs that enable them to flourish in important ways.

Since just war is basically a punitive response to grave injustice, whether directed at one's own people or another's, it follows that the justification for killing enemy combatants is paradigmatically that they are culpable of objective injustice, or presumably so. In rare cases unjust agents might not be at all guilty in fact, because although responsible for judging the moral quality of their own cause, their ignorance of its injustice might be completely excusable; and in rarer cases this might be known to their just opponents. Nevertheless, their possession of a right not to be harmed does not lie entirely in the control of their own moral choices. Its loss can be caused by factors other than their incurring guilt. Their threatening or causing objective injustice is one factor, necessary but not sufficient. What is also necessary is that those who kill them do not intend (that is, maliciously want) their deaths, that they kill only as a last resort, and that they do so with proportionate reason. Thus will wrongdoers be rendered the respect that is due. Thus will the harshness they suffer be made kind.

6

On not always giving the Devil benefit of law

Legality, morality, and Kosovo[1]

I. Natural law as trumps

Law is given before it is made. Legal statutes and social contracts are not crafted in a moral wasteland. They are born accountable to a higher, natural law, and their word is neither first nor last. If that were not so, then Nuremberg was nothing but victors' vengeance dressed up in a fiction of 'justice', and today's high-blown rhetoric of universal human rights is just so much wind.

Such is the moral realism that the Christian doctrine of just war, both early and late, takes for granted. It assumes that there is a universal moral order that transcends national legal systems and applies to international relations even in the absence of positive international law. It believes that there are human goods and moral obligations that exist in and with the nature of things (in some sense), and which exercise a guiding and constraining moral authority long before human beings articulate them in statutes or treaties. It holds that the principles of moral law are given before positive laws are made. One thing that this implies is that military action can sometimes be morally justified in the absence of, and even in spite of, statutory international law. Therefore, the doctrine's proponents cannot join those who believe that the

1. This chapter contains elements of two essays published elsewhere: 'On Giving the Devil Benefit of Law in Kosovo', in *Kosovo: Contending Voices on Balkan Interventions*, ed. William Joseph Buckley (Grand Rapids: Eerdmans, 2000), pp. 409–18; and 'The Ethics of Forgiveness and the Doctrine of Just War: A Religious View of Righting Atrocious Wrongs', in *The Religious in Responses to Mass Atrocity*, ed. Brudholm and Cushman, pp. 105–23.

legitimacy of military intervention to prevent or halt grave injustice is decided simply by the presence or absence of authorization by the United Nations Security Council. Positive law cannot have the final word.

This view is theological at least insofar as it is consonant with, and supported by, monotheism. Part of the meaning of the assertion that there is only one God is that the world of space and time in all its variety and change has a fundamental point of unity that gives it a basic coherence, order, rationality, and intelligibility. Part of the meaning of the assertion that there is one quasi-personal God is that this order is not just physical, but benevolent. That is to say, the world's physical processes are governed by God's intention to bring it to fulfilment. This cosmic fulfilment involves the emergence and securing of beings capable of appreciating, and freely committing themselves to, what is true and good and beautiful—that is, it involves the growth and establishment of a community of virtuous human persons. This is the human good: the condition where persons flourish. The virtuous commitment that intends such good is the foundation of morality, for moral rules are but the explication of what that commitment requires of behaviour: right action is demanded by it, permissible action is consonant with it, and wrong action contradicts it.

Monotheism implies a real, universal human good, with regard to which particular moralities try to order human conduct. Anyone, then, who affirms such moral realism will find allies in orthodox Jews, Christians, and Muslims. Clearly, however, not all moral realists are monotheists. Many of them feel able to affirm a culturally transcendent moral order without having to resort to theology. Whether they should feel so able depends upon the upshot of the long-standing debate about whether belief in a universal moral order logically requires monotheism (which is not the same, of course, as the belief that monotheism logically implies a universal moral order), or whether a universal order at least needs monotheism for optimal intelligibility.[2] We do not need to settle that question here. For our purposes it suffices to say

2. In favour of the view that a universal moral order needs monotheism for optimal intelligibility, this monotheist would urge the following claims: that human striving to realize the good cannot remain sufficiently intelligible if it is understood to occur in a cosmos whose fundamental driving energies are blind and heartless; that human dignity and rights cannot long continue to command authority among those who are convinced of a relentless cosmic indifference; that the project to realize a community of virtuous persons cannot inspire motivation if in the end death reduces all of its members forever to dust; and that Kant was therefore correct to argue that the coherence of a commitment to do human persons justice ultimately requires the postulates of immortality and therefore of an immortalizing agent, God.

that, insofar as it remains true to its theological roots, just war doctrine is morally realist and therefore holds that the claims of positive law can be trumped by appeal to natural morality. And insofar as they are morally realist on other grounds, non-theological versions of the doctrine will hold likewise.

A common objection to appeals to natural moral law is that it is indeterminate and controversial. Positive law, however, is itself not beyond controversy—as we shall see shortly. What is more, one truth made manifest by the experience of Nazi rule is that the deliberate and indiscriminate killing of the innocent can be legally permissible, and that its condemnation therefore requires appeal to principles of justice that transcend positive law.[3] Further still, the widespread view that NATO's intervention in Kosovo was at once formally illegal and morally right implies that a significant measure of international consensus on natural principles of justice transcending positive international law is not only possible, but actual.

II. The (conditional) authority of positive law

None of this is to say that, in the eyes of morally realist just war doctrine, positive international law carries no moral weight itself. There are good moral reasons of a prudential sort why we should be loath to transgress positive law even for the noblest of motives.[4] The case for this is made with

3. The distinction between justice and positive, statutory law came to be recognized in German law in the wake of the Nazi regime. Before the Second World War, Gustav Radbruch, professor of law and a politician, was a legal positivist. In 1946, however, he wrote a now famous essay, 'Gesetzliches Unrecht und übergesetzliches Recht', arguing that there can be cases where the discrepancy between positive law and justice reaches such an 'unbearable' degree that the former must be deemed 'erroneous' (*unrichtiges*). Indeed, there may be cases where positive law does not even attempt justice, and where equality is abandoned, in which case the statute does not partake of the nature of law at all. 'That,' he wrote, 'is because law, including positive law, can only be defined as an order and statute, whose very meaning is precisely to serve justice' (G. Radbruch, 'Gesetzliches Unrecht und übergesetzliches Recht', *Süddeutsche Juristenzeitung* [1946], p. 107). This view is referred to as the 'Radbruch Formula', which has been applied many times by both the German Federal Constitutional Court and the Federal Court of Justice, originally in cases concerned with Nazi crimes.

4. My view of the conditional moral authority of positive law aligns itself very largely with that of Joseph Raz. According to Raz, there is no 'general obligation applying to all the law's subjects and to all the laws on all the occasions to which they apply' to do what the law requires simply because the law requires it (Joseph Raz, 'The Obligation to Obey the Law' [1979], in *The Authority of Law*, 2nd edn [Oxford: Oxford University Press, 2009], pp. 233–4). Indeed, it is 'morally pernicious' to 'suggest that every individual is inevitably obliged to obey the law of his

memorable rhetorical force in *A Man for All Seasons*, Robert Bolt's play about Sir Thomas More. In one scene More is urged by his daughter, Margaret, and his future son-in-law, Nicholas Roper, to arrest Richard Rich, an informer. The subsequent argument rises to this climax:

MARGARET (exasperated, pointing to Rich): While you talk, he's gone!
MORE: And go he should if he was the Devil himself until he broke the law!
ROPER: So now you'd give the Devil benefit of law!
MORE: Yes. What would you do? Cut a great road through the law to get after the Devil?
ROPER: I'd cut down every law in England to do that!
MORE: Oh? And when the last law was down, and the Devil turned round on you —where would you hide, Roper, the laws all being flat? This country's planted thick with laws from coast to coast—Man's law's, not God's—and if you cut them down—and you're just the man to do it—d'you really think you could stand upright in the winds that would blow then? Yes, I'd give the Devil benefit of law, for my own safety's sake.[5]

The law's power to order a society, national or international, and so to safeguard the rights of its members, consists primarily in its authority (as distinct from its capability of physical force); and this authority consists in the willingness to obey of those it commands. Obedience can be volunteered for a variety of reasons, including the conviction that what the law requires is morally right and socially beneficial. Certainly—*pace* Hobbes and his followers—the fear of sanction is not the only motive for compliance, nor is it a necessary one.[6] That is evidenced by the fact that most citizens feel bound

society regardless of how good or bad that law may be' (ibid., p. 240). However, there can be *prima facie* reasons of a moral or prudential kind to obey the law—for example, not setting a bad example, encouraging others to become lawbreakers, and so contributing to a general breakdown in the rule of law (ibid., pp. 237–8). Nonetheless, '[i]f the facets of law which make it morally valuable are pervasive, systemic features, e.g., that it—the law—is a way of securing public order through subjecting social activity to a framework of openly ascertainable rules, then it affects an individual's reasons only to the extent that his action will tend to undermine the law' (ibid., p. 240). The view dominant among philosophers, which Raz appears to share, is 'that the obligation to obey the law is not violated when an offence is committed in circumstances where there are strong moral reasons for committing it' (ibid., p. 235). My only point of dissent from Raz's account concerns the sharp distinction that he draws between 'moral' reasons and 'prudential' ones.

5. Robert Bolt, *A Man for All Seasons* (London: Heinemann, 1960), pp. 38–9.
6. Among Hobbes's eminent disciples on this point are John Austin and Hans Morgenthau, who hold that the law's authority and obligatory force consist simply in the subject's fear of the sovereign's threat of sanction against lawbreakers (Mary Ellen O'Connell, *The Power and Purpose of International Law: Insights from the Theory and Practice of Enforcement* [New York: Oxford University Press, 2008], pp. 4, 40, 63).

by domestic laws that are only haphazardly enforced, and that most states comply with international law, despite the absence of a global executive authority.[7] Nevertheless, the readiness of subjects to volunteer obedience is partly sustained by confidence that perpetrators of grave violations of the law expose themselves to serious threat of proportionate sanction, and that not infrequently they suffer it. If the law is not so enforced, and if grave lawbreakers are seen to act with frequent impunity, then the respect of the obedient for the law will be shaken and its authority will tend to diminish. If this diminution proceeds far enough, then the rule of law will disintegrate and society will dissolve into anarchy, and those who have taken advantage of others' law-abidingness will find themselves reduced to an equality of defencelessness—the laws all being flat.[8]

Usually, of course, those who disobey the law do so in order to gain some private advantage—material goods, say, or an increase in political power. But sometimes people are moved to break the law in pursuit of justice. This is because there are occasions when those with the power to enforce the law cannot do so, typically because they do not have sufficient evidence to make an arrest or secure a conviction; and in those cases private bodies might be moved to take the law into their own hands, in order to administer rough justice to those whom they know—or presume to know—are criminals. As a rule, however, they should not. Why? Because the laws governing law enforcement are in place to protect the innocent against wrongful arrest and excessive punishment on mistaken or fraudulent grounds. This is a protection that would-be vigilantes expect for themselves; so they cannot consistently deny it to others. Further, if they do so without penalty, their action would diminish the law's authority and discourage its observance by suggesting that it serves only to disadvantage the weak in relation to the strong. So for the sake of the general order and peace that ensue from prevalent respect for the law, particular pursuits of justice must be legally constrained—even at the expense of letting the Devil himself escape.

7. Thus Louis Henkin: '[i]t is probably the case that *almost all nations observe almost all principles of international law and almost all of their obligations almost all of the time*' (quoted by O'Connell in *Power and Purpose*, p. 76; emphasis original). O'Connell also observes that even Morgenthau acknowledged that compliance with international law is the norm (ibid., p. 66).

8. H.L.A. Hart renders the same point thus: sanctions are 'the guarantee that those who would voluntarily obey shall not be sacrificed to those who would not. To obey, without this, would be to risk going to the wall' (*The Concept of Law* [Oxford: Clarendon Press, 1961], p. 193).

III. Kosovo: a case of legal controversy

Or, if not quite the Devil, then, as some argued in relation to the Kosovo War in 1999, Slobodan Milošević and his forces. One of the most basic objections raised by critics of NATO's military intervention in Kosovo was that, lacking authorization by the Security Council, it presumed to run roughshod over international law, thereby weakening the law's authority and setting a precedent for any sufficiently powerful state to invade another's sovereign territory on moral grounds of its own choosing. As a result, it was argued, the security of states everywhere had been weakened and relations between them made more distrustful. NATO's high-handed action had made the world a considerably more dangerous place.

That, however, was only one view, for the legal status of NATO's action was—and is—a point of controversy, on which eminent experts in international law have taken opposing sides.[9] There is no doubt that the UN Charter forbids the unilateral use of force, except in self-defence; and that it restricts all other use of force to what is specifically mandated by the UN's Security Council for the maintenance of international security and peace. Controversy arises, however, over whether or not this is the last word on the matter of armed intervention for humanitarian purposes. On the one hand, Ian Brownlie, former Professor of Public International Law at Oxford University, thought that it is. He argued that the Charter's position is clear and that it remains unqualified. In support of his argument he made the following points: that the preparatory work of the Charter indicates unequivocally that intervention for special motives was ruled out; that the Charter's position was confirmed in 1970 by the Declaration on Principles of International Law concerning Friendly Relations and Cooperation in its restatement of 'the principle concerning the duty not to intervene in matters within the domestic jurisdiction of any State'; and that there is no evidence of the development of a doctrine of humanitarian intervention in customary international law. To demonstrate this last point, Brownlie cited statements made between 1971 and 1999 by seven legal authorities of vari-

9. For example, on 10 May 1999 at the International Court of Justice in the Hague, Oxford's Ian Brownlie argued on behalf of the government of the Federal Republic of Yugoslavia that NATO's action was illegal, while his counterpart at the London School of Economics, Christopher Greenwood, argued the opposite on behalf of the government of the United Kingdom.

ous nationalities, including (most powerfully) a British Foreign Office document that contains this passage:

> In fact, the best case that can be made in support of humanitarian intervention is that it cannot be said to be unambiguously illegal... But the overwhelming majority of contemporary legal opinion comes down against the existence of a right of humanitarian intervention, for three main reasons: first, the UN Charter and the corpus of modern international law do not seem specifically to incorporate such a right; secondly, state practice in the past two centuries, and especially since 1945, at best provides only a handful of genuine cases of humanitarian intervention, and, on most assessments, none at all; and finally, on prudential grounds, that the scope for abusing such a right argues strongly against its creation... In essence, therefore, the case against making humanitarian intervention an exception to the principle of non-intervention is that its doubtful benefits would be heavily outweighed by its worth in terms of international law.[10]

On the other hand, against this position it can be argued that the UN Universal Declaration of Human Rights (1948) and subsequent treaties on the maintenance of human rights have subjected the internal conduct of sovereign states to international norms: 'From their inception these texts were regarded as a significant attack in the shell of state sovereignty.'[11] It is doubtful, however, that they establish a right of unilateral intervention in defence of the rights they affirm.[12] Such a right might be inferred from Article 1 of the Genocide Convention (1948), where the signatories 'undertake to prevent and punish' genocide. However, arguably, this is then qualified by Article 8, according to which contracting parties 'may call upon' the United Nations to take action under its Charter. Certainly, it is generally taken for granted that all subsequent treaties are to be read as subordinate to the Charter.

Nevertheless, there remains good reason to doubt whether the Charter's rule of non-intervention should be understood as absolute, applying always and everywhere. Like any other human document, the Charter's inception

---

10. Foreign Policy Document No. 148, *The British Year Book of International Law*, 57 (1986), p. 619. Brownlie's argument as a whole may be found in the record of the public session of the International Court of Justice, 10 May 1999, to hear the case of Yugoslavia v. Belgium et al. concerning the legality of the use of force.

11. J. Bryan Hehir, 'Just War Theory in a Post-Cold War World', *Journal of Religious Ethics*, 20/1 (Fall 1992), p. 244.

12. *Pace* Hehir, who seems to assert such a unilateral right: 'the UN texts affirm an obligation on the part of states to defend human rights in states found guilty of persistent and gross violations of rights' (ibid.).

had an historical context—one in which particular concern about certain kinds of intervention was predominant. Like any others, its rules draw their specific meaning from certain typical cases. In 1945 the typical cases of intervention were expansionist and (neo)-colonialist. This is borne out in the aforementioned 1970 Declaration on Principles of International Law, whose commentary on the principle of non-intervention specifies its meaning in these terms:

> No State may...coerce another State in order to obtain from it the subordination of the exercise of its sovereign rights and to secure advantage of any kind...Every State has an inalienable right to choose its political, economic, social and cultural systems, without interference in any form by another State.[13]

So far, as Brownlie claimed, this confirms the UN Charter's position. But it also develops it by making specific mention of a case that is unlikely to have been in the minds of the Charter's authors in 1945:

> no State shall organise, assist, foment, finance, incite or tolerate subversive, terrorist or armed activities directed toward the violent overthrow of the regime of another State.[14]

If the meaning of the Charter can be developed in the light of a new case, surely it can also be revised by one. Is it not highly improbable that the Charter's signatories, acting in the immediate aftermath of the Holocaust, envisaged a case where a state is perpetrating genocide against a minority within its own borders, and is thereby posing a threat to international peace and security; but where the UN is powerless either to act itself or to authorize another body to act instead, because a single member of the Security Council would veto action for reasons of regional politics? And is it not highly probable that they agreed to outlaw unilateral intervention on the (idealistic) assumption that the UN would be able both to recognize genocide when it saw it, and to decide to act against it—by force of arms, if need be?[15] If this is

---

13. Quoted by Brownlie before the International Court of Justice, 10 May 1999. See Section III of his speech.
14. Ibid.
15. Richard Lillich made this historical-contextual point in an exchange with Ian Brownlie as far back as 1974, when he wrote that '[d]octrinal analysis of Article 2(4), much of it written shortly after the Charter's adoption or based upon attitudes and expectations formed during the immediate post-war period, frequently fails to mention that, to the extent that states consciously relinquished the right to use forcible self-help, they took action under the assumption

not so, then the signatories to the Charter must be deemed to have agreed that in a case where a Hitler decides upon a Final Solution for a minority group within the borders of his own state, cannot be dissuaded from this policy by diplomatic or economic pressure, and restrains himself from invading a neighbour; and where the politics of the Security Council preclude sufficient unanimity to enable armed intervention by an authorized body; then international law would forbid any state to intervene instead. Those who do not find this supposition plausible (and I am among them) have good reason, therefore, to regard the case of NATO's military action in Kosovo as an exception to the UN Charter's rule prohibiting unilateral intervention, rather than a transgression of it.

Whatever the intentions of the original signatories to the UN Charter, it is clear that many of their successors recognize that, under present circumstances (where the power of the United Nations to enforce international law is so weak and trammelled), an unconditional prohibition of unauthorized humanitarian intervention is intolerable. This is evidenced in part by the tendency of international lawyers and diverse states to undertake 'creative exegesis'[16] of international law. So, for example, while it is true that India did eventually justify its intervention in East Pakistan in 1971 in terms of a strained claim to self-defence,[17] she did so only for the political reason of winning support from the Security Council. Her preferred, original justification was humanitarian,[18]

---

that the collective implementation measures envisaged by chapter VII soon would be available. Yet even staunch supporters of the collective approach, such as Judge Jessup, admitted that unilateral humanitarian interventions might be permissible if the United Nations lacked the capacity to act speedily' ('Humanitarian Intervention: A Reply to Ian Brownlie and a Plea for Constructive Alternatives', in J.N. Moore, ed., *Law and Civil War in the Modern World* [1974]; reprinted in Mary Ellen O'Connell, ed., *International Law and the Use of Force: Cases and Materials* [New York: Foundation Press, 2005], p. 309).

16. The phrase is Tom J. Farer's in 'A Paradigm of Legitimate Intervention', in Lori Fisler Damrosch, ed., *Enforcing Restraint: Collective Intervention in Internal Conflicts* (New York: Council on Foreign Relations Press, 1993), pp. 330, 340.

17. Proponents of a legal basis for unauthorized humanitarian intervention commonly claim India's 1971 intervention as a supporting case of state practice, and so of customary law. Opponents commonly point out that India's primary ground of justification was self-defence, not humanitarian intervention (e.g. Simon Chesterman, 'Hard Cases Make Bad Law: Law, Ethics, and Politics in Humanitarian Intervention', in Anthony F. Lang, ed., *Just Intervention* [Washington, DC: Georgetown University Press, 2003], p. 49), and that this ground was weak (e.g. Nigel D. White, *Democracy Goes to War: British Military Deployments under International Law* [Oxford: Oxford University Press, 2009], p. 209). What opponents fail to point out is that self-defence was only offered *faute de mieux*, politically speaking.

18. David Fisher, *Morality and War: Can War be Just in the Twenty-first Century?* (Oxford: Oxford University Press, 2011), p. 225.

and the international community's reluctance to countenance it moved the Indian ambassador to berate other members of the Security Council. 'What ... has happened to our conventions on human rights, self-determination, and so on?' he asked on one occasion; and on another, 'What has happened to the justice part [of the UN Charter]?'[19] Further evidence of dissatisfaction with reading international law simply in terms of the express statements of treaty law is furnished by the wide acceptance in the 1990s of humanitarian interventions that were not explicitly authorized by the Security Council—this 'wide acceptance' being expressed in the form either of a supportive Security Council resolution in prospect, or of a refusal by a majority of the Security Council to issue a condemnatory resolution in retrospect. Two examples of the former are the Anglo-American intervention in northern Iraq in 1991 to save the Kurds, and the imposition of a no-fly zone in southern Iraq to aid the Shi'ite Muslims.[20] An example of the latter is the Council's refusal, by twelve votes to three, of Russia's proposed resolution condemning NATO's intervention in Kosovo in 1999.[21]

There is, therefore, a widespread view that international treaty law, strictly read, prohibits what it should not. Implied in this is an appeal to a moral authority that transcends treaty texts—proximately, customary law. Since dissatisfaction with a strict reading of treaty law is not universal, and since evidence of the recognition of customary law in the history of state practice is controversial, the appeal to customary law carries limited social authority. Nevertheless, according to Christian just war thinking, as expressed by that patriarch of international law, Hugo Grotius, the appeal is entirely rational. In cases of *iudicium cessans*, where public authority fails to enforce the law

---

19. UN Security Council Resolutions, 1606th Meeting, 4 December 1971, and 1608th Meeting, 6 December 1971; quoted in Fisher, *Morality and War*, p. 225.

20. Stanley Hoffman wonders whether the protection of the Kurds might have been 'a simple extension of the classical security operation against Iraq, that would have never have occurred if Iraq had not invaded Kuwait', rather than the application of a new principle of humanitarian intervention on behalf of oppressed minorities (*The Ethics and Politics of Humanitarian Intervention* [Notre Dame: University of Notre Dame Press, 1996], p. 28). While it was, no doubt, diplomatically convenient to have the intervention ride on the coat-tails of the Security Council's authorization of the Allies' defence of Kuwait against Iraq, it is hard to see how it could plausibly be described as an 'extension' of that defence.

21. In their highly tendentious article, 'Has US power destroyed the UN?', Simon Chesterman and Michael Byers say that Russia's proposal was defeated 'in large part' by the votes of the five NATO countries then on the Council (*London Review of Books*, 29 April 1999, p. 29). They discreetly omit to mention the role of the other *seven* votes cast against Russia by non-NATO states. Quite how a minority of five votes can inflict a defeat 'in large part' is a puzzle.

against grave and massive injustice, the natural unilateral right to oppose it by force revives—other, prudential, things being equal.[22] In addition, sceptical readings of the history of state practice are vitiated by the simplistic assumption that where national interests are at play, humanitarian motives must be either absent or spurious. The appeal to customary law is rationally stronger and more authoritative than many recognize.

The crucial question then arises as to whether this unwritten law should be allowed to interpret and qualify that which is inscribed in treaties such as the UN Charter.[23] I believe that it should, because otherwise international law would become so rigid as to be incapable of learning from situations that its original authors never envisaged, and of revising itself accordingly—and that would certainly detract from its authority. If customary law is permitted to play this qualifying role, then NATO's intervention in Kosovo has a reasonable claim to legality.

IV. The politics and ethics of legal interpretation

Let us pause here for a moment, lift our eyes from the particulars of the Kosovo case, and reflect directly on the nature of the legal controversy about military intervention. On the one hand, Ian Brownlie argued that international law's prohibition of unauthorized military intervention for humanitarian purposes is unequivocal. In support, as we have seen, he cited the text of the UN Charter, the Declaration on Principles of International Law, and the statements of a variety of national legal authorities over a period of

---

22. Grotius, *Rights of War and Peace*, II.XX.VIII.5, p. 970: '[T]he antient [sic] liberty, which the law of nature at first gave us, remains still in force where there are no courts of justice,' or when they malfunction—for example, 'when complaint having been made to the judge, he does not render justice in a certain time'; ibid., II.XX.IX.5, p. 975: 'even in this punishment [for the satisfaction of the offended party] . . . there remain some footsteps of the antient [sic] right in those places, and among those persons, who are not subject to any established courts of judicature; and even among those too who are so subject, in some particular cases'. The phrase '*iudicium cessans*' derives from Grotius: 'in a private war, the right of defence is as it were, only momentary, and ceases as soon as one can apply to a judge. Whereas a publick war, arising only between those that acknowledge no common judge, or when the exercise of justice is interrupted [*ubi cessant iudicia*]; the right of defence has here some continuance, and is perpetually maintained, by fresh injuries and damages received' (ibid., II.I.XVI, p. 416 and note).

23. This is the basic point of disagreement between Brownlie (who denied it) and Greenwood (who affirmed it). For Brownlie's position, see his speech before the International Court of Justice. For Greenwood's, see his article in the *Observer*, 28 March 1999, p. 22 ('Yes, but is the war legal?'); and the report on 'Law and Right' in the *Economist*, 3 April 1999, pp. 19–20.

almost thirty years. He also denied that the history of state practice evidences an informal international consensus about a unilateral right to intervene, which could be held to constitute customary international law.[24] On the other hand, Richard Lillich argued that the doctrine of humanitarian intervention can claim the authority of jurists such as Grotius and Vattel; that pre-Charter history furnishes ample evidence of relevant state practice; that the Charter does not 'specifically abolish the traditional doctrine'; that the Charter attributes *two* main purposes to the post-war international legal regime, the maintenance of peace *and* the protection of human rights; that humanitarian intervention serves the latter purpose; and that it only offends against Article 2(4) if it threatens the 'territorial integrity' or 'political independence' of the state subject to intervention.[25] Brownlie implied that such a 'flexible and teleological interpretation of treaty texts' is weak;[26] while Lillich approvingly cited another commentator's view of Brownlie's interpretation as 'an arid textualist approach'.[27]

The struggle between textualist and contextualist lawyers for the true meaning of international law resembles nothing so much as the struggle between conservative and liberal theologians for the true meaning of the Bible. In both cases, while the text itself does constrain what can plausibly be attributed to it, the variety of plausible interpretations is considerably determined by extra-textual factors. In the case of the interpretation of international law, prominent among these factors are the empirical, political, and moral assumptions that legal interpreters bring to the texts of treaties and to the 'text' of the history of state practice. So we observe that Brownlie assumed a generally cynical view of the motives of governments when he wrote of 'the near impossibility of discovering an aptitude of governments

---

24. In his 1974 exchange with Richard Lillich, Brownlie argued that before 1945 history can be found to yield only 'one possible genuinely altruistic action', namely, the intervention of 1860 in Syria to prevent further massacres of Maronite Christians. The collective intervention in Greece in 1827, he said, did not use a legal justification; and the American intervention in Cuba in 1898 was justified by the Joint Resolution of Congress in terms of American interests. In the period between the UN Charter and 1974 Brownlie found state practice of humanitarian intervention 'totally lacking' (Brownlie, 'Humanitarian Intervention', p. 301).

25. Lillich, 'Humanitarian Intervention: A Reply to Ian Brownlie', pp. 307–8. As evidence of pre-Charter state practice of humanitarian intervention, Lillich cited collective action against Ottoman suppression of the Greeks in 1827; against Ottoman persecution of Christian Cretans in 1866–8; against Turkish oppression in the Balkans 1877–8; and against Turkish oppression in Macedonia 1903–8.

26. Brownlie, 'Humanitarian Intervention', p. 300.

27. Lillich, 'Humanitarian Intervention: A Reply to Ian Brownlie', p. 308.

in general or carefully moderated, altruistic, and genuine interventions to protect human rights'[28] and that '[t]he whole field [of humanitarian intervention] is driven by political expediency and capriciousness'.[29] Along the same lines, Simon Chesterman judges that '[t]he capriciousness of state interest is a theme that runs throughout the troubled history of humanitarian intervention';[30] and the fact that '[m]ilitary action under... [the Security Council's] auspices has taken place only when it was in the national interests of a state that was prepared to act' he deems 'a troubling trend through the 1990s'.[31] That genuinely moral action is altruistic and entirely lacking in self-interest is a particular moral view and, as I hope to show, a false one. Similarly, it is not necessary to attribute the selectivity of humanitarian intervention to grubby expediency and capriciousness. Sometimes the decision to intervene in one place rather than another can be an expression of the moral virtue of prudence—as was the case, I shall shortly argue, with NATO's intervention in Kosovo.

Brownlie also expressed scepticism about the efficacy of military action, arguing that civil conflicts 'cannot be "solved" by a use of force', and that those advocating military intervention 'need to produce more evidence' that such action achieves benefits greater than the costs it imposes.[32] It is clear enough that he doubted that such evidence can be produced, because he did not believe that intervention is worthwhile. Whatever its truth, this is not a textual claim but an empirical one—and an empirical claim that involves an inarticulate and controversial moral ranking of the values that comprise costs and benefits (for example, bare lives, a just political environment, and the maintenance of international order), together with an opaque and spurious 'calculation' of them. Such scepticism about military action also fuels another legal scholar's opposition to unilateral humanitarian intervention, which stiffens her interpretation of international law. Mary Ellen O'Connell reckons that one of the two main objections to military intervention for humanitarian purposes is 'the severe pragmatic difficulty of protecting human rights through war'.[33] She suggests that the desire to see more military force used to enforce human rights 'may result from an unrealistic

28. Brownlie, 'Humanitarian Intervention', p. 303.
29. Ibid., p. 304.
30. Chesterman, 'Hard Cases Make Bad Law', p. 47.
31. Ibid., p. 55.
32. Brownlie, 'Humanitarian Intervention', p. 304.
33. O'Connell, *Power and Purpose*, p. 181. The other main objection is that intervention weakens the legal regime for peace (ibid.).

understanding of the good that can actually be accomplished by major armed force'.[34] '[O]ne can question,' she writes, 'whether the US attack [on Libya in 1986] was proportional.'[35] She refers to '[t]he deaths and devastation caused by the bombing [of Yugoslavia by NATO in 1999] and the terrible aftermath, during which Serbs and UN Peacekeepers were killed'.[36] And she suggests that the continued use of massive aerial bombardment after the fall of the Taliban regime in 2001 'was arguably disproportionate'.[37] The issue that Brownlie and O'Connell raise is both appropriate and important, but it is a moral-empirical issue, not a legal-textual one. Moreover, as we would expect in the light of our discussion in Chapter Four above, their judgements of proportionality are necessarily less than scientific, highly controversial, and difficult to substantiate. O'Connell herself signals this by the consistently tentative manner of her assertions: 'may result', 'one can question', 'arguably'.

The interpretation of international law offered by Richard Lillich is, of course, no less influenced by extra-textual considerations. However, unlike the textualists, Lillich thought that international law *should* be interpreted with reference to such factors. Thus he quoted with approval Michael Reisman's comment that Brownlie lives 'within the paper world of the Charter',[38] and he complained that 'there is little evidence that Brownlie has contemplated the costs in terms of life and dignity his construction of the Charter demands'[39] and that he makes no mention of the problem of 'the obvious procedural defects' of the United Nations and is 'wholly devoid' of constructive alternatives.[40]

My own view should be clear from the previous section on the legal controversy about Kosovo. I do not believe that the meaning of international law lies in texts as distinct from their context. What the UN Charter means must be understood in terms of the historical context of its origin. That context includes the authors' intentions and expectations. One expec-

---

34. Ibid., p. 148. See also Mary Ellen O'Connell, 'Responsibility to Peace: A Critique of R2P', *Journal of Intervention and Statebuilding*, 4/1 (2010).
35. Ibid., p. 183.
36. Ibid., p. 180.
37. Ibid., p. 188.
38. Lillich, 'Humanitarian Intervention: A Reply to Ian Brownlie', p. 313.
39. Ibid., p. 311. Martti Koskenniemi agrees: a formalistic, strictly textual reading of international law 'seems arrogantly insensitive to the humanitarian dilemmas involved' ('"The Lady Doth Protest Too Much": Kosovo and the Turn to Ethics in International Law', *The Modern Law Review*, 65/2 [March 2002], p. 163.
40. Lillich, 'Humanitarian Intervention: A Reply to Ian Brownlie', p. 313.

tation that they did not have—I think it plausible to argue—was that the new international regime would serve to guarantee the sovereign rights of the next Hitler to liquidate a domestic minority. Other extra-textual factors that are bound to shape the interpretation of legal texts are the interpreters' views of the motivation of governments and the efficacy of military action in defence of human rights. On both of these matters my own views are considerably less cynical, or at least pessimistic, than those of Brownlie and O'Connell.

V. Kosovo: a case of international beneficence

Some doubt that, in intervening in Kosovo, NATO's motives were genuinely humanitarian. I myself have yet to hear a plausible account of the alternatives. No one, to my knowledge, has suggested that NATO was really covetous of physical resources or territory. Ian Brownlie spoke knowingly and darkly of 'a geopolitical agenda unrelated to human rights', while declining to elaborate.[41] Harold Pinter, expressing the traditional prejudices of the British Left, proposed the motive of American domination:

> The truth is that neither Clinton nor Blair gives a damn about the Kosovar Albanians. The action has been yet another blatant and brutal assertion of US power using NATO as its missile. It sets out to consolidate one thing—American domination of Europe.[42]

Never mind that earlier in the 1990s European nations had proven perfectly capable of distancing themselves from American foreign policy when they saw fit to do so—for example, over Iraq. Never mind that in the forefront of NATO's military intervention stood France, which has made a post-war career of not doing whatever America wants. Never mind that America's military involvement in Kosovo was patently reluctant—to the frustration of at least one European leader, Tony Blair. And never mind that America's reluctance is intelligible precisely because its national interest in the outcome of the Kosovo conflict, as distinct from the interest of its European allies, was so weak.

41. See his speech before the International Court of Justice, Section V.
42. As reported by Audrey Gillan in 'Bombing Shames Britain, Pinter Tells Protesters', *Guardian*, 7 June 1999.

In an article whose cynicism almost rivals Pinter's, the Australian Simon Chesterman and the Canadian Michael Byers identified NATO simply with the United States and asserted that its military interventions throughout the 1990s—including that of Kosovo—were simply self-interested. They conclude with this:

> One might well conclude that the greatest long-term threat to peace is neither Slobodan Milošević nor Saddam Hussein, but the impulsive (if well meaning) sole remaining superpower—undeterred by rules and procedures, driven only by the inconstant winds of its own self-interest.[43]

Before reaching this conclusion, however, the authors themselves mention, with a rather unattractive superciliousness, two occasions in the 1990s when American action was impelled by humanitarian motives: Somalia in 1992 ('Driven by images of starvation in Somalia, the US once again led the good fight'); and Bosnia in 1995 ('Frustrated at the Serbian massacre of Bosnians in UN "safe havens" and at Europe's powerlessness to stop the madness, NATO found a cathartic release in air-strikes').[44] What is more, in the conclusion itself, the parenthetical qualification, 'if well meaning', serves to undermine the claim that the United States was 'driven only by...self-interest'. By Chesterman and Byer's own inadvertent admission, then, US foreign policy in the years leading up to 1999 had shown evidence of humanitarian motivation. But if in Somalia and Bosnia, then why not also in Kosovo?

Edward Said, too, preferred to collapse NATO into the United States[45] and asserted that the Kosovo intervention was basically 'a display of [American] military might' to 'show the world who is boss'.[46] This account also depends on the fiction that NATO is simply an American tool. It passes over the deep reluctance with which the United States became involved. It raises the question of why America chose to show off its military might by way of such a half-hearted and precarious strategy. And it

---

43. Chesterman and Byers, 'Has US power destroyed the UN?', p. 30.
44. Ibid.
45. 'In its arrogance, the US has forced NATO to go along with it' ('It's Time the World Stood up to the American Bully', *Observer*, 11 April 1999, p. 19).
46. Harold Pinter took a similar tack in a BBC2 television programme, broadcast on 4 May 1999, when he described NATO's intervention as 'an act of deplorable machismo' (as reported by Timothy Garton Ash in his sharp critique, 'Vivid, Dark, Powerful and Magnificent—but Wrong', *The Independent*, 6 May 1999).

gains what little plausibility it has only by dogmatically ignoring the alternatives.[47]

It is certainly true that NATO—but much less its North American than its European members—had an interest in the stability of the Balkans, and therefore in curbing the activity of the main source of recent disturbance, Milošević and his regime.[48] But this interest was not private to NATO. It was shared, presumably, by the Balkan peoples themselves. Indeed, it was also shared by the United Nations, whose Security Council had adopted resolutions (1160, 1199, and 1203) in 1998, which legally bound the Federal Republic of Yugoslavia to cease all action by its security forces affecting the civilian population of Kosovo; to withdraw all security units used for civilian repression; and to implement in full all agreements with NATO and the Organization for Security and Co-operation in Europe (OSCE). These, together with the statements following the Račak massacre in January 1999, judged that the government in Belgrade had created a humanitarian emergency in Kosovo that constituted a threat to peace and security in the Balkans.

It may also be true, as Tony Coady reports, that General Wesley Clark, supreme commander of NATO's forces during the Kosovo intervention, has claimed that the primary motive for NATO's bombing of Serbia was to preserve the credibility of the NATO alliance.[49] However, the phrase 'primary motive' is ambiguous, one of its meanings being plausible, the other not. It is plausible that, *having decided* to address the problem of Serbian ethnic cleansing in Kosovo, NATO felt (quite rightly) that it had to carry through with its threat of military action, should Milošević not come to reasonable terms. What is implausible is the claim that NATO first decided to address the issue of Kosovo, *in order* to make a general demonstration of its credibility. In other words, the motive of maintaining credibility might well have become 'primary' in the sense of 'dominant' at a late point along

47. Said told us that 'not even the Kosovo Albanians believe that the air campaign is about independence for Kosovo or saving Albanian lives: this is a total illusion' (ibid.). However, NATO did not claim that its campaign was for Kosovan independence—that certainly would have been unacceptable to Russia and China; and there is ample evidence that the Albanian Kosovars welcomed NATO's action wholeheartedly as a means of saving their life as a people—even after NATO airstrikes had killed some of them by accident.

48. Resolutions 1199 and 1203 both spoke of 'impending humanitarian catastrophe' and asserted that the situation in Kosovo 'constitutes a threat to peace and security in the region'.

49. C.A.J. Coady, *The Ethics of Armed Humanitarian Intervention*, Peaceworks No. 45 (Washington, DC: United States Institute of Peace, 2002), p. 24. Coady relies here on Michael Ignatieff, 'Chains of Command', *New York Review of Books*, 19 July 2001, p. 18.

the diplomatic way. But it was never 'primary' in the sense of the original and basic reason for intervening in the first place.

VI. The morality of national interest

I have just admitted that NATO's intervention in Kosovo did contain elements of self-interest—primarily in Balkan stability, secondarily in NATO's credibility. I have also noted that Ian Brownlie supposed genuinely moral action to be 'altruistic'. Since 'altruism' is commonly understood to exclude self-interest, I infer that Brownlie would have concluded from my admission that NATO's motivation for intervening was not moral. I mentioned earlier that I regard the equation of genuinely moral action with disinterested altruism as a mistake. Now I shall explain why.

In the popular Kantian view of ethics, self-interest is regarded as an immoral motive.[50] According to this view, therefore, where national interests motivate military intervention, they vitiate it. There is, however, an alternative and, I think, superior eudaimonist tradition, which found classic expression in Thomas Aquinas. Combining the Book of Genesis's affirmation of the goodness of creation with Aristotle, Thomist thought does not view all self-interest as selfish and immoral. Indeed, it holds that there is such a thing as morally obligatory self-love. The human individual has a duty to care for himself properly, to seek what is genuinely his own good. As with an individual, so with a national community and the organ of its cohesion and decision, namely its government: a national government has a moral duty to look after the well-being of its own people—and in that sense to advance its genuine interests. As Yves Simon wrote, 'What should we think, truly, about a government that would leave out of its preoccupations the interests of the nation that it governs?'[51] This duty is not unlimited, of course. There cannot be a moral obligation to pursue the interests of one's own nation by

50. The ethics of Immanuel Kant are usually held to be simply 'deontological', viewing the only truly moral act as one that is done out of a pure sense of duty or reverence for the moral law. So conceived, the truly moral act stands in stark contrast to a merely prudential one, which seeks to promote the agent's interests. Whether this common, deontological view of Kant fully captures his thought I doubt. I think that a better reading has him argue that truly moral acts are those where the duty of justice as fairness disciplines—rather than excludes—the pursuit of interest.
51. Yves R. Simon, *The Ethiopian Campaign and French Political Thought*, ed. Anthony O. Simon, trans. Robert Royal (Notre Dame: University of Notre Dame, 2009), p. 55.

riding roughshod over the rights of others. Still, not every pursuit of national interest does involve the committing of injustice; so the fact that national interests are among the motives for military intervention does not by itself vitiate the latter's moral justification.

This is politically important, because some kind of national interest needs to be involved if military intervention is to attract popular support; and because without such support intervention is hard, eventually impossible, to sustain. One such interest can be moral integrity. Nations usually care about more than just being safe and fat. Usually they want to believe that they are doing the right or the noble thing, and they will tolerate the costs of war—up to a point—in a just cause that looks set to succeed. I have yet to meet a Briton who is not proud of what British troops achieved in Sierra Leone in the year 2000, even though Britain had no material stake in the outcome of that country's civil war, and even though intervention there cost British taxpayers money and British families casualties.[52] Citizens care that their country should do the right thing.

The nation's interest in its own moral integrity and nobility alone, however, will probably not underwrite military intervention that incurs very heavy costs. So other interests—such as national security—are needed to stiffen popular support for a major intervention. But even a nation's interest in its own security is not simply selfish. After all, it amounts to a national government's concern for the security of millions of fellow countrymen. Nor need it be private; for one nation's security is often bound up with others'. As Gareth Evans puts it: 'these days, good international citizenship is a matter of national self-interest'.[53]

So national interest need not vitiate the motivation for military intervention. Indeed, some kind of interest will be necessary to make it politically possible and sustainable. It is not unreasonable for a national people to ask why they should bear the burdens of military intervention, especially in remote parts of the world. It is not unreasonable for them to ask why *they* should bear the burdens *rather than others*. It is not unreasonable for them to ask why *their* sons and daughters should suffer and die. And the answer to those reasonable questions will have to present itself in terms of the nation's

---

52. The British casualties were very light: one dead, one seriously injured, and twelve wounded (<http://www.eliteukforces.info/special-air-service/sas-operations/operation-barras/>, as at 24 November 2009).

53. Gareth Evans, *The Responsibility to Protect: Ending Mass Atrocity Crimes Once and for All* (Washington, DC: Brookings Institute, 2008), p. 144.

own interests. And it could and ought to present itself in terms of the nation's own morally legitimate interests.

VII. The morality of 'hypocritical' intervention

One of the most common ways of objecting to a humanitarian justification of unauthorized military intervention is to cast doubt on its sincerity by pointing to inconsistency of practice. The argument runs thus: 'You say that you care about the victims of oppression in country A. If that is really so, why didn't you intervene to save the victims in countries B, C, and D? The fact that you didn't intervene in those cases shows that you don't really care; and it implies that your claim to care in this case is hypocritical. Your real reason for intervening in A must therefore be something else, some selfish material or geopolitical interest.' Accordingly, the fact that the United States and other Western countries did not intervene in Rwanda or Kurdish Turkey or the Krajina (where 600,000 Serbs were 'ethnically cleansed' by the Croats in 1995) is taken to imply that NATO's intervention in Kosovo was not genuinely humanitarian. And the fact that the West did not intervene in Chechnya or Tibet is taken as evidence that its intervention in Iraq or Afghanistan must have been selfish. This is why Ian Brownlie judged that '[t]he whole field [of humanitarian intervention] is driven by political expediency and capriciousness'.[54]

There are two ways of responding to the charge of hypocritical inconsistency. One is to say that, even if we should have intervened elsewhere, that would still not amount to a reason not to have intervened here—unless there were some virtue in maintaining, as one journalist very nicely put it, 'a level apathy field'.[55] Surely, it is better to be inconsistently responsible than consistently irresponsible.

Another response to the charge is to deny it altogether and to say, 'There were good moral reasons why we *didn't* intervene in B, C, and D; and there were good moral reasons why we *did* intervene in A.' These moral reasons can be of three kinds: practical, prudential, or political. One reason why the United States and others intervened in Kosovo was that there was to hand

---

54. Brownlie, 'Humanitarian Intervention', p. 304.
55. Steve Crawshaw, 'A Journey into the Unknown', *The Independent on Sunday*, 28 March 1999, p. 15.

an international body that had the political cohesion and military power to act effectively—namely NATO. This was not the case in Rwanda. So one reason why Western countries did not intervene there was practical: effective means were not readily available to them. But how is a practical reason also a moral one? In this sense: that usually one ought not to attempt even a worthy goal by means that are likely to fail.

A second moral reason that justifies intervention in some cases but not in others is prudential. In much discussion of international relations, prudential reasons are usually regarded as alternatives to moral ones. Moral reasons are supposed to operate in terms of the principle of absolute duty, which obliges heroic action that disdains the calculating concern for consequences. By comparison, prudential reasons seem selfish and grubby, native to the discourse of merchants rather than of moral heroes. As implied in the previous section, such suppositions express a particular, Kantian view of morality. In the alternative, Thomist view—as in much classical Greek and Roman thought—prudence is a virtue. It is not the only virtue, and it is not the only or the primary consideration in moral deliberation, but it is one of them. Applied to cases where military intervention is under consideration, prudence forbids action that is likely to be disproportionate. The moral virtue of prudence and its offspring, the criterion of proportionality, therefore, help to justify the difference between NATO's responses to Chechnya and Kosovo. Had NATO intervened in Chechnya in 1994–6 or in 1999–2000, it would certainly have provoked war with Russia, thereby risking escalation to the point of an exchange of nuclear weapons. While it would have been good to save Chechen civilians from indiscriminate and disproportionate injury by Russian troops, it is reasonable to argue that it would not have been proportionate to do so at the risk of nuclear war. By contrast, there was no serious risk of direct war with Russia, and so of nuclear escalation, in the case of Kosovo. Yes, Russia had cultural and political interests in Serbia, which motivated her support of the Milošević regime; but her interests were not so vital as to make it likely that she would go to war with NATO in defence of them.

The third kind of moral reason that can warrant different behaviour in different cases is political. If any regime is to go to war and stay at war, it must be able to win and maintain popular support. This is especially so in the case of democracies, but not only so. Even a regime as undemocratic as that of Tsar Nicholas II proved unable to sustain either war against Germany or its own survival in the face of overwhelming popular dissent in 1917. After all, it is invariably the *people* who must fill the uniforms of the soldiers that a regime would send to war; and if sufficient of the people object to a war strongly enough, then the regime can neither begin nor continue to prosecute it. This is certainly a practical, political consideration; but how is it moral? It is moral insofar as the *raison d'être* of any regime is its service of the good of its own people; and while it is quite possible that a regime might have a better grasp of that good than the people themselves, there nevertheless comes a point where, having failed to convince, a regime is morally obliged to defer to the popular will. Accordingly, one reason why the British government intervened in Afghanistan in 2001 was its ability to win the support of a large majority of the British electorate. It is very unlikely that it would have won similar support for direct intervention on the same scale in Darfur.

VIII. The efficacy of military intervention

In my judgement, the claim that NATO's intervention in Kosovo was ill motivated has often been expressive of instinctive anti-Western—and especially anti-American—prejudice. It has not been the conclusion of careful moral reflection or of a fair assessment of political phenomena. NATO's motivation was considerably humanitarian; and where national interests were involved, they were legitimate and public. What, then, about the claim that military intervention, especially in civil conflicts, does more harm than good? Is it true?

To answer that question I call two witnesses, both of whom have served as soldiers, diplomats, and politicians, both of whom have had direct experience of responsibility for nation-building, and both of whom have written books about it: Paddy Ashdown and Rory Stewart. Ashdown, the international High Representative for Bosnia and Herzegovina from 2002 to 2006, argues that '[h]igh profile failures like Iraq should not... blind us to the fact that, overall, the success stories outnumber the failures by a wide margin'.[56] In support he appeals to two studies, one of which finds that military intervention by the international community is the best way of stabilizing peace

---

56. Paddy Ashdown, *Swords and Ploughshares: Bringing Peace to the 21st Century* (London: Weidenfeld & Nicolson, 2007), p. 14.

and reconstructing nations after conflict,[57] and the other of which shows that the increasing incidence of intervention has helped to halve the number of wars in the world.[58] Notwithstanding the fact that he thinks we got it wrong in Iraq and Afghanistan, Ashdown remains convinced that there is a way of getting it right:

> remember... that an army of liberation has a very short half-life before it risks becoming an army of occupation. Dominate the security space from the start; then concentrate first on the rule of law; make economic regeneration an early priority; remember the importance of articulating an 'end state' which can win and maintain local support; but leave elections as late as you decently can. When rebuilding institutions be sensitive to local traditions and customs. Understand the importance to the international community effort of coordination, cohesion, and speaking with a single voice. And then at the end, do not wait until everything is as it would be in your country, but leave when the peace is sustainable.[59]

Rory Stewart was the Coalition Provisional Authority's deputy governor of two provinces of southern Iraq from 2003 to 2004. He approached the task of building a more stable, prosperous Iraq with optimism, but experience brought him disillusion.[60] He now thinks that foreigners' short-term commitment, ignorance of local conditions, and consequent inability to build on local strengths hamstrings many of their well-intentioned efforts.[61] His co-author, Gerald Knaus, takes direct issue with Ashdown's top-down model of success.[62] Nevertheless, Stewart and Knaus write that:

---

57. P. Collier, V. L. Elliot, H. Hegre, A. Hoeffler, M. Reynal-Querol, and N. Sambanis, *Breaking the Conflict Trap: Civil War and Development Policy*, A World Bank Policy Research Report (Oxford: Oxford University Press, 2000).

58. Human Security Centre, *Human Security Report 2005* (Oxford: Oxford University Press, 2005).

59. Ashdown, *Swords and Ploughshares*, p. 213.

60. Rory Stewart and Gerald Knaus, *Can Intervention Work?* Amnesty International Global Ethics Series (New York: W. W. Norton, 2011), p. xv. For the full account of Stewart's experience in Iraq, see his *Occupational Hazards: My Time Governing in Iraq* (London: Picador, 2006).

61. Stewart and Knaus, *Can Intervention Work?*, pp. xix, xxi. Stewart's first-hand witness goes a long way toward corroborating Michael Walzer's position: 'The common brutalities of authoritarian politics, the daily oppressiveness of traditional social practices—these are not the occasion for intervention; they have to be dealt with locally, by the people who know the politics, who enact or resist the practices... Foreign politicians and soldiers are too likely to misread the situation, or to underestimate the force required to change it, or to stimulate a 'patriotic' reaction in defense of the brutal politics and the oppressive practices. Social change is best achieved from within' (Michael Walzer, 'The Argument about Humanitarian Intervention' [2002], in *Thinking Politically: Essays in Political Theory*, ed. and intro. David Miller [New Haven: Yale University Press, 2007], p. 238).

62. Stewart and Knaus, *Can Intervention Work?*, pp. xv, xvii–xviii, xxv.

[w]e both agree that there are certain occasions—such as genocide—that can justify an international intervention...[W]e accept the basic intuitions of many interveners around the world, and a worldview that seems to permit, for example, the intervention in Kosovo, even without the full legal sanction of the UN Security Council...Bosnia and Kosovo were successes...We both believe that it is possible to walk the tightrope between the horrors of over-intervention and non-intervention; that there is still a possibility of avoiding the horrors not only of Iraq but also of Rwanda; and that there is a way of approaching intervention than can be good for us and good for the country concerned...Intervention may be a necessary, indispensable ingredient of the international system. It is certainly capable, as in the Balkans, of doing good.[63]

Ashdown and Stewart know whereof they speak: they have both had first-hand experience of trying to make intervention work. Stewart admits that the experience chastened him, and he disagrees with Ashdown about the conditions of success. Nevertheless, both of them agree that interven-tion *can* be done well. Given the right conditions, success is possible. Their consensus, it seems to me, is powerful testimony against merely academic scepticism.

IX. International law after Kosovo

The Kosovo crisis augmented the grist, but Kofi Annan's mill was already grinding. Upon his appointment as Secretary General of the United Nations in 1997, Annan had begun to press the international community to achieve a greater measure of collective clarity over humanitarian intervention by explicitly affirming what he asserted to be 'this developing international norm in favour of intervention to protect civilians from wholesale slaugh-ter', and by agreeing rules for its effective application under international law. 'The choice,' he told the UN's General Assembly in September 1999, '...must not be between [Security] Council unity and inaction in the face of geno-cide—as in the case of Rwanda, on the one hand; and Council division, and regional action, as in the case of Kosovo, on the other.'[64] Sadly, notwithstanding the support he received from the report of the Canadian government's International Commission on Intervention and State Sovereignty (ICISS),

---

63. Ibid., pp. xii, xiv, xvi, xxvi.
64. Quoted by Edward C. Luck in *UN Security Council: Practice and Promise*, Global Institutions series (London: Routledge, 2006), p. 85.

The Responsibility to Protect,[65] Annan's efforts proved to be in vain. The debate he had stimulated was overshadowed by the highly controversial invasion of Iraq in 2003, which stiffened opposition to any loosening of the reins on unilateral action. As a consequence, the report of the Secretary General's High Level Panel on United Nations Reform in 2004, the Secretary General's own report of September 2005, and the Outcome Document of the 2005 UN World Summit all reaffirmed the prohibition on the use of force without prior Security Council authorization, except in the case of armed attack;[66] and the Panel expressly rejected the claim that force can sometimes be legitimate, even if unlawful.[67]

On the other hand, the World Summit did declare that '[e]ach individual state has the responsibility to protect its population from genocide, war crimes, ethnic cleansing and crimes against humanity', and the gathered heads of state and government did pledge that 'we accept that responsibility and will act in accordance with it', promising to take collective action in a timely and decisive manner through the Security Council, should a national authority 'manifestly fail' in its responsibility to protect.[68] Moreover, since the end of the Cold War, the Council has increasingly tended to view internal conflicts as threats to international security, and to authorize military intervention on that ground—for example, in the former Yugoslavia, Somalia, Rwanda, and Haiti. Some see this as an expression of 'a deeper understanding of security'.[69] Others see it as a ploy to adorn illegal action

---

65. Report of the International Commission on Intervention and State Sovereignty, *The Responsibility to Protect* (Ottawa: International Development Research Centre, 2001).

66. O'Connell, *Power and Purpose*, p. 227. Thus they rejected the ICISS's recommendation that, where the Security Council rejects a proposal or fails to deal with it in a reasonable time, unilateral action by a regional or sub-regional organization under chapter VII of the UN Charter would be permissible, subject to its seeking subsequent authorization from the Security Council (*Responsibility to Protect*, XIII).

67. O'Connell, *Power and Purpose*, p. 147. This claim had been made by the Swedish government's Independent International Commission on Kosovo in its report in 2000 (ibid., p. 225).

68. Luck, *UN Security Council*, p. 85.

69. Adam Roberts and Dominik Zaum, *Selective Security: War and the United Nations Security Council since 1945*, Adelphi Paper 395 (London: International Institute for Strategic Studies, 2008), p. 57. See also Terry D. Gill and Dieter Fleck, eds, *The Handbook of the International Law of Military Operations* (Oxford: Oxford University Press, 2010), pp. 221–2: 'Experience has shown on numerous occasions that...large-scale and systematic human rights violations very often lead to regional and even wider destabilization and aggravation of international tension, in addition to constituting violations of fundamental *jus cogens* norms and qualifying as international crimes in their own right... [T]he practice of the Council over many years has demonstrated that it has viewed such large-scale violations of human rights as a threat to the peace on repeated occasions.'

with the fig leaf of legality.[70] Whatever the truth—and it is probably a bit of both—post-Cold War practice, together with the World Summit's public commitments, make it more likely than ever that the Security Council will gird its loins to authorize intervention to stop gross oppression within the borders of a state. The Council's 2011 authorization of military intervention in Libya—notwithstanding the long shadow of Iraq—is evidence of this.

Nevertheless, there is no guarantee that the Council will act when, arguably, it should—as its current paralysis over Syria demonstrates. And the question of what should happen in such a case remains unresolved.[71] According to *The Handbook of the International Law of Military Operations*, the minority view is that humanitarian intervention either does not violate Art. 2 (4) of the UN Charter or is part of customary law. Most legal authorities, however, judge that unauthorized humanitarian intervention is *prima facie* illegal, but that it can be 'legitimized and wholly or partially *justified*' under certain conditions, which provide grounds for partial or complete 'mitigation' of responsibility for otherwise illegal conduct.[72] Normally mitigation is understood to reduce the responsibility of the agent, not the unlawfulness of his act.[73] However, if it is true that international lawyers suppose that mitigating circumstances can render an apparently illegal act legal, or an

70. Thus Mary Ellen O'Connell comments of the Security Council's authorization of peacekeeping in the former Yugoslavia in 1991 that 'there was no tangible threat to other independent states' (*Power and Purpose*, p. 208); and of its authorization of military intervention in Haiti in 1994 that 'there was no threat to international peace' (ibid., p. 209). This latter she describes as 'likely the zenith of the Security Council's *reinterpretation* of the Charter' (ibid., p. 209; my emphasis).

71. *The Handbook of the International Law of Military Operations* (2010) judges that the notion of the 'responsibility to protect' (R2P) has reinforced the Security Council's responsibility to undertake, if necessary, military measures 'in response to large-scale and systematic human rights violations as part of a wider effort to protect populations from violations of their fundamental human rights, and promote stability and the creation of conditions aimed at preventing further such violations'. R2P 'also serves as a clear indication that a State cannot use its sovereignty as a cover for the perpetration of atrocities against its citizens, and that such acts cannot be seen as a wholly internal matter falling outside the scope of international law or the concern of the international community'. 'Nevertheless,' it warns, 'there is no guarantee that the Council will invariably be able to come to a decision to undertake measures which are likely to end such violations,' in part because of the need for a two-thirds majority and the possibility of a veto by one of the Permanent Five (Gill and Fleck, *Handbook*, pp. 222–3).

72. Ibid., p. 224 and n. 9. The emphasis is mine.

73. The authors of the Oxford *Handbook* recognize this, when they write that 'mitigation of responsibility' 'is based on the consideration that there are degrees of wrongfulness relating to an illegal act and that the actions and motivations of the party committing a violation of any legal rule or principle should be taken into account in determining the consequences of unlawful conduct' (Ibid., p. 226).

illegal act (morally) legitimate or justified, then that would be satisfactory.[74] I say this because I do not consider the Kosovo intervention to be a morally wrong action, for which NATO had diminished responsibility. I think that NATO was entirely responsible and that its intervention was morally right, if legally ambiguous or even wrong. Insofar as this view is the one that predominates among international lawyers, a looser concept of mitigation is at work here.[75]

X. The prospects for global government

Some express great faith in the growth of international legal consensus, and in the consequent capacity of international courts to make objective and authoritative judgments that will govern international law enforcement. Thus, for example, Mary Ellen O'Connell describes international law as 'the closest thing we have to a neutral vehicle for taking on the world's most complex issues and pressing problems'.[76] She writes enthusiastically of increasing worldwide participation in the formation of the law, and in the discovery of international values. She endorses Abdullahi an-Na'im and Christopher Weeramantry's Habermasian quest for universal consensus through dialogue, commenting that they understand that international laws should be those 'to which all possibly affected persons could agree as participants in rational discourses'.[77] She acknowledges that international law enforcement still functions considerably through self-judging and self-help, but reckons that 'with the growth of courts and tribunals this problematic aspect of the law is diminishing'.[78] And while, in the search for higher norms and general principles, different courts and tribunals may yield conflicting

---

74. Ian Brownlie lent support to this view, when he wrote that 'in the context of *practice* of States, mitigation and acceptance in principle are not always easy to distinguish' ('Thoughts on Kind-Hearted Gunmen', in *Humanitarian Intervention and the United Nations*, ed. Richard B. Lillich [Charlottesville: University Press of Virginia, 1973], p. 146. Emphasis in the original).

75. It seems that a majority of international lawyers are willing to countenance the notion that an action might be at once illegal and (morally) legitimate. According to Edward Luck, 'the Kosovo and Afghanistan interventions were generally regarded as legitimate regardless of their ambiguous legal status' (*UN Security* Council, p. 55); and according to Martti Koskenniemi, 'most lawyers—including myself—have taken the ambivalent position that it [NATO's intervention in Kosovo] was both formally illegal and morally necessary' (' "The Lady Doth Protest Too Much" ', p. 162).

76. O'Connell, *Power and Purpose*, p. 14.

77. Jürgen Habermas, *Between Facts and Norms* (1997), p. 107; quoted by O'Connell, *Power and Purpose*, p. 141.

78. O'Connell, *Power and Purpose*, p. 7–8.

results, she reckons that these can be ordered in terms of the hierarchy of courts.[79] In the closing paragraph of her book she writes that the world's problems 'will not be solved by armed conflict.... People everywhere believe in law, believe in this alternative to force . . . International law reflects that the international community's shared goals today are peace, respect for human rights, prosperity, and the protection of the natural environment'.[80]

I fully respect the aspiration; but I cannot share the faith. My Protestant view of human community and institutions will not allow it.[81] I do not think that we can expect human society—even as it manifests itself in international courts—to be free of moral disagreement and political conflict.[82] I do not deny that it would be ideal if international law were to specify the full range of kinds of state action or state neglect that constitute crimes and warrant international intervention. It would be ideal if there were a global government with a global police force, which would act impartially and efficiently to uphold international law by stopping criminal acts, arresting those responsible, and bringing them to court. We are, however, a very long way from the ideal; and I, for one, am sceptical that we will ever realize it.

Why am I sceptical? Because it seems to me that moral and political norms across the globe are too diverse, and international mistrust is accordingly too great, to permit the high degree of consensus required for comprehensive legal specification of state crimes and for impartial and efficient enforcement of international law. We might agree abstract norms, and we might even agree upon certain specifications of those norms. We are less

---

79. Ibid., p. 144.
80. Ibid., p. 370.
81. My disagreement with Mary Ellen O'Connell might have something to do with our divergent ecclesial allegiances—she teaches at the University of Notre Dame, one of the United States' leading Roman Catholic institutions of higher learning; I am an Anglican clergyman. This possibility first occurred to me when reading her statement, quoting Alfred Rubin, that the international authority of the Pope and the Holy Roman Emperor declined because of 'the Reformation's perception of the Church as a human institution with fallible officers' (O'Connell, *Power and Purpose*, p. 23), and that just war doctrine 'broke down when the authority of the Church was lost to determine the justness of any cause' (ibid., p. 148 n. 192). It strikes me that that O'Connell looks to the UN to recover what was lost to international order at the Reformation, whereas my Inner Protestant regards the church and the UN with equal scepticism.
82. According to O'Connell's account, it seems that I am aligned here with the New Haven School of international law in its 'skepticism about the possibility of cabining law from policy or politics, as well as skepticism about the possibility of objectivity in the law' (ibid., p. 70). For an explanation of why I regard Habermas's aspiration to universal consensus as naïve, see 'Not Translation, but Conversation: Theology in Public Debate about Euthanasia' and 'Conclusion' in Nigel Biggar and Linda Hogan, eds, *Religious Voices in Public Places* [Oxford: Oxford University Press, 2009], esp. pp. 162–73, 191–3, 312–24).

likely to agree that a given case offends against a specified norm, and we are much less likely to agree upon what action, if any, should be taken against the offence. To agree that a given case constitutes an offence involves controversial moral and political judgements about whether a state's use of force is proportionate to the threat posed, and about the justice of the opposing cause. To agree that action should be taken—and by whom—involves political judgements about international reputation, equitable burden-sharing, and domestic support.

Of course, if we had a global state as cohesive and centralized as nation-states now often are, then the judgement of cases and decisions about action could be efficient (even if still controversial). However, even if it were desirable,[83] such a prospect seems so remote as to be utopian. In Europe, national judicial and policing systems came into being because they were imposed, often coercively, by strong royal central government. Yes, the history of the formation of the federal United States and of the confederal European Union (EU) suggests that judicial and policing coherence can be negotiated, and need not always be coerced. However, in the case of the United States such negotiation was made possible by a very high degree of cultural homogeneity and by the short histories of the individual constituent colonies. The much longer histories of the member states of the EU, and their much more limited cultural similarity, have meant that the process of unification has been much more prolonged and will probably never be as complete. In the absence of a single state that is able and willing to use force to create and sustain a comprehensively global empire, therefore, we can expect that the deep cultural differences between the West and the likes of China, India, and even Russia—differences that have been entrenched by centuries and even millennia of largely separate historical development—will continue to hinder agreement about what sovereign states should not be allowed to do, on when interference is warranted, on the creation of a standing global police force, and on the delegation of enforcement to it.

For the foreseeable future, therefore, we will remain in our current situation, which is irreducibly political, if not simply so. Indeed, since political conflict and negotiation are indelible features of human life, we will, I think, remain in something like this situation forever. As Adam Roberts and Dominik Zaum have observed, 'the era since 1945 has witnessed—alongside

---

83. One common objection to a global state is that its monopoly of armed force would make it prone to tyranny, and that its tyranny would be beyond challenge.

the new institutions of the United Nations and the multilateral diplomacy that it embodies—the continuation of all the classical institutions of the international system: great powers, alliances, spheres of interest, balances of power and bilateral diplomacy'.[84] They judge the 2004 report of the UN High Level Panel on Threats, Challenges, and Change to be 'hopelessly optimistic' in aspiring to set up a comprehensive security system through the UN,[85] which they regard as an 'impossible ideal'.[86] This is because the fault lies not simply with the unruly behaviour of particular states nor even with the right to veto in the Security Council,[87] but with 'deep and enduring problems of world politics'.[88] 'The Security Council,' they write, 'is not an impartial judicial body, but a deeply political organisation',[89] whose members have 'very different perspectives on the world and the threats it faces'.[90]

Accordingly, on the one hand, many nations (such as China and India) continue to insist that *only* the Security Council may authorize military intervention, and that only directly authorized intervention is legal. They insist on this because they do not trust the grounds on which others might want to intervene, because they fear that they themselves might become subject to such intervention, and because they therefore want to control it as much as they can. On the other hand, there are other nations who are not content with an international system that allows the politics of the Security Council, and especially the casting of a veto, to stymie effective action, sometimes military, against a state's grossly atrocious behaviour. The recent fate of *The Responsibility to Protect* report in international debate gives no ground for hope that this crucial point of disagreement is going to be resolved any time soon.[91]

---

84. Roberts and Zaum, *Selective Security*, p. 24.
85. Ibid., p. 18.
86. Ibid., p. 76.
87. They point out that no veto prevented the Security Council from addressing the Khmer Rouge's auto-genocide in Cambodia from 1975–9, and that Council members have sometimes acted in spite of a veto, e.g. over the Suez crisis in 1956 (ibid., p. 37).
88. Ibid., p. 19.
89. Ibid., p. 20.
90. Ibid., p. 28. Edward Luck concurs: 'As an innately political body composed of member states with individual interests...the [Security] Council's determinations about...whether a government's...suppression of some of its population...threaten[s] its neighbors or more distant states...may often be controversial' (*UN Security Council*, pp. 82–3).
91. See Alex J. Bellamy, *Responsibility to Protect: The Global Effort to End Mass Atrocities* (Cambridge: Polity Press, 2009).

XI. The legal component of moral justification

Notwithstanding the manifest inadequacies of present—and probably future—international legal arrangements, it remains optimal that the Security Council should authorize effective action to stop states from perpetrating grave atrocities within their own borders. Such authorization is legally uncontroversial, carries maximal international authority, and is least susceptible to suspicion of being motivated primarily by private and illegitimate national interests. Therefore any state that would see an end to another's atrocious domestic oppression should do its utmost to secure Security Council authorization of intervention.

Suppose, however, that the supplicant state fails, perhaps because of the threat of veto. What, then? Must it stand by and confine its action to the wringing of hands? Not necessarily. International law bears more than one plausible interpretation. It may be that the dominant view is that legality requires Council authorization, but dominance does not make right. Majority opinion does not constitute truth. As I have argued, the strict, textualist reading of the law is sometimes—perhaps often—informed by dubious moral concepts and empirical judgements. Once those concepts and judgements are exposed and challenged, the plausibility of the majority view diminishes.

The making of a *bona fide* legal case is integral to the moral justification of intervention, because it is right that serious respect be paid to the law and that its authority be thereby acknowledged and confirmed. It is right, because the rule of law fosters the good of international order. Even those who continue to doubt the legal reasoning proposed will appreciate the proposer's readiness to be accountable before the law. A measure of trust, of moral community will be maintained; and because the advocate of unilateral action shows himself not to be a contemptuous rogue elephant, the law's authority will be preserved. Right, responsible process may not secure agreement on the truth, but it does help to preserve community and authority in the midst of substantive disagreement.[92]

---

92. The authority of international law consists fundamentally in the moral obligation of one state to be accountable to others in terms of norms of conduct that have been publicly agreed at some level or other. Thus, according to Michael Doyle, '[l]aw.... is intersubjective, determined by multilateral agreement' ('Striking First', in Michael W. Doyle, *Striking First: Preemption and Prevention in International Conflict*, ed. and intro. Stephen Macedo [Princeton: Princeton University Press, 2008], p. 60), and the UN Security Council embodies a process whereby judgements are subjected to 'structured deliberation and contestation in the presence

Further, there is more than one way to corrode the law's authority. Wanton violation is the obvious one; but failure to act against gross and massive violation of human rights is surely another. That is precisely why Kofi Annan sought to move the international community to affirm the norm of humanitarian intervention, together with a legal way of undertaking it in case of Security Council paralysis. So by interpreting the law in such a way as to permit intervention without Council authorization—as can be plausibly done—the supplicant state might actually serve to save the law's face and preserve its authority.

Most states most of the time will strive to find a legal justification for what they do. After all, they are ruled and represented by rational human beings, who are troubled by their own inconsistency and who like to think of themselves as doing the right thing. (Even the Nazis felt the need to rationalize legally and morally.) They also care to maintain their reputation as law abiding, for the sake of international trust and diplomatic leverage. Moreover, having participated in the creation, interpretation, and development of international law, they will have come to own its norms (or at least a certain version of them).[93] For those reasons alone, it is unlikely that a state will seek to justify military intervention in moral terms *rather than* legal ones.[94]

Nevertheless, states, like international lawyers, have been moved to recognize the distinction between legality and (moral) legitimacy, and that the latter can override the former. So, with regard to military intervention in defence of the Kurds of Northern Iraq in 1991, the French argued that '[t]he law is one thing, but the safeguard [sic]of a population is another, quite as precious, to which humanity cannot be indifferent'.[95] And of international lawyers on NATO's intervention in Kosovo, Martti Koskenniemi

of... multiple... decision-makers... in order to reflect a decent respect for the opinions of mankind' (ibid., p. 30). Thus, too, Henry Shue, who writes of 'the limiting effects of the need to offer plausible justifications appealing to shared standards' ('What Would a Justified Preventive Military Attack Look Like?', in Shue and Rodin, *Preemption*, p. 240).

93. See Harold Honju Koh, 'Why Do Nations Obey International Law?', *Yale Law Journal*, 106 (1996–7). This implies a rejection of an atomistic view of states and their international relations. Michael J. Smith puts the point nicely: 'states were never billiard balls impermeable to transnational norms, influences, and activities' ('Humanitarian Intervention: Overview of the Ethical Issues', in Joel H. Rosenthal, ed., *Ethics and International Affairs: A Reader*, 2nd edn [Washington, DC: Georgetown University Press, 1999], p. 273).

94. Paraphrasing Roger Fisher, Mary Ellen O'Connell writes that governments 'rarely if ever announce they are in violation of the law', preferring to exploit the law's ambiguities (*Power and Purpose*, p. 82).

95. Ibid., p. 206.

has written that 'most lawyers—including myself—have taken the ambivalent position that it was both formally illegal and morally necessary'.[96] In addition to a legal case for intervention, a supplicant state may also need to offer a supplementary, moral one; for sometimes the letter of the law prohibits what is morally obligatory, and the moral obligation is so stringent as to warrant transgression. If this were not so, then those who plotted Hitler's death in July 1944 would be simply criminals and not primarily moral heroes.

Some regard this line of thinking with great suspicion. Mary Ellen O'Connell, for example, refers to the 'the dangerous idea about force sometimes being legitimate, even if unlawful',[97] complains that its advocates do not show how the authority of the UN Charter and Security Council can survive it,[98] notes that it is espoused by 'some just war scholarship',[99] and argues that the doctrine 'can have little restraining force when the determination of justice is a subjective one'.[100] Martti Koskenniemi raises similar objections to what he calls 'shallow and dangerous moralisation' in international law.[101] To appeal beyond the law's text to its deeper logic or purposes is to claim access to 'an objective moral world', which is controversial,[102] as is the interpretation of any public criteria for humanitarian intervention.[103] To rise above formal law and decide its meaning is to make a decision that is, to quote Carl Schmitt, 'born out of legal nothingness'.[104] Moral conscience, being emotional, subjective, and private,[105] is no substitute. What purports to be ethics is really nothing but politics.[106] Therefore, what the 'exception' of Kosovo reveals is the will and power of a handful of Western leaders,[107] and a preoccupation with the morality of their decision-making serves to obscure the violent injustice of a global system, where 'it is never Algeria that will intervene in France, or Finland in Chechnya'.[108] 'Intervention remains a politi-

---

96. Koskenniemi, '"The Lady Doth Protest Too Much"', p. 162.
97. O'Connell, *Power and Purpose*, p. 147.
98. Ibid., p. 227.   99. Ibid., p. 147.
100. Ibid., p. 148 n. 192.
101. Koskenniemi, '"The Lady Doth Protest Too Much"', p. 162.
102. Ibid., pp. 165, 170.
103. Ibid., pp. 167–8.
104. Carl Schmitt, *Political Theology: Four Chapters on the Concept of Sovereignty*, trans. Georg Schwab (Cambridge, MA: MIT Press, ca 1985), pp. 31–2; quoted by Koskenniemi, '"The Lady Doth Protest Too Much"', p. 170.
105. Koskenniemi, '"The Lady Doth Protest Too Much"', p. 173.
106. Ibid., p. 173: the turn to ethics reveals 'the *political* moment' in official decision-making (author's italics).
107. Ibid., p. 171.   108. Ibid., p. 172.

cal act however much it is dressed in the language of moral compulsion or legal technique.'[109] Set against this, the value of legal formalism becomes clear: it keeps decision-makers accountable to other members of the international community, and it constrains them to serve common interests.[110]

To these objections I make the following response. First of all, the fact that foreign policy decisions include political considerations does not render them *ipso facto* immoral. Politics and ethics need not be mutually exclusive. Second, the ethical deliberations of conscience are not essentially private. Their reasoning can be articulated, exposed to public criticism, and found more or less cogent. Koskenniemi himself admits that most international lawyers are persuaded that the Kosovo intervention was both illegal *and morally right*, which strongly suggests that ethics is not a merely private, capricious, irrational endeavour. Third, it is rarely, if ever, possible to understand a text (whether the UN Charter or the Bible) from the bare words on its pages and without reference, often debatable, to what those words assume and intend. Fourth, formal law, as we have seen, is not objective in the sense that either it or its import commands universal assent. As Koskenniemi admits, 'in the interesting cases, non-compliance [with the law] is not a technical or a bad faith problem but a political [or, better, an interpretative, moral, and political] one: substantive disagreement about what the party accused of non-compliance undertook to comply with'.[111] Fifth, moral reasoning (at its best) and legal reasoning are very similar, and since international law embodies so many moral concepts, moral argumentation is hardly alien to it. Sixth, as I have already argued, the cynical interpretation of NATO's motivation in intervening in Kosovo simply does not withstand the facts. There is good reason to suppose that it was genuinely humanitarian. Seventh, the fact that there were larger and deeper injustices in the world deserving attention in 1999 does not mean that Serbian 'ethnic cleansing' in Kosovo was either just or unimportant, and that it was wrong of NATO to give it the time of day. Eighth and finally, how far unauthorized, formally illegal intervention will weaken the authority of international law and institutions depends very largely on how successful are the intervening states in persuading others of their ethical case.[112] States that fear international

---

109. Ibid., p. 173.   110. Ibid., p. 174.   111. Ibid., p. 165 n. 23.

112. Thus Gareth Evans: 'The effectiveness of the global collective security system, as with any other legal order, depends ultimately not only on the legality of decisions but also on *the*

intervention, should they ever embark on genocide and its like, will of course never be persuaded. Others, however, might be. In the case of Kosovo the Security Council had been unable to authorize NATO's intervention, because Russia threatened to cast its veto. However, when Russia subsequently proposed a resolution condemning the intervention, the Council refused by a vote of twelve to three. NATO's action, then, was at once *not expressly authorized* and yet *expressly not condemned* by a majority of four to one. When the Security Council itself refuses to condemn unauthorized intervention by such a margin, is it not reasonable to infer that a majority of the international community has been persuaded of the humanitarian motivation, the public-spiritedness, the necessity, and the proportionality of the action? What is more, such action has not actually set a precedent for rogue states to ride roughshod over international law. And if that is so, then how exactly has the law's authority been weakened at all?[113]

XII. The moral marks of just intervention

The moral justification of military intervention is bound to take the form of a legal case. The legal case is bound to involve moral elements. Morality and legality are not separable. Nevertheless, let us put aside legal considerations in this concluding section and concentrate our attention on the relevant moral criteria. What are they? First, given the terrible destructiveness and hazardous unpredictability of even justified military intervention, the reason for embarking upon it—its 'cause'—would have to be sufficiently grave if the intervention is to be just. The only kind of sufficiently grave reason that international law specifies is 'genocide'—and that, arguably, is still intended only as a motive for military intervention that is authorized by the Security Council. Morally speaking, however, it is

common perception of their legitimacy: their being made on solid evidentiary grounds, for the right reasons, morally as well as legally' (*Responsibility to Protect*, p. 139. My emphasis).

113. I note that Gareth Evans reaches a conclusion that is close to my own: 'While it is obviously optimal for any military action to be both unquestionably legal under international law and more or less universally accepted as legitimate (as was the case, for example, with the 1991 Gulf War), it is fair to suggest that military action that is technically illegal but widely perceived to be legitimate (as with Kosovo in 1999) does far less damage than action which is generally perceived to be neither legal nor legitimate (Iraq in 2003)' (*Responsibility to Protect*, p. 139).

arguable that murderous oppression on a massive scale that is not genocidal could be grave enough to warrant risking the evils and hazards of
war. It seems to me, for example, that saving Kosovar Albanians from indiscriminate killing by the troops of a Serbian regime that had Srebrenica on
its curriculum vitae was proportionate cause. Therefore I agree with the
ICISS report, *The Responsibility to Protect*, that just cause should be extended
beyond genocide to include any 'large scale loss of life' or 'large scale
"ethnic cleansing"'.[114]

Must, however, the atrocity be 'actual or [imminently] apprehended [that
is, anticipated]' for intervention to be warranted—as the report stipulates?[115]
One obvious reason for such a condition is that only then could intervention claim to be about protecting victims. After the event is over, there is
presumably no protecting left to do. Well, actually, no. A regime that has
shown itself willing to carry out mass atrocities, and which succeeds in
doing so with impunity, will have no compunction about perpetrating fresh
atrocities, should it see fit to do so. For that reason the international community has a responsibility to punish state atrocities after the fact, and not
merely to stop them in mid-flight. *The Responsibility to Protect* comes close
to my point here when it says that while '[o]verthrow of regimes is not, as
such, a legitimate objective', 'disabling that regime's capacity to harm its
own people may be essential to discharging the mandate of protection—
and what is necessary to achieve that disabling will vary from case to case.
Occupation of territory may not be able to be avoided.'[116]

Other marks or criteria of morally justified but legally unauthorized
military intervention, which *The Responsibility to Protect* lays down, are the
usual just war doctrine suspects: namely, that the intention must be to halt
or avert (unjust) human suffering; that it should be a last resort, every other
available and *effective* alternative having been tried; that the military means
(and their destructiveness) should be proportionate—that is, limited to what
is necessary to protect (and, I would add, therefore punish); and that there
must be a reasonable prospect of success—success being taken to include
both military victory *and* post-war reconstruction.[117]

---

114. ICISS, *The Responsibility to Protect*, pp. 32–3, s.4.19–21.
115. Ibid., p. 32, s.4.18–19. The ICISS, in *The Responsibility to Protect*, stipulates that for military
    intervention to be warranted, 'there must be serious and irreparable harm *occurring to human
    beings, or imminently likely to occur*' (p. 32, s.4.18. My emphasis).
116. Ibid., p. 35, s.4.33.   117. Ibid., pp. 35–7, ss.4.32–43.

In addition to these primary, necessary marks of moral justification, there are two other secondary ones that strengthen an intervention's claim to serve international public interests, rather than selfish national ones. The first is the consonance of the ends of intervention with those expressly asserted by the United Nations in the Resolutions of its Security Council. The second is highlighted by the case of Kosovo: that military intervention, with or without formal authorization by the Security Council, should nevertheless be undertaken by as broad an alliance of states as possible. The moral significance of this is that the broader the alliance, the less likely its motives for intervention will be purely private, rapaciously self-interested ones.

7

Constructing judgement
The case of Iraq

I. The order of judgement

The just war tradition does not hand us a random list of disparate criteria for
judging the rightness and wrongness of belligerency. The various criteria are
connected by an internal logic that orders them, making some logically prior
to others and imposing on the complex act of judgement a certain structure.
The issue of just cause is logically basic and therefore first in the process of
judging. Without just cause nothing that follows can be justified, even if it
can be more or less virtuous: the fact that some fought honourably on the
Nazi side in the Second World War did nothing to redeem their cause.
According to the Christian tradition, a just cause must comprise an injustice.
Justified war, then, is basically a reaction to injustice that seeks to curb it or
rectify it. An intention to improve the world is not sufficient. Why? Because
the evils and hazards of war are too great to be warranted by an attempt to
raise a people's condition from good to better. They are even too great to be
warranted by an attempt to raise it from tolerably bad to better. What alone
justifies belligerency is an injustice that is intolerably grave.

A grave injustice calls for punishment, but who may do the punishing?
Enter the criterion of legitimate authority. Traditionally and basically, a just
belligerent is one who is responsible for defending a community against
external injury as well as against internal crime.[1] To this we moderns might
add that he is also one publicly accountable for the manner of his caring,
and whose authority to exercise it is therefore publicly recognized. What
is at stake here is partly the good of public order, since this will be less

---

1. See, for example, Aquinas, *Summa Theologiae*, 2a 2ae, Q.40, a.1.

disturbed if punitive coercion is used by a body that is publicly approved. There is also a concern for the higher probability of justice, since a body is more likely to exercise its responsibility in the public interest if it is publicly accountable. The criterion of authority that is 'legitimate' in the sense of 'publicly accountable' is therefore connected to the prudential criteria of last resort, proportionality, and prospect of success. Since in the end it is the citizenry of a state that must supply the necessary resources of manpower and materiel, a government cannot wage war without public support. (Historically, at least in England, it was frequently the monarch's need to raise money and troops for war that *made* him accountable to parliament.) Since no one wants to see their resources wasted, citizens will rightly require their government to give a persuasive account of why punishment cannot take a less costly form than war, why war will be proportionate, and why it has an appropriate prospect of success.

Grave injustice and the political authority to punish it, however, are not sufficient. The injustice must be the *basic reason* for the authority's reaction. It must form what it does in response. It must inform its responsive intention, directing it either to curb or to rectify what is unjust. No matter how legitimate, an authority may not use an objective injustice as a mere pretext for intending something quite unrelated—say, expanding its political and military dominance. Right intention, therefore, is at once logically secondary to grave injustice and equally necessary.

Before we go to war, prudence requires us to consider whether there are other, less hazardous and less costly means of achieving what we intend. We must consider whether or not our going to war would be a last resort. This does not require us to stay our belligerent hand for so long as an alternative route is conceivable. A conceivable alternative might be so improbable as to make deference to it nothing better than an act of evasion—for example, the continuation of diplomatic negotiations with an opponent who has shown persistent bad faith. In order to be justified, belligerency must defer only to alternatives that seem feasible and likely to be effective.

To be right, a responsive intention must aim to oppose, perhaps reverse, grave injustice. What it aims to achieve, however, must be proportionate. However limited in scale and duration a war looks set to be, its effects are invariably evil in depth, if not in breadth: the violent killing of even one person is something not to be done lightly. What is more, once we relax the leash on the dogs of war, we should expect to be dragged where we do not want to go. Long experience has taught that war has a momentum of its own—partly military, partly political—that is not readily controlled. Before we launch ourselves into war, therefore, it behoves us to satisfy ourselves that its evils, which will very probably be higher than we anticipate, will be incurred for a sufficiently important reason, that they will not undercut the end we seek, and that they will be militarily and politically sustainable.

Breathing down the neck of the criterion of proportion is that of the prospect of success. The benefit that we intend might be the correction of grave injustice and it might be worthy of the evils incurred by war. The question remains, however: Is it feasible? Can we actually realize what we intend? If we cannot, then our belligerency might be an enormously expensive exercise in futility. This is obviously a sensible question to ask. In answering it, however, we need to take into account that high stakes can warrant higher risks, that taking high risks can sometimes be heroic and not foolish, and that failure can sometimes be caused by misfortune and not mere imprudence.

In addition to the six criteria of justice in going to war (*ius ad bellum*), there are two that concern justice in the course of waging it (*ius in bello*). One of these is the prohibition of intentional attacks upon non-combatants— the requirement of discrimination. The other is the consideration of proportionality at the operational and tactical levels: the evils caused by military means must be proportionate to the military objectives. That is to say, the means should be as efficient as possible, causing only such damage as is militarily necessary. These criteria of *ius in bello* are relatively independent of those of *ius ad bellum*, insofar as the former continue to bind those who fight without the latter. While it is true that those fighting without just cause or right intention wound and kill without justification, it is also true that it is better that their unjustified wounding and killing are done discriminately and proportionately. It is better for their just enemies, for non-combatants, and for their own moral integrity.

In the case of a basically justified war, however, the means are not independent of the intended ends. Specifically, operational or tactical means need to avoid subverting—being ill-proportioned to—the basic, strategic aims of fighting. So, for example, if a strategic aim is to win popular support for a government, then killing civilians in the course of a counter-insurgency campaign might well be strategically disproportionate, even when it is discriminate (or at least unintentional) and operationally proportionate. More generally, discriminate and proportionate means serve to minimize the overall sum of evil incurred, and so to support the basic justification for going to war in the first place—namely, the achievement of a just peace.

II. The 2003 invasion of Iraq:
not so morally simple

For many people, the immorality of the invasion of Iraq in 2003 is plain. The exact constellation of factors varies from critic to critic, of course, but certain views are so common that they can be composed into the following stereotype, which is not far from what is often actually thought and expressed. The Bush administration was intent on revenge, on remaking the world according to its imperialist whim, and on stealing oil. Tony Blair was in the grip of a Christian, moralistic, messianic megalomania,[2] and was pathetically desperate to be allowed to paddle in the shallows of American power. Both Bush and Blair lied—Bush, about the connection between Saddam Hussein and al-Qaeda; Blair, about the threat posed by Iraqi weapons of mass destruction (WMD). In going to war, they ignored viable and less costly alternatives, and they violated international law. They were woefully unprepared for the task of national reconstruction in the aftermath of invasion. As a consequence, Iraq has been plunged into a state even worse than it suffered under Saddam Hussein, and the costs to the United States and the United Kingdom have far exceeded any gains.

Much of this stereotypical view is, I think, quite wrong. As I see it, and as I hope to show, the crafting of a satisfactory, comprehensive moral judgement about the invasion and occupation of Iraq is complicated and difficult. In what follows, I intend to build such a judgement and to explicate the important lessons it teaches about the practical application of just war theory in general.

III. *Ad bellum*: just cause (i): an atrocious regime

Whether or not the 2003 invasion and occupation of Iraq were basically just or unjust depends, fundamentally, on whether they had just cause. According to the Christian tradition of thought on these matters, just belligerency is

---

2. So, for example, the highly esteemed commentator on British politics, Andrew Rawnsley, writes of Mr Blair's 'biblical Manichaeism' (*The End of the Party: The Rise and Fall of New Labour* [London: Viking, 2010], pp. 20, 42, 85, 249), his 'moral imperialism' (ibid., p. 43), and of his 'messianic tendency' (ibid., p. 45). As a theologian, I must risk pedantry in pointing out that Manichaeism was actually *post*-biblical and, according to Augustine, *anti*-biblical.

motivated by love for neighbours in the specific form of righting a grave wrong done to them. That is, it depends at bottom on the objective fact of grave injustice. One kind of such injustice is a state's murder of its own citizens on a massive scale. Let us call this state atrocity.[3]

Was Saddam Hussein's regime guilty of such atrocity? Undoubtedly, it was. The 1988 Anfal campaign saw the repeated use of chemical weapons against Kurdish civilians. The Kurdistan government claims that this caused 182,000 deaths[4]—and of these the Iraqi military commander with sole responsibility for the region, Ali Hassan al-Majidi, was happy to own 100,000.[5] Between 1991 and 2003, according to Western human rights groups, at least a further 300,000 people were victims of the state.[6] So Saddam Hussein's regime was responsible for the murder of at least 400,000—perhaps close to half a million—of its own people in the fifteen years from 1988 to 2003. To these must be added many others who were raped, tortured, or rendered destitute by the demolition of their homes. That record certainly makes the regime atrocious; and according to Human Rights Watch, it also makes it genocidal.[7] This is, without doubt, a grave injustice, and it therefore constitutes just cause for military intervention. Note: it is *not* sufficient to make intervention *morally right*, because there are other criteria yet to be met; but it is sufficient to satisfy the single criterion of just cause.

3. Peter Lee tells us that self-defence is 'the most ancient of just causes', that Tony Blair's aim of regime-change in Iraq contradicted 'the long established principles of just war', and that his moral arguments therefore amounted to a 'moral sleight of hand' and created only 'the illusion of morality' (*Blair's Just War: Iraq and the Illusion of Morality* [London: Palgrave MacMillan, 2012], pp. 99–100; see also pp. 5, 12). Lee errs here in conflating the whole of just war tradition with Michael Walzer's modern version (ibid., p. 113). In fact, Blair's affirmation of the use of military force to overthrow atrociously tyrannical regimes stands squarely within Christian just war tradition, both early and late. But this is unlikely to impress Lee, who, notwithstanding his service as an RAF chaplain during the Iraq invasion and the three biblical quotations that preface his book, is more Foucauldian than Christian in his cynicism about (theological) appeals to 'true' principles of morality and justice that transcend positive international law (ibid., pp. 10, 187 n. 12, 37, 138–9).

4. Peter W. Galbraith, *The End of Iraq: How American Incompetence Created a War without End*, 2nd edn (New York: Simon & Schuster, 2007), p. 49.

5. Anne Clwyd, 'Why Did it Take You so Long to Get Here?', in Thomas Cushman, *A Matter of Principle: Humanitarian Arguments for War in Iraq* (Berkeley: University of California, 2005), pp. 311–12.

6. William Shawcross, *Allies: The U.S., Britain, Europe, and the War in Iraq* (New York: Public Affairs, 2004), p. 160. Galbraith specifies this figure as referring to Shi'ites killed by the Iraqi army and security forces from March to September 1991 (*The End of Iraq*, p. 49).

7. Human Rights Watch, 'Genocide in Iraq: The Anfal Campaign against the Kurds', July 1993, <http://www.hrw.org/reports/1993/iraqanfal/> (as at 28 March 2011).

It is true, however, that these atrocities lay in the past when the United States and its allies invaded in 2003. Saddam Hussein's regime was not actually in the process of carrying out mass murder when American and British troops crossed the border into Iraq. For some this is significant. As mentioned in the previous chapter, the ICISS's report, *The Responsibility to Protect*, stipulated that an atrocity has to be 'actual or apprehended [that is, 'imminently likely to occur']' for intervention to be warranted;[8] and one obvious reason for such a condition is that only then can intervention claim to be about protecting victims. Against this, I argued that a state that has shown itself willing to carry out mass atrocities, and which succeeds in getting away with it, will have no qualms about perpetrating fresh atrocities and creating fresh victims, should *raison d'état* and opportunity present themselves. This is all the more so where it has succeeded in getting away with mass murder several times over. As individuals have characters that are formed by their histories, so have regimes. Characters comprise habitual inclinations: as one has acted repeatedly in the past, so one will be inclined to act in the future. Therefore, a state that has become habituated to mass murder may be expected, *ceteris paribus*, to do so again. Of course, *cetera* might not be *paria*. Individuals might undergo a change of heart, and regimes might undergo a significant change in leadership and direction. In that case, there would be no reason to expect the future to run along historical lines. Absent such change, however, there would be reason. Therefore an unrepentant regime is liable to punishment after the fact, and not merely to opposition *in flagrante delicto*. Such punishment should not be about the undisciplined and indiscriminate wreaking of vengeance upon the heads of mass murderers. Rather, it should intend to rescue probable victims from present terror and future murder.

More than this, however, perhaps punishment owes something to the dead as well as to the living. Perhaps the already murdered deserve not to be abandoned to history as lost causes, but to be paid respect—to be vindicated—by punishing their murderers, first of all by removing them from power. Suppose, for example, that Hitler had succeeded in completing the Final Solution. Would the rationale for the Allies' prosecution of war against him really be only the preservation of the still living, and not also the vindication of the already dead? I doubt it. We do not cease to love the familiar dead, and we feel strong obligations of loyalty to them. This is so

8. ICISS, *Responsibility to Protect*, p. 32, s.4.18 and 19.

true that sometimes we devote the rest of our lives to clearing their names of guilt or bringing their persecutors to justice—to vindicating them. That is a fact. It may be difficult to rationalize, but our faithfulness to the dead makes us more morally beautiful, and beauty is a reason.

I do not think, therefore, that the fact that Saddam Hussein was not actually engaged in the process of perpetrating mass atrocity removes just cause from the invasion of 2003. While the regime had an historical record of mass atrocity, its atrociousness was not all history: in April 2002 the UN Commission on Human Rights adopted a resolution proposed by the European Union, which held Iraq responsible for 'systematic, widespread and extremely grave violations of human rights and international humanitarian law'.[9] The regime of Saddam Hussein had not changed its spots. It remained a standing insult to its innocent victims, both dead and living, and a standing threat to future ones.[10]

I believe that the atrocious record and character of the Iraqi regime were a just cause for war, and this belief is basic to the structure of the argument that follows. It is very significant that Craig White's impressively systematic and painstaking analysis of the 2003 invasion does not share it. He does mention the regime's 'evil' character, but only in the specific form of international recklessness and aggressiveness, and in relation to the alleged threat of its possession of weapons of WMD.[11] He also mentions President Bush's claim that liberation from tyranny was among the aims of invasion, but dismisses it as 'a kind of addendum' that was 'not a part of the core of the announced reasons for war'.[12] I disagree with White over this, for reasons that I shall explain more fully below. For now let me point out that whether

---

9. <http//: news.bbc.co.uk/1/hi/world/middle_east/1940050.stm> (as at 16 December 2011).
10. In support of this view of the persistently atrocious character of Saddam's regime, I note that Peter Galbraith, a professional diplomat and Kurdish expert, whose 2006 book, *The End of Iraq*, is highly critical of the 2003 invasion, nevertheless describes Iraq under Saddam Hussein as 'Stalinist' (ibid., p. 22) and as subject to 'pervasive fear' (ibid., p. 21), and confesses that in September 1991, '[a]fter all that I heard and saw, I was convinced that the use of force to remove Saddam Hussein was morally justifiable' (ibid., p. 65). I note, too, that Emma Sky, the British Arabist who opposed the invasion of Iraq but served there from 2003 to 2010 in a variety of senior political capacities, has been reported as saying, 'I had arrived [in 2003] ready to apologise to every Iraqi for the war. Instead I had listened to a litany of suffering and pain under Saddam for which I was quite unprepared. The mass graves, the details of torture, the bureaucratisation of abuse. The pure banality of evil' (Nick Hopkins, 'The British volunteer, the US army, and Iraq's descent into civil war', *Guardian*, 16 July 2012, p. 11).
11. Craig M. White, *Iraq: The Moral Reckoning. Applying Just War Theory to the 2003 War Decision* (Lanham, Maryland: Lexington Books, 2010), pp. 43, 58–62.
12. Ibid., p. 87.

or not one reckons that the domestic record of the Iraqi regime was a just cause for war, and whether or not one counts its correction among the Coalition's intentions, are considerations crucial for the construction of a final judgement. It is not a coincidence that my conclusion turns out to be morally complex, whereas White's is simply damning.

IV. *Ad bellum*: just cause (ii): the threat of WMD

The atrocious character of a regime is sufficient just cause for punishment—if need be, by means of war. It might not, however, be sufficient just cause to motivate any body in particular to inflict the punishment. If there were a global government responsible for law and order, and competent to maintain them, then the task would naturally fall to it; but there is no such government. Whether or not action is taken under the auspices of the United Nations, therefore, it will be taken by nation-states; and states must be motivated by national interest. As we have already argued, national interest need not be ignoble.[13] Nations do care about their own moral integrity, they want to believe that they are virtuous, and their moral indignation is sometimes appropriately aroused by news of mass murder in foreign parts. In other words, they have a national interest in opposing gross injustice. However, while this interest might be sufficient to motivate punitive action in faraway places, which is swift or at least cheap, it is unlikely to sustain it alone if the costs and casualties mount. Then, the motivating force of some additional interest will be necessary. However, not any kind will do, morally speaking. The additional interest must be rooted in a further just cause, otherwise injustice will be less the reason for action than a mere pretext for it, and the guise of just punishment will serve to cloak an act of domination or theft.

Here, in the case of Iraq, is where the issue of WMD comes into play. It was the perceived threat posed by the prospect of Saddam Hussein coming to possess WMD that gave the United States and the United Kingdom sufficient national interest to motivate belligerent action against Iraq. What, exactly, was the threat? What would have been so evil about Saddam Hussein's possession of WMD, especially nuclear weapons? First, it would have given a characteristically atrocious regime immunity from military punishment for mass murder, whether past, present, or future. If this seems

13. See Chapter Six, VI.

unlikely, then imagine how Muammar Gaddafi's possession of nuclear weapons would have constrained NATO's intervention to prevent the slaughter of the rebellious citizens of Benghazi in 2011. Second, it would have made the regime immune from military retaliation on the next occasion it invaded the likes of Kuwait. Third, it would have heightened the possibility of nuclear war in the Middle East—between Iraq and Israel or, if it also acquired nuclear weaponry, Iran. Fourth, it would have made it possible for the regime to supply WMD to al-Qaeda or other terrorists seeking to maximize civilian casualties, not least in Western cities.

This fourth threat is the one that bore most closely on the national interests of the United States and the United Kingdom. What kind of threat was this? Was it merely speculative or actual or somewhere in between? This first thing to say in response is that al-Qaeda and associated jihadist networks represent a significantly novel form of terrorism. Hitherto, terrorist organizations—such as the IRA—have had strong political reasons for being discriminate in their killing, for limiting it. Since their intent has been to attract the loyalty of citizens away from the established regime, and to win the support of foreign governments, it has not been to their political advantage to cause the indiscriminate slaughter of civilians. The form of terrorism perpetrated in New York and Washington, DC on 11 September 2001 (9/11), however, did not suffer from those political constraints. It was not interested in gaining the support of Americans, nor did it care how governments around the world would receive its deed. In a single day it succeeded in killing almost 3,000 people, which is not far short of the total number (3,593) of people killed in Northern Ireland's 'Troubles' over three decades.[14] It is important to bear in mind that the damage wrought by such mass murder is not to be measured simply in terms of lives lost. It also casts a menacing shadow over subsequent civilian life, exacerbates social and political tensions, and threatens the loss of civil liberties.

---

14. Philip Bobbitt, *Terror and Consent. The Wars for the 21st Century* (London: Allen Lane, 2008), pp. 46, 48–9, 60. Of the total number of Troubles-related deaths between 1969 and 1998, members of the Irish Republican Army or the Irish National Liberation Army are reckoned to be responsible for 55.7 per cent (Marie Smyth, 'Putting the Past in its Place: Issues of Victimhood and Reconciliation in Northern Ireland's Peace Process', in Nigel Biggar, *Burying the Past*, pp. 137–8 [Tables 7.3 and 7.4]. In May 2008 I wrote to Dr Smyth to ask whether her 2001 apportionment of responsibility for Troubles-related killings was still reliable. With a minor qualification, she responded in the affirmative).

Had the perpetrators of 9/11 possessed the means to kill ten times or a hundred times as many people, I can see no reason to doubt that they would have done so. Certainly, there is evidence that al-Qaeda was working to acquire WMD,[15] and the possibility of its succeeding was not remote. The technology involved in such weaponry has been getting ever smaller in scale and easier to construct and operate. This is especially true of chemical, biological, and radiological weapons.[16] Even though the successful construction of a nuclear weapon would require high standards of engineering design and manufacture, 'according to some analysts these standards are becoming steadily more attainable'.[17] It is clear, then, that there is the will to acquire and use WMD on the part of terrorists, and that the means are becoming increasingly feasible. What is more, there is an international black market in nuclear materials and expertise—most infamously instanced by the commercial operations of Dr A.Q. Khan[18]—that could bring together terrorist will and WMD means. In the light of all this, it seems to me that the fear of the terrorist use of WMD is not the fabrication of the overwrought imaginations of securocrats, and that it is not far-fetched to suppose

15. According to Philip Bobbitt, after the collapse of the Taliban government in Afghanistan, the discovery of documents and disks revealed that al-Qaeda had a biological weapons programme, including the location of sites containing commercial production equipment and cultures of a biological agent; and that members of al-Qaeda had met with Pakistani scientists to discuss the development of nuclear weapons (*Terror and Consent*, p. 119. The latter claim has been confirmed to me by an authoritative source in Britain's Secret Intelligence Service.) Under interrogation, one of these scientists, Sultan Bashiruddin Mahmood, reported that Osama Bin Laden had insisted that he already possessed sufficient fissile material to build a nuclear bomb, having obtained it from former Soviet stockpiles through a militant Islamic group, the Islamic Movement of Uzbekistan (ibid.). In January 2003 British officials found documents in Herat that led them to believe that al-Qaeda had succeeded in building a small 'dirty bomb' (ibid., p. 100).

16. According to Paul Cornish, highly toxic industrial chemicals 'are relatively easy to acquire and would need minimal processing and preparation before use...Although the large-scale production, weaponisation and delivery of chemical weapons would be challenging, scientifically and logistically, as well as extremely expensive, a small number of low-yield chemical weapons would be relatively easy to hide and transport' (*The CBRN System. Assessing the threat of terrorist use of chemical, biological, radiological and nuclear weapons in the United Kingdom* [London: Royal Institute for International Affairs, 2007], p. v); 'As with chemical weapons, a covert biological weapons programme would make use of easily available dual-use material and equipment...Unlike chemical weapon manufacture, however, a bio-weapon progamme might require only a small research, development and production process...Delivery of a biological weapon could be a relatively straightforward matter'; 'Radioactive material of various types can be acquired from a wide range of sources, including industry, hospitals and university research laboratories...[W]hile the physical harm from a RW attack might be limited, the blast could provoke panic...The technical challenges would not...be insurmountable' (ibid., p. vi).

17. Ibid., p. vii.

18. Bobbitt, *Terror and Consent*, pp. 107–21.

that, 'with demand rising and marginal cost falling, as is...the case with...WMD technologies, it is only a matter of time before such weapons, including nuclear weapons, become available to terrorist groups'.[19] In fact, at least one terrorist group has *already* used a chemical weapon in an attack upon an urban civilian population: in 1995 five members of the religious cult Aum Shinrikyo released sarin gas on the Tokyo underground, killing twelve, severely injuring fifty, and moderately injuring almost one thousand others.

The international black market is one medium through which terrorists willing to use WMD could obtain the means. States are another. There are plenty of instances of states collaborating with terrorist groups—for example, Libya with the IRA, Iran with Hezbollah. Would such a state ever take the risk of supplying WMD or the means to construct them? According to familiar, Western lines of rational political calculation, that might seem very unlikely; but rationality always depends on certain assumptions, and not all political leaders share ours. In 1945 Hitler preferred to take 'unworthy' Germany into the abyss with him, rather than spare tens of millions of his fellow countrymen needless suffering. In 2003 Saddam Hussein preferred to risk invasion rather than suffer the shame of revealing that the emperor really had no WMD clothes. Tyrants tend to surround themselves with people who tell them what they want to hear, with the result that they are even less tolerant of uncongenial reality and more prone to self-delusion than the rest of us. The truth is that we cannot know whether a tyrannical state with an atrocious character and a record of collaboration with terrorists would be prepared to enable them to use massively destructive weapons. It may seem improbable to us, but we cannot be sure; and given the height of the stakes, reluctance in yielding benefit of doubt would be reasonable.

Nevertheless, it is not responsible simply to assume the worst in the absence of any evidence whatsoever that a feared possibility is being actualized. So was there any evidence of cooperation between Saddam Hussein's regime and relevant terrorists—that is, with those who have shown themselves willing to kill indiscriminately on a massive scale? There is evidence that the regime had a connection with al-Qaeda. According to the 2004 Butler report, between October 2002 and February 2003 the UK's Joint Intelligence Committee (JIC) reckoned that al-Qaeda agents had been involved in the production of chemical and biological agents in Kurdish

---

19. Michael Intriligator and Abdullah Toukan, quoted by Bobbitt in ibid., p. 99.

northern Iraq *and* that they had been in contact with the Iraqi Directorate
General of Intelligence over four years since 1998, perhaps in search of toxic
chemicals.[20] It is true that in November 2001 the JIC concluded that 'there
is no evidence that these contacts led to practical cooperation: we judge it
unlikely because of mutual mistrust'.[21] This judgement of likelihood, however, seems too confident, since common interests can make unlikely allies.
No one ever imagined that Hitler and Stalin would overcome their pro-
found ideological hostility to agree a non-aggression pact, but this they did
in 1939; and unlikely though it is, Shi'ite Iran has in fact managed to hold
its nose sufficiently to collaborate with Sunni groups such as Hamas and
Palestinian Islamic Jihad, as well as with Salafists such as the Taliban.[22] In the
case of secular, Ba'athist Iraq and militantly Islamist al-Qaeda, the JIC's subsequent assessments tend to confirm this point. In October 2002 it noted
that 'Saddam's attitude to Al Qaida has not always been consistent', and that
'Abu Musab al-Zarqawi (a senior Al Qaida figure) was relatively free to
travel within Iraq proper and to stay in Baghdad for some time'; and in
March 2003 it observed that al-Zarqawi had been sufficiently at liberty to
establish sleeper cells in Baghdad for activation during a US occupation of
the city.[23] In sum, there was evidence that communication had been sustained over several years between al-Qaeda and the Iraqi regime, perhaps on
the topic of toxic chemicals, and that a senior al-Qaeda agent had been free
to operate in the heart of Iraq. On the other hand, there was no evidence of
practical cooperation in the construction of WMD for terrorist use. This
lack of evidence, however, does not drain all reason from the concern. Given
the backdrop of 9/11, given the self-delusion of tyrants, given the atrocious
character of the Iraqi regime, given the evidence of its prolonged communication with and tolerance of al-Qaeda, and given the assumption that it

---

20. *Review of Intelligence of Weapons of Mass Destruction*, HC 898 (London: The Stationery Office,
    2004), p. 119, paras 481–4. Craig White observes that al-Zarqawi's al-Qaeda camp in north-
    eastern Iraq was outside Baghdad's control (*Iraq*, p. 63), but he makes no mention of the evi-
    dence of communication between al-Zarqawi and the Iraqi regime.
21. *Review of Intelligence*, para. 481. In June 2004 the National Commission on Terrorist Attacks
    upon the United States confirmed the JIC's earlier assessment, reporting that 'while there had
    been contacts between al-Qaeda and Saddam Hussein's Iraq, it has seen no evidence of "a
    collaborative operational relationship"' (Thomas Ricks, *Fiasco: The American Military Adventure
    in Iraq* (New York: Penguin, 2006), p. 377).
22. Tony Blair makes this point in his 2010 autobiography: 'How many times did I hear, in respect
    of the Iranian government, people tell me that they, as Shia, would never forge an alliance with
    Sunni groups in the Middle East? But where they conceive it serves a tactical purpose, they
    do' (*A Journey* [London: Hutchinson, 2010], pp. 386–7).
23. Ibid., p. 120.

continued to possess WMD, there was reason to remain concerned that cooperation for which there was not yet evidence was happening nonetheless or would happen shortly. The concern was not merely fanciful; it did have grounds.

However, these grounds have proven weaker than first appeared. Since the invasion it has become clear that Iraq did not actually possess WMD. How, then, should we assess the claim that it did? Was it manufactured in bad faith by Washington and London? If so, then the concern about Iraq feeding them to al-Qaeda was spurious. In my view, the claim that Iraq possessed WMD was not a lie. It was an error, but it was an error on the part of the intelligence services, not just of the United Kingdom and the United States, but also of all other Western countries[24] and of Russia.[25] The President of France believed it. In February 2003, two months before his government threatened to veto United Nations Security Council authorization of military action against Iraq, Jacques Chirac told *Time* magazine: 'There is a problem—the probable possession of weapons of mass destruction by an uncontrollable country, Iraq. The international community is right...in having decided Iraq should be disarmed.'[26] Even the head of the 2003 UN weapons inspection team, Hans Blix, believed it. Writing in 2004 of his views on the eve of the invasion, he confessed that '[m]y gut feelings...suggested to me that Iraq still engaged in prohibited activities and retained prohibited items, and that it had the documents to prove it'.[27]

In fact, the belief was not entirely false. If Iraq did not actually possess the weapons, it did possess active research programmes in chemical and biological weaponry; and according to at least one credible authority, this was sufficient to constitute a serious threat. Rolf Ekeus, Swedish head of the UN Special Commission on Iraq (UNSCOM) from 1991 to 1997—in which

24. David Fisher, formerly a senior official in the UK's Ministry of Defence and Foreign Office, who served as the senior defence adviser to the Prime Minister in the Cabinet Office, with responsibilities including Iraq, 1997–9, has written that 'all experts advised, not just in the UK and US but in all other Western countries' that SH [Saddam Hussein] had retained some CBW [chemical and biological weapons] (*Morality and War*, p. 200).
25. Since Russia supported UNSC Resolution 1441 in November 2002, which declared Saddam Hussein to be in material breach of his disarmament obligations, we may infer that Russian intelligence did not disagree that Iraq possessed WMD. David Fisher made this point to me in personal correspondence.
26. Kenneth Pollack, 'Spies, Lies, and Weapons', *The Atlantic Monthly*, January/February 2004, (online) p. 3.
27. Hans Blix, *Disarming Iraq. The Search for Weapons of Mass Destruction* (London: Bloomsbury, 2004), p. 112.

capacity he had resisted US attempts to use the Commission for the purposes of espionage—and later chairman of the board of the Stockholm International Peace Research Institute, wrote in June 2003:

> Detractors of Bush and Blair have tried to make political capital of the presumed discrepancy between top-level assurances about Iraq's possession of chemical weapons (and other WMD) and the inability of invading forces to find such stocks. The criticism is a distortion and trivialization of a major threat to international peace and security... [The] combination of researchers, engineers, know-how, precursors, batch production techniques and testing is what constituted Iraq's chemical threat—its chemical weapon. The rather bizarre political focus on the search for rusting drums and pieces of munitions containing low-quality chemicals has tended to distort the important question of WMD in Iraq...The real chemical warfare threat from Iraq has had two components. One has been the capability to bring potent chemical agents to the battlefield to be used against a poorly equipped and poorly trained enemy. The other is the chance that Iraqi chemical weapons specialists would sign up with terrorist networks such as al Qaeda...The chemical and biological warfare structures in Iraq constitute formidable international threats through potential links to international terrorism.[28]

There are, of course, significantly different kinds of WMD: chemical, biological, and nuclear. Whereas many people were persuaded that Iraq possessed chemical and/or biological weapons, there was little evidence that it either possessed nuclear weapons or was about to acquire them imminently. Richard Haas, special assistant to President George H. W. Bush and senior director on the staff of the National Security Council from 1989 to 1993, judges that 'the case that Iraq was close to possessing NW [nuclear weapons] did not bear cursory scrutiny',[29] citing in support the National Intelligence Estimate of October 2002, which had reckoned that, 'if left unchecked, [Iraq] probably will have a nuclear weapon during this decade'.[30] Richard Clarke, National Coordinator for Security, Infrastructure Protection, and Counterterrorism under Presidents Clinton and George W. Bush, agrees: 'Nothing in 2002 indicated Saddam intended to build nukes, much less use them, and certainly not imminently.'[31] Thus, too, Peter Galbraith, a US

---

28. Rolf Ekeus, 'Iraq's Real Weapons Threat', *Washington Post*, 29 June 2003, <http://www.usembassy.it/file2003_07/alia/A3070202.htm> (as at 24 August 2012).
29. Richard N. Haas, *War of Necessity. A Memoir of Two Iraq Wars* (New York: Simon and Schuster, 2010), p. 218.
30. Haas, *War of Necessity*, p. 230.
31. Richard A. Clarke, *Against All Enemies: Inside America's War on Terror* (New York: Free Press, 2004), p. 268.

diplomat with expertise on Kurdistan: 'based on what the United States knew or could assume in 2002, the maximum possible threat from Iraq was from previously produced chemical weapons and, more remotely, an experimental quantity of biological weapons'.[32]

On the other hand, *pace* Clarke, many were convinced that Saddam Hussein was intent on acquiring nuclear weapons;[33] and in February 2000 the BND (Bundesnachrichtendienst), the German intelligence agency, estimated that by 2005 Iraq would have at its disposal nuclear missiles capable of hitting targets in Europe and Central Asia.[34] Moreover, whatever the truth about nuclear weapons, the fact remains that evidence and reason had persuaded a wide range of experts in a variety of countries that Iraq still possessed chemical and/or biological weapons. This alone was ground for serious concern. As Galbraith concedes: 'Although Iraq was the least dangerous member of the Axis of Evil, there were reasons to be concerned about Iraq's WMD programmes, and in particular about the regime's ambitions.'[35] Even an opponent of the invasion such as Haas still agreed that there was a genuine threat: 'I assumed that Iraq did possess biological and chemical weapons and might act with greater aggressiveness because of them, actually use them, or conceivably transfer them to some other state or group.'[36]

The belief that Iraq possessed WMD, and that this was a threat, was not just an expedient fabrication by President Bush's administration or by Mr Blair. It was widespread, held even by some of the best-known critics of the invasion. Why was this? Five cogent reasons present themselves. First was the shocking revelation in the mid-1990s that before the Gulf War Iraq had succeeded in enriching uranium without being detected, and that it had been only six to twenty-four months away from having a nuclear weapon. This severely reduced the inclination of Western intelligence agencies to give Iraq the benefit of any subsequent doubt. Second, this inclination was even further reduced by their failure to anticipate 9/11.[37] Third was the

---

32. Galbraith, *The End of Iraq*, pp. 72–3, 78.

33. These included critics of the invasion such as Peter Galbraith. See ibid, p. 76.

34. William Shawcross, *Allies. The U.S., Britain, Europe, and the War in Iraq* (New York: PublicAffairs, 2004), p. 151. This point was confirmed to me in personal correspondence by Charles Duelfer, who was deputy executive chairman of the UN Special Commission on Iraq from 1993 to 2000, deputy head of the United Nations weapons inspections team from 2003 to 2005, and leader of the Iraq Survey Group from January 2004.

35. Galbraith, *The End of Iraq*, p. 76.

36. Haas, *War of Necessity*, p. 214.

37. Ricks, *Fiasco*, pp. 32, 54.

paucity of 'human intelligence'—that is, intelligence gathered directly from human sources within Iraq.[38] Fourth was the regime's constant resistance—culminating in the complete withdrawal of cooperation in 1998 and continuing to some degree right up until the very eve of war in 2003—to the UN's attempts to ensure disarmament, which served to confirm the scepticism engendered by the first reason. Fifth was the problem of what the Butler Report called 'mirror-imaging', that is, of reading and predicting others' behaviour according to one's own canons of prudential rationality.[39] In retrospect it seems that Saddam Hussein's obstructiveness was a symptom not of his actually having weapons to hide but of his overriding need to *pretend* so for domestic and regional political purposes. To use Hans Blix's memorable metaphor, he had posted a warning, 'Beware of the dog,' even though he had no dog to beware of.[40] To shoulder the risks of such pretence might seem crazy to Western democrats, but not to an Arab despot. These are the reasons why so many experts in so many countries believed that Iraq possessed WMD. Insofar as the claim was an error, it was a reasonable and widespread one and not a lie invented by George Bush and Tony Blair.[41]

V. *Ad bellum*: just cause (iii): how substantial a threat?

Before the invasion in March 2003, concern that Iraq might help al-Qaeda acquire massively destructive weaponry was a reasonable one. However, it cannot be said with any degree of certainty that the possibility of the threat was actual or that the probability of it becoming so was high. Was it therefore a *just* cause for war?

According to the 16th-century proponent of just war thinking, Alberico Gentili, the fear of attack is sufficient just cause. It is true that he distinguished fear from mere suspicion, and implied that its object should be not merely speculative but already 'meditated' by an enemy, somewhat developed

---

38. Ricks, *Fiasco*, pp. 22, 57; Haas, *War of Necessity*, p. 231.
39. The concept is Butler's (*Review of Intelligence*, p. 15, para.56), but Fisher applies it to Iraq (*Morality and War*, p. 202).
40. Oliver Burkeman, 'Iraq dumped WMDs years ago, says Blix', *Guardian*, 18 September 2003.
41. Craig White insists that there was 'no clear evidence' of Iraq's chemical or nuclear programmes after 1991, or of proscribed weapons or weapons programmes after 1995 (*Iraq*, pp. 50, 54). This is quite true, but it misses the point, namely, that the British and American governments were required to make grave decisions on the basis of an *interpretation* of *un*clear evidence.

('it is safer to meet [violence] halfway'), and even 'impending'. Elsewhere, however, he was more permissive, writing that a just defence is one that anticipates dangers that are not only 'already meditated and prepared', but also 'not meditated... probable and possible'.[42] Such permissiveness, however, is not usual in the just war tradition. For Suárez the unjust threat has to be 'about to take place'[43] and for Vitoria it must be 'immediate'.[44] Grotius distinguishes between private and public self-defence. In the case of the former, the danger should be 'present'.[45] He explains why: 'Time gives us frequent opportunities of remedy, and there may many things happen, as the proverb has it, betwixt cup and lip.' Therefore, even in the face of a threat that is actually developing, we should stay our hand, unless it is quite clear that it cannot be avoided by other means.[46] Public authorities, however, 'may lawfully prevent an insult which seems to threaten them, even at some considerable distance... by punishing a crime that is only begun [but not yet carried through (*consummatum*)]'.[47] Notwithstanding that,

> to pretend to have a right to injure another, merely from a possibility that he may injure me, is repugnant to all the justice in the world: for such is the condition of the present life [*vita humana*], that we can never be in perfect security. It is not in the way of force, but in the protection of Providence [*divina providentia*], and in innocent precautions, that we are to seek for relief against uncertain fear.[48]

In order for war to be just, it must be necessary—that is to say, we must be 'sure, with a moral certainty, that [our neighbour] has not only forces sufficient, but a full intention to injure us'.[49]

---

42. Gregory Reichberg, 'Preventive War in Classical Just War Theory', *Journal of the History of International Law*, 9 (2007), pp. 16–17; and Alberico Gentili, *On the Law of War*, I.XIV, in Reichberg et al., *The Ethics of War*, p. 377.
43. Suárez, 'On Charity', Disputation XIII.I.6, p. 804.
44. Vitoria, *On the Law of War*, q. 1. art. 2, p. 300. It is true that, when Vitoria stipulates that the danger must be immediate, he does so in a discussion of private self-defence. Nowhere, however, does he say or imply that this stipulation does not also apply to public defence.
45. Grotius, *Rights of War and Peace*, II.I.V.1, p. 398.
46. Ibid., II.I.V.2, p. 401.
47. Ibid., II.I.XVI. The clause in square brackets appears in Reichberg, *Ethics of War*, p. 404, which presents the translation by Francis W. Kelsey as revised by Peter Haggenmacher (ibid., p. 387 n. 5). Reference to the original Latin text confirms that Kelsey's translation is more accurate than that in the Liberty Fund's edition. See Hugo Grotius, *De Iure Belli ac Pacis*, 3 vols, ed. B.J.A. De Kanter-van Hettinga Tromp (Leiden: E.J. Brill, 1939; Aalen: Scientia Verlag, 1993).
48. Ibid., II.I.XVII, p. 417. The phrases in square brackets represent the original Latin text.
49. Ibid., II.XXII.V.1, p. 1102.

The reason why the mere fear or suspicion or possibility of a threat is not a sufficient cause of just war is twofold: first, the invariable evils of war are so grave that it should be avoided except when necessary; and second, international relations are so infused with mistrust, suspicion, and paranoia that such a permissive concept of just cause would legitimate a lot of unnecessary war—for example, the German invasion of Belgium and France in 1914. The only kind of threat that warrants a belligerent response is one that is substantial, not imaginary. Someone must intend it and the intention must have materialized in action. The action need not be mature, so that a fully developed threat is about to be launched. In that sense, the threat need not be imminent or immediate. For sure, if its immaturity affords the time and opportunity to try non-military means of thwarting it, if the opportunity is realistic, and if one can afford the risks of failure, then resort to war would be less than necessary and therefore wrong. However, an immature threat might be so grave, its maturation so likely, and non-military alternatives so unrealistic that war is warranted.

In the light of these considerations, how fares the threat of Saddam Hussein's Iraq transferring WMD capability to al-Qaeda? On the one hand, the gravity of the horrendous threat to civilian life that would be posed, and the extreme difficulty of detecting and tracking its development, reduces the degree of probability required to justify the use of defensive force. On the other hand, there was no substantial evidence that Saddam Hussein had any intention of making such a transfer, and there were reasons to doubt that he would have. This threat alone, therefore, does not constitute sufficient just cause.

VI. *Ad bellum*: 'spinning' the data, making a case, and telling a story

Critics of the invasion on both sides of the Atlantic accused the Bush and Blair governments of mishandling the data in advocating their chosen policy of invasion. Thus Sir Richard Dearlove reported in July 2002 that in Washington '[t]he intelligence and the facts were being fixed around the policy';[50] and Richard Haas has written in retrospect, 'I know of no attempt to falsify intelligence by anyone in the U.S. government. It was more a case

---

50. Haas, *War of Necessity*, p. 215.

of people selecting ("cherry-picking") reports that supported a certain position and going with them despite questions about their accuracy.'[51] Others are less charitable and accuse US officials of wilfully misrepresenting the intelligence.[52] The Blair government was also famously accused of 'sexing-up' the evidence in its dossier of September 2002, *Iraq's Weapons of Mass Destruction: The Assessment of the British Government*, especially in its claims that Iraq had recently sought to acquire uranium in Niger, and that the regime had the capability of launching WMD within forty-five minutes. Its subsequent publication of January 2003, *Iraq: Its Infrastructure of Concealment, Deception and Intimidation*, was quickly dubbed 'the Dodgy Dossier', when it was revealed that some of its material had been lifted verbatim and without acknowledgement from an academic article based on documents captured when Iraq withdrew from Kuwait in 1991. In Britain it is now widely taken for granted that Blair lied.

To some extent the complaint that the governments were arranging the data to suit their policy is odd. Unlike journalists and academics—unlike even intelligence experts—governments have to decide on a policy in response to the data. If the data are ambiguous, and the issue seems urgent, they do not have the luxury of prevarication. They cannot rest with the ambiguity. They have to venture an interpretation of the data, decide on the optimal policy response, and then advocate a case for it in the legislature and in the media. In this sense, they have no choice but to 'spin' the evidence. Of course, if fresh data emerge that prove their interpretation wrong, then they should pay attention and change course. If, however, adverse evidence presents itself in a prevailing context of ambiguity, it could still be quite reasonable to discount it. In the case of the plan to invade Iraq, doubts did arise, but there were good reasons—as already explained—not to give Saddam Hussein the benefit of them.

If governments' public advocacy is to be successful, it needs to be tailored politically. It needs to be rhetorically astute, catching the wind of its audience's concerns and riding on it. The moral danger here is that of distorting the case in order to make it more appealing. It seems that both Washington and London succumbed to this temptation at certain points. Washington persisted in claiming substantial collaboration between Iraq and al-Qaeda, when the lack of evidence for that could and should have been known.

51. Haas, *War of Necessity*, p. 231.
52. Ricks, *Fiasco*, pp. 52–3, 55; White, *Iraq*, pp. 70, 73.

It also appears to have been unscrupulous in publicizing raw intelligence that was supportive of its case, but which had not been verified or corroborated.[53] The Blair government's record was also mixed, although not nearly as black as many of its critics would have it. The accusation of plagiarism against the dossier of January 2003 was as overwrought as it was trivial. Intelligence reports regularly contain data provided by open sources as well as secret ones.[54]—as any journalist could have found out upon asking. Indeed, the very first sentence of the dossier claimed only that 'it draws upon a number of sources, including intelligence material'.[55] Within days of the row breaking out, the author of the article from which the material had been taken, Ibrahim al-Marashi, told BBC2's *Newsnight* that 'in my opinion, the UK document overall is accurate, even though there are a few minor cosmetic changes'.[56] *The Middle East Review of International Affairs*, in which the article had been published, confirmed that 'the fact is that the [government] report is a good one. The information was correct and highly useful.'[57] Had the dossier been a piece of academic work, it would have been marked down for failing to reference its source. Since it was not a piece of academic work, fastidious referencing was not obviously required of it. This makes its lack at very most a discourtesy, not at all a sin of substance.

The dossier's claim that Iraq had been attempting to acquire uranium from Niger for the purpose of producing nuclear weapons later appeared to come under challenge from the International Atomic Energy Agency (IAEA). In March 2003, after examining evidence purporting to prove that Niger had agreed to sell uranium to Iraq, which had originated from a journalistic source and had been furnished by Colin Powell, the US Secretary of State, the IAEA judged that it was fraudulent. However, Lord Butler in his 2004 report demonstrated that the British government had never claimed—either in its September dossier or in the person of Tony Blair—that Iraq had succeeded in purchasing uranium, and that their more modest claim that Iraq had been seeking to purchase it was 'well founded' on other evidence. It concludes: 'The forged documents were not available to the British

53. White, *Iraq*, p. 70.
54. David Omand, *Securing the State* (London: Hurst, 2010), pp. 31–2.
55. *Iraq—its Infrastructure of Concealment, Deception, and Intimidation* (London: UK Government, January 2003), p. 1.
56. Michael White and Brian Whitaker, 'British 'intelligence' lifted from academic articles', *Guardian*, 7 February 2003.
57. Barry Rubin, 'British Government Plagiarises MERIA Material: Our Response': <http://meria.idc.ac.il/british-govt-plagiarizes-meria.html> (as at 17 December 2011).

Government at the time its assessment was made, and so the fact of the forgery does not undermine it.'[58]

The claim that Iraq could launch WMD within forty-five minutes became controversial when it was revealed that it concerned tactical weapons, not strategic ones—a distinction that the dossier had failed to make, and which the government had failed to clarify when the media wrongly assumed a strategic threat. It does seem that the government was content to let the media run the story under a mistaken assumption. It did not positively mislead the media, which could have interrogated the claim before it ran the story. Had a journalist sought clarification, and had the government then claimed a threat from strategic weapons, the government would have lied. As it happened, the media ran the story first and only paused to ask questions later. The government did not lie, but it did decline to take the initiative in correcting the misunderstanding, presumably because it was politically advantageous. This was a political advantage that it should have foregone, at least for the sake of preserving every appearance of integrity.

Andrew Rawnsley, a highly respected journalist and commentator on British politics, suggests that Tony Blair misled parliament when presenting the dossier. Mr Blair claimed that Saddam Hussein was 'a current and serious threat', after intelligence officials and WMD experts had told him that the threat was not 'imminent'.[59] Here Mr Rawnsley is himself guilty of the sin of 'spinning', since his story exceeds the strict logic of the evidence: a threat can be 'current' in the sense of 'growing', without being 'imminent' in the sense of 'about to mature'. Blair's precisely phrased claim in parliament did not contradict what the experts had told him. Rawnsley then quotes Lord Butler, who wrote in his report of July 2004: 'More weight was put on it than the intelligence was strong enough to bear. The interpretation was stretched to the limit.' Rawnsley comments that Butler refused to call Blair mendacious 'directly',[60] and that his report 'pulled its punches by clearing Blair of "deliberate distortion or of culpable negligence"'.[61] Here Rawnsley 'spins' Butler in favour of a strong, eye-catching storyline of high political villainy. Lord Butler has a well-deserved reputation for judiciousness, and can be expected to have chosen his words with care. Had he found

---

58. *Review of Intelligence*, pp. 122–5, paras 493–503.
59. Rawnsley, *The End of the Party*, p. 119.
60. Ibid., p. 121.
61. Ibid., *The End of the Party*, p. 269, referring to the Butler report (*Review of Intelligence*, p. 152, para. 21).

the government guilty of deliberate distortion and lying, he would doubt-less have said so. He did not. Perhaps that is because, after a lifetime's experi-ence as a civil servant, he is more aware than journalists like Rawnsley of the burden upon government of having to fix on a policy and navigate it through a fog of ambiguity in the face of political opposition. Under such circumstances, any interpretation is going to have to vie with some of the data, struggle to keep it on side, maybe even bend it. However, it seems to me that to stretch an interpretation to the very limits of plausibility is still to fall short of lying; and so it seemed to Lord Butler.[62]

Nevertheless, there are two elements of truth in Rawnsley's accusation. One is that the September 2002 dossier did not make clear to its public readership the paucity and weakness of the evidential base for the conclu-sions that the intelligence experts were drawing. As Lord Butler told Rawnsley: 'The intelligence community warned the Prime Minister that, though they concluded that Saddam Hussein had weapons of mass destruc-tion and was trying to develop more, their intelligence for this conclusion was very weak. That was explicitly explained to the politicians, but it wasn't the impression that the public had.'[63] It appears that John Scarlett, then head of the JIC, had been pressed by Alastair Campbell, the Prime Minister's Director of Communications and Strategy, to remove qualifications from the dossier's claims about WMD 'for political reasons'.[64] Many critics, including Rawnsley, are inclined to read this as evidence of deliberate decep-tion. There is, however, a more charitable explanation: the status of the September dossier was inadvertently ambiguous. On the one hand, it was unprecedented in its presentation of intelligence data to the public; on the other hand, it was obviously not an academic report but a piece of political advocacy, tailored to support the government's case against Iraq. It deliber-ately construed the evidence so as to make a case, focusing on the support-ive conclusion of the intelligence experts rather than on the uncertainty of the evidence. I do not think that the government can be faulted for that. All the Western intelligence agencies agreed that Iraq had WMD, and the British intelligence experts' reading of the evidence agreed with the govern-ment's assumptions. Nevertheless, it was a mistake to conflate the operations of

---

62. I note that even a critic as relentlessly uncharitable as Peter Lee concedes, not only that no evidence of Blair's lying has yet emerged, but that 'no such evidence exists' (*Blair's Just War*, p. 40).
63. Rawnsley, *The End of the Party*, p. 109.
64. Ibid., p. 113.

intelligence assessment and political advocacy, thereby gracing the 2002 dossier with an aura of scientific objectivity that it did not deserve.

The second element of truth in Rawnsley's accusation is that Tony Blair, in failing to correct the media's misapprehension of the 'forty-five minutes' claim, was culpable of a certain negligence. This, however, is culpable negligence that members of Rawnsley's own profession must share, since it was they who neglected to ask questions that they should have asked. It is also negligence that, if what Blair writes in his autobiography is true, was of very limited political significance. While the 'forty-five minutes' claim was taken up by some of the media, it was not referred to afterwards, nor was it mentioned by Blair at any time later, including the crucial parliamentary debate of 18 March 2003. Of the 40,000 parliamentary questions posed between September 2002 and the end of May 2003, when the BBC made their broadcast about it, only two asked about the 'forty-five minutes' issue; and of the 5,000 oral questions, not one mentioned it. 'So,' Blair concludes, 'the idea that we went to war because of this claim is truly fanciful.'[65]

If that is so, the negligence caused little damage. Yet it still remains culpable, as does Washington's persistence in making the unfounded claim about substantial terrorist cooperation between Iraq and al-Qaeda. In each case government was guilty—be it passively or actively—of misleading in the course of advocating its policy. Does that serve to make the policy unjust? Not necessarily. After all, in 1941 President Roosevelt attempted to bolster American support for Britain by 'sexing up' the *Greer* incident into a Nazi act of aggression;[66] and he claimed to possess a 'secret map' of Nazi designs on Latin America—a map far more dodgy than any Iraq dossier, since its very probable forgery by the British was probably known by Roosevelt.[67] Does that make US belligerency against Hitler wrong? Hardly.

VII. *Ad bellum*: legitimate authority

Grave injustice, whether in the form of domestic atrocity or international threat, warrants a punitive reaction. But who had the authority to do the

---

65. Blair, *A Journey*, p. 406.
66. Robert Dallek, *Franklin D. Roosevelt and American Foreign Policy, 1932–1945* (New York: Oxford University Press, 1979), pp. 286–9.
67. Nicholas John Cull, *Selling War: the British Propaganda Campaign against American 'Neutrality' in World War II* (New York: Oxford University Press, 1995), pp. 168–75.

punishing? Many assume that the relevant authority was the Security Council of the United Nations and that, since the invasion of Iraq was not authorized by the Council, it was clearly and simply illegal. I disagree. I think that the invasion had a substantial claim to legality, although not the strongest one. Whether or not the authorization of the Security Council *was* given to the 2003 invasion is itself a matter of unresolved dispute. UN resolutions are the fruit of political agreement; and political agreement is often achieved through creative ambiguity. Different parties agree to the same form of words, while meaning different things by them. Of course, the words agreed cannot reasonably be said to mean *anything* whatsoever: they do impose semantic limits. Nevertheless, they can often admit more than one reasonable interpretation. Accordingly, Washington and London understood UNSC Resolution (UNSCR) 1441 (November 2002) to be sufficient to authorize military action; others did not. There is no court with international authority to determine which understanding is the correct one. What we have instead are advocates, who mount more or less arguable cases for rival interpretations. Sometimes the controversy is simply intra-textual—about how the meanings of some words on the page are best understood in relation to other words. Sometimes the controversy is more contextual—about what the text means in the light of the history of its negotiation and of preceding and relevant Resolutions. What is more, as I argued in the previous chapter, these textual interpretations are bound to be shaped by the empirical, moral, legal, and political assumptions of their interpreters.

Craig White's forensic analysis of the 2003 invasion of Iraq damns it on almost every count. Although he acknowledges that grave injustice can comprise just cause, he doubts that it does so in this case, since he believes it to be an empirical fact that the correction of atrocious wrong was not among Washington's motives. Further, his faith in the UN Security Council as the proper and final arbiter of the international use of force seems entirely untroubled by the unavoidably political nature of its deliberations and by the damage done to the authority of international law through the Council's paralysis. White, therefore, is not disposed to find in favour of the invasion's legality, and he works hard—too hard, I think—to find against it. He argues that UNSCR 1441 (November 2002) was not sufficient to authorize military action against Iraq. Against Christopher Greenwood's claim that 'the only possible interpretation' of the Resolution's preamble is that it confirms the authorization by UNSCR 678 (1990) of the use of 'all necessary means' (i.e. force),[68] White contends that 678 authorized the use of force *in order to eject Iraq from Kuwait*, and that it is 'absurd' to argue that the authorization of means survived the achievement of its end.[69] UNSCR 687 (1991) effected a formal, permanent ceasefire, which 'by definition suspends earlier authorizations to use force'.[70] Even if the authorization of the use of force had survived the agreement of a permanent ceasefire, White argues that 'it is rarely the case, and certainly was not here, that a cease-fire violation authorizes either party to re-launch full-scale war unilaterally'.[71] Besides, in this case the authorizing authority was the Security Council, not the US government.[72]

I read the law differently. This is partly because I believe it to be a matter of fact—as I shall seek to demonstrate in the following section—that the correction of the atrocious injustice of the regime of Saddam Hussein *was* among the motives of both Washington and London, and because I think that, given the flawed nature of international institutions, abiding by the law's black letter can sometimes do more harm to the law's authority than transgressing it. But my alternative interpretation of the law is also attributable to what the words of UNSCR 1441 say and how they relate to other words in the same text and in preceding Resolutions. It seems to me that the logic of the text of UNSCR 1441 tells clearly against some of White's interpretation.[73] In its preamble, the Resolution first 'recalls' UNSCR 678's authorization to use 'all necessary means' to remove Iraq from Kuwait '*and to restore international peace and security in the area*' (my emphasis). Note that the end of the coercive means authorized here is *two*fold, not single: it is not just about expelling Iraq from Kuwait. The Resolution then goes on to recall that UNSCR 687 'imposed obligations on Iraq *as a necessary step for achievement of its stated objective of restoring international peace and security in the area*' (also my emphasis). These obligations included fresh ones that had received no mention in 678, namely the unconditional acceptance of disarmament of chemical and biological weapons and an unconditional agreement not to acquire or develop nuclear ones. What this implies is that the aims of the United Nations in authorizing the use of force had expanded in

68. Christopher Greenwood, 'International Law and the Pre-emptive Use of Force: Afghanistan, Al-Qaida, and Iraq', 4 *San Diego International Law Journal*, 7 (2003), p. 34.
69. White, *Iraq*, p. 130. See also pp. 96, 101.
70. Ibid., pp. 98–9.
71. Ibid., pp. 119.
72. Ibid., pp. 105.
73. The text of UNSCR 1441 can be found at <http//daccess-dds-ny.un.org/doc/UNDOC/GEN/N02/682/26/PDF/N0268226.pdf?OpenElement> (as at 14 August 2012).

the course of the conflict. Because Saddam Hussein had threatened the use of WMD during the war, the restoration of international peace and security had come to require not only Iraq's removal from Kuwait but—*pace* White—also her unconditional renunciation of such weapons. Next, Resolution 1441 recalls that UNSCR 687 had declared that a ceasefire would be 'based' on acceptance by Iraq of the obligations imposed. This implies that the ceasefire was conditional upon Iraq meeting its obligations under UNSCR 687, and that the use of force had been suspended rather than simply terminated. White agrees: 'It is true … that a cease-fire is generally seen as a suspension rather than a termination of the earlier authority … to use force.'[74] The Resolution then proceeds to decide that Iraq had been and was still 'in material breach' of its disarmament obligations.

Here is where the crucial and controversial question arises: What may happen next and who should decide? White argues that 'it is rarely the case, and certainly was not here, that a cease-fire violation authorises either party to re-launch full-scale war unilaterally'[75] and that here the Security Council was the legitimate authority. Against this reading, however, are two considerations. First, as White acknowledges, on 14 January 1993 the United Nations' Secretary-General, Boutros Boutros-Ghali, affirmed that British and American military action against Iraq the previous day had 'received a mandate' from the Security Council, according to UNSCR 678, on the ground of Iraq's violating the ceasefire conditions of UNSCR 687.[76] In other words, Boutros-Ghali affirmed that a violation of the terms of ceasefire justified the immediate revival of the use of force, without the need for a further, explicit decision by the Council. White dismisses this, however, on the ground that that the Secretary-General's opinions are not 'legally binding' and he does not make 'official UN determinations' of what is and is not in accord with the UN Charter or Security Council Resolutions.[77] This may be true, but it is also true that the determination of such things is highly controversial and that the Secretary-General's judgement is no mean authority in this field. The second consideration that tells against White's interpretation is this. To say that the use of force is 'suspended' rather than 'terminated' is to imply that the threat of its resumption is immediate—that while it has been lifted, it remains hanging and can be let fall again at a moment's notice.

74. White, *Iraq*, p. 119.   75. Ibid.
76. Ibid., p. 114.   77. Ibid., pp. 122–3.

If, however, its resumption must wait on a fresh decision by majority vote in a politically divided Security Council, then the threat is neither certain nor immediate. So in such a case how exactly does 'suspension' differ from 'termination'?

As it happened, the members of the Security Council agreed in Resolution 1441 'to afford Iraq a final opportunity to comply'. The Resolution warns that future failure to comply or offer full cooperation 'at any time' will amount to a further material breach of obligation, which will be reported to the Council for consideration. 'In that context' it also recalls that the Council has repeatedly warned that Iraq will face 'serious consequences' if it persists in violating its obligations. After the Resolution had been formally agreed by the Security Council, the US ambassador to the United Nations, John Negroponte, confirmed that further material breaches by Iraq would not automatically trigger the resumption of force but would be considered by the Council. However, he added that '[i]f the Security Council fails to act decisively in the event of further Iraqi violations, this resolution does not constrain any Member State from acting to defend itself against the threat posed by Iraq or to enforce relevant United Nations resolutions and protect world peace and security'.[78] The British ambassador, Sir Jeremy Greenstock, spoke along similar lines: 'There is no "automaticity" in this resolution. If there is a further Iraqi breach of its disarmament obligations, the matter will return to the Council for discussion...We would expect the Security Council then to meet its responsibilities.'[79]

The following January, Hans Blix, the Executive Chairman of the UN Monitoring, Verification and Inspection Commission (UNMOVIC), reported to the Security Council that 'Iraq appears not to have come to a genuine acceptance—not even today—of the disarmament, which was demanded of it and which it needs to carry out to win the confidence of the world and to live in peace';[80] and in March he reported that:

after a period of somewhat reluctant cooperation, there has been an acceleration of initiatives from the Iraqi side since the end of January...the question is now asked whether Iraq has cooperated 'immediately, unconditionally and

---

78. UNSC Verbatim Report, 4644th meeting, 8 November 2002, <http://www.globalissues.org/external/1441Speeches.pdf>, p. 3 (as at 17 August 2012).
79. Ibid., p. 5.
80. Hans Blix, an 'update on inspection' to the UNSC, 27 January 2003, <http://www.un.org/Depts/unmovic/Bx27.htm>, p. 2 (as at 17 August 2012).

actively' with UNMOVIC, as required under paragraph 9 of resolution 1441
(2002)...It is obvious that, while the numerous initiatives...can be seen as
'active', or even 'proactive', these initiatives three to four months into the new
resolution cannot be said to constitute 'immediate' cooperation. Nor do they
necessarily cover all areas of relevance.[81]

In response to this the United States administration asserted that Iraq
remained in material breach of its ceasefire obligations and that, under
UNSCR 1441, the Security Council must now meet to consider the case.
Together with the United Kingdom and Spain, it proposed a further resolution that would give Iraq a final deadline of 17 March to demonstrate 'full,
unconditional, immediate and active cooperation'. Three days later, however, the President of France, Jacques Chirac, told an interviewer on French
television that, 'regardless of circumstances', France would veto any further
resolution that included an ultimatum, 'thus giving the international green
light to war'.[82] The British, American, and Spanish attempt to secure a further resolution was then abandoned.

From their agreement to Resolution 1441 and their subsequent attempt
to secure a further one, it could be inferred that Washington and London
had conceded that further Security Council authorization was indeed
required for the legal resumption of the use of force; and that since this
authorization was not forthcoming, the subsequent invasion was clearly illegal. Such an inference, however, would not be correct. First, the Resolution's
description of what the Council was doing as 'affording a final opportunity
to comply', following repeated warnings of 'serious consequences as a result
of...continued violations', connotes a measure of indulgence, a generous
concession that exceeds what is strictly required. Second, the Council had
determined *in advance* that 'failure by Iraq at any time to comply with, and
cooperate fully in the implementation of [the] resolution' would constitute
'a further material breach' of its obligations, fulfilment of which was the basis
of the 1991 ceasefire. Third, the history of the negotiation of Resolution 1441
shows that some members of the Council had attempted to insert an explicit
requirement of the Security Council to authorize any resumption of the

---

81. Hans Blix, oral introduction to the 12th quarterly report of UNMOVIC to the UNSC, 7
March 2003, <http://www.un.org/Depts/unmovic/SC7asdelivered.htm>, p. 4 (as at 17
August 2012).

82. 'Interview with M. Jacques Chirac, President of France, French Ministry of Foreign Affairs,
10 March 2003': <http://www.iraqwatch.org/government/France/MFA/france-mfa-chirac-
031003.htm>, p. 5 (as at 17 August 2012).

use of force, but that they had not succeeded. Fourth, the British negotiators had succeeded in excluding a statement that the Council would 'decide' on the situation in case of a further material breach, and in deliberately substituting one that has the Council merely 'consider' it.[83]

It seems to me, therefore, that a reasonable case can be made that the use of force originally authorized by UNSCR 678 to expel Iraq from Kuwait 'and to restore international peace and security in the area' had only been suspended and not terminated. The authorization had been extended by UNSCR 687 to apply to the enforcement of Iraq's WMD disarmament obligations under the terms of the 1991 ceasefire, then revived in 1993 without a further Security Council decision, and then reaffirmed by UNSCR 1441, which explicitly recalled that Resolution 687 had 'based' the ceasefire on Iraq's meeting its obligations *and* decided that Iraq 'has been and remains in material breach' of them. The fact that the United Kingdom and the United States sought a further resolution, which would explicitly or implicitly authorize the use of force, does imply that their legal case would have been the stronger for it. Indeed, in his advice of 7 March 2003, the UK's Attorney General wrote that 'the safest legal course' would be to secure the adoption of a further resolution.[84] A 'safest' legal course is one that is least controvertible and so commands the greatest international support. Nevertheless, a course that does not command the greatest support can still be 'reasonable'.[85] The fact that a coherent argument can be made for the coercive enforcement of unmet ceasefire conditions in terms of the texts of a series of Resolutions, upon which the Security Council had already agreed, does give the 2003 invasion a claim to legality. Indeed, it gives a greater claim to legality than the Kosovo intervention of 1999, whose lack of positive authorization by any Resolution is beyond dispute.[86]

---

83. 'Legality of Military Action in Iraq: Disclosure Statement', made by the UK government's Cabinet Office and the Legal Secretariat to the Law Officers to the Information Commissioner's Office (undated), <http://www.ico.gov.uk/upload/documents/library/freedom_of_information/notices/appendix_6_disclosure_statement.pdf> (as at 17 August 2012).
84. Attorney General, 7 March 2003 advice, <http://www.ico.gov.uk/upload/documents/library/freedom_of_information/notices/annex_a_-_attorney_general%27s_advice_070303.pdf>, para. 27.
85. Ibid., para. 28.
86. I note that, writing in 2003, Adam Roberts judged that '[t]he argument that past Security Council resolutions provide a continuing, or revived, authority to use force...has substance' ('Law and the Use of Force after Iraq', *Survival*, 45/2 [Summer 2003], p. 40). Even a critic of the invasion such as Richard Haas believes that that the US (and UK) position that a second

However, even if the original authorization of force were somehow suspended rather than terminated, the mere violation of a condition of ceasefire would not justify its automatic resumption. Justification would require proportion: the violation would have to be sufficiently grave to warrant a return to war. This is part of what White means, and he is quite correct. However, he goes on to assert that only the Security Council had the authority to decide the matter. Here lies the nub of the problem. The judgement of an invasion's proportionality in this case depends on answers to a series of questions: Has there in fact been a violation? How significant is it? Must we mete out retribution? If so, what form should it take? The answer to the first question is simply empirical and it is clear. There had been a series of violations spanning more than a decade and provoking several Security Council Resolutions (707 [August 1991] and 1205 [November 1998], as well as 1441).[87] According to UNSCR 1441, the Security Council agreed on this. The answers to the remaining questions are not so straightforward, because they depend on the moral and political stance of the one giving them. Members of the Council whose political interests were not threatened by Iraqi possession of chemical and biological weapons and ambition to acquire nuclear ones, or who were indifferent to the atrocious character of the defiant regime, or whose commercial interests would be jeopardized by war, or who were not much concerned about the damage done to the authority of international law by the ineffectual enforcement of the Council's Resolutions, or who were very much concerned to constrain American power, would naturally downplay the significance of the violations

resolution was unnecessary 'was not without merit', since UNSCR 1441 could be construed as providing the authority to use force. Iraq was not providing the information necessary for inspectors to verify that it was in compliance with its obligations, and was therefore in violation of the 1991 ceasefire. By early March 2003 the material provided by Iraq 'was widely seen as inadequate and therefore another sign that Iraq had no intention of complying fully with what the United Nations and the international community had required. This is consistent with the February 14 report of Hans Blix, the chief weapons inspector, who noted that he had found no weapons of mass destruction, but that many proscribed weapons and items remained unaccounted for' (*War of Necessity*, pp. 243–5).

87. According to Nicholas Rostow, 'Resolution 1441 (2002)'s use of the words "material breach" to characterize Iraq's repeated failures over more than a decade to implement the 1991 ceasefire agreement was the ninth such Security Council finding since the end of the Gulf War. In addition...from 1993 [sic: 1991] to the end of 2002, the Council concluded three times that Iraq was in "flagrant violation" of its obligations, twelve times that Iraq was not complying, once that Iraq was in "clear-cut defiance" of its obligations, three times that Iraq had committed a "clear violation", twice that its violations were "clear and flagrant", and once that Iraq was in "gross violation" of Resolution 687 (1991)' ('Determining the Lawfulness of the 2003 Campaign against Iraq', *Israel Yearbook on Human Rights* [2004], pp. 22–3).

and the need for belligerent retribution. Other members with different moral and political views would judge differently.[88] In the case of deadlock in the Security Council, what should happen? According to some, nothing may happen: if the Council is not able to authorize the use of force, then it is illegal and should not be used. According to others, following Grotius, where the Council is paralysed by moral and political differences and cannot do what ought to be done—that is, in a case of *iudicium cessans*, where positive judgement is remiss or absent—the use of force can be justified by appeal to the authority of natural justice.

In the end, my view is that the use of force against Iraq in 2003 had substantial claim to legality, but not the strongest claim. It had a substantial claim on four grounds. First, its end was one agreed upon by the Security Council and reaffirmed in numerous Resolutions: the *permanent* disarmament of Iraq of WMD. Second, the invasion sought to enforce Resolutions that, it was agreed, had been repeatedly violated. Third, the resumption of the use of suspended force was proportionate, according to the moral and political views of *some* members of the Council. And fourth, the United States and the United Kingdom showed respect for international law in taking the trouble to argue a legal case for invasion at the UN, thereby rendering themselves accountable to the international community. While its case was not the strongest, because the Security Council could not agree that the use of force in 2003 was proportionate, and therefore did not collectively authorize its resumption, the invasion was not clearly or simply illegal. But even if it had been illegal, that could not be the final word, since positive law is always subject to moral law. Beyond the legal question always lies the moral question. No one may park his or her conscience in the space marked 'law'.

VIII. *Ad bellum*: right motive and intention

I have argued that there were two just causes for invading Iraq. Were these in fact, however, the reasons that motivated the United States and the United

88. Tony Blair is quite right to argue, therefore, that 'the law and the politics were inextricably intertwined. If people disagreed with war, they tended to think a second UN resolution [additional to UNSC Resolution 1441] specifically and expressly authorising military action was legally necessary; if they agreed with removing Saddam, they didn't... [W]hether we got a second resolution or not basically depended on the politics of France or Russia and their calculation of where their political interests lay' (*A Journey*, pp. 421, 433).

Kingdom in 2003? It is not enough that there are just causes for war, objectively speaking. These causes must also constitute the basic reasons or motives for waging war, if it is to have the form of a punitive reaction. If the causes do not determine the war's intentionality, then its goals will be independent of them, and its nature will be something other than an act of curbing or rectifying injustice.

The reasons for the invasion of Iraq were multiple. One analyst counted twenty-one.[89] In part this was the result of cabinet government, wherein policy is decided by several minds, not just one, and where decision often has the character of a compromise. In part, it is also the result of the invasion being conducted from two centres, Washington and London. Since Washington was overwhelmingly the senior partner, it might be argued that London's motives should be discounted. However, Tony Blair's advocacy had a significant influence on audiences throughout the United States, and it was *his* reasons that helped to move many Americans to support the Bush administration. Insofar as the administration was sensitive to domestic opinion, its thinking was indirectly shaped by Blair's reasons. Therefore, I shall not discount them.

Nevertheless, I begin by marshalling Washington's motives. In doing so, I depend almost entirely on five accounts, three by senior members of the US government (Richard A. Clarke,[90] Peter W. Galbraith,[91] and Richard N. Haas[92]) and two by journalists (George Packer[93] and Thomas Ricks[94]). None of these accounts is an apologia for the invasion, and every one contains severe criticism of it.

Both Packer and Ricks agree that Paul Wolfowitz played a central role in forming Washington's policy.[95] Packer describes him as 'the intellectual architect' of the war, and tells us that he cared about Iraq and was genuinely concerned to set it free.[96] Ricks agrees: Wolfowitz viewed the regime of Saddam Hussein as evil and believed in Iraq's liberation.[97] This concern to

---

89. Davon Largio, 'Rationales for War', *Foreign Policy* (September/October 2004), p. 18.
90. Clarke, *Against All Enemies*.
91. Galbraith, *The End of Iraq*.
92. Haas, *War of Necessity*.
93. George Packer, *The Assassins' Gate. America in Iraq* (London: Faber & Faber, 2006). Packer is a staff writer for *The New Yorker*.
94. Thomas Ricks, *Fiasco*. Ricks is the *Washington Post*'s senior Pentagon correspondent.
95. Ricks, *Fiasco*, p. 7; Packer, *Assassins' Gate*, p. 114.
96. Packer, *Assassins' Gate*, p. 114. Packer is clear in asserting that Wolfowitz's driving concern was the plight of Iraq, *not* the security of Israel (ibid., pp. 32, 115).
97. Ricks, *Fiasco*, p. 378.

end the injustice of political oppression was also owned by Wolfowitz's colleagues, since, according to Richard Clarke, the relief of the suffering of the Iraqi people was one of three reasons publicly urged by the Bush administration in favour of invasion.[98] If Packer, Ricks, and Clarke are correct, Craig White is wrong to relegate the liberation of Iraq from tyranny to the margins of Washington's intentions.

The second and third of Clarke's reasons were the separate threats of terrorism and of a rogue state's possession of WMD, combining into an even greater threat. Iraq had not been an issue in the 2000 presidential campaign, when Bush and Richard Cheney intended to continue President Clinton's policy of containment.[99] Then, hurtling through a gap in the intelligence net, came the sudden attacks of 9/11. In the wake of this, members of the administration 'were really scared. They were afraid of what they did not know.'[100] By the following July, it was evident that priorities had changed. Returning from a meeting in Washington, Sir Richard Dearlove, then head of the Secret Intelligence Service (MI6), reported to Downing Street that military action was viewed by the Americans as justified because of the conjunction of terrorism and WMD.[101]

The three reasons that Clarke lists as comprising the administration's public case for invasion are identical to those given by Wolfowitz in an interview in May 2003. While concern about WMD was the one 'core reason' that commanded consensus among the members of the Bush administration, Wolfowitz said, 'there have always been three fundamental concerns. One is weapons of mass destruction, the second is support for terrorism, the third is the criminal treatment of the Iraqi people.'[102]

In addition to these primary motives, there were others. Prominent among them was the desire to change the course of history for the better in the crucial region of the Middle East.[103] In 2002, Middle East experts

---

98. Clarke, *Against All Enemies*, p. 265.
99. Ricks, *Fiasco*, p. 24.
100. According to Jack Goldsmith, an official at the Department of Defense, in 'An Oral History of the Bush White House', *Vanity Fair* (February 2009); quoted by Rawnsley in *The End of the Party*, p. 84.
101. According to a Downing Street Memo of 23 July 2002; reported in Haas, *War of Necessity*, p. 215.
102. In *Vanity Fair* (May 2003); quoted by Galbraith in *The End of Iraq*, pp. 78–9. Packer reports Wolfowitz as saying, 'The truth is that for reasons that have a lot to do with the US government bureaucracy, we settled on the one issue that everyone could agree on, which was weapons of mass destruction' (*Assassins' Gate*, p. 60).
103. Haas, *War of Necessity*, pp. 169, 235.

Bernard Lewis and Fouad Ajami were summoned by Cheney, to whom they said: 'American power has helped to keep the Arab world in decline by supporting sclerotic tyrannies; only an American break with its own history in the region can reverse it. The Arabs cannot pull themselves out of their own rut. They need to be jolted by some foreign-born shock. The overthrow of the Iraq regime would provide one.'[104] Regime-change in Iraq would establish 'a beachhead of democracy',[105] which would spread to the likes of Egypt and Saudi Arabia.[106] Lewis and Ajami's advocacy of intervention appears to have had its desired effect, since Ricks attributes to both Cheney and Bush the view that the United States' previous policy of stability in the Middle East had produced 'decrepit regimes, sallow economies, and growing terrorism'.[107] George Packer reckons that this aim of transforming the politics of the Middle East preceded concern about WMD, and while not the *casus belli* sold to the American people, it was still a serious factor in the decision to invade Iraq.[108]

A further motive was to enable the United States to withdraw its troops from Saudi Arabia, where they had been stationed since 1991 to counter Iraqi aggression, but had become a source of anti-Americanism that at once threatened the regime[109] and was being exploited by al-Qaeda. (Many of the hijackers on 9/11 had been Saudi citizens.[110]) Clarke reckons that concern about the long-term stability of the House of Saud was a pervasive factor in the administration's motivation. Many US officials were worried that it would suffer the same fate as the Pahlavi dynasty in Iran: 'This fear probably played a role in the thinking of some in the Bush administration, including Dick Cheney, who wanted to go to war with Iraq. With Saddam gone, they believed, the US could reduce its dependence on Saudi Arabia, could pull forces out of the Kingdom, and could open up an alternative source of oil.'[111] This Saudi factor helps to explain why the administration focused its worries about terrorism and WMD on Iraq rather than on Iran, which was more actively engaged in both.[112]

104. Packer, *Assassins' Gate*, pp. 51–2.
105. Paul Berman, quoted by Packer in ibid., p. 58.
106. Clarke, *Against All Enemies*, p. 265. See also Galbraith, *The End of Iraq*, pp. 9–10.
107. Ricks, *Fiasco*, p. 47.
108. Packer, *Assassins' Gate*, pp. 395–6.
109. Clarke, *Against All Enemies*, p. 265.
110. Packer, *Assassins' Gate*, p. 60.
111. Clarke, *Against All Enemies*, pp. 265, 283.
112. Ibid., p. 284.

Finally, there was the desire to improve Israel's strategic position,[113] although none of our five sources attributes primary importance to this, and most do not mention it at all.

Since Tony Blair was by far the strongest and most influential advocate of invasion in London, the British government's motives were basically his. According to Andrew Rawnsley, Blair's position was 'a mix of the moral case, the violations case and the menace case', the menace case being the only one that would provide legal, diplomatic, and political cover.[114] He was genuinely revolted by Saddam Hussein: 'He could never fathom why so many on the left could not see a moral imperative to act against such a tyrant when opportunity presented itself. When protesters against war massed opposite Downing Street, he would react by asking: "Why aren't they out there demonstrating against the junta in Burma? Where are the protests against North Korea?" '[115] He had already given original voice to a new doctrine of liberal interventionism in his Chicago speech of April 1999, 'The Doctrine of International Community',[116] which he came to feel had been vindicated by NATO's subsequent action in Kosovo.[117] According to this doctrine—which strongly echoes the Christian just war tradition—the first questions to ask are moral ones: '[S]hould this be allowed to happen or not? Should this regime remain in power? Should these people continue to suffer?'[118] '[I]ntervention to bring down a despotic dictatorial regime could be justified on the ground of the nature of the regime, not merely its immediate threat to our interests.'[119] Moreover, in this age of global interdependence, '[the] moral question is part of the national interest'.[120] People care about other people, even outside their own borders.[121] The choice between idealism and realism in foreign policy is false.[122]

This brings us from the moral case—or better, the injustice case—to the violations one. Blair was deeply exercised at the international community's willingness to allow Iraq to defy a long series of UN resolutions with virtual

---

113. Ibid., p. 265.
114. Rawnsley, *The End of the Party*, p. 108.
115. Ibid., pp. 91, 155, 275.
116. Ibid., p. 43; Blair, *A Journey*, pp. 248–9.
117. Rawnsley, *The End of the Party*, pp. 92, 103.
118. Blair, *A Journey*, p. 229.
119. Ibid., pp. 248–9.   120. Ibid., p. 229.
121. Ibid., p. 224.   122. Ibid., p. 368.

impunity. His doctrine of liberal interventionism was, of course, a reaction to what he saw as the chronic ineffectuality of international institutions in the face of the fact or threat of grave injustice. As he wrote in his 2010 auto-biography, 'the primary instinct of the international community was...to pacify, but not to resolve'.[123] He also tells of going to see the film *Schindler's List* in April 1994, and then comments 'You take sides by inaction as well as action...If we know and we fail to act, we are responsible. A few months later Rwanda erupted in genocide. We knew. We failed to act. We were responsible.'[124] '[T]he absence of credibility actually increases the likelihood of confrontation...Indecision is also decision. Inaction is also action. Omission and commission both have consequences.'[125] Non-intervention in Bosnia in the mid-1990s, for example, had led Milošević to think that he could get away with Kosovo in 1999.[126] Blair gave these views ample public expression on many occasions before the invasion of Iraq on 20 March 2003, not least in his politically crucial speech to the House of Commons two days before on 18 March:

> Of course Iraq is not the only part of this threat [i.e., of WMD finding their way into the hands of terrorists]. But it is the test of whether we treat the threat seriously. Faced with it, the world should unite. The UN should be the focus, both of diplomacy and of action. That is what [Resolution] 1441 said. That was the deal. And I say to you, to break it now, to will the ends but not the means, that would do more damage in the long term to the UN than any other course.
>
> To fall back into the lassitude of the last twelve years, to talk, to discuss, to debate but never act; to declare our will but not enforce it; to combine strong language with weak intentions: a worse outcome than never speaking at all. And then, when the threat returns from Iraq or elsewhere, who will believe us? What price our credibility with the next tyrant?...
>
> I have come to the conclusion after much reluctance that the greater danger to the UN is inaction: that to pass Resolution 1441 and then refuse to enforce it would do the most deadly damage to the UN's future strength, confirming it as an instrument of diplomacy but not of action, forcing nations down the very unilateralist path we wish to avoid.[127]

The evidence is that Blair was genuinely concerned that the international community should gird its loins, rise to the occasion, and vindicate its reso-

---

123. Ibid., p. 227.   124. Ibid., p. 61.
125. Ibid., pp. 230, 239.   126. Ibid., p. 229.
127. Tony Blair, 'Full Statement to the House of Commons, 18 March 2003', in Cushman, *A Matter of Principle*, pp. 336–7.

lutions against Iraq's serial violation of them; and that he regarded multilateral action as far preferable to unilateral. Here is the one point where London and Washington diverged in their motives. Blair continued to believe in the strategic importance of the United Nations; the Bush administration did not. According to Richard Haas, such concern as the administration expressed about Iraq's non-compliance with the UN was mere 'window-dressing'.[128]

In addition to the injustice and violations factors in Blair's case for invasion, there was also the menace one. In the wake of 9/11, and of the subsequent anthrax attack upon prominent political and government figures in the United States, the Prime Minister became seriously concerned about the threat of terrorists using WMD, and he was very disturbed when briefed about the effects of a dirty bomb being exploded in the middle of London.[129] The prospect of terrorists acquiring WMD had been 'unthinkable', he wrote after the invasion, and it had produced a '[w]holly different kind' of attitude to proliferation.[130] He became convinced of the need for pre-emption.[131] In this he was heavily influenced by Robert Cooper, who had expressed the view that there would be circumstances in which 'we need to revert to the rougher methods of an earlier era—force, pre-emptive attack, deception, whatever is necessary to deal with those who still live in the 19th century world of every state for itself'.[132] As for Iraq in particular, Blair believed that Saddam Hussein was a menace with ambitions to acquire nuclear weaponry, who had successfully corrupted the oil-for-food programme run by the UN, and who could not be adequately contained by the sanctions regime.[133]

Disgust at the atrocious character of the regime of Saddam Hussein, fear that the regime would become a conduit of WMD to terrorists intent on maximizing civilian casualties, and the conviction that Iraq's decade-long cat-and-mouse game with the UN had to be finally decided in favour of permanent disarmament—these were the main motives that led Tony Blair

---

128. Haas, *War of Necessity*, p. 235.
129. Rawnsley, *The End of the Party*, pp. 24, 37, 90; Blair, *A Journey*, pp. 357, 385–6.
130. Blair, *A Journey*, pp. 357.
131. Rawnsley, *The End of the Party*, p. 89.
132. Robert Cooper, 'The Next Empire', *Prospect* (October 2001); quoted by Rawnsley in *The End of the Party*, p. 89.
133. Rawnsley, *The End of the Party*, p. 88.

to support invasion in March 2003. Given that the issue had to be brought
to a head, other geopolitical motives then came into play, which concerned
the strategic context in which invasion would take place. Blair was convinced that, to be effective, the struggle against terrorism and WMD proliferation had to be a concerted international effort. The growing gulf
between America and Europe therefore alarmed him. As he wrote in 2010:
'I find the insouciance towards the decline of the transatlantic relationship,
on both sides of the water, a little shocking.'[134] Partly in order to narrow
the transatlantic gulf, and partly to address the main focus of Muslim
resentment of the West, he urged the Bush administration to revive the
Middle East peace process.[135] He regarded the stagnating plight of the
Palestinians as 'a vital and persistent proof that the West was inimical to
Islamic interests',[136] and he believed that progress to a Palestinian state was
of 'huge importance'.[137]

There, according to our sources, we have the full array of reasons that
impelled Washington and London to invade Iraq. It has been argued, however, that not all of these reasons should be taken into account. David Fisher
refers to 'the declared basis' for going to war, as set out in the British government's 'published war aims.'[138] According to this, the prime objective was to
rid Iraq of WMD and thereby to enforce UNSC Resolutions.[139] Regime-
change was strictly instrumental to that purpose. While noting that the US
government believed that the tyrannical nature of Saddam Hussein's regime
furnished humanitarian grounds for military action—hence the name of
the operation, 'Iraqi Freedom'—Fisher insists that the British government
did not appeal to humanitarian grounds. Nor did it argue in terms of pre-
emptive self-defence against collaboration between Iraq and al-Qaeda, a
threat which it considered too uncertain.[140] Because of this stringent reading of the intentions of at least one of the belligerents, Fisher disallows Tony
Blair's post-invasion appeal to the just cause of toppling an atrocious regime,

134. Blair, *A Journey*, p. 677.
135. Rawnsley, *The End of the Party*, pp. 34, 88, 177, 444.
136. Blair, *A Journey*, pp. 387, 405.
137. Ibid., p. 409.
138. These were published in March 2003, and may be found in Annex C of the Butler report,
     'Iraq: Military Campaign Objectives' (*Review of Intelligence*, pp. 177–9).
139. Fisher, *Morality and War*, p. 196.
140. Ibid., pp. 196–9.

commenting that '[t]he just war tradition looks unkindly on the expansion of war aims as wars run into difficulties'.[141]

What should we make of this? First of all, Fisher is not fair to Blair, whose conviction that atrocious oppression is sufficient just cause for military intervention preceded the invasion of Iraq by many years and had been made very public in his famous Chicago speech of 1999. Second, as Fisher himself acknowledges, Blair felt that the current terms of international law 'had boxed him into going to war on the too narrow grounds of WMD disarmament'.[142] This is a genuine problem. I have already made plain in Chapter Six that the black letter of international law governing the use of armed force is at odds with just war thinking and therefore morally problematic. The consequence is that governments motivated on sufficient moral grounds to intervene for humanitarian purposes, but who also wish to respect international law, are forced to suppress valid motives and either to make strained interpretations of the law or to pay its letter lip service in bad faith. Third, why should our understanding of a government's real intentions be limited to a single formal declaration of war aims? In the case of the invasion of Iraq, as we have seen, a range of different grounds motivated Messrs Bush and Blair and their governments, none of which was inconsistent with the others, and all of which were made public in one way or another. Because the British government in particular rightly wanted to pay international law due respect, it felt compelled to suppress its stated desire to see the regime of Saddam Hussein toppled because of its atrocious character, and not only as a means to a permanent solution to the problem

141. Ibid., p. 208. Brian Orend makes a similar complaint against what he calls the 'scatter-shot' approach to justifying war, 'when you throw out every possible argument in favour of war, hoping some will stick in terms of persuading the public or attracting evidence which will stand the test of time and scrutiny' (*The Morality of War* [Peterborough, Ontario: Broadview Press, 2006], p. 49). As an instance of this he cites Washington's case for the 2003 invasion of Iraq (ibid.). While admitting that the reasons for going to war may be multiple, he first doubts that more than one can 'plausibly' be intended, since human attention is finite and if the intended action is to be coherent. Shortly afterwards he takes a more sophisticated stance, arguing that there must be one 'main reason' that 'disciplines' the others (ibid., pp. 49–50). I agree, of course, with the need for a coherent ordering of intentions, and so of their practical embodiment in action. I disagree, however, that coherence requires one main reason only. Coherence of intention and of corresponding action is possible with more than a single main reason, although it will be more complicated and fragile as a consequence. Unity can be complex as well as simple: ask any Trinitarian monotheist. As for the multiple reasons adduced for invading Iraq, I find no incoherence among them or among their practical implications: the intentions to punish an atrocious regime, to end the threat of its wielding WMD, and to vindicate repeated Resolutions of the UNSC were all served by concerted action to bring about regime-change in Baghdad.

142. Ibid., p. 208. Fisher quotes Blair's speech in his Sedgefield constituency in March 2004.

of WMD. One possible reason for confining attention to declared war aims is that these are the aims that actually shape policy. Maybe so; but they need not be the only formative aims. Suppressed motives and their corresponding aims do not cease to operate just because they are suppressed. Another possible reason for focusing on formally declared aims is that it is in response to *these* that citizens give or withhold their support for government policy. Formally declared aims, however, are not the only publicly stated or publicly understood ones. (One piece of evidence for this is that, whereas I have been reflecting on the British government's reasons for invading Iraq ever since 2003, it was only in 2011, when I first read David Fisher's book, that I became aware that the government had published a formal statement of war aims at all.) Besides, in deliberating whether or not to support a proposed policy, citizens are not confined to the terms in which the policy presents itself. A citizen might well support a policy for reasons other than those given by the government—and, indeed, he might support it *in spite of them*. The motives and corresponding intentions that are relevant to assessing a policy of belligerence are those that actually shape it; and we have good reason to suppose that the motives and intentions that informed UK government policy regarding Iraq were not limited to those presented in the British government's statement of war aims in early 2003. They included the motive of revulsion at the atrocious character of Saddam Hussein's regime and the corresponding intention to topple it. It is quite clear that this motive and intention inspired Tony Blair, as well as the Bush administration.

Let us return to the full range of motives and intentions that we adduced earlier. How are we to assess them? The fact that the leading motives were common to both centres makes our task much simpler. The desires to liberate Iraq from the tyranny of Saddam Hussein's regime, to prevent that regime from acquiring WMD, and to preclude it from conveying them to terrorists—these were all shared by both governments. Morally speaking, they are entirely unobjectionable. Born of disgust at atrocious tyranny, the intention to rectify it is quite right. So is the intention to fend off a murderous threat. If these intentions were basic—and my reading of the evidence strongly suggests that they were—then just cause was the invasion's motive, and not merely its pretext.

Given those basic, focal intentions, others then gathered around them. Some were intrinsic to the invasion. Regime-change in Baghdad was itself the inaugural realization of the intention to change US policy from propping up friendly tyrants to kick-starting the democratic transformation of the region. Democratic transformation was the specific form of rectification chosen in response to the original injustice. Regime-change was also the necessary precondition of realizing the intentions to reduce dependence on Saudi Arabia and remove the offensive presence of US forces on its soil, and to improve Israel's strategic position. Other secondary intentions were extrinsic and accidental. Iraq was hardly invaded *in order to* maintain the transatlantic alliance, to rouse the UN to decisive action, and to revive the Middle East peace process. However, once the decision to invade—or at least the decision to carry out the threat to invade in the absence of unequivocal capitulation—had been made, further intentions were then formulated with a view to shaping its geopolitical significance and effects.

Not one of these secondary intentions is immoral. None of them is incompatible with the primary intentions, which are themselves morally justified. Some of them are morally admirable; others are politically prudent (and prudence is a moral virtue). The goal of strengthening Israel's strategic position seems to me rather less important than that of reviving the peace process. If such strengthening would militate against that revival, then I would consider it wrong. However, some have argued the reverse, namely that a more confident Israel would be readier to come to acceptable terms with the Palestinians. I myself doubt this very much, but whatever the truth of the case, it cannot be said that freeing Israelis from Saddam Hussein's threat of annihilation was in itself a wicked thing to do; and it can be said that the political consequences of so doing were indeterminate.

In sum, therefore, it seems to me that that the primary motives for invading Iraq and their corresponding intentions, which were shared by Washington and London, were indeed responses to the just causes of rectifying injustice and fending off unjust aggression; that none of the secondary motives was immoral; that some of them were admirable; that others were prudent; and that only one was morally uncertain, and that was marginal. In this I agree with the conclusion of David Fisher, who, although judging the invasion overall to have been unjust, concedes that 'in the main, the reasons for undertaking the war were honourable and the concerns over WMD proliferation in general and Saddam's contribution to this in particular were genuinely held... [T]hose responsible were trying to make the world a better and safer place.'[143]

143. Fisher, *Morality and War*. p. 215. Fisher judges that both the American and British governments 'genuinely believed' that Saddam Hussein had WMD capability, that they were concerned over the regional and global threat that this posed, and that this was their 'primary motivation' for undertaking military action (ibid., p. 205).

IX. *Ad bellum*: the motive of imperial ambition?

It is possible that my analysis so far of the motivation for invading Iraq completely misses the main point. It is possible that it overlooks a deep hinterland of formative assumptions and attitudes and aspirations, which were never voiced in the White House, because they were so taken for granted that they did not need to be. It is possible that my hermeneutic has not been suspicious enough—or, to be more exact, not Marxist enough.

Michael Northcott would say so, I imagine. He approximates Augustine to '[t]he imperial theologians who lauded Constantine as the angel of God',[144] and dismisses just war thinking as involving 'the imperial belief that violence is necessary for the restraint of evil'.[145] He reads the invasion and occupation of Iraq against the background of an American messianic nationalism, which sees the United States as uniquely chosen (by God) to re-form the world in the image of its own neo-liberal 'democracy', where the state is weak and corporate interests call the shots.[146] This form of imperialism combines biblical apocalypticism, Enlightenment progressivism, and Zionism. The first divides the world sharply into the righteous and the wicked; the second is unrelentingly confident in its own power to impose a New World Order; and the third regards the fulfilment of the Zionist dream as a necessary preliminary to the eschatological End of History.[147]

In the light of this cultural hinterland, Northcott thinks that the United States invaded Iraq to secure oil, to establish a strategic military presence, to profit American corporate and financial interests, and to make the Middle East safe for Israel.[148] He also seems to imply that America went to war *in order*

---

144. Michael Northcott, *An Angel Directs the Storm. Apocalyptic Religion and American Empire* (London: SCM, 2007), p. 153.
145. Ibid., p. 154.
146. Ibid., pp. 3–6, 9, 12, 22, 81–2.
147. Ibid., chapter 1 (esp. pp. 13, 16) and pp. 61–8.
148. Ibid., pp. 11, 29, 68 ('Making the Middle East safe for a newly aggressive and assertive Israel was...a central aim of the Bush administration in its war and subsequent occupation of Iraq...[T]he installation in Iraq of an American economic regimen of privatised public services, and a democratic polity subservient to American corporate, financial, and strategic interests, is the core rationale for the American invasion and occupation of Iraq...With a long-term American military presence, the Bush administration intends to make it possible for Israel to defeat the Palestinians'), 80, 91, 166 ('This was a war not only about oil...but about trying to bomb people into accepting a value system, and a set of institutional and economic arrangements, that imperial America would impose upon them by brute force, and by colonial government').

to sacrifice its young, when he writes that 'blood sacrifice is the organising principle of the United States', because it is 'effective in uniting the nation around its totem flag'; and that this 'helps to explain' why America has been prepared to sacrifice 100,000 dead and 250,000 wounded in Korea, Vietnam, and the two Gulf Wars.[149] Lest anyone should think this too cynical a reading of the United States' motives and intentions, Northcott points to the historical record: its manufacturing a *coup d'état* in Iran in 1953 so as to keep control of oil production, its use of military power to defend corporate interests at the expense of democracy in Latin America in the 1960s and 1970s, its supplying Saddam Hussein with chemical weapons in the 1980s, and its collusion in blaming Iran for the mass gassing of Kurds at Halabja in 1988.[150]

On America's historical record from 1953 to 1988 I am not competent to comment. However, even if what Michael Northcott reports is true, we should still judge each case on its own merits. In trying to determine what motivated Washington to invade Iraq in 2003, we should examine the most directly relevant evidence, and give it priority over what our reading of historical precedent has led us to expect. Evidence that I shall shortly adduce does show some traces of the ideological background to which Northcott points: the assumption that Iraqis were all really latent Americans, eager to seize their natural, liberal destiny the moment the stone of tyranny was lifted; excessive confidence in the top-down, managerialist imposition of rational order; the arrogant refusal to pay serious attention to local difference; and the prominent role of US corporations in post-invasion reconstruction.

On the other hand, according to the professional and journalistic witnesses that I have already called, the securing of Israel was a secondary motive at best. As for the claim that the United States invaded Iraq in order to seize direct control of its oil, this is hard to credit, since it did not in fact happen. Indeed, today American oil companies are not especially keen on investing in post-Saddam Iraq, whose oil industry is now dominated by the Chinese. It is perhaps plausible that the United States hoped that regime-change, by ending the need for sanctions, would lift the constraints on Iraqi oil-production, weaken OPEC's grip, and drive down prices. However, there is nothing intrinsically wicked about such a hope, and even if there were, none of the evidence that I have adduced suggests that it was a primary

149. Ibid., pp. 97–8.   150. Ibid., pp. 28–30.

motive.[151] Similarly, the fact that US corporations were enabled to make a profit on the back of the invasion does not establish that that was a motive for invading in the first place. On the matter of establishing a permanent, strategic military presence, all that I have read confirms what David Fisher writes, namely that there is 'little evidence' of the United States planning it before the invasion, and that, on the contrary, 'the overwhelming evidence' is that Rumsfeld was planning for a swift exit after an efficient military victory.[152]

As for going to war with Iraq *in order* to reinvigorate national fervour by way of blood sacrifice, it is, I suppose, possible. The notion does smack, however, of left-wing apocalypticism, painting America blood-red as the Great Moloch. Still, sadly, Molochs are not confined to comic books; they have been known to walk the earth within living memory. So it is possible such a macabre motive lurked in the mental basement of the White House in the run-up to March 2003. Whether or not it actually did, however, needs to be carefully argued for; and that would involve displacing the more plausible case that national ideals and perceived interests motivated the readiness of America to put its sons and daughters in harm's way.[153]

X. *Ad bellum*: last resort

Given the attendant evils and hazards, one of the characteristics of a just war is that it is undertaken as a last resort. By this is not meant that war may be launched only when every other conceivable alternative has been exhausted. Some conceivable alternatives have no realistic prospect of succeeding, and to opt for them is but to prevaricate: to engage in yet another round of negotiations with a party who has shown serial bad faith can express less the patience of a saint than the folly of a coward. What is more, sometimes the early and resolute use of military force can be far more efficient—and so less expensive of human life—than use that is delayed and hesitant.[154] What the

151. My understanding of the role of oil as a motive for the 2003 invasion I owe almost entirely to Derek Brower, editor of *Petroleum Economist*.

152. Fisher, *Morality and War*, p. 204.

153. To complete my response to Michael Northcott, I should add, first, that the mature Augustine who began to adumbrate the theory of just war was certainly not one of the '[t]he imperial theologians [like Eusebius or Orosius] who lauded Constantine as the angel of God'; and that the idea 'that violence is necessary for the restraint of evil' is surely as Pauline (Romans 13:4) as it is 'imperial'.

154. Rupert Smith, *The Utility of Force: the Art of War in the Modern World* (London: Allen Lane, 2005), pp. 243, 310, 350, 358, 388.

criterion of last resort requires is that, in deciding whether or not to go to war at all, every non-violent means of achieving the desired end of just peace should first be tried, which has a reasonable prospect of success. How reasonable it looks will depend partly on how affordable is the risk of failure.

In the case of Iraq, the United States and the United Kingdom chose to solve the problem of an atrocious regime coming to possess WMD by invading it. Was this an act of last resort? On the one hand, the regime gave no reason to suppose that it had undergone a radical change in character: in March 2003 there was no reason to suppose that it would be less atrocious in the future than it had been in the recent past. Moreover, there was good cumulative reason to suppose that Iraq had WMD and was in the process of acquiring nuclear weapons. Part of the reason was the regime's persistent resistance to complying with a decade's worth of UN resolutions, repeatedly calling upon it to give up its WMD ambitions once and for all, and to do so manifestly. German intelligence reckoned that Iraq could have nuclear arms within two years.[155] So, the atrocious injustice of the regime remained unpunished, and the threat posed by its coming to possess WMD, especially of a nuclear kind, appeared to be persistent and growing. Invasion aimed at regime-change was one way of dealing with this dual problem, but were there available other, non-violent means, which had a reasonable prospect of success?

Containment is the obvious candidate. What were the prospects in early 2003 of prolonged containment being successful? Some argue that the post-invasion discovery that Iraq did not in fact possess WMD proves that containment was working and that the invasion was unnecessary, less than a last resort, and therefore unjust. What needs to be proven, however, is not that containment had been effective, but that it would have continued to be so. Richard Clarke and Peter Galbraith both reckon that continued control of relevant Iraq imports and further intrusive inspections by the IAEA would have been sufficient to avert the threat of WMD.[156] Against this, however, Kenneth Pollack wrote in 2002 that containment was collapsing beyond repair. In that year smuggling conducted by Syria, Turkey, Jordan, and Iran was reckoned to earn Iraq between $2.5 billion and $3 billion (15–22 per cent of Iraq's total revenue).[157] What is more, since 1997 France, Russia, and

155. That is to say, within two years of the beginning of 2003. See note 34 above.
156. Clarke, *Against All Enemies*, p. 268; Galbraith, *The End of Iraq*, pp. 69, 78.
157. Kenneth Pollack, *The Threatening Storm: The Case for Invading Iraq*, a Council on Foreign Relations book (New York: Random House, 2002), pp. 214–15, 218–21.

China—all members of the Security Council—had been pressing for a relaxation of sanctions and inspections, in order to obtain oil and military contracts and to collect debts owed.[158] In particular, China had been constructing a nationwide fibre-optic communication system, which would have enabled Iraqi anti-aircraft batteries to target American and British aircraft enforcing the no-fly zones.[159] However, since Pollack's book is well known for mounting one of the most cogent and influential cases in favour of regime-change, one might assume that his views on containment are biased and untrustworthy. If so, we should note that Thomas Ricks—whose damning account of the intervention bears the indicative title, *Fiasco*—nevertheless regards Pollack as sufficiently authoritative to rely upon him in citing the Chinese transgression.[160] What is more, Ricks also suggests that maintaining the no-fly zones in northern and southern Iraq was so straining the US military that they could not have been enforced much longer.[161]

Richard Haas confirms Pollack's general assessment of the state of the sanctions regime before the invasion. They 'were generally seen as being in bad shape and getting worse'. They were too blunt, hurting the people and sparing the regime; and Jordan, Syria, Turkey were increasingly ignoring them for the sake of lucrative trade.[162] Nevertheless, Haas believes that the United States could have done much more to make sanctions more effective. It could have compensated Turkey and Jordan for the loss of revenues from illicit trade;[163] and it could have shut down the Iraq–Syria oil pipeline, which was a major source of revenue to Saddam Hussein, either as part of a programme of normalizing relations with Syria or by using military force.[164] At the same time, however, Haas reports that Colin Powell's attempts to tighten sanctions before the invasion met with no success. The fruition of his efforts, namely, the passage of UNSC Resolution 1409 in May 2002, facilitated Iraq's importation of a wider variety of goods, but did nothing to ensure that proscribed items did not enter the country or to slow the illegal exports of oil that provided the regime with income.[165] The fact that only such an inadequate Resolution could be agreed during a period when Iraq was widely believed to possess WMD implies a significant lack of collective

158. Ibid., pp. 100–1, 216–17, 224–7.
159. Ibid., chapter 7, 'The Erosion of Containment', esp. pp. 224–7.
160. Ricks, *Fiasco*, pp. 19, 26–7, 453.   161. Ibid., pp. 43–5.
162. Haas, *War of Necessity*, p. 17.   163. Ibid., pp. 179, 233.
164. Ibid., p. 179.   165. Ibid., p. 175.

international will to contain the problem. That implication is corroborated by the fact that a majority of the members of the Security Council was clamouring for sanctions to be relaxed, not tightened;[166] and that one of them was actually supplying Iraq with technology that could be used to subvert the no-fly zones. Haas offers no explanation as to what could have been done to secure the common resolve of the Security Council to maintain watertight sanctions against Iraq indefinitely.

The prospect of effective sanctions was by no means assured. The prospect of successful inspections was little better. Hans Blix is frank in admitting that without the Coalition's build-up of an invasion force in the summer of 2002 'Iraq would probably not have accepted the resumption of inspections',[167] and that 'the US could not keep troops idling in the area for months' in rising temperatures.[168] And Haas feared the risk of 'Potemkin inspections', which would enable the regime to argue for the relaxing of sanctions in reward for superficial improvements in behaviour.[169]

In sum, it seems to me that Peter Baehr expressed common sense when he wrote that containment is at best only a short-term measure since '[t]he unanimity of interest and durability of resolve that are required to institutionalize it do not exist in the real world of geopolitics'.[170] Therefore it also seems to me that the sadly famous Dr David Kelly, Britain's expert on biological weapons and a former UN weapons inspector, was correct when he wrote shortly before the invasion that '[a]fter twelve unsuccessful years of UN supervision of disarmament, military force regrettably appears to be the only way of finally and conclusively disarming Iraq . . . The long-term threat . . . remains Iraq's development to military maturity of weapons of mass destruction—something only regime change will avert.'[171]

---

166. Tony Blair reports that in mid-2001 Russian commercial interests obstructed agreement about new sanctions: 'When Vladimir [Putin] and I discussed sanctions at the July 2001 Genoa G8 summit, he joked he was all in favour of them, provided we compensated him for the $8 billion that Iraq owed Russia' (*A Journey*, p. 395).
167. Blix, *Disarming Iraq*, p. 11.
168. Blix, *Disarming Iraq*, p. 130; see also p. 14.
169. Haas, *War of Necessity*, p. 174.
170. Peter Baehr, 'The Critical Path', *Times Literary Supplement*, 31 January 2002, pp. 3–5.
171. David Kelly, 'Only regime change will avert the threat', *Observer*, 31 August 2003. Although written before the invasion, the article was not published by the *Observer* until afterwards—and after the author's tragic suicide.

On the eve of the invasion the belief that Saddam Hussein possessed chemical and biological weapons, and was intent on acquiring nuclear ones, had reasonable grounds and was widespread. His regime had refused to comply fully and unreservedly with ten years' worth of UN resolutions. The policy of containment was breaking down and attempts to repair it were being frustrated by a lack of collective resolve on the part of the international community. There was evidence of sustained liaison, so far falling short of collaboration, between the regime and al-Qaeda. If the threat posed by Iraq coming to possess nuclear weapons was grave—and, judging by its repeated Resolutions on the matter, the Security Council thought so— then, given these facts and reasonable beliefs, invasion intending a significant change in regime could claim to have been the only sure and available means of solving the problem. That is, it could reasonably claim to have been a last resort.

Moreover, regime-change was always the only way of solving the other problem: chronic oppression by a characteristically atrocious state. It is quite true that such change does not always require invasion. It can happen through economic collapse (precipitated by an arms race), as in the case of the USSR in 1989. It can happen through spontaneous and widespread popular disobedience, as in Egypt's 'Arab Spring'. It can happen through domestic armed rebellion (with foreign support and air strikes), as in Libya during 2011. Could the regime of Saddam Hussein have been changed without the invasion of 2003? Of course it *could*, for many things are possible. But was it at all *likely*? Before the invasion, it did not seem so. After all, Saddam Hussein's regime had survived a gruelling war with Iran in the 1980s, expulsion from Kuwait and defeat in the Gulf War of 1991, rebellion in the south and in the north, the imposition of no-fly zones, and subjection to economic sanctions. In March 2003 there was no sign at all that the regime was on the verge of collapse. However, the 'Arab Spring' reminds us that unlikely things do happen, and it makes us wonder whether, if the United States and the United Kingdom had waited, what happened eight years later in Tunisia, Egypt, and Libya would have happened also in Iraq. Perhaps it would have done. But equally without the invasion of Iraq, the 'Arab Spring' might not have happened at all and certainly would not have been the same. The coerced fall of Saddam Hussein appears to have been one of the factors that moved Muammar Gaddafi to enter into the 2003 negotiations that led to the termination of Libya's efforts to develop nuclear and chemical weapons.[172] Had he not been persuaded to yield, and had he come to wield nuclear weapons by 2011, it is unlikely that NATO would have intervened militarily on behalf of the Benghazi rebels, and it is very likely that the rebels would have been crushed as a consequence. The invasion of Iraq also seems to have been an inspiration for Lebanon's 'Cedar Revolution' in 2005.[173]

We now know, of course, that Saddam Hussein did not possess WMD and that the threat he actually posed in March 2003 was not imminent. Should we therefore judge that, while the invasion *looked* like a last resort, it *was* not in fact so? With respect to Iraq as a WMD threat, I think that we are bound to reach that conclusion. It is true that, while the problem of the threat of Iraqi possession of WMD was not as pressing as it looked, it still remained, since Saddam Hussein was intent on acquiring them, especially nuclear weapons.[174] Containment was collapsing, and the collective will to shore it up was lacking—*even* when it was widely believed that Iraq retained WMD. The prospect of frustrating Saddam Hussein's enduring intention by

172. So claims Tony Blair (*A Journey*, p. 391), as does Jack Straw, Blair's Foreign Secretary at the time of the Iraq invasion: 'I have no doubt that what convinced him [Gaddafi] to abandon these [WMD] programmes was Iraq. But don't take that from me. Just three days after Libya had agreed to have its WMD programmes dismantled under international supervision, CNN reported that "Gaddafi acknowledged that the Iraq war may have influenced him" in his decision. In the same report Hans Blix, the former UN weapons inspector, said he imagined that "Gaddafi could have been scared by what he saw happen in Iraq"' ('Gaddafi makes me glad we toppled Saddam', *The Times*. 5 March 2011, p. 21). Christopher Hitchens corroborates this, asserting that Gaddafi's 'abject fear at watching the fate of Saddam Hussein...has been amply reconfirmed by many Libyan officials in the hearing of many of my friends. He did, after all, approach George W. Bush and Tony Blair, not the United Nations' ('The Iraq effect: If Saddam Hussein were still in power, this year's Arab uprisings could never have happened', *Slate*, 28 March 2011, at <http://www.slate.com/articles/news_and_politics/fighting_words/2011/03/the_iraq_effect.html> [as at 23 December 2011]).

173. Walid Jumblatt, patriarch of the Druze Muslim community and a leader of the 2005 'Lebanese intifada' against Syrian interference in Lebanon, is reported to have remarked: 'It's strange for me to say it, but this process of change has started because of the American invasion of Iraq. I was cynical about Iraq. But when I saw the Iraqi people voting three weeks ago, 8 million of them, it was the start of a new Arab world. The Syrian people, the Egyptian people, all say something is changing. The Berlin Wall has fallen. We can see it' (David Ignatius, 'Beirut's Berlin Wall', *Washington Post*, 23 February 2005, page A19).

174. The Iraq Survey Group's final report of September 2004 (commonly known as the 'Duelfer Report' after its head, Charles Duelfer) concluded that '[t]he regime [of Saddam Hussein] made a token effort to comply with the disarmament process, but the Iraqis never intended to meet the spirit of the UNSC's resolutions. Outward acts of compliance belied a covert desire to resume WMD activities. Several senior officials also either inferred or heard Saddam say that he reserved the right to resume WMD research after sanctions' (*Comprehensive Report of the Advisor to the DCI [Director of Central Intelligence] on Iraq's WMD*, 3 vols. [Washington, DC: Central Intelligence Agency, 2004], Vol. 1, p. 49).

this means, therefore, was not at all high; and there is no reason to suppose that it *would* have been enhanced by the deferral of military action. Nevertheless, there is reason to suppose that containment *might* have been enhanced; and since the threat posed by Iraq was not imminent, the United States and the United Kingdom could in fact have afforded to wait—in case the regime should unexpectedly implode or the international community should suddenly find itself possessed of unusual collective resolve. History sometimes holds happy surprises for us, and we should allow it the opportunity to pull them, if it seems that we can afford to. In March 2003 it was not clear to Washington or London that they could afford to wait—on grounds that, while erroneous, were reasonable. So I do not think that they can be blamed for acting when they did. Nevertheless, in retrospect it seems clear that delay was affordable. So, with regard to the threat of WMD, the invasion was not in fact a last resort.

That threat, however, was not the only injustice requiring correction. There was also the injustice of the survival of a characteristically atrocious regime, whose dead and living victims cried out for vindication, and whose future ones for protection. Since there was no sign of internal revolution or reason to suppose its likelihood, external regime-change was the only effective means of remedy. In this respect, therefore, the 2003 invasion was a last resort.

XI. *Ad bellum*: proportionality

When deliberating the rightness and wrongness of going to war, the criterion of proportionality requires political leaders to consider, among other things, whether military means in general, and the particular ones at their disposal, are suited to achieve the end of rectifying the injustice that comprises just cause. In the case of the 2003 invasion of Iraq, the just cause was a combination of a characteristically atrocious regime and the threat posed by its possession of WMD. Basic to the rectification of these two forms of injustice was regime-change, and the first part of this was regime-removal, which is something that military force could achieve—and under the circumstances was necessary to achieve.

The removal of the old, however, is but the beginning of change. Its completion requires the establishment of the significantly new (and better). While military force has a vital role in this—the securing of borders and the maintenance of law and order—it is nevertheless a limited one. Within the space secured and pacified by military forces the task of political reconstruction falls to civilians. If the intention of the United States and the United Kingdom was genuinely regime-*change* and not merely regime-toppling, then we may expect them to have made plans not only for the invasion itself but also for *post bellum* pacification and reconstruction. They *did* make plans. According to Tony Blair, these focused on avoiding humanitarian disaster when a country dependent on food coupons suddenly lost the tightly controlled system of government distribution; on neutralizing the effects of the possible use of chemical and biological weapons; and on coping with the possibility that the oilfields would be set ablaze and threaten major environmental disaster. The second never happened; the first and third were successfully prevented.[175] Thomas Ricks corroborates Blair's testimony to the extent that he writes that there was 'a lot' of pre-war planning for the post-war situation by 'at least' three groups inside the military and one at the State Department in Washington.[176]

Notwithstanding this, it is widely acknowledged that the Coalition's plans for pacification and reconstruction were woefully inadequate. As Ricks also writes: 'much of the planning was shoddy, there was no one really in charge of it, and there was little coordination between the various groups'.[177] A major reason for this was an excessive optimism, which gathered its momentum from several sources. One was the Jeffersonian assumption that political liberty and democracy naturally spring up wherever the stone of tyranny is lifted.[178] According to George Packer, '[i]n his [Rumsfeld's] view

---

175. Blair, *A Journey*, pp. 442–3.
176. Ricks, *Fiasco*, p. 79. Craig White claims that before the invasion 'detailed U.S. government plans to manage Iraq after conquering it simply did not exist' (*Iraq*, p. 139), that 'no real plan to govern Iraq had been drawn up' (ibid., p.143), and that 'there is no evidence of any serious planning at all for vital purposes: no means were chosen for the stated end of "liberation" and enabling a peaceful, well-governed society' (ibid., p. 154). In substantiation of this claim he appeals almost entirely to Ricks. He then argues that the mismatch between the US Government's non-existent plans and its stated intention of creating a better Iraqi government indicates that the latter was not sincere (ibid., p. 136): 'Failure to choose the necessary means is a failure to intend the stated end' (ibid., p. 154). White's argument would be unanswerable, had there been no planning at all. However, according to Ricks' report, there was 'a lot' of planning, although 'much' of it was poor. The significance of a lot of inadequate planning is ambiguous. It *could* be symptomatic of an insincere intention to create a better Iraq, but equally it could express naïveté about what a sincere intention's realization would require. I argue in the following paragraph that it was the latter.
177. Ricks, *Fiasco*, p. 79.
178. According to one biographer, Jefferson 'did not worry about public order, believing as he did that individuals liberated from the last remnants of feudal oppression would interact freely to create a natural harmony of interests that was guided, like Adam Smith's marketplace, by invisible or veiled forms of discipline' (Joseph J. Ellis, *American Sphinx: The Character of Thomas Jefferson* [New York: Vintage, 1998], pp. 359–60).

and that of others in the administration, but above all the president, freedom was the absence of constraint. Freedom existed in divinely endowed human nature...Remove a thirty-five-year-old tyranny and democracy will grow in its place, because people everywhere want to be free.'[179]

This Enlightenment optimism was allied with a certain impatience toward hindered humanity, which refuses the notion that the poor will be with us, if not always, then for a very long time. Thus George Packer observes that Rumsfeld allowed 'no contingency for psychological demolition'—that is, he did not countenance the demoralizing and debilitating effects upon a people of prolonged subjection to tyranny.[180] He believed that the international efforts at national reconstruction in the Balkans in the 1990s had bred a culture of dependency.[181] Accordingly, Rumsfeld's spokesman, Larry Di Rita, dismissed the claim that the 2003 invasion needed to show early benefits to the Iraqi people by saying, 'We don't owe the people of Iraq anything. We're giving them their freedom. That's enough.'[182] Later Rumsfeld himself said: 'I don't believe it's our job to reconstruct the country. The Iraqi people will have to reconstruct that country over a period of time.'[183]

A second spring of over-optimism appears to have been an excessive managerialist confidence in the power to impose 'progress' from above. This is something that Rory Stewart has identified and begun to articulate, most recently in relation to Afghanistan, but drawing from his own experience as a Coalition Provisional Authority (CPA) official in Iraq: the rude dismissal of local wisdom and of piecemeal, organic growth in favour of abstract, prefabricated, top-down, technical 'solutions'.[184] What Stewart observed in Afghanistan was that '[a] culture of country experts had been replaced by a culture of consultants'.[185] Signs of the same mentality are evident in accounts of the planning for, and running of, post-invasion Iraq. Quoting retired US army colonel Andrew Bacevich, Thomas Ricks refers to Rumsfeld's 'contempt for the accumulated wisdom of the military profession' and 'the assumption among forward thinkers that technology—above all information technology—has rendered obsolete the conventions traditionally governing

179. Packer, *Assassins' Gate*, pp. 136–7.
180. Ibid., pp. 137, 144, 178.   181. Ibid, p. 114.
182. Ibid., p. 133.   183. Ibid., p. 242.
184. Rory Stewart, 'Afghanistan: Ambition and Reality' and 'The Rhetoric of War', The Leonard Stein Lectures, Balliol College, Oxford, May 2010 (unpublished).
185. Stewart and Knaus, *Can Intervention Work?*, p. 17.

the preparation and conduct of war'.[186] Peter Galbraith observes that before the war the Bush administration gave little thought to the nature of Iraqi society, thanks to 'a culture of arrogance', and he reports how several (American) participants in the occupation of Iraq were struck by American ignorance of the country and indifference to it.[187] And George Packer writes of the second Administrator of the CPA, Paul Bremer, that he 'would approach the running of Iraq like a demanding corporate executive, insisting on fast and quantifiable results from his staff, hating surprises and setbacks.'[188]

These two ideological propensities toward excessive optimism were undoubtedly encouraged by the rosy accounts given by certain Iraqi exiles of their people's political maturity. Galbraith writes that Ahmed Chalabi's role in bringing about the 2003 invasion 'cannot . . . be overstated. If it were not for him, the United States military likely would not be in Iraq today. This does not make him a con man, as his critics allege. Through a twenty-year cultivation of America's foreign policy elite, Chalabi made a convincing case for a democratic Iraq and Arab democracy.'[189]

Determined over-optimism did not just infect the planning; it also infected the execution. Thus, when he replaced Jay Garner at the head of the CPA in May 2003, Bremer reversed Garner's plans to get the Iraqi government up and running as soon as possible.[190] With no previous experience of Iraq and only a fortnight of preparation, three days after his arrival Bremer decided that he, not the Iraqis, would run the country.[191] He immediately proceeded to make the fateful decision to radically de-Ba'athify the state's security institutions by disbanding the Iraqi army and police. This resulted in lots of young men, many of them armed, being thrown out onto the streets with no legitimate way of earning an income, and so becoming ready recruits for insurgency.

Warnings had been given by regional, military, and intelligence experts against top-down de-Ba'athification, about the risks of insurgency, and about the difficulty of installing democracy.[192] They were ignored. Contrary views, according to Peter Galbraith, were not just rejected, but banned.[193]

186. Ricks, *Fiasco*, p. 75.
187. Galbraith, *The End of Iraq*, pp. 83, 97–8.
188. Packer, *Assassins' Gate*, p. 190.
189. Galbraith, *The End of Iraq*, p. 86. George Packer's account accords a prominent role to Kanan Makiya (*Assassins' Gate*, *passim*).
190. Ricks, *Fiasco*, 165.
191. Galbraith, *The End of Iraq*, p. 9.
192. Ricks, *Fiasco*, pp. 65, 72–3; Packer, *Assassins' Gate*, p. 298.
193. Galbraith, *The End of Iraq*, p. 89.

Thomas Ricks cites two testimonies that Bremer was 'a talker, not a listener'.[194] He also quotes Andrew Rathmell, a British defence expert who served as a strategic planner at the CPA, who observes that an 'unwillingness to challenge assumptions and question established plans persisted during the course of the occupation, giving rise to the ironic refrain among disgruntled Coalition planners that "optimism is not a plan". This failure was compounded by a persistent tendency... to avoid reporting bad news and not to plan for worst case, or other case, contingencies.'[195] George Packer confirms this, reporting that in the CPA bad news was unwelcome and no one wanted to be the one to ask unsettling questions.[196]

In addition to Enlightenment over-optimism, correlative impatience with human demoralization, excessive managerialist confidence in remaking the world, and a resultant refusal to heed expert advice or bad news, a further set of flaws in the planning and execution of post-invasion operations were military. Scarred by Vietnam, the US military was averse to assuming a counter-insurgency role. Instead, in the wake of the end of the Cold War and inspired by its efficient victory in the Gulf War of 1991, it was in the process of being reorganized with a focus on Special Forces, air power, and advanced weapons systems.[197] When the US army invaded Iraq in 2003, it was committed to short, blitzkrieg-style warfare,[198] and it was quite unready to shoulder responsibility for restoring peace, which was unexpectedly thrust on it after the invasion.[199] It was also far too small for the job. The swift victory over the Taliban regime in Afghanistan in 2001, achieved by air power and small numbers of Special Forces operating with local militias, had confounded the army's prediction of the need for huge numbers of troops.[200] Donald Rumsfeld was therefore able to force General Tommy Franks of Central Command to reduce his Iraq invasion force from an original half million to around 160,000.[201] This was sufficient for a successful invasion; but it was not sufficient for a successful occupation. Combined with the disbandment of the Iraqi army, it meant that the CPA was unable to seal Iraq's borders and to starve native insurgents of foreign support.

194. Ricks, *Fiasco*, pp. 187, 325.   195. Ibid., *Fiasco*, p. 169.
196. Packer, *Assassins' Gate*, p. 319.   197. Ibid., p. 117.
198. Ricks, *Fiasco*, pp. 130–3, 264.   199. Ibid., *Fiasco*, p. 151.
200. Packer, *Assassins' Gate*, pp. 117–18.   201. Ibid., p. 118.

The United States and the United Kingdom did make plans to secure the peace after a successful invasion. They were serious in intending regime-change and not merely regime-toppling. Their plans were vitiated, however, by naïve optimism, impatience with human frailty and inconvenient counsel, unwise disdain for regional and local expertise, and consequent imprudence. These were serious moral failings, and they lack persuasive excuse. Nonetheless, all wars are waged by sinners, and even just wars give rise to vice. The war against Hitler provided a stage for Montgomery's conceit, Patton's vainglory, and Zhukov's ruthlessness; and the liberation and occupation of eastern Germany in 1945 involved vengeful incontinence on a massive scale, as an estimated two million German women were raped by Soviet troops.[202] Vice alone, therefore, does not an unjust war make.

Moreover, it is morally significant that, after their initial failures, the occupying powers did not simply walk away. Over six years and at great cost they sought to compensate for their errors. And judging by General Petraeus's 'Surge' and its aftermath, their compensation met with considerable success.[203] Right and sincere intention to exchange the regime of Saddam Hussein for something significantly better was not lacking at the beginning, and over time that intention proved itself serious.

In deliberating whether or not to go to war, the fitting—or proportioning—of means to ends is one factor to consider. Well-proportioned means are efficient in achieving their ends. In Iraq, the efficiency of the chosen military means in achieving a successful invasion was very high, but the efficiency of the military, administrative, and political means of achieving better government was very low. Over time, however, the efficiency of the latter was improved.

Another kind of proportion that might be considered is that of costs to benefits. As I argued in Chapter Four, this is seldom susceptible of any rational comparative 'weighing'. This is partly because what needs to be weighed is constantly evolving. The effects of any human act develop and change over time according to the subsequent interventions of other human agents or natural forces. Today's 'overall balance' will not be tomorrow's. History does not run along fixed lines: novel factors are constantly emerging that suddenly throw a black balance into the red, or haul a red one back

202. Antony Beevor, *Berlin: The Downfall 1945* (London: Viking, 2002), p. 410.
203. Thomas Ricks, *The Gamble: General Petraeus and the Untold Story of the American Surge in Iraq*, 2006–8 (London: Allen Lane, 2009), chapter 11.

into the black. But even more problematic than the evolution of effects is their frequent incomparability and incommensurability: they cannot be compared, because they do not submit to the same measure. There is no single scale that can measure, for example, lives lost against justice gained.

Notwithstanding this, there are cases where one can say with some confidence that the benefit is *not* worth the cost. For example, the end of supporting the Hungarian uprising of 1956 or the Czech Spring of 1968 was clearly not worth military means that risked the cost of a full-scale exchange of nuclear weapons with the USSR, since that would have rendered uninhabitable the very territory to be liberated—and much more besides. The costs would not have been worth it, in the sense that they would have undermined the very benefit that they were supposed to be purchasing. The means would have subverted the end. Similarly, one can determine with some certainty when the cost in blood and treasure is not worth bearing, because it is militarily, economically, or politically unsustainable, and therefore futile.

Most of the time, however, the costs and benefits are so unpredictable and incommensurate that any 'calculation' can be little more than a well-informed guess, when it is not simply prejudice dressed up as reason. Tony Blair has written: 'The leader has to decide whether the objective is worth the cost. What's more, he or she must do so unsure of what the exact cost might be, or the exact cost of failing to meet the objective.'[204] Quite so. Staring into an uncertain future, the best that a sovereign decision-maker can do, having judged just cause, right motive and intention, and last resort, is to consider whether the military and other means seem capable of achieving their end, whether the likely costs in blood and treasure seem tolerable, whether the national interest is sufficiently engaged to maintain enough political support at home, and whether the risk of failure can be borne.

Before the invasion of Iraq there was reason to return a positive answer to each of these questions. However, the grounds for confidence in the means for regime-*change* were much weaker than the White House supposed, and its wilful ignorance was culpable. After the invasion, and as a consequence of this culpable naïvete, the costs proved to be much higher than expected. It also became clear that the extent to which the national interests of the United States and the United Kingdom were in fact engaged had been (non-culpably) overestimated, and political support declined

204. Blair, *A Journey*, pp. 238–9.

accordingly. Nevertheless, even now, ten years after the invasion, it is not manifest to me that the invading parties had no significant interest in regime-change, that the means eventually employed undermined the end and failed to make a crucial and significant contribution to improving upon the regime of Saddam Hussein, that domestic political support was insufficient to sustain those means, or that the costs and risks were intolerable.

XII. *Ad bellum*: the prospect of success

Before the invasion the prospect of the US and British military prevailing over Iraq's regular forces appeared good, and the appearance did not deceive. The prospect of installing liberal democracy also appeared good, given the Bush administration's excessive optimism and managerialist confidence, given what they were told by Chalabi and his like, and given their dismissal of adverse counsel. Expert warnings that the task would be much more difficult and hazardous, however, have since been proven correct. Had the planning and the early implementation taken account of those warnings, had the aim been relaxed from the ambitious imposition of Western-style democracy to the gradual growth of (more) responsible government, had Franks got the 500,000 troops that he originally wanted, and had the military prepared to seal the borders and impose peace within them, then the *realistic* prospect would have been much better. Before the invasion, therefore, the prospect of success seemed better than it deserved to seem. Had different means been chosen, the realistic prospect could have been much better than it was. Nevertheless, it cannot be said that before the invasion there was no actual prospect of success, since much would depend on how the invaders responded to their own early mistakes.

It would also depend on the responses of other people and on whether or not Providence were to smile on their endeavours. Well-meaning and earnest intentions, even when fortified with meticulous plans, can be frustrated by accidents of history: the just may be robbed of victory by a change in the wind. And sooner or later the fate of what one rightly, sincerely, and seriously intends inevitably moves out of one's own hands and into others'. Whether, and how far, the Iraq intervention will achieve a political regime that is a significant improvement on Saddam Hussein's depends increasingly on what *Iraqis* do and fail to do, and whether the efforts of the well-intentioned among them meet with good fortune or bad.

What the settled upshot will be is not clear—and it cannot be clear. Different people of different political persuasions and different temperaments give different estimates at different times. Judging by reports made between 2006 and 2009, on the one hand Iraqi politics and the security forces continued to be divided along ethnic and religious lines;[205] political Islamism was flourishing;[206] politically motivated violence continued;[207] the government in Baghdad was tending to become more authoritarian;[208] Iranian influence had grown;[209] and the American military—and perhaps the British, too—had suffered demoralization.[210] According to some reckonings, involvement in Iraq had been strategically counterproductive—in alienating mainstream Muslim support and enhancing the appeal of al-Qaeda, in hindering international cooperation in combating al-Qaeda, in distracting the United States and its allies from dealing with more urgent threats of nuclear proliferation posed by the likes of Pakistan, Iran, and North Korea.[211] On the other, positive hand, the threat of Iraq coming to possess and proliferate WMD has been removed unequivocally; Iraq's Shi'ite majority has been liberated from eight decades of oppression to participate fully in political life; the Kurds, no longer standing in fear of a regime that once deployed WMD against them, now rightly enjoy virtual independence; and the adoption of a counterinsurgency strategy focused on population protection, combined with the 2007–8 'Surge', had succeeded in reducing sectarian killings by 50 per cent (in April 2007), in bolstering trust between the Sunnis and the Coalition's forces, and in persuading many indigenous Sunnis that their foreign extremist *confrères* were a threat to their future.[212] Even a critic such as Richard Haas wrote in 2009 that '[b]y mid-2008 something of a virtuous cycle appeared to be developing, in which improved security was leading to improved economic conditions, which in turn was reinforcing more stable politics and security'.[213]

205. Galbraith, *The End of Iraq*, p. 3 (2006); Ricks, *Fiasco*, p. 448 (2007); Ricks, *Gamble*, pp. 298, 322 (2009).
206. Galbraith, *The End of Iraq*, p. 89 (2006).
207. Ricks, *Gamble*, pp. 294–6, 318 (2009).
208. Ricks, *Gamble*, p. 318 (2009).
209. Galbraith, *The End of Iraq*, pp. 7, 89 (2006).
210. Ricks, *Gamble*, p. 305 (2009). My evidence for the demoralizing impact of Iraq on the British military is anecdotal.
211. Clarke, *Against All Enemies*, pp. 246, 264, 280, 286 (2004); Galbraith, *The End of Iraq*, pp. 10, 73, 75 (2006); Haas, *War of Necessity*, pp. 176–7, 270 (2009).
212. Galbraith, *The End of Iraq*, pp. 5, 11 (2006); Ricks, *Fiasco*, p. 450 (2007); Haas, *War of Necessity*, p. 263 (2009).
213. Haas, *War of Necessity*, p. 264.

Haas's reading has since been confirmed. By December 2011 monthly civilian casualties had been brought down to 382 from a peak of 3,208 in July
2006 (although there had been no further improvement since 2009);[214] and
a second peaceful transfer of governing power by democratic election had
taken place in March 2010. By the summer of 2012, the level of security and
political stability was such as to support dramatic growth in investment,
construction, general business activity, and oil production. According to
Amir Taheri, a supporter of the invasion,

> [b]y all measures, Iraq is experiencing an economic revival: living standards are
> on an upward trend for the first time since the 1970s. For much of the past
> decade, Iraq's growth rate has hovered around 12 per cent, according to esti-
> mates by the World Bank, making it the fastest growing economy in the
> Middle East... [H]elping the economic uplift are the nation's growing oil
> revenues. In 2007, Iraq's oil income fell to just a few hundred million dollars.
> By 2011, however, it had reached $87 billion, an all-time record... [B]oasting
> one of the largest... reserves of oil in the world, Iraq is destined to emerge as
> an energy superpower.[215]

In March 2011, the *Guardian* newspaper, no friend of Bush or Blair and a
consistent critic of the invasion, reported that Iraq 'remains broadly supportive of [NATO's] military campaign' to curb or oust Colonel Gaddafi—
which would presumably not have been the case if Iraqi views of foreign
intervention in their own country in 2003 had been predominantly negative.[216] On the international front, Tony Blair and others argue plausibly
that the toppling of Saddam Hussein was an important factor in persuading
Gaddafi to give up his efforts to develop nuclear and chemical weapons.[217]
Since the Iraq invasion was launched partly to stop the proliferation of
WMD, this is an indirect effect that should be allowed to count in its
favour.

Even if we accept all these effects as presented, we cannot give them a
numerical value in order to make a calculation, determine whether or not
the benefits outweigh the costs, and decide upon overall success or failure.

---

214. According to Iraq Body Count, <http://www.iraqbodycount.org/analysis/numbers/2011>
     (as at 22 August 2012).
215. Amir Taheri, 'A Democratic Beacon in the Fractious Arab World', *Standpoint* (July/August
     2012), pp. 45–6. The credibility of Taheri's report is bolstered by his candid admission of
     persistent problems of corruption in government and of political violence (ibid., p. 46).
216. Martin Chulov, Katherine Marsh, and Saeed Kamali Dehghan, 'It is the right of the people
     to protest against tyrants', *Guardian*, 22 March 2011, p. 7.
217. See note 172 above.

There is no common currency: how can one possibly value the lighter step of a Kurdish mother freed from the threat of genocide against the temporary distraction of US policy-makers from the task of sorting out Pakistan? What is more, history does not stand still: the effects change daily, rendering today's 'calculation' obsolete tomorrow. Yet further, not all of the ill effects of the 2003 intervention can be laid simply at the feet of the United States and the United Kingdom: the invasion and occupation did not *compel* insurgents to dispatch suicide bombers into marketplaces. We cannot judge the success or failure of the intervention in Iraq by way of a comprehensive weighing of its actual effects, since these are often indeterminable and incommensurable, always constantly evolving, and attributable to a variety of agents. However, we can make a judgement in crude and approximate terms. The invasion did succeed in toppling an atrocious regime and in removing the threat of its acquiring WMD. Formally, it provided an opportunity for Iraqis to create a new political system, which would be a significant improvement on Saddam Hussein's. Substantially, it did far less than it should have done to create favourable conditions for such reconstruction. Had it not been vitiated by excessive optimism and confidence, it would have known to do more. After their initial failures, however, the intervening powers—and especially the United States—did strive to recover lost ground, and their efforts met with a significant measure of success. For sure, it looks most unlikely that the intervention will achieve the creation in Iraq of Western-style liberal democracy. That aim was always fantastically overambitious.[218] Full-blown liberal democracy, however, is not the only form of tolerably good government. Political justice did not take on earthly form for the very first time in late 17th-century England or late 18th-century America. Even if liberal democracy is the ideal, other political forms are tolerably just; and Iraq might yet settle upon one of them. In sum, on the success or failure of the 2003 invasion in creating significant regime-*improvement* in Iraq, I plant my flag in the position articulated by the spokesman of the group of young, professional Iraqis who visited me in Oxford in March 2010. At the end of our meeting, I asked them bluntly, 'Should the invasion of 2003 have happened?' Without hesitating, their spokesman responded: 'It was good that it happened. It could have been done better. And it isn't over.'

218. I say this on the ground of accounts of the experience of two Britons, Rory Stewart and Mark Etherington, charged with realizing the political ambitions of the Coalition Provisional Authority in southern Iraq (Stewart, *Occupational Hazards*; Mark Etherington, *Revolt on the Tigris. The Al-Sadr Uprising and the Governing of Iraq* [London: Hurst, 2005]).

XIII. *In bello*: discrimination and proportionality

The two traditional criteria of justice in the course of war—and insurgency—are discrimination and proportionality. The first requires that the belligerents do not intentionally kill or harm non-combatants, and that they strive to avoid killing them incidentally. The second requires that military operations cause no more evil than is necessary—that is, that wounding, killing, and wider destruction be governed and constrained by the just end of rectifying injustice.

In the invasion itself and during subsequent counter-insurgency operations, The Coalition's forces sought to avoid non-combatant deaths, not least because of the political damage that they would cause both domestically and internationally. If James Turner Johnson is correct, during the invasion itself those forces 'set a new standard' for discriminate conduct in major military operations, including:

> the selection of targets for the air campaign, with particular sites marked off in advance as not to be struck...care in the choice of weapons, angles of attack, and delivery vehicles both in the air campaign and on the ground; a structure for command decisions that incorporated legal advice at various levels to help deal with ambiguous cases...and...the availability of technology that allowed close and accurate targeting and choice of means to match the purpose of a specific action.[219]

In the early years of the insurgency, however, the US military remained in war-fighting mode, and was therefore less careful to avoid harm to civilians—for example in Fallujah and Najaf in April 2004—than it would become after adopting a counter-insurgency strategy focused on population protection in early 2007. Since harm to civilians tends to alienate them, and since the alienation of the civilian population is counterproductive in fighting an insurgency, we may say that the early conduct of the US military was disproportionate. This appears not to have been the case with their British colleagues, who applied lessons learned (the hard way) from thirty years of combating paramilitaries in Northern Ireland.[220]

---

219. James Turner Johnson, *The War to Oust Saddam Hussein: Just War and the New Face of Conflict* (Lanham, MY: Rowman and Littlefield, 2005), pp. 133–4.

220. The British mode of military operations in the aftermath of the invasion was frequently and favourably contrasted with the American mode by British soldiers themselves and then by the British press. This seems not to have been merely an expression of professional competitiveness or national chauvinism. George Packer, an American journalist, reports that the

Some suppose that the sheer scale of civilian casualties in Iraq is sufficient to establish the immorality of the intervention in Iraq. Estimating the number of deaths by violence directly attributable to the invasion is fiercely controversial, not only politically but also scientifically. Figures for the period March 2003 to June 2006 range from 601,027 (G. Burnham et al., 11 October 2006[221]), through 151,000 (Iraq Family Health Survey, January 2008[222]), down to 49,692 (Iraq Body Count, 6 December 2011). We can be sure that the actual figure is higher than the conservative tally given by Iraq Body Count, since that includes only the violent deaths of non-combatants, which have been reported by the press and validated. Both the Burnham study and the Iraq Family Health Survey (IFHS) report were peer-reviewed and published in distinguished scientific journals, the *Lancet* and the *New England Journal of Medicine*, respectively. Both arrived at their figures by surveying a sample of households, calculating mortality rates, extrapolating to the national population as a whole, and then subtracting an estimate of pre-invasion mortalities to arrive at the number of 'excess deaths'. There are two reasons to prefer the findings of the IFHS over those of Burnham and his colleagues: the IFHS interviewed 9,345 households in 1,086 clusters, compared with Burnham's 1,849 in 47; and several experts believe that Burnham's estimate of the pre-invasion mortality rate is much too low.[223] Between June 2006 and December 2011 the cautious Iraq Body Count's tally rose by over 128 per cent to 113,505. If we take the IFHS figure for March 2003 to June 2006 and multiply it by 1.284, then we get a total of 193,884 violent civilian

Iraqis themselves made the same comparison; and he confirms it from his own experience (*Assassins' Gate*, pp. 238–9, 426–7). I should add that I have heard several senior British officers express deep admiration for the remarkable efficiency with which the US military adapted itself, once it had decided to do so.

221. G. Burnham, R. Lafta, S. Doocy, and L. Roberts, 'Mortality after the 2003 invasion of Iraq: a cross-sectional cluster sample survey', *The Lancet*, 11 October 2006. The total given here refers to the direct deaths of combatants and non-combatants. It rises to 654,965, if indirect ones due to increased lawlessness, degraded infrastructure, poor healthcare etc. are added.

222. Iraq Family Health Survey Study Group, 'Violence-Related Mortality in Iraq from 2002 to 2006', *New England Journal of Medicine*, 31 January 2008. The IFHS was conducted by federal and regional ministries in Iraq in collaboration with the World Health Organization.

223. For example, Beth Osborne Daponte in 'Wartime estimates of Iraqi civilian casualties', *International Review of the Red Cross*, 89/868 (December 2007), pp. 950–1. Daponte reports that the UN Population Division, whose figures are 'generally deemed to be of very high quality', reckoned that Iraq's pre-invasion mortality rate was 10 per thousand—almost twice the 5.5 per thousand assumed by Burnham. She also observes that the UN reports that Iran's mortality-rate in the 2000–5 period was 5.3—and that before the invasion 'most thought that the situation in Iraq was considerably worse than in Iran, mostly due to the impact of sanctions' (ibid., p. 951).

deaths attributable to the invasion and its aftermath up until the end of 2011. This excludes those whose deaths were caused indirectly—through damage to the national infrastructure and systems of public hygiene and health;[224] but it includes the deaths of civilian insurgents and of their victims.[225]

Even though it is considerably lower than the Burnham estimate, this figure of almost 200,000 violent civilian deaths betokens suffering on a massive scale. However, the liberation of Europe from Nazi domination cost the lives of 70,000 French civilians and about 600,000 German ones through British and American bombing. Estimates of the number of German civilians who died as a result of expulsion by the Red Army rise as high as 2.2 million, though recent analysis suggests a more sober figure of 500,000 to 600,000. The point here is not that Saddam Hussein was a tyrant as evil as Adolf Hitler (although the difference between them was more one of opportunity than of inclination). Nor does it assert a general analogy between the war against Hitler and the invasion of Iraq. The point is rather that Allied belligerency, which is very widely regarded as just, nevertheless involved massive civilian casualties; and that therefore massive civilian casualties in Iraq do not *by themselves* suffice to render the 2003 invasion unjust.

Moreover, whereas the deaths of French and German civilians in the Second World War were the direct responsibility of the British and Americans, the majority of Iraqi civilian deaths are directly attributable to foreign or native insurgents. Not being a utilitarian, I do not regard an agent as *equally* responsible for *all* the effects of his action. No agent is primarily responsible for the reactions of other agents. Sunni or Shia insurgents and al-Qaeda agents were not compelled to send suicide bombers into crowded marketplaces or to hack off the heads of hostages. They chose to do so. And even if they were motivated by nationalist or Islamist resentment at foreign or Western intrusion, that is not a sufficient warrant. Neither nationalism nor Islamism is its own moral justification. Sometimes foreign intervention is morally right, and should be accepted. So, yes, the occupying powers had an obligation to maintain law and order, in which they failed initially. But the insurgents also had a moral obligation not to intentionally target civilians; and that is one in which they have failed persistently.

224. Burnham et al. estimate 53,938 indirect deaths ('Mortality after the 2003 invasion of Iraq', p. 1421).
225. Burnham et al. report that 31 per cent of violent deaths were attributable to the Coalition's forces and 24 per cent to 'others'; 46 per cent were unattributable ('Mortality after the 2003 invasion of Iraq', p. 1425).

In addition to causing disproportionate damage, the Coalition's forces sometimes intentionally harmed non-combatants, most infamously at Abu Ghraib. The invasion and occupation of Iraq, therefore, was morally blemished. But, then, so was the war against Hitler—by the RAF's (arguably) indiscriminate bombing of German cities, by the not uncommon shooting in cold blood of German prisoners of war by US troops during the Battle of Normandy,[226] and by the Red Army's rape of an estimated two million German women.[227] Action by human individuals is often morally marred. Collective action of any kind, involving tens of thousands or even millions of individual agents, is *bound* to be marred. This raises a particular question about the relationship between parts and wholes: When do instances of negligence or malice so vitiate the whole of a collective action so as to make it basically unjust and oblige that it cease? Answer: when the instances are symptoms of a basic flaw. For example, it might be that carelessness about harm to non-combatants is widespread in a particular military, because the basic intention in fighting is not actually the rectification of injustice at all, but rather the assertion of dominance or the wreaking of revenge. On the other hand, the root of criminal carelessness might be local rather than systemic: for example, poor leadership by officers in the field. One sign that vice is accidental rather than essential to an operation is that, upon discovery, it is publicly renounced and rooted out. The fact that the Coalition's troops have been prosecuted and convicted of crimes therefore serves to limit the significance of their wrongdoing.

XIV. Collecting the elements

We have now considered the Iraq invasion and its aftermath in the light of all of the criteria of just war. With a view to constructing an overall judgement, I shall first gather together its main elements. The invasion's cause was a twofold injustice: a characteristically and massively atrocious state, together with the international threat posed by its possession of WMD. The first was sufficient cause for just regime-change. Had Saddam gov-

---

226. Beevor, *D-Day*, pp. 24, 106, 121, 153, 158, 438.
227. Beevor, *Berlin*, p. 410.

erned one of the member states of the United States, or even one of the German *Länder*, he would not have been tolerated by Washington or Berlin and would have been removed years before. He was only able to remain in power for lack of responsible and effective global government. The second injustice was not required to render the first sufficient as a cause for war, but it was required to give the United States, the United Kingdom, and others sufficient interest in taking that cause up.

The invasion was not clearly—in the sense of simply and uncontroversially—illegal. The Coalition rendered itself accountable to the international community at the UN. It made a reasonable case that Security Council authorization for the use of force had already been given, albeit a case that was not the strongest and did not win majority support. In addition, a primary aim of invasion—Iraq's permanent disarmament of WMD—was one that the Council itself had repeatedly affirmed. At very least, all this serves to give the invasion a measure of legality. Whether or not this measure was sufficient is moot; but even if it were not, the case of Kosovo has established the precedent of an intervention that is widely regarded (even by lawyers) *as at once illegal and (morally) legitimate*. So the invasion of Iraq was not clearly illegal, but even if it was, that alone does not prevent it from being morally right.

In going to war, the Coalition's intention was rooted in the just causes. There is no evidence that the invasion was undertaken *primarily* to secure oil supply or to improve Israel's strategic position. If these were motives at all, they were secondary and peripheral. The invasion was undertaken primarily out of revulsion at the character of Saddam Hussein's regime, and to avert what was perceived to be the threat of such a regime possessing WMD, especially nuclear weapons. The basic intention of the invasion was to bring about a change of regime for the better, both internally and externally. Adjunct to this were the hopes that regime-change in Iraq would deter similar regimes from the pursuit of WMD, and that it would naturally encourage beneficial political change throughout the Middle East. I call these 'hopes' rather than intentions, because they had not been crystallized into a plan of action.

Was invasion in 2003 a last resort? With regard to dealing effectively with the threat posed by Iraq's possessing chemical and biological weapons and coming to possess nuclear ones, invasion seemed (reasonably) at the time like a last resort. In retrospect, however, it was not. Yet, with regard to removing a characteristically atrocious regime, it was.

On the eve of the invasion of Iraq, there was no reason to suppose that any intolerable risks were about to be taken—for example, that Iraq would retaliate with nuclear weapons against Western cities. The invasion held out hope of a range of significant benefits: an efficient conventional military victory, issuing in the liberation of the Iraqi people, spontaneous national self-reconstruction, the removal of a particular WMD threat, the deterrence of others, and the establishment of a regional beacon-on-the-hill. The national interest seemed sufficiently engaged to maintain domestic political support. The cost in blood and treasure looked affordable.

However, with the benefit of hindsight, it is now clear that decision-makers in Washington and London made misjudgements, some of them vincible and culpable. Non-culpably, they overestimated the imminence of the WMD threat. Culpably, they considerably underestimated the challenges attending the task of national reconstruction, and so the difficulty of regime-*change*. In particular, they were quite unrealistic in their assumption that Iraq was ready for rapid transformation into a viable liberal democracy. Consequently, they seriously underestimated the costs even of replacing Saddam Hussein's regime with something tolerably better. These are all valid criticisms. Nevertheless, it cannot be said that the ends sought were unworthy, the eventually adopted means subversive of the ends, the risks intolerable, or the actual costs unaffordable.

The invasion of Iraq intended worthwhile goals, without taking intolerable risks, and at costs that, while much higher than expected, were still affordable. Notwithstanding all this, the prospect of success could still have been poor or negligible. Was it, in fact? The prospect of defeating Iraq's military forces was high. The *realistic* prospect of transforming Iraq swiftly into a viable liberal democracy was always low, but that of creating a tolerably better regime was higher; and had the pre-war planning been less optimistic, it would have been higher still. In some cases it can be right to go to war with little prospect of success—say, to defend oneself against a wicked enemy whose triumph would be ruthlessly and widely atrocious. Sometimes it is noble to fight in a virtually lost cause. The Coalition's belligerency against Iraq in 2003 was not such a desperate case. It would not have been prudent to entertain the risks and hazards of war, if the prospect of exchanging Saddam Hussein's regime for something significantly better had been clearly negligible. However, given what has *in fact* been achieved since 2003— democratically elected governments no longer in pursuit of WMD, accountable to the international community, and responsible to the Shi'ite majority; sufficient political stability and security to host an economic revival; and a semi-autonomous Kurdistan freed from the shadow of state terror—a pre-invasion assessment that rated the prospect of success as considerable would have been realistic.

The conduct of the invasion, and especially of post-invasion counter-insurgency operations, was marred by instances of indiscriminate and disproportionate harm to civilians and prisoners. Such instances deserve moral criticism, for sure, but do they establish the basic injustice of the invasion, such that it should never have been launched? They would establish it if they betokened a deeper, basic flaw—such as the insincerity of the declared intention to exchange Saddam Hussein's regime for something tolerably better. However, the fact that many of those accused of abuses have been tried, convicted, and sentenced is strong evidence that their conduct was incidental, not essential.

Let me summarize these various points in a crude list of the credits and debits of the 2003 invasion of Iraq. To its credit are: two just causes; a reasonable legal case in favour of the Security Council's authorization; right intention; last resort with regard to the just cause of rectifying a characteristically atrocious regime; the reasonable belief in last resort with regard to the just cause of stopping Iraq's acquisition of WMD; proportionate means of invasion; a high prospect of success in toppling the regime; and some prospect of changing it for the better.

In the debit column are the following factors: the threat of WMD appeared more imminent than it actually was, and the invasion was therefore not in fact a last resort in dealing with *that* injustice; the legal case was not optimal and did not persuade many states; the means of regime-reconstruction were originally ill-proportioned to the end, resulting in greater evils than were necessary; realistically, the prospect of success in establishing full-blown liberal democracy was not high, while the prospect of doing so in short order was non-existent; and the occupation was flawed by instances of indiscriminate abuse of civilian detainees and, arguably, by disproportionate harm to civilians. Several of these flaws are susceptible of mitigation: the Coalition worked successfully to improve the proportion of its means to beneficial regime-change; although the prospect of installing liberal democracy was negligible, that of replacing Saddam Hussein's regime with something tolerably better was higher; at least some of those responsible for abusing detainees were punished; and heavy-handed military tactics resulting in disproportionate civilian casualties were changed for a counter-insurgency strategy focused on population protection.

XV. How should we construct judgement?

There lie the materials. Now we must build a judgement out of them. But how is that to be done? For Craig White, the answer is straightforward. For the Iraq war to have been just, it must meet all of the relevant criteria: '[g]enerally, the failure to say "yes" to any of the criteria, should lead to the evaluation "unjust" for the entire war...[A]ny planned war that failed to meet even one of the criteria would, in fact, be seriously unjust in some way.'[228] In asserting the equal importance of all the criteria and the equal necessity of meeting each of them, White aligns himself with the *Catholic Catechism*[229] against James Turner Johnson's distinction between 'the deontological core of the tradition' and the prudential criteria, and against his downgrading of the latter as merely 'supportive'.[230] Rhetorically (and with a telling degree of exaggeration) White asks: 'How could a war be just if the planners made no calculations about the likely harm a war would cause, or, worse, calculated beforehand that it was likely to cause more harm than it solved?'[231] Such a calculation 'must include all the likely or reasonably possible consequences of war', although, to be at all reliable, it 'should generally be limited to five years in the past, and five years in the future'.[232] Specifically, regime-change should only be attempted 'if you can be reasonably confident that the balance of good and evil in the future regime, MINUS the evil involved in war, scores higher than leaving the existing regime in place (including goods and evils over the next five years)'.[233] According to White's own analysis, the 2003 Iraq war 'clearly' failed to satisfy five of the six classic just war criteria.[234] While my own analysis is far less damning than his, it still fails to meet his demanding standard. As I see it, the war's legal footing was not optimal, it was not a last resort with respect to the problem of WMD, its realistic prospects of success in regime-reconstruction were uncertain, its means were initially ill proportioned to that end, and it involved some indiscriminate and disproportionate killing of civilians. Thus to the question,

---

228. White, *Iraq*, p. 12; see also p. 21.
229. Ibid., pp. 20, 21, 257.
230. Johnson, *War to Oust Saddam Hussein*, pp. 38, 59.
231. White, *Iraq*, p. 21.
232. Ibid., pp. 162, 173.
233. Ibid., p. 174. The capitalization of 'minus' is the author's.
234. Ibid., p. 257. The one criterion that it did meet, according to White, was the requirement of sovereign authority (ibid., p. 31).

'Did the Iraq war meet all the relevant criteria?', I return only a qualified 'Yes' on five counts and a 'No' on a sixth. Judging my analysis by White's standard, therefore, we must conclude that the invasion was unjust.

David Fisher's reasoning is similar to White's. He tells us that just war criteria 'are designed to make it difficult to go to war';[235] that they set '[t]he evidential bar...high...[because of] the grim logic of war, where the suffering caused is certain, while the gains...are less certain';[236] that in particular 'the benefits of regime-change are uncertain, whereas the disadvantages of military action are only too evident';[237] and that therefore steps need to be taken 'to *ensure* that war would not cause more harm than good'.[238] With regard to the case of Iraq, he argues that there were 'doubts' and 'concerns' about each of the criteria; that '[t]he war failed fully to meet any of the criteria that need to be satisfied'; that 'crucially, no adequate assessment was undertaken before military action was authorized to *ensure* that the harm likely to result would not be disproportionate to the good achieved'; and that 'such individual failures, when taken together, mutually reinforced each other, so building up cumulatively to support the conclusion that the war was undertaken, in particular, without sufficient just cause and without adequate planning to ensure a just outcome. It thus failed the two key tests.'[239] Again, even if we take my less damning analysis, it still produces a negative verdict, when subjected to Fisher's standard.

I doubt, however, that White's and Fisher's standards are reasonable. First, I disagree with Craig White that each of the criteria carries equal weight, and I agree with Johnson that the deontological criteria of just cause, legitimate authority, right intention, and last resort are clearly decisive with regard to *ius ad bellum*, while the prudential criteria of prospect of success and proportionality are not. This is partly because the former are always required, whereas a good prospect of success is not. In some cases it might be right, indeed heroic, to fight against a very evil enemy with quite poor prospects of prevailing—as did Britain in the wake of Dunkirk in May 1940. The higher the stakes, the higher are the risks worth taking. Further, I agree with Johnson because the deontological criteria are susceptible of definite determination to a degree that proportionality is not. Whereas an agent has control over whether his

235. Fisher, *Morality and War*, p. 205.
236. Ibid., p. 206.
237. Ibid., p. 209.
238. Ibid., p. 206. The emphasis is mine.
239. Ibid., pp. 208, 216–17. The emphasis is mine.

intention is rooted in just cause and whether he is patient in exhausting all available and reasonable alternatives to war, he does not have control over the future. Consequently, his painstaking efforts to choose the most efficient (least costly) means of achieving his just end can easily be thwarted by a multitude of variable factors that he could not possibly have foreseen or predicted. Further still, lack of just cause, legitimate authority, right intention, or the status of last resort is always sufficient to render a war irredeemably unjust. So too is ill-proportion between war *as war* and the end of rectifying grave injustice. However, *particular strategic, operational, and tactical forms of warfare* can be disproportionate (in the sense of inefficient) and yet not render the war as a whole irredeemably unjust. Thus, as I argued in Chapter Four, Britain's sometimes culpably inefficient attritional warfare did not subvert the basic justice of her war against Wilhelmine Germany. A basically just enterprise can be marred without being corrupted. Defective parts do not always infect their whole. Unless the *in bello* disproportion is somehow rooted in the very intentionality of a war (in which case the intentionality itself must already be corrupt), it can be corrected without disturbing the war's basic and just rationale. In brief, I do not agree that failure to meet the criteria of prospect of success or *in bello* proportionality is sufficient to render a war unjust as a whole.

Second, as will now be clear, I regard as impossible the kind of consequential calculation required by White, with its pretension to mathematical precision ('the balance of good and evil...MINUS...scores higher'). The fact that he feels the need to impose a 'somewhat arbitrary' limit of five years in the future indicates that he recognizes the problem of capturing all the relevant effects. However, the problem is not solved—at least not rationally—by arbitrarily deciding to ignore what cannot be seen. But what else can we do? We can remember how much we do not and cannot know. We can be mindful of the known unknowns, and require only a conscientious estimate, not an accurate calculation.

Third, I do not quite agree with David Fisher that just war criteria are designed 'to make it difficult' to go to war. Of course, since war invariably causes grave evils, the criteria are designed to govern and constrain it—and in that sense 'to make it difficult'. By the same token, however, they are designed to permit war—even to oblige it—under certain conditions, and not to make it so difficult in practice to wage morally as to issue in 'a functional pacifism'.[240] Yet this is what Fisher does when he enjoins that

---

240. Johnson, *The War to Oust Saddam Hussein*, pp. 26–32. Johnson traces this kind of just war thinking back to the US Catholic bishops' 1983 pastoral letter, *The Challenge of Peace*.

steps must be taken 'to ensure' the consequential predominance of good over harm. As I have already made plain, I think that determining the future consequences of one's actions with any precision or finality is impossible, given their vulnerability to the free choices of other agents and to natural hazards; that the so-called 'weighing up' of goods and evils is usually irrational, given their incommensurability; that what purport to be 'net balances' produced by 'calculations' are invariably little more than the rationalizations of prejudice; and that it is therefore entirely beyond human power to ensure the predominance of good over evil.

How should we explain this loading of the dice against the permission of war? One reason that Fisher gives is that the evils of war are certain, while its gains are less certain. That is both true and untrue. It is certain *that* war will cause evils, but it is not certain *what* evils a particular war will cause. So we are not weighing a certain quantity of evil against an uncertain quantity of good. For sure, it is certain that war of any kind will cause some evil, and it might not be certain that it will achieve any good. And yet, depending on the circumstances, a war's efficient achievement of great good might be highly probable. Besides, the evils and goods of war are not the only factors to be taken into account. We must also factor in the evils of peace. It might well be quite as certain that peace will permit great evils as that punitive war will cause them. Peace is not simple, but complex. Of course, *our* not continuing war in 1991 and *our* not going to war in 1994 and 1995 meant peace for *us*. But it also meant leaving at peace Saddam Hussein, the Rwandan Hutus, and the Bosnian Serbs to perpetrate mass murder. And it did not mean peace at all for hundreds of thousands of Marsh Arabs, Tutsis, and Bosnian Muslims. We cannot make the general presumption that war results in more evil than not-war.

Nevertheless, we might make a presumption against permitting war, because we think that governments are prone to go to war when they should not, rather than not to go to war when they should. That might have been the case at certain times and in certain places, and it might still be the case today; but it is not so universally. In particular, it is not so in contemporary Europe. General Sir Rupert Smith, who commanded the United Nations' forces in Bosnia in 1995 and went on to be Deputy Supreme Allied Commander in NATO, nicely describes (European) international deliberation about the use of military force as 'a hotbed of cold feet',[241] and concludes

241. Smith, *The Utility of Force*, p. 344. The memorable phrase was coined by Field Marshall Lord Vincent.

from his experience that 'one of the endemic problems of our modern conflicts is the lack of political will to employ force rather than deploy forces—meaning will is close to zero—which is why many military interventions fail'.[242]

For these reasons, among others already stated, I am disinclined to load the dice against the justification of war by foregrounding the prudential criteria of the prospect of success and proportionality in its consequentialist form—that is, the allegedly 'overall' weighing of goods and evils, as distinct from the proportioning of means to ends—and then by insisting upon spurious 'calculations' that pretend to predict the future and weigh up incommensurables with an impossible accuracy.

In addition to insisting upon an ensured predominance of good over harm, Fisher also requires that the criteria be met 'fully', that is, beyond doubt and concern. My objection to this is that if wars are required to be beyond doubt or concern, then no war can be just, since any war is vulnerable to *someone's* doubting it. So whose doubt counts?

Finally, Fisher tells us that, in the case of Iraq, multiple individual shortcomings accumulated—added up—to a comprehensive injustice. But *how*, exactly? Large-scale, corporate human ventures invariably suffer from an array of shortcomings, but we do not usually think that this invalidates them. Why should we do so with regard to Iraq? We need to see the 'arithmetic' spelt out. And when it is, I wager that we will see that, while it might be reasonable, it is not arithmetic at all.

So, I disagree with White that the criteria are all equally decisive and I disagree with Fisher that they can ever be met beyond doubt. The criterion of just cause is absolutely basic. Without it, none of the other criteria gets off the ground. With it, the question arises of who has the authority to take it up belligerently. If that is not satisfied, we need proceed no further. But if we may proceed, then we must ask whether the legitimate authority will wage war *in order* to rectify the basic injustice or in order to do something else merely on its pretext. If the answer is the former—if the intention really is governed by the desire to correct the basic injustice—then it is likely that the choice of means will be governed by what that correction requires. For why else would it have come under consideration at all? That is to say, it is likely that war, generally speaking, will be well-proportioned to its end. However, even if war would serve to realize our good intention, there might be an alternative instrument that promises to be equally effective

242. Smith, *The Utility of Force*, p. 243.

and far less hazardous and costly. If so, then war would not be a last resort. At this point we have entered the foggier territory of the unavoidably crude estimation of risk and prediction of future consequences, and in considering the prospect of success and *in bello* proportionality we enter even deeper. Our estimations are morally bound to be conscientious and circumspect, but they are not bound to be accurate. They cannot be, for it is humans, not gods, who must make them.[243]

XVI. Iraq: the verdict

Now, at long last, we have to hand both the materials and a method for building a judgement and reaching a verdict. What should it be? Was it right or wrong to invade Iraq? Was it just or unjust? Had the invasion lacked

---

243. I observe that my view here echoes that of von Clausewitz in 1807–8:

> The skill and all the moral qualities that can be evoked in war are extremely difficult to estimate and compare with the [weak] physical forces, for which one wants them to compensate. Moreover, the realm of possible occurrences—the series of consequences—that a human action generates is infinite, and human understanding can never arrive at the final result of this whole calculation. This consideration should be borne in mind by those who, with some kind of demanding precision, want never to transgress the limit of what is probable. In the court of reason it justifies those who get involved in ventures whose good success is just possible, but nevertheless improbable. Therefore the motivating cause should be sufficient—that is, the importance of the end must be proportionate to the danger incurred. There is no political end more important than that of the independence of the state and the nation. This must be pursued in even the greatest of dangers. [Das Talent und alle moralischen Grössen, welche man im Kriege geltend machen kann, sind äusserst schwer zu schätzen und mit den phisischen Kräften zu vergleichen, welche man dadurch ausgleichen will. Ueberdem is das Reich möglicher Ereignisse, die Reihe von Folgen, welche eine Handlung erzeugt, unendlich und das endliche Resultat dieses ganzen *Calculs* also auch nie für den menschlichen Verstand zu erreichen. Diese Betrachtung sollten diejenigen anstellen, welche mit einer Art anspruchsvoller Praezision die Grenze des Wahrscheinlichen nie überschreiten wollen. Sie rechtfertigt vor dem Richterstuhl der Vernunft diejenigen, welche sich auf Unternehmungen einlassen, deren guter Erfolg blos möglich, übrigens aber unwahrscheinlich ist.. Nur muss dann die bewegende Ursache hinreichend seyn, d.h. die Wichtigket des Zwekes im Verhältniss stehen zu der Gefahr, welche man dabey läuft. Es giebt aber keiner politisch wichtigern Zwek als die Unabhängigkeit des Staates und der Nation. Diesen muss man unter den größten Gefahren verfolgen. ('Über die künftigen Kriegs-Operationen Preußens gegen Frankreich', in Carl von Clausewitz, *Schriften—Aufsätze—Briefe*, Deutsche Geschichtsquellen des 19. und 20. Jahrhunderts, vol. 45, ed. Werner Hahlweg, 2 vols [Göttingen: Vandenhoeck & Ruprecht, 1966], pp. 78–9)]

I agree that precision in estimating consequences and success is impossible, and that therefore considerations of the importance of the motivating cause and consequent intended end, and the latter's relation to the risks incurred, should move to the forefront of deliberation. I do not agree, however, that the independence of the nation-state is the most important end. That is rather the rectification of grave injustice, which may—or may *not*—involve the maintenance of national independence.

a sufficient just cause or a reasonable claim to legitimate authority, had its primary intentions not been generated by the just cause, had war been launched when alternative effective means were available, or had it been a means ill-proportioned to the rightly intended end, then it would have been clearly unjust. According to my analysis, however, the Iraq invasion commanded two just causes (a characteristically atrocious regime and the threat of its possession of WMD), a reasonable (if not optimal) claim to legitimate authority, right intention grounded in both just causes, last resort with regard to one and non-culpable lack of last resort with regard to the other.

The fact that the second just cause—the threat of WMD—turned out not to be imminent, that a belligerent defence need not have been offered in March 2003, and that time could have been allowed to permit alternative solutions to emerge, does weaken the domestic political case for war. It weakens the national interest of the United States and the United Kingdom in taking up the first just cause, and so it weakens the reason why American and British soldiers (as distinct from any others) should have sacrificed their lives. It weakens, but it does not dissolve. As I argued in Chapter Five, nations have an interest in moral self-respect, and my perception is that what soldiers want is a basic assurance that they are risking life and limb for some good purpose, not necessarily that this comprises the safety of their kith and kin.[244] Dislodging an atrocious tyrant like Saddam Hussein and opening up the possibility of a healthier political future for the Iraqi people were good things to do. What is more, even though the WMD threat to the United States and the United Kingdom was neither direct nor mature, it remained substantial and persistent. By itself it did not warrant war. But there was nothing wrong in solving it in the course of correcting the grave injustice of a characteristically atrocious regime, for which war was necessary. The invasion therefore served two kinds of legitimate national interest.

The remaining prudential and *in bello* criteria can be decisive in determining the overall justice of the war, but only indirectly. If the realistic prospect of success in beneficial regime-change had been nil, then that would suggest that the Coalition's purported intention to rectify the injustice

---

244. Richard B. Miller discusses this issue in his article, 'Justifications of the Iraq War Examined' (*Ethics and International Affairs*, 22/1 [Spring 2008], pp. 54, 57, 65). I agree with him that military intervention for humanitarian purposes carries a heavier burden of moral proof than defensive war, since, beyond establishing that there is a grave injustice to be corrected, one must also explain why *we* should be the ones to bear the costs of correcting it. I think, however, that he distinguishes too sharply between national interest and altruism.

of an atrocious regime was insincere. The same would be true if the initially disproportionate counter-insurgency strategy had not been corrected, and if the indiscriminate abuse of detainees had not been stopped and those responsible punished. In fact, the prospect of regime-change for the better was a lot better than nil, the initial strategy was changed, the abuses were stopped and (at least some of) the abusers convicted and punished.

For sure, the war against Saddam Hussein suffered from some serious flaws. Excessive optimism, impatience with human frailty, managerial over-confidence, heedlessness of uncongenial counsel—all these vices generated an imprudence in the choice of means that caused unnecessary loss of life and jeopardized the establishment of security and the rule of law. Yet wars are human enterprises and all human enterprises are flawed, reflecting the limitations and the weaknesses and the disordered loves of the human agents who operate them. Of course, such vices and wrongdoing deserve criticism, even condemnation. Nevertheless, of themselves they do not determine that the operation as a whole should never have been started or that it should have ceased earlier than it did. The Allied war against Hitler was vitiated by instances of chauvinistic arrogance, personal conceit, overweening profes-sional ambition, vindictive hatred of the enemy, and ruthless carelessness of one's own troops; and it was marred by lies, the slaughter of prisoners, and, arguably, the indiscriminate killing of civilians on a massive scale. Yet none of that tells us that the Allies should have ceased fighting.

All things considered, therefore, I judge that the invasion of Iraq was justified.

Conclusion

I. Is it worth it?

In 2010 ninety-year-old Geoffrey Wellum looked back over seven decades to the summer he spent as an RAF fighter pilot in the Battle of Britain. 'I ask myself,' he mused, '"Was it worth it? Was it worth it? All those young men I fought and flew with? All those chaps who are no longer with us?" I ask myself that question and I can't answer it. I suppose it must have been. I suppose it must have been. I am still struggling.'[1]

So are we all. I have argued in this book that it is impossible to calculate with any precision or certainty whether the evils incurred by war outweigh the benefits achieved. It is impossible even in retrospect, because of the incommensurable variety of goods and evils. It is also impossible because the consequences of a war—as of any human act—run down the whole length of human history, and ramify throughout its breadth; and because that history is not yet over. What is impossible even in retrospect is all the more so in prospect.

From this one might conclude, as pacifists both Christian and otherwise do, that war can never be justified. Surely the burden of proof lies on those urging belligerency to demonstrate that its terrible costs will be outnumbered and outweighed by the benefits secured. If they cannot, the case for war has not been made and a non-belligerent response to grave injustice is morally preferable. This, as I said in Chapter One, is the strongest card in the pacifist's hand. Yet, as I have also argued, it cannot be presumed that a non-belligerent response would be less costly *overall*. It might well be less costly for us, but not necessarily for distant or future victims. Not-war is not

---

1. In 'First Light', Matthew Whiteman's 2010 BBC television dramatization of Wellum's wartime memoir, *First Light* (London: Viking, 2002).

simple: peace also has its evils. Therefore pacifism is obliged to justify itself, too.

In oblique testimony to this, most pacifists evidently feel the need to be optimistic about the future, holding that not-war will produce a happier result in the long run. Non-religious pacifists plant their hope for this in human nature. Thus Robert Holmes claims that a visitor from outer space, observing 'individual [human] beings' only in their 'personal lives' and apart from human history and international affairs, would conclude the following:

> Undoubtedly that virtually everyone values peace, happiness, and friendship; that most people love their families, desire basic creature comforts, and seek neither to suffer nor to cause pain to others; that they only rarely harm one another, and then do so mainly under duress or in fits of anger directed against friends or loved ones and regretted soon after; that while they can all be insensitive, and a few of them cruel, they for the most part treat those they know with friendly feeling and others with civility; and that most of them wish nothing more than to be left alone to work out their life plans according to their lights, which they do with varying degrees of success when given the chance.[2]

Holmes calls for the ditching of the Christian notion of the corruption of human nature. The ancient Greeks thought that 'wrongdoing is ultimately from ignorance.... that we have within ourselves the resources to lead a good life, provided only we put reason to work... Christianity reversed all of this.'[3] In the footsteps of Rousseau, or perhaps Jefferson, he finds the root of the problem not in human nature but in government:

> Human nature is not corrupt. But it can be tricked by the subtleties of complex social, political, and international systems... What is needed is a new perspective that sees the people of the world as arrayed, not basically against one another, but against the deceit, ignorance, and arrogance of governments and the ways of thinking that have produced them.[4]

In the light of this, Holmes suggests that, if enough people could be persuaded to renounce violence, they would make it impossible for their wicked political leaders to launch wars:

2. Holmes, *On War and Morality*, p. 9.
3. Ibid., pp. 263–4.
4. Ibid., pp. 290–1.

Now whether or not non-violence could have stopped Hitler once the war began, had enough German citizens acted responsibly with or without a commitment to nonviolence, but particularly with it, say, in the 1920s and early 1930s, fascism could never have advanced to the stage where it could be deemed necessary to reverse it by military means.[5]

Holmes was writing in 1989. Much more recently, his Enlightened anthropological optimism has found fresh expression in Steven Pinker's 800-page-long argument that violence among human beings is dramatically on the decline, and has been for several thousand years.[6]

What do I make of all this? As a considerably Augustinian Christian, rather than a Hobbesian atheist, I am not cynical about human beings. As I have made clear, I think that we are sometimes capable of moral nobility and heroism. At the same time, however, I do think that Augustine's biblically inspired insight into human psychology is far more deeply illuminating than that attributed to the ancient Greeks. The cause of our wrongdoing is not always or basically ignorance, but rather ill-ordered *love*. Our deepest problem is not that we do not know what is good or right or what are the facts, but that we love great goods too little and lesser goods too much.

Therefore I do not doubt that many, maybe most, human beings in a basically secure environment have no strong desire to harm others, might well be inclined to help them, and simply want to get on with living a tolerably satisfactory life, perchance to improve it. Nevertheless, my own tiny window onto the sum of human experience suggests that, even in a very comfortable environment, disordered loves give rise to reckless lusts, ruthless ambitions, and irritable frustrations that harm neighbours and rupture relationships. And when the environment becomes insecure—say, through economic crisis or the breakdown of law and order—human anxieties can easily become toxic. For sure, political leaders (and journalists) often play a major role in inciting the insecurities of ordinary citizens to the point of violence—not just Hitler in 1930s Germany, but also Radio-Television Libre des Mille Collines in Rwanda and Slobodan Milošević in Serbia in the 1990s. But, equally, it is ordinary citizens who lend themselves to incitement. Perhaps in 1989 it was plausible to blame belligerency on governments. Since then, however, we have witnessed mass atrocity at the hands of

---

5. Ibid., p. 275.
6. Steven Pinker, *The Better Angels of our Nature: The Decline of Violence in History and its Causes* (London: Viking, 2011).

popular mobs in Rwanda, of irregular militia in the Balkans, of graduate terrorists over Manhattan, and of part-time insurgents in Iraq and Afghanistan. It seems clear enough that the roots of violence come up from below as well as down from above.

It *might* be true that, *if* enough people could be persuaded to repudiate violence, war would become impossible. On this score, however, history is not encouraging. The common interests of the cannon-fodder class of international socialists throughout Europe did not prevent war in 1914, and the unprecedented strength of pacifist reaction to the carnage of the First World War did not prevent the rise of aggressive dictatorships and their provocation of a thrice more costly war two decades later. Besides, the unilateral renunciation of violence would not always solve the problem. Sometimes it would take two not to tango, since the absence of defence does not always remove the will to attack. Too often the defencelessness of the innocent fills the aggressor not with disarming shame but with contemptuous hatred. As for Pinker's own thesis, much of what he offers as empirical substantiation is little more than well-meaning speculation. My view is that of Mark Micale at the end of his *Times Literary Supplement* review: 'Pinker's book is a personal expression of moral idealism but not, alas, an account of historical reality.'[7]

Non-religious pacifists put their faith in the fundamental and ineradicable goodness of human nature. Christian pacifists doubt this, and they do so, I think, for good empirical and historical reasons. As a consequence they feel the need to put their faith in something (arguably) rather more reliable—the *super*human power of the goodness of God.[8] As we have seen, John

---

7. Mark Micale, 'Improvements', *Times Literary Supplement*, 9 March 2012, p. 25. Micale explains his fundamental criticism of Pinker's book thus: 'Methodologically, to compare and quantify all types of human violence across world cultures over the past 7,000 years is an impossible project...[T]he Pinker thesis is a vast over-simplification...I strongly doubt that any of the types of human hostility that he discusses—suicides, war deaths, civilian murders, wife beatings, criminal executions—have anything remotely like the sort of stable and coherent source base necessary to permit reliable statistical measurement on a long-term, universal scale' (ibid., p. 24).

8. I cannot help but point out the irony attending Robert Holmes's choice of the following quotation of Anne Frank for the closing page of his non-religious argument for pacifism: '[I]n spite of everything I still believe that people are really good at heart. I simply can't build up my hopes on a foundation consisting of confusion, misery, and death...I can feel the sufferings of millions and yet, *if I look up into the heavens*, I think that it will all come right, that this cruelty too will end, and that peace and tranquillity will return again' (*On War and* Morality, p. 295. The emphasis is mine). What can Frank's reference to the heavens be other than an expression of religious hope in divine aid? Some might retort that it was merely a figure of speech. But if so, what *exactly* did it signify?

Howard Yoder and Stanley Hauerwas are both highly sceptical of the power of human beings to control history and make it turn out right, especially by violent means. They therefore renounce any such attempt, assuming a pacifist stance in faithful reflection of, and witness to, God's saving power. They insist that such a stance is right regardless of its efficacy. That may well be so, but their insistence sometimes sports such nonchalance as to give the impression that they care not one way or another whether their testimony is effective. That makes no sense. While not every witness need care about the outcome of what he says, a Christian witness must. One cannot reflect and testify to the God who invested himself deeply in the world through Jesus, in order to rescue it and bring it to fulfilment, without sharing in such an investment. One cannot reflect God without loving the world that God loves. To love is to want to benefit, and to love sincerely is to *try* to benefit. Christian pacifists, therefore, must take their pacifist stance out of love for the world and so because they view the unilateral renunciation of violence as optimally beneficial in the (very) long run. That it should prove to be so is, given the vicissitudes of history, not in their control. Nor, therefore, is it in their power to predict or demonstrate. But if that is so, then Christian pacifists are in exactly the same boat as Christian just warriors: they too cannot *demonstrate* that their chosen response to grave injustice will be less costly and more beneficial than the alternative. They trust and hope and pray that it will be, but they cannot prove it.

What reason might we have, then, to choose just war over not-war? One reason is this: that human experience teaches that wickedness, unpunished, tends to wax. Sometimes, of course, wrongdoers are so shamed by defenceless innocence that they renounce their wrongdoing. But history suggests at most that this is rare, and at least that it cannot be relied upon. It is highly doubtful, it seems to me, that Gandhi would have embarrassed and softened Hitler, Stalin, Mao, Pol Pot, the Interahamwe, Ratko Mladić, or Saddam Hussein. Violent domination can be a powerful addiction; and, judging not only by SS fanatics but also by the civilian policemen who committed mass murder in Poland and the USSR as members of the *Einsatzgruppen*,[9] human beings are quite capable of hardening themselves against compassion. Their wickedness is excited, not sickened, by impunity. We have already seen atrocious power at work on a continental scale (the Nazi empire) and endure

---

9. Christopher R. Browning, *Ordinary Men: Reserve Police Battalion 101 and the Final Solution in Poland* (New York: HarperCollins, 1992).

for generations (in the Stalinist USSR and in Maoist China). There is no reason in principle, nor any in practice, why it could not come to achieve global dominance. That is why effective retribution is so important.

When Geoffrey Wellum found himself perplexed by the question of whether the deaths of all his comrades in the Battle of Britain were 'worth it', he might have been flirting with the possibility that they were not. But I doubt it. More likely he was recognizing that the question is an impossible one to answer either way. However good it was to contribute to regime-change in Berlin, the premature and violent deaths of his young comrades were an irreducible and tragic loss, for which no benefit can compensate. Had he posed himself an alternative question, 'Was it right?' I suspect that he would have been less puzzled. Given the atrocious nature and ambition of the unjust aggression that the young RAF pilots faced, given its serially cynical lack of good faith in pacific negotiation, and given the lack of *manifest* disproportion in their opposition, Wellum's comrades were right to fight.

II. Epilogue: reflection on the role of the ethicist

In this book I have not confined myself to articulating general moral principles and rules, but have ventured to craft moral judgements about three particular military ventures: the British prosecution of the First World War in 1914–18, NATO's intervention in Kosovo in 1999, and the American-led Coalition's invasion of Iraq in 2003. In order to do this, I have had to make historical and empirical judgements about the facts of the case, and prudential ones about consequences and probabilities. I am, however, merely a moral theologian. I am not a minister of state, a diplomat, an intelligence officer, or a soldier. I am not even a political scientist, a scholar of international relations, or an expert on the Middle East. Have I not, then, ventured far beyond my competence?

Some would appear to suggest so. James Turner Johnson, for example, follows Paul Ramsey in holding that 'as a class, moralists have no particular experience with the prudential exercise of statecraft'.[10] While they can

---

10. Johnson, *The War to Oust Saddam Hussein*, p. 37. Concern about the presumptuousness of professional ethicists motivates Johnson's assertion of the primacy of the just war criterion of legitimate authority. In Aquinas's treatment of war, he tells us, 'the requirement of sovereign authority has the first priority. The logic of his argument places the responsibility to determine whether there is a just cause, [etc.]...among the responsibilities of the sovereign...This

judge what is just or unjust, on matters of prudence or wisdom they may only advise.[11] Oliver O'Donovan, formerly Ramsey's student, assumes a similar position, when he writes that '[a]ny private contribution to a current political debate...is not...in a position to offer precise recommendations'.[12] These words of caution are especially cogent, where (as in O'Donovan's case) they address academic and ecclesiastical critics of government policy *in medias res* or at least just before, since those not in the driving seat might be able to ask the right questions but are very probably not in a position to give conclusive answers. However, since Johnson was writing about twenty months after the Iraq invasion, his remarks apply more generally. They apply after the fact, and not just before and during it.

I appreciate the problem, but I doubt the solution. The problem is that of the ethicist overreaching his competence, speaking with greater confidence than he has a right to, impressing others more than he deserves to, and eventually damaging his own moral authority. The solution proposed is that he should withhold himself from making definite judgements—especially over matters of prudence. I both agree and disagree. I agree that, in order to compose a judgment, ethicists are bound to depend heavily on others for trustworthy information about the historical, political, military, and technical facts, and for estimates of probability and risk. I also agree that they need to show appropriate sympathy for those who are burdened with the responsibilities of democratic government, without the leisure for reflection and prevarication that academics, journalists, and clergy enjoy. I agree, too, that, in uncertain advance of the event and in the foggy midst of it, the judgement of an ethicist should often be conditional ('*If* x is the case, *then*...').

I disagree, however, for three reasons. One reason is that, if an informed ethicist is not in a position to offer precise judgements, albeit conditional,

contrasts markedly with a recent trend in just war thought to consider just cause as prior to right authority. One wonders whether contemporary moralists wish implicitly to reserve to themselves the right to make the final judgment as to just cause, even though they bear no responsibility for the consequences of their decision' (James Turner Johnson, 'Thinking Morally about War in the Middle Ages and Today', in Henrik Syse and Gregory Reichberg, eds, *Ethics, Nationalism and Just War: Medieval and Contemporary Perspectives* [Washington, DC: Catholic University of America, 2007], p. 6).]

11. Johnson, *The War to Oust Saddam Hussein*, pp. 24, 67.
12. O'Donovan, *The Just War Revisited*, p. 127. I note that O'Donovan's view here differs from taken by William Temple, who in *Christianity and the Social Order* (New York: Penguin, 1942) argued that whereas the church as a corporate body should deal only in the currency of general principles, individual churchmen may offer casuistic counsel in a private capacity (pp. 18–19).

then I do not know who else is. What the academic lacks in experience of public decision-making, for example, the politician lacks in time for mature reflection; and what the ethicist lacks in expertise about, say, Iraq, the Iraq pundit in the Foreign and Commonwealth Office is likely to lack in just war reasoning. So if moral judgements are to be made at all, then any judge will have to shoulder risks in making them, by entering territory where he is not entirely expert.

Second, an ethicist can best help a decision-maker by giving him options as thoroughly thought through as possible. It is not enough to hand him a set of abstract norms and rules, and then leave him to work out from scratch what they might require in the case before him. The meaning of moral rules is made manifest in terms of concrete cases. Therefore a fraternally responsible ethicist is bound to show the decision-maker, as concretely as he can, how the relevant rules impact on the empirical matter in hand—and, ideally, how that impact changes according to different understandings of the matter.

Finally, a third reason for pushing moral reasoning to a definite conclusion is that the very process of interpreting moral principles in relation to concrete particulars refines the principles and illuminates the reasoning. So, for example, it is only in the process of crafting judgements about the First World War and the Iraq invasion, for example, that the sheer impossibility of rational 'calculations' about proportion (in the sense of an overall 'net balance' of good over evil) has become clear to me; and it is only in relation to the Iraq invasion that the primacy of the criteria of just cause, right intention, and last resort—as well as the possibility of the *indirect* decisiveness of the prudential factors of discrimination and proportionality as they betoken intention—has become plain.

The *manner* of judgement matters, of course. To presume on clerical or academic status, and to pontificate or prophesy grandly out of political prejudice or factual ignorance or practical inexperience is one thing. But it is only one thing. An alternative is to work one's way laboriously to a definite judgement, laying out one's reasons for it as thoroughly as possible, dealing with objections as carefully and charitably as possible, taking for granted that any moral argument's cogency depends on its fallible grasp of the facts, and then to offer it up as a contribution to public deliberation and wait to see how it fares. Maybe it will survive the fire of public criticism and prove to be right—or at least, as right as anyone knows. But even if it should prove to be seriously mistaken, whether in fact or logic or premise, it will still have performed the good service of being a pebble in the shoe of public deliberation or understanding, provoking reflection and refinement. Sometimes one can think long and hard and conscientiously—and still turn out to be wrong. But where is the shame in that? And besides, if the truth wins out, then who loses? To adapt Martin Luther, we should risk erring boldly (though considerately) that truth may abound.

Bibliography

Aquinas, Thomas. *Summa Theologiae*. Ed. Thomas Gilby. London: Blackfriars with Eyre & Spottiswoode, 1964–81.

Arendt, Hannah. *The Human Condition*. Chicago: University of Chicago, 1958.

Ash, Timothy Garton. 'Vivid, Dark, Powerful and Magnificent—but Wrong'. In *The Independent*, 6 May 1999.

Ashdown, Paddy. *Swords and Ploughshares: Bringing Peace to the 21st Century*. London: Weidenfeld & Nicolson, 2007.

Augustine. *Against Faustus*. In O'Donovan and O'Donovan, *From Irenaeus to Grotius*.

——. *Contra Faustum Manichaeum*. In *Patrologia Cursus Completus*, Series Latina, ed. J.-P. Migne, vol. 42, *Augustini Opera Omnia*, vol. 8. Paris: J.-P. Migne, 1844–65.

——. *Letters*. Vol. I (1–82). Trans. Wilfrid Parsons. The Fathers of the Church, vol. 12. Washington, DC: Catholic University of America Press, 1951.

——. *On Free Will*. In *Augustine: Earlier Writings*. Ed. and trans. J.H.S. Burleigh. Library of Christian Classics. Philadelphia: Westminster Press, 1953.

——. *Reply to Faustus the Manichaean*. Trans. R. Stothert. In *A Select Library of the Nicene and Post-Nicene Fathers of the Christian Church*, ed. Philip Schaff, vol. IV (Grand Rapids: Eerdmans, 1956).

——. *The City of God*. Trans. Henry Bettenson. London: Penguin, 1972.

——. *Political Writings*. Ed. E.M. Atkins and R.J. Dodaro. Cambridge Texts in the History of Political Thought. Cambridge: Cambridge University Press, 2001.

Baehr, Peter. 'The Critical Path'. In the *Times Literary Supplement*, 31 January 2002.

Barnes, Jonathan. 'The Just War'. In *The Cambridge History of Later Medieval Philosophy*. Ed. Norman Kretzman, Anthony Kenny, Jan Pinborg, Eleonore Stump. Cambridge: Cambridge University Press, 1982.

Barr, Niall and Sheffield, Gary. 'Douglas Haig, the Common Soldier, and the British Legion'. In Brian Bond and Nigel Cave, *Haig: A Reappraisal Seventy Years On*. London: Leo Cooper, 1999.

Barry Rubin, 'British Government Plagiarises MERIA Material: Our Response': <http://meria.idc.ac.il/british-govt-plagiarizes-meria.html> (as at 17 December 2011).

Barth, Karl. *Church Dogmatics.* Vol. II, Part 2, 'The Doctrine of God'. Ed. G.W. Bromiley and T.F. Torrance. Edinburgh: T. & T. Clark, 1957.

——. *Church Dogmatics.* Vol. IV, Part 3.1, 'The Doctrine of Reconciliation'. Ed. G.W. Bromiley and T.F. Torrance. Edinburgh: T. & T. Clark, 1962.

Bean, C.E.W. *The Official History of Australia in the War of 1914–18.* Vol. III: 'The A.I.F. [Australian Imperial Force] in France, 1916'. Sydney: Angus and Robertson, 1929.

Beevor, Antony. *Berlin: The Downfall 1945.* London: Viking, 2002.

——. *The Battle for Spain: The Spanish Civil War, 1936–1939.* London: Weidenfeld and Nicholson, 2006.

——. *D-Day: The Battle for Normandy.* London: Viking, 2009.

Bellamy, Alex J. *Responsibility to Protect: The Global Effort to End Mass Atrocities.* Cambridge: Polity Press, 2009.

Bernard of Clairvaux. *Liber ad Milites Templi de laude novae militiae.* In *S. Bernardi Opera*, 8 vols, vol. III, ed. J. Leclerq and H.M. Rochais (Rome: Editiones Cistercienses, 1963).

Bernhardi, Friedrich von. *Germany and the Next War.* Trans. A.H. Powles. London: Edward Arnold, 1912.

Biggar, Nigel. 'On Giving the Devil Benefit of Law in Kosovo'. In *Kosovo: Contending Voices on Balkan Interventions.* Ed. William Joseph Buckley. Grand Rapids: Eerdmans, 2000.

——. *Burying the Past: Making peace and doing justice after civil conflict.* Washington, DC: Georgetown University Press, 2003.

——. *Aiming to Kill: The Ethics of Suicide and Euthanasia.* London: Darton, Longman, and Todd, 2004.

——. 'Anglican Theology of War and Peace'. In *Crucible*, 43/4 (October–December 2004): 7–20.

——. 'Between Development and Doubt: The Recent Career of Just War Doctrine in British Churches'. In Reed and Ryall, *The Price of Peace.*

——. 'Forgiving Enemies in Ireland'. In *Journal of Religious Ethics*, 36/4 (December 2008): 559–79.

——. 'The Ethics of Forgiveness and the Doctrine of Just War: A religious view of righting atrocious wrongs'. In *The Religious in Responses to Mass Atrocity: Interdisciplinary Perspectives.* Ed. Thomas Brudholm and Thomas Cushman. Cambridge: Cambridge University Press, 2009.

——. 'Specify and Distinguish! Interpreting the New Testament on "non-violence"'. In *Studies in Christian Ethics*, 22/2 (May 2009): 164–84.

——. 'Not Translation, but Conversation: Theology in Public Debate about Euthanasia'. In Biggar and Hogan, *Religious Voices in Public Places.*

——. 'Conclusion'. In Biggar and Hogan, *Religious Voices in Public Places.*

——. 'The New Testament and Violence: round two'. In *Studies in Christian Ethics*, 23/1 (February 2010): 73–80.

——. 'Reinhold Niebuhr and the Political Possibility of Forgiveness'. In *Reinhold Niebuhr and Contemporary Politics: God and Power.* Ed. Richard Harries and Stephen Platten. Oxford: Oxford University Press, 2010.

——'Melting the Icepacks of Enmity: Forgiveness and reconciliation in Northern Ireland'. In *Studies in Christian Ethics*, 24/2 (May 2011): 199–209.

——and Linda Hogan (eds). *Religious Voices in Public Places*. Oxford: Oxford University Press, 2009.

Bishop, Patrick. *Fighter Boys: Saving Britain 1940*. London: HarperCollins, 2003.

——. *3 Para*. London: Harper Press, 2007.

Black, Jeremy. *Warfare in the Western World, 1882–1975*. Chesham: Acumen, 2002.

Blair, Tony. 'Full Statement to the House of Commons, 18 March 2003'. In Cushman, *A Matter of Principle*.

——. *A Journey*. London: Hutchinson, 2010.

Blix, Hans. 'United Nations Security Council verbatim report', 4644th meeting, 8 November 2002: <http://www.globalissues.org/external/1441Speeches.pdf>, p. 3 (as at 17 August 2012).

——. 'Update on inspection' (to the UNSC), 27 January 2003: <http://www.un.org/Depts/unmovic/Bx27.htm> (as at 17 August 2012).

——. 'Oral introduction to the 12th quarterly report of UNMOVIC to the UNSC', 7 March 2003: <http://www.un.org/Depts/unmovic/SC7asdelivered.htm>, p. 4 (as at 17 August 2012).

——. *Disarming Iraq. The Search for Weapons of Mass Destruction*. London: Bloomsbury, 2004.

Bobbitt, Philip. *Terror and Consent. The Wars for the 21st Century*. London: Allen Lane, 2008.

Boesak, Willa. *God's Wrathful Children: Political Oppression and Christian Ethics*. Grand Rapids: Eerdmans, 1995.

Bolt, Robert. *A Man for All Seasons*. London: Heinemann, 1960.

Botman, H. Russel and Peterson, Robin M. (eds). *To Remember and to Heal: Theological and Psychological Reflections on Truth and Reconciliation*. Cape Town: Hutman and Rousseau, 1996.

Bourke, Joanna. *An Intimate History of Killing. Face-to-face Killing in Twentieth Century Warfare*. London: Granta, 1999.

British Broadcasting Corporation. 'UN Condemns Iraq on Human Right', 19 April 2002: <http://news.bbc.co.uk/1/hi/world/middle_east/1940050.stm> (as at 26 August 2012).

——. (BBC4). "Sandhurst". First broadcast on 3 October 2011.

——. (BBC Radio 4). "While the Boys are Away". First broadcast on Wednesday 16 March 2011.

Browning, Christopher R. *Ordinary Men: Reserve Police Battalion 101 and the Final Solution in Poland*. New York: HarperCollins, 1992.

Brownlie, Ian. 'Humanitarian Intervention'. In O'Connell, *International Law and the Use of Force*.

——. 'Thoughts on Kind-Hearted Gunmen'. In *Humanitarian Intervention and the United Nations*. Ed. Richard B. Lillich. Charlottesville: University Press of Virginia, 1973.

Burkeman, Oliver. 'Iraq Dumped WMDs Years Ago, says Blix'. In the *Guardian*, 18 September 2003.

Burleigh, Michael. *Moral Combat: A History of World War II*. London: HarperPress, 2010.

Burnham, G.; Lafta, R.; Doocy, S.; and Roberts, L. 'Mortality after the 2003 Invasion of Iraq: a Cross-sectional cluster sample survey'. In *The Lancet*, 368, 21 October 2006: 1421–8.

Burridge, Richard. *Imitating Jesus: An Inclusive Approach to New Testament Ethics*. Grand Rapids, MI: Eerdmans, 2007.

Bury, Patrick. 'Pointing North'. Unpublished paper, May 2009.

——. *Callsign Hades*. London: Simon & Schuster, 2011.

Butler, Joseph. *Fifteen Sermons*. Ed. W.R. Matthews. London: G. Bell & Sons, 1953.

Butler, Lord (Robin). *Review of Intelligence of Weapons of Mass Destruction*. HC 898. London: The Stationery Office, 2004.

Cajetan. *Commentary on Summa Theologiae*. In Reichberg, *The Ethics of War*.

Cavanaugh, T.A. *Double-Effect Reasoning: Doing Good and Avoiding Evil*. Oxford: Clarendon Press, 2006.

Chesterman, Simon. 'Hard Cases Make Bad Law: law, ethics, and politics in humanitarian intervention'. In *Just Intervention*. Ed. Anthony F. Lang. Washington, DC: Georgetown University Press, 2003.

——and Byers, Michael. 'Has US Power Destroyed the UN?' In *London Review of Books*, 29 April 1999.

Chirac, Jacques. 'Interview with M. Jacques Chirac, President of France', French Ministry of Foreign Affairs, 10 March 2003: <http://www.iraqwatch.org/government/France/MFA/france-mfa-chirac-031003.htm>, p. 5 (as at 17 August 2012).

Chulov, Martin; Marsh, Katherine; and Dehghan, Saeed Kamali. 'It is the Right of the People to Protest against Tyrants'. In the *Guardian*, 22 March 2011.

Churchill, Winston. *Great Contemporaries*. London: Thornton Butterworth, 1937.

Clark, Ian. *Waging War: A Philosophical Introduction*. Oxford: Clarendon Press, 1988.

Clarke, Richard A. *Against All Enemies: Inside America's War on Terror*. New York: Free Press, 2004.

Clausewitz, Carl von. 'Über die künftigen Kriegs-Operationen Preußens gegen Frankreich'. In Carl von Clausewitz, *Schriften—Aufsätze—Briefe*. Deutsche Geschichtsquellen des 19. und 20. Jahrhunderts, vol. 45. Ed. Werner Hahlweg. 2 vols. Göttingen: Vandenhoeck & Ruprecht, 1966.

——. *On War*. Ed. M. Howard and P. Paret. Princeton: Princeton University Press, 1976.

Clwyd, Anne. 'Why Did it Take You so Long to Get Here?'. In Cushman, *A Matter of Principle*.

Coady, C.A.J. *The Ethics of Armed Humanitarian Intervention*. Peaceworks No. 45. Washington, DC: United States Institute of Peace, 2002.

——*Morality and Political Violence*. Cambridge: Cambridge University Press, 2008.

Coates, A.J. *The Ethics of War*. Manchester: Manchester University Press, 1997.

Collier, P., Elliot, V.L., Hegre, H., Hoeffler, A., Reynal-Querol, M., and Sambanis, N. *Breaking the Conflict Trap: Civil war and development policy*. A World Bank Policy Research Report. Oxford: Oxford University Press, 2000.

Cooper, Robert. 'The Next Empire'. In *Prospect*, 67 (October 2001): 22–6.

Cornish, Paul. *The CBRN System. Assessing the Threat of Terrorist Use of Chemical, Biological, Radiological and Nuclear Weapons in the United Kingdom*. London: Royal Institute for International Affairs, 2007.

Corrigan, Gordon. *Mud, Blood, and Poppycock: Britain and the First World War*. London: Cassell, 2003.

Crawshaw, Steve. 'A Journey into the Unknown'. In *The Independent on Sunday*, 28 March 1999.

Cull, Nicholas John. *Selling War: The British Propaganda Campaign Against American 'Neutrality' in World War II*. New York: Oxford University Press, 1995.

Cushman, Thomas (ed.). *A Matter of Principle: Humanitarian Arguments for War in Iraq*. Berkeley, CA: University of California, 2005.

D'Este, Carlo. *Bitter Victory: The Battle for Sicily 1943*. Glasgow: Collins, 1988.

Dallek, Robert. *Franklin D. Roosevelt and American Foreign Policy, 1932–1945*. New York: Oxford University Press, 1979.

Daponte, Beth Osborne. 'Wartime estimates of Iraqi civilian casualties'. In *The International Review of the Red Cross*, 89/868 (December 2007): 943–57.

Daube, David. *The New Testament and Rabbinic Judaism*. London: Athlone, 1956.

Dennis, Gerald V. 'A Kitchener Man's Bit (1916–1918)'. London: Imperial War Museum, 1928.

Dill, Janina. 'Applying the Principle of Proportionality in Combat Operations'. Policy Briefing. Oxford: Oxford Institute for Ethics, Law, and Armed Conflict, 2010.

Doyle, Michael W. 'Striking First'. In *Striking First: Preemption and Prevention in International Conflict*. Ed. and intro. Stephen Macedo. Princeton: Princeton University Press, 2008.

Dunn, James D.G. *Romans 9–16*. Word Biblical Commentary, vol. 38B. Dallas: Word, 1988.

Egremont, Max. *Siegfried Sassoon ... A Biography*. London: Picador, 2005.

Ekeus, Rolf. 'Iraq's Real Weapons Threat'. In the *Washington Post*, 29 June 2003: <http://www.usembassy.it/file2003_07/alia/A3070202.htm> (as at 24 August 2012).

Ellis, Joseph J. *American Sphinx: The Character of Thomas Jefferson*. New York: Vintage, 1998.

Elshtain, Jean Bethke. *Just War against Terror: The burden of American power in a violent world*. New York: Basic Books, 2003.

Etherington, Mark. *Revolt on the Tigris. The Al-Sadr Uprising and the Governing of Iraq*. London: Hurst, 2005.

Evans, Gareth. *The Responsibility to Protect: Ending Mass Atrocity Crimes Once and for All*. Washington, DC: Brookings Institute, 2008.

Farer, Tom J. 'A Paradigm of Legitimate Intervention'. In *Enforcing Restraint: Collective Intervention in Internal Conflicts*. Ed. Lori Fisler Damrosch. New York: Council on Foreign Relations Press, 1993.

Fay, Sidney B. *The Origins of the World War*. 2 vols. New York: Macmillan, 1928.

Fiddes, Paul. *Past Event and Present Salvation: The Christian Idea of Atonement*. London: Darton, Longman, and Todd, 1989.

Finkel, David. *The Good Soldiers*. London: Atlantic Books, 2009.

Finnis, John. 'Intention and Side-Effects'. In *Liability and Responsibility*. Ed. R. Frey and C. Morris. Cambridge: Cambridge University Press, 1991.

Fischer, Fritz. *Germany's Aims in the First World War*. London: Chatto & Windus, 1967.

——. *War of Illusions: German Policies from 1911 to 1914*. London: Chatto & Windus, 1975.

Fisher, David. *Morality and War: Can War Be Just in the Twenty-first Century?* Oxford: Oxford University Press, 2011.

Foreign and Commonwealth Office. Foreign Policy Document No. 148, *The British Year Book of International Law*, 57 (1986): 614–20.

Freyne, Seán. *Jesus: A Jewish Galilean: A New Reading of the Jesus Story*. London and New York: T. & T. Clark, 2004.

Fromkin, David. *Europe's Last Summer: Why the World Went to War in 1914*. London: Heinemann, 2004.

Galbraith, Peter W. *The End of Iraq: How American Incompetence Created a War Without End* 2nd edn. New York: Simon & Schuster, 2007.

Gentili, Alberico. *On the Law of War*. In Reichberg, *Ethics of War*.

Gilbert, Martin. *Winston S. Churchill*. Volume III, Companion, Part 2, Documents, May 1915–December 1916. London: Heinemann, 1972.

——. *Somme: The Heroism and Horror of War*. London: John Murray, 2006.

Gill, Terry D and Fleck, Dieter (eds). *The Handbook of the International Law of Military Operations*. Oxford: Oxford University Press, 2010.

Gillan, Audrey. 'Bombing Shames Britain, Pinter Tells Protesters'. In the *Guardian*, 7 June 1999.

Ginsberg, Morris. 'On the Diversity of Morals'. In *On the Diversity of Morals*. London: Mercury, 1962.

Goldsmith, Jack. 'An Oral History of the Bush White House'. In *Vanity Fair*, 582 (February 2009).

Gratian. *Decretum*. In Reichberg, *Ethics of War*.

Greenwood, Christopher. 'Yes, But is the War Legal' In the *Observer*, 28 March 1999.

——. 'International Law and the Pre-emptive Use of Force: Afghanistan, Al-Qaida, and Iraq'. In 4 *San Diego International Law Journal*, 7 (2003): 8–38.

Gray, J. Glenn. *The Warrior: Reflections on Men in Battle*. Intro. Hannah Arendt. Lincoln, Nebraska: University of Nebraska Press, 1998.

Grossman, Dave. *On Killing: The Psychological Cost of Learning to Kill in War and Society*. Boston: Little Brown, 1995.

Grotius, Hugo. *De Iure Belli ac Pacis*. 3 vols. Ed. B.J.A. De Kanter-van Hettinga Tromp. Leiden: E.J. Brill, 1939; Aalen, Scientia Verlag, 1993.

——. *The Rights of War and Peace*. 3 vols. Ed. Richard Tuck. Indianapolis: Liberty Fund, 2005.

Guelich, Robert A. *The Sermon on the Mount: A Foundation for Understanding*. Waco, Texas: Word, 1982.

Guthrie, Charles and Quinlan, Michael. *Just War. The Just War Tradition: Ethics in Modern Warfare*. London: Bloomsbury, 2007.

'Harry Patch' (obituary). In *The Times*, 27 July 2009.

Haas, Richard N. *War of Necessity. A Memoir of Two Iraq Wars*. New York: Simon and Schuster, 2010.

Haig, Douglas. *War Diaries and Letters, 1914–1918*. Ed. Gary Sheffield and John Bourne. London: Weidenfeld & Nicolson, 2005.

Harries, Richard. *Should a Christian Support Guerrillas?* Guildford: Lutterworth, 1982.

Harris, J.P. *Douglas Haig and the First World War*. Cambridge: Cambridge University Press, 2008.

Hart, H.L.A. *The Concept of Law*. Oxford: Clarendon Press, 1961.

Hart, Peter. *The I.R.A. and its Enemies: Violence and Community in Cork, 1916–1923*. Oxford: Oxford University Press, 1998.

Hastings, Adrian. *The Construction of Nationhood: Ethnicity, Religion, and Nationalism*. Cambridge: Cambridge University press, 1997.

Hauerwas, Stanley. *The Peaceable Kingdom. A Primer in Christian Ethics*. Notre Dame: University of Notre Dame, 1981.

——. *Unleashing the Scripture. Freeing the Bible from Captivity to America*. Nashville: Abingdon, 1993.

——. *Dispatches from the Front: Theological Engagements with the Secular*. Durham, NC: Duke University Press, 1994.

——. *The Hauerwas Reader*. Ed. John Berkman and Michael Cartwright. Durham, NC: Duke University Press, 2005.

——. *Matthew*. London: SCM Press, 2006.

——. *Learning to Speak Christian*. London: SCM Press, 2009.

——. *War and the American Difference. Theological Reflections on Violence and National Identity*. Grand Rapids: Baker, 2011.

Hays, Richard B. *The Moral Vision of the New Testament: A Contemporary Introduction to New Testament Ethics*. Edinburgh: T. & T. Clark, 1996.

——. 'Narrate and Embody! A response to Nigel Biggar, "Specify and Distinguish"'. In *Studies in Christian Ethics*, 22/2 (May 2009):185–98.

——. 'The Thorny Task of Reconciliation: Another response to Nigel Biggar'. In *Studies in Christian Ethics*, 23/1 (February 2010): 81–6.

Hegel, G.W.F. *Elements of the Philosophy of Right*. Trans. H.B. Nisbet. Cambridge: Cambridge University Press, 1991.

Hehir, J. Bryan. 'Just War Theory in a Post-Cold War World'. In *Journal of Religious Ethics*, 20/1 (Fall 1992): 237–57.

Hennessey, Patrick. *The Junior Officers' Reading Club: Killing Time and Fighting Wars*. London: Penguin, 2010.

Hitchens, Christopher. 'The Iraq effect: If Saddam Hussein Were Still in Power, This Year's Arab Uprisings Could Never Have Happened. In *Slate*, 28 March 2011: <http://www.slate.com/articles/news_and_politics/fighting_words/2011/03/the_iraq_effect.html> (as at 23 December 2011).

Hoffman, Stanley. *The Ethics and Politics of Humanitarian Intervention*. Notre Dame: University of Notre Dame Press, 1996.

Holmes, Richard. *Acts of War: The Behaviour of Men in Battle*. London: Cassell, 2003.

——. *Dusty Warriors: Modern Soldiers at War*. London: HarperPress, 2006.

Holmes, Robert. *On War and Morality*. Princeton: Princeton University Press, 1989.

Horne, John and Kramer, Alan. *German Atrocities, 1914: A History of Denial* New Haven: Yale, 2001.

Horsley, Richard. *Jesus and the Spiral of Violence: Popular Jewish Resistance in Roman Palestine*. San Francisco: Harper and Row, 1987.

Human Rights Watch. 'Genocide in Iraq: The Anfal campaign against the Kurds', July 1993: <http://www.hrw.org/reports/1993/iraqanfal/> (as at 28 March 2011).

Human Security Centre. *Human Security Report 2005*. Oxford: Oxford University Press, 2005.

Hunter, David G. 'A Decade of Research on Early Christians and Military Service'. In *Religious Studies Review*, 18/2 (April 1992): 87–94.

Hurka, Thomas. 'Proportionality and Necessity'. In May, *War*.

——. 'Proportionality in the Morality of War'. In *Philosophy and Public Affairs*, 33/1 (2005): 34–66.

Ignatieff, Michael. 'Chains of Command'. In *New York Review of Books*, 48/12, 19 July 2001: 16–19.

Ignatius, David. 'Beirut's Berlin Wall'. In the *Washington Post*, 23 February 2005, page A19.

International Commission on Intervention and State Sovereignty. *The Responsibility to Protect*. Ottawa: International Development Research Centre, 2001.

Iraq Body Count: <http://www.iraqbodycount.org/analysis/numbers/2011> (as at 22 August 2012).

Iraq Family Health Survey Study Group. 'Violence-Related Mortality in Iraq from 2002 to 2006'. In *The New England Journal of Medicine*, 358/5, 31 January 2008: 484–93.

Iraq Survey Group. *Comprehensive Report of the Advisor to the DCI [Director of Central Intelligence] on Iraq's WMD*. 3 vols. Washington, DC: Central Intelligence Agency, 2004.

Johnson, James Turner. *The War to Oust Saddam Hussein. Just War and the New Face of Conflict*. Lanham, Maryland: Rowman & Littlefield, 2005.

——. Just war Thinking in Recent American Religious Debate over Military Force'. In Reed and Ryall, *The Price of Peace*.

——. 'Thinking Morally about War in the Middle Ages and Today'. In *Ethics, Nationalism and Just War: Medieval and Contemporary Perspectives*. Ed. Henrik Syse and Gregory Reichberg. Washington, DC: Catholic University of America, 2007.

Joll, James. *The Origins of the First World War.* London: Longman, 1984.

Jones, L. Gregory. *Embodying Forgiveness: A Theological Analysis.* Grand Rapids: Eerdmans, 1995.

Jünger, Ernst. *Storm of Steel.* Trans. Michael Hoffman. London: Allen Lane, 2003.

Junger, Sebastian. *War.* London: Fourth Estate, 2010.

'*Justice: Rights and Wrongs:* Critical and Interdisciplinary Engagements with Nicholas Wolterstorff'. In *Studies in Christian Ethics,* 23/2 (May 2010): 115–224.

Kaczor, Christopher. *Proportionalism and the Natural Law.* Washington, DC: Catholic University of America Press, 2002.

Kannengiesser, Hans. *The Campaign in Gallipoli.* Intro. Liman von Sanders. Trans. C.J.P. Ball. London: Hutchinson, 1927.

Keegan, John. *The Face of Battle: A Study of Agincourt, Waterloo, and the Somme.* London: Pimlico, 1976.

——. *The First World War.* London: Pimlico, 1999.

Kelly, David. 'Only Regime-change will Avert the Threat'. In the *Observer,* 31 August 2003: 3–5.

Knox, John. *On Rebellion.* Ed. Roger A. Mason. Cambridge Texts in the History of Political Thought. Cambridge: Cambridge University Press, 1994.

Koh, Harold Honju. 'Why Do Nations Obey International Law?' In *Yale Law Journal,* 106 (1996–7): 2599–659.

Koskenniemi, Martti. '"The Lady Doth Protest Too Much": Kosovo and the Turn to Ethics in International Law'. In *The Modern Law Review,* 65/2 (March 2002): 159–75.

Kramer, Alan. *Dynamics of Destruction. Culture and Mass Killing in the First World War.* Oxford: Oxford University Press, 2007.

Lang, Anthony F. 'Punitive Intervention: Enforcing Justice or Generating Conflict?'. In *Just War Theory: A Reappraisal.* Ed. Mark Evans. Edinburgh: University of Edinburgh Press, 2005.

—— *Punishment, Justice, and International Relations: Ethics and order after the Cold War.* London: Routledge, 2008.

Largio, David. 'Rationales for War'. In *Foreign Policy,* 144 (September/October 2004): 18.

'Law and Right'. In the *Economist,* 3 April 1999.

Lee, Peter. *Blair's Just War: Iraq and the Illusion of Morality.* London: Palgrave MacMillan, 2012.

Leith, John (ed.). *Creeds of the Churches: A Reader in Christian Doctrine from the Bible to the Present.* Rev. edn. Atlanta: John Knox, 1973.

Liddell Hart, Basil. *History of the Second World War.* London: Cassell, 1970.

Lieber, Keir A. 'The New History of World War I and What It Means for International Relations Theory'. In *International Security,* 32/2 (Fall 2007): 155–89.

Lillich, Richard. 'Humanitarian Intervention: A Reply to Ian Brownlie and a Plea for Constructive Alternatives'. In O'Connell, *International Law and the Use of Force.*

Lindemann, Thomas. *Les doctrines darwiniennes et la guerre de 1914.* Hautes Études
    Militaire. Paris: Institut de stratégie comparée & Economica, 2001.
Locke, John. *Two Treatises of Government.* Cambridge: Cambridge University Press,
    1960.
Luban, David. 'Preventive War and Human Rights'. In Shue and Rodin, *Preemption.*
Luck, Edward C. *UN Security Council: Practice and Promise.* Global Institutions series.
    London: Routledge, 2006.
Ludendorff, E. *My War Memories, 1914–1918.* 2 vols. London: Hutchinson, n.d.
Luis de Molina. *De iustitia et iure.* In Reichberg, *Ethics of War.*
McMahan, Jeff. 'Aggression and Punishment'. In May, *War.*
——. *Killing in War.* Oxford: Clarendon Press, 2009.
Marlantes, Karl. *What it is Like to Go to War.* New York: Atlantic Monthly Press,
    2011.
May, Larry (ed.). *War: Essays in Political Philosophy.* Cambridge: Cambridge
    University Press, 2008.
Micale, Mark. 'Improvements'. In the *Times Literary Supplement,* 9 March 2012: 24–5.
Miller, Richard B. 'Justifications of the Iraq War Examined'. In *Ethics and International
    Affairs,* 22/1 (Spring 2008): 43–67.
Minow, Martha. *Between Vengeance and Forgiveness: Facing History after Genocide and
    Mass Violence.* Boston: Beacon, 1998.
Morgan, Robert. 'The New Testament'. In *The Oxford Handbook of Biblical Studies.*
    Ed. J. W. Rogerson and Judith M. Lieu. Oxford: Oxford University Press, 2006.
Murphy, Séamus. 'Easter Ethics'. In *1916: The Long Revolution.* Ed. Gabriel Doherty
    and Dermot Keogh. Cork: Mercier Press, 2007.
Nehad Bey, Mehmed. 'Les Opérations de Sedd ul Bahr Campagne des Dardanelles,
    25 avril au 13 juillet 1915'. Trans. by M. Larcher from a lecture given in Turkish
    in 1919. In *Revue d'histoire de la guerre mondiale,* vol. 3 (Paris: A. Costes, 1925).
Neillands, Robin. *The Great War Generals on the Western Front, 1914–18.* London:
    Robinson, 1999.
Niebuhr, Reinhold. *Moral Man and Immoral Society.* New York: Scribner's, 1960.
——. *An Interpretation of Christian Ethics.* New York: Seabury, 1979.
Northcott, Michael. *An Angel Directs the Storm. Apocalyptic Religion and American
    Empire.* London: SCM, 2007.
O'Connell, Mary Ellen (ed.). *International Law and the Use of Force: Cases and
    Materials.* New York: Foundation Press, 2005.
——. *The Power and Purpose of International Law: Insights from the Theory and Practice
    of Enforcement.* New York: Oxford University Press, 2008.
——. 'Responsibility to Peace: A Critique of R2P', *Journal of Intervention and
    Statebuilding,* 4/1 (2010): 39–52.
O'Donovan, Oliver. *Measure for Measure: Justice in Punishment and the Sentence of
    Death.* Grove Booklet on Ethics no. 19. Bramcote: Grove Books, 1977.
——. *The Just War Revisited.* Oxford: Oxford University Press, 2003.
——. 'The Language of Rights and Conceptual History'. In *Journal of Religious
    Ethics,* 37/2 (June 2009): 193–207.

——and O'Donovan, Joan Lockwood (eds). *From Irenaeus to Grotius: A Sourcebook in Christian Political Thought*. Grand Rapids: Eerdmans, 1999.

——and O'Donovan, Joan Lockwood. *Bonds of Imperfection: Christian Politics, Past and Present*. Grand Rapids: Eerdmans, 2004.

O'Driscoll, Cian. *The Renegotiation of the Just War Tradition and the Right to War in the Twenty-First Century*. New York: Palgrave MacMillan, 2008.

Omand, David. *Securing the State*. London: Hurst, 2010.

Orend, Brian. *The Morality of War*. Peterborough, Ontario: Broadview Press, 2006.

Orr, Philip. *Field of Bones: An Irish Division at Gallipoli*. Dublin: Lilliput Press, 2006.

Owen, Wilfred. *Collected Letters*. Ed. Harold Owen and John Bell. London: Oxford University Press, 1967.

Packer, George. *The Assassins' Gate. America in Iraq*. London: Faber & Faber, 2006.

Parfit, Derek. *On What Matters*. 2 vols. Oxford: Oxford University Press, 2011.

Philpott, William. *Bloody Victory: The Sacrifice on the Somme and the Making of the Twentieth Century*. London: Little, Brown, 2009.

Pinker, Steven. *The Better Angels of our Nature: The Decline of Violence in History and its Causes*. London: Viking, 2011.

Pinnock, Kenneth. 'November Thoughts'. In *The Oriel Record 2002*. Oxford: Oriel College, 2002.

Pitt, Barrie. *The Crucible of War*. 2 vols. Vol. 1: 'Year of Alamein 1942'. London: Jonathan Cape, 1982.

Pollack, Kenneth. *The Threatening Storm: The Case for Invading Iraq*. A Council on Foreign Relations book. New York: Random House, 2002.

——. 'Spies, Lies, and Weapons'. In *The Atlantic Monthly* (January/February 2004).

Quinlan, Michael. 'A British Political Perspective'. In Reed and Ryall, *The Price of Peace*.

Radbruch, G. 'Gesetzliches Unrecht und übergesetzliches Recht'. *Süddeutsche Juristenzeitung*, 5 (1946): 105–8.

Ramsey, Paul. *The Just War. Force and Political Responsibility*. Savage, Maryland: Littlefield Adams, 1983.

——. *Speak Up for Just War or Pacifism: A Critique of the United Methodist Bishops' Pastoral Letter, 'In Defense of Creation'*. London: Pennsylvania State University Press, 1988.

Rawnsley, Andrew. *The End of the Party: The Rise and Fall of New Labour*. London: Viking, 2010.

Raymond, Ernest. *The Story of My Days: An Autobiography 1882–1922*. London: Cassell, 1968.

Raz, Joseph. 'The Obligation to Obey the Law'. In Joseph Raz, *The Authority of Law*. 2nd edn. Oxford: Oxford University Press, 2009.

Reed, Charles and Ryall, David (eds). *The Price of Peace. Just War in the Twenty-First Century*. Cambridge: Cambridge University Press, 2007.

Reichberg, Gregory. 'Preventive War in Classical Just War Theory'. In *Journal of the History of International Law*, 9 (2007): 5–34.

——Gregory M.; Syse, Henrik; and Begby, Endre (eds). *The Ethics of War: Classic and Contemporary Readings*. Malden, MA: Blackwell, 2006.

Renouvin, Pierre. *Les origines immédiates de la guerre (28 juin–4 août 1914)*. Paris: A. Costes, 1925.

——. *La crise européene et la grande guerre, 1914–1918*. Paris: Félix Alcan, 1934.

Reynolds, David. 'The Churchill Government and the Black American Troops in Britain during World War II'. In *Transactions of the Royal Historical Society*, Fifth Series, 35 (1985): 113–33.

——. *Rich Relations: The American occupation of Britain, 1942–1945*. London: HarperCollins, 1995.

Richards, Norvin. 'Double Effect and Moral Character'. In *Mind*, XCIII (1984): 381–97.

Ricks, Thomas. *Fiasco: The American Military Adventure in Iraq*. New York: Penguin, 2006.

——. *The Gamble: General Petraeus and the Untold Story of the American Surge in Iraq, 2006–8*. London: Allen Lane, 2009.

Roberts, Adam. 'Law and the Use of Force after Iraq'. In *Survival*, 45/2 (Summer 2003): 31–56.

——and Zaum, Dominik. *Selective Security: War and the United Nations Security Council since 1945*. Adelphi Paper 395. London: International Institute for Strategic Studies, 2008.

Roberts, Andrew. *The Holy Fox. A Life of Lord Halifax*. London: Papermac. 1992.

Rodin, David. *War and Self-Defense*. Oxford: Clarendon Press, 2002.

——. 'The Problem with Prevention'. In Shue and Rodin, *Preemption*.

Roman Catholic Church. *Catechism of the Catholic Church*. London: Geoffrey Chapman, 1994.

Rostow, Nicholas. 'Determining the Lawfulness of the 2003 Campaign against Iraq'. In *Israel Yearbook on Human Rights*, 34 (2004): 15–34.

Russell, Frederick J. 'Just War'. In *The Cambridge History of Medieval Philosophy*, vol. 2, ed. Robert Pasnau and Christina Van Dyke (Cambridge: Cambridge University Press, 2010).

Said, Edward. 'It's Time the World Stood up to the American Bully'. In the *Observer*, 11 April 1999.

Sassoon, Siegfried. *Siegfried's Journey*. London: Faber & Faber, 1945.

Semple, Michael. *Reconciliation in Afghanistan*. Washington, DC: United States Institute of Peace Press, 2009.

Shaffer, Peter. *The Gift of the Gorgon*. London: Viking, 1993.

Shawcross, William. *Allies. The U.S., Britain, Europe, and the War in Iraq*. New York: PublicAffairs, 2004.

Sheffield, Gary. 'The Shadow of the Somme: The Influence of the First World War on British soldiers' Perceptions and Behaviour in the Second World War'. In

Time to Kill: the soldier's experience of war in the West 1939–1945. Ed. Paul Addison and Angus Calder. London: Pimlico, 1997.

——. *The Somme.* London: Cassell, 2003.

——. *The Chief: Douglas Haig and the British Army.* London: Aurum, 2011.

Sheldon, Jack. *The German Army on the Somme, 1914–1916.* Barnsley: Pen & Sword, 2005.

Shue, Henry. 'What Would a Justified Preventive Military Attack Look Like?' In Shue and Rodin, *Preemption*.

——and Rodin, David (eds). *Preemption. Military Action and Moral Justification.* Oxford: Oxford University Press, 2007.

Simpson, Peter Phillips. 'Just War Theory and the I.R.A.'. In *Vices, Virtues, and Consequences. Essays in Moral and Political Philosophy.* Washington, DC: Catholic University of America Press, 2001.

Skinner, Quentin. *The Foundations of Modern Political Thought.* 2 vols. Vol. 2: 'The Age of Reformation'. Cambridge: Cambridge University Press, 1978.

Smith, Michael J. 'Humanitarian Intervention: Overview of the Ethical Issues'. In *Ethics and International Affairs: A Reader.* Ed. Joel H. Rosenthal. 2nd edn. Washington, DC: Georgetown University Press, 1999.

Smith, Rupert. *The Utility of Force: the Art of War in the Modern World.* London: Allen Lane, 2005.

Special Air Service. 'Special Air Service (SAS): Operation Barras, Sierra Leone', <http://www.eliteukforces.info/special-air-service/sas-operations/operation-barras> (as at 24 November 2009).

Stevenson, David. *1914–1918. The History of the First World War.* London: Penguin, 2004.

Stewart, Rory. 'Afghanistan: Ambition and Reality' and 'The Rhetoric of War'. The Leonard Stein Lectures, Balliol College, Oxford, May 2010 (unpublished).

——. *Occupational Hazards: My Time Governing in Iraq.* London: Picador, 2006.

——and Knaus, Gerald. *Can Intervention Work?* Amnesty International Global Ethics Series. New York: W.W. Norton, 2011.

Stouffer, Samuel A., et al. *The American Soldier: Combat and its Aftermath.* 2 vols. Princeton, NJ: Princeton University Press, 1949.

Strachan, Hew. 'The Battle of the Somme and British Strategy'. In *Journal of Strategic Studies*, 21/1 (1998): 79–95.

——. *The First World War.* Vol. I: 'To Arms'. Oxford: Oxford University Press, 2001.

——. *The First World War.* London: Pocket Books, 2006.

——. 'Preemption and Prevention in Historical Perspective'. In *Preemption: Military Action and Moral Justification.* Ed. Henry Shue and David Rodin. Oxford: Oxford University Press, 2007.

Straw, Jack. 'Gaddafi Makes Me Glad We Toppled Saddam'. In *The Times*, 5 March 2011.

Suárez, Francisco de. 'De Caritate: Disputatio XIII'. In *Opus de triplici virtute theologica, fide, spe, et charitate.* Paris: Edmundus Martin, 1621.

———. 'On Charity: Disputation XIII', *A Work on the Three Theological Virtues, Faith, Hope, and Charity* (1621). In Francisco Suárez, S.J., *Selections from Three Works*. 2 vols. Vol. II: 'The Translation'. Ed. Gwladys L. Williams et al. The Classics of International Law. Oxford: Clarendon Press, 1944.

Swartley, Willard M. *Covenant of Peace: The Missing Peace in New Testament Theology and Ethics*. Grand Rapids, MI: Eerdmans, 2006.

Swinburne, Richard. *Responsibility and Atonement*. Oxford: Clarendon Press, 1989.

Taheri, Amir. 'A Democratic Beacon in the Fractious Arab World'. *Standpoint*, 44, July/August 2012: 44–7.

Tawney, R.H. *'The Attack' and Other Papers*. London: George, Allen, Unwin, 1953.

Temple, William. *Christianity and the Social Order*. New York: Penguin, 1942.

Tertullian, 'On the Soldier's Chaplet' [De Corona]. In *Ante-Nicene Christian Library*. Ed. Alexander Roberts and James Donaldson. Vol, XI: 'The Writings of Tertullian, vol. I'. Edinburgh: T. & T. Clark, 1869.

The Straits of War: Gallipoli Remembered. Introduced by Martin Gilbert. Stroud: Sutton, 2000.

Thielicke, Helmuth. *Theological Ethics*. 2 vols. Grand Rapids: Eerdmans, 1979. Vol. 2: 'Politics'.

Thorne, Christopher. 'Britain and the Black GIs: Racial issues and Anglo-American relations in 1942'. In *Border Crossings: Studies in International History*. Oxford: Blackwell, 1988.

Tierney, Brian. *The Idea of Natural Rights: Studies in Natural Rights, Natural Law, and Church Law, 1150–1625*. Emory Studies in Law and Religion. Grand Rapids: Eerdmans, 1997.

Tremlett, Giles. *Ghosts of Spain: Through a Country's Hidden Past*. London: Faber and Faber, 2006.

United Kingdom Government. *Iraq—its Infrastructure of Concealment, Deception, and Intimidation*. London: UK Government, January 2003.

———. 'Attorney General, 7 March 2003 advice': <http://www.ico.gov.uk/upload/documents/library/freedom_of_information/notices/annex_a_-_attorney_general%7s_advice_070303.pdf>.

———. 'Legality of Military Action in Iraq: Disclosure Statement'. Made by the UK Government's Cabinet Office and the Legal Secretariat to the Law Officers to the Information Commissioner's Office (undated): <http://www.ico.gov.uk/upload/documents/library/freedom_of_information/notices/appendix_6_disclosure_statement.pdf> (as at 17 August 2012).

United Nation Security Council Resolution 1441: <http//daccess-dds-ny.un.org/doc/UNDOC/GEN/N02/682/26/PDF/N0268226.pdf?OpenElement> (as at 14 August 2012).

Villa-Vicencio, Charles (ed.) *Theology & Violence: The South African Debate*. Grand Rapids: Eerdmans, 1988.

Vitoria, Francisco de. *Relectiones theologiae tredecim partibus per varias sectiones in duos libros divisae*. Lyon: Petrus Landry, 1587.

—— 'De Bello', In *Comentarios a la Secunda secundae de Santo Tomás*, ed. Vicente Beltrán de Heredia, vol. II: 'De Caritate et Prudentia (qq. 23–56)' (Salamanca: Apartado 17, 1932).

——. 'De Bello: On St Thomas Aquinas, *Summa Theologiae*, 2a 2ae, Question 40'. Trans. Gwladys L. Williams. In James Brown Scott, *The Spanish Origin of International Law: Francisco de Vitoria and his Law of Nations*, Appendix F (Oxford: Clarendon Press, 1934).

——. 'On Dietary Laws, or Self-Restraint'. In *Political Writings*.

——. 'On the American Indians'. In *Political Writings*.

——. 'On the Law of War'. In *Political Writings*.

——. *Political Writings*. Ed. Anthony Pagden and Jeremy Lawrance. Cambridge Texts in the History of Political Thought. Cambridge: Cambridge University Press, 1991.

Wajda, Andrzej (dir.). *Katyń*. 2007,

Walzer, Michael. 'World War Two: Why was this War Different?'. In *War and Moral Responsibility*. Ed. Marshall Cohen, Thomas Nagel, and Thomas Scanlon. Princeton: Princeton University Press, 1974.

——. *Just and Unjust Wars: A Moral Argument with Historical Illustrations*. London: Allen Lane, 1978.

——. 'The Argument about Humanitarian Intervention'. In Michael Walzer, *Thinking Politically: Essays in Political Theory*. Ed. and intro. David Miller. New Haven: Yale University Press, 2007.

Weir, Peter (dir.). *Master and Commander*. 2003.

Wellum, Geoffrey. *First Light*. London: Viking, 2002.

White, Craig M. *Iraq: The Moral Reckoning. Applying Just War Theory to the 2003 War Decision*. Lanham, Maryland: Lexington Books, 2010.

White, Martin and Whitaker, Brian. 'British "intelligence" lifted from academic articles'. In the *Guardian*, 7 February 2003.

White, Nigel D. *Democracy Goes to War: British Military Deployments under International Law*. Oxford: Oxford University Press, 2009.

Whiteman, Matthew (dir.). *First Light*. London: BBC, 2010.

Wiesenthal, Simon. *The Sunflower: On the Possibilities and Limits of Forgiveness*. Rev. edn. New York: Schocken, 1997.

Wilson, Richard A. 'Reconciliation and Revenge in Post-Apartheid South Africa: Rethinking legal pluralism and human rights'. In *Current Anthropology*, 41 (2000): 74–98.

——. *The Politics of Truth and Reconciliation: Legitimizing the Post-Apartheid State*. Cambridge: Cambridge University Press, 2001.

Winter, Jay and Prost, Antoine. *Great War in History: Debates and Controversies, 1914 to the Present*. Cambridge: Cambridge University Press, 2005.

Wolterstorff, Nicholas. *Justice: Rights and Wrongs*. Princeton: Princeton University Press, 2008.

Yoder, John Howard. *The Politics of Jesus: Vicit Agnus Noster.* Grand Rapids: Eerdmans, 1972.

———. *The Priestly Kingdom. Social Ethics as Gospel.* Notre Dame: University of Notre Dame Press, 1984.

———. *The Politics of Jesus: Vicit Agnus Noster,* 2nd edn. Grand Rapids: Eerdmans, 1994.

———. *When War is Unjust. Being Honest in Just-War Thinking.* Rev. edn. Maryknoll, NY: Orbis, 1996.

———. *Christian Attitudes to War, Peace, and Revolution.* Ed. Theodore J. Koontz and Andy Alexis-Baker. Grand Rapids: Brazos, 2009.

———. *The War of the Lamb: The Ethics of Nonviolence and Peacemaking.* Ed. Glen Stassen, Mark Thiessen Nation, and Matt Hamsher. Grand Rapids: Brazos, 2009.

Index